THE
ELGAR–ATKINS
FRIENDSHIP

THE
ELGAR–ATKINS
FRIENDSHIP

E. WULSTAN ATKINS

DAVID & CHARLES
Newton Abbot   London   North Pomfret (Vt)

Frontispiece
Sir Edward Elgar and Sir Ivor Atkins in August 1922, photographed in front of
the Atkins home, 8 College Yard, Worcester, where Elgar was then staying.
Elgar's small-bowled pipe, his left hand in his pocket with the thumb
protruding—a characteristic attitude—and his smart grey spats will be noted

British Library Cataloguing in Publication Data
Atkins, E. Wulstan
  The Elgar–Atkins friendship.
  1. Elgar, Edward   2. Atkins, Ivor
  I. Title
  780′.092′4   ML410.E41
  ISBN 0–7153–8583–6

© E. Wulstan Atkins 1984
First published 1984
Second impression 1985

Filmset by Latimer Trend & Company Ltd, Plymouth
and printed in Great Britain
by Butler & Tanner Limited, Frome and London
for David & Charles (Publishers) Limited
Brunel House Newton Abbot Devon

Published in the United States of America
by David & Charles Inc
North Pomfret Vermont 05053 USA

FOREWORD

By the late Sir Adrian Boult, CH

It is well known that one of Sir Edward Elgar's greatest friends for most of his life was Sir Ivor Atkins, organist of Worcester Cathedral from 1897 to 1950.

It will be a great addition to Elgar literature that Sir Ivor's son Wulstan, who was Elgar's godson, has written a book about this friendship which has a great human interest apart from its account of all the links between Elgar and a friend whom he met almost every week for the greater part of his life. From 1923 until Elgar's death Wulstan was privileged to accompany his father on many of these visits.

We welcome this fresh and vital contribution to the still growing Elgar literature.

PREFACE

This book portrays the interrelated lives of two musicians and two great friends against the background of the times in which they lived, and shows something of the personalities of two wonderful and deeply human men—my father and my godfather.

I have used seven main sources in writing the book:
The letters between them;
Diaries and engagement books;
My father's written notes and jottings;
My father's concert and Three Choirs Festival programmes;
My father's and Elgar's conversations when I have been in their company;
My own notes after visits to Elgar;
My own memories.

Great care has been taken, wherever possible, to check all details from original sources; the author would, however, be grateful if any reader finding a mistake would notify him via the publisher.

The photographs, unless otherwise indicated, are all reproduced from photographs taken by myself, or from those given to my father, either by Elgar or his niece May Grafton. Dates given are either from the negatives or from notes written by my father on the back of the prints as he received them.

NOTE

In accordance with convention, words underlined once by Elgar or Atkins have been represented in this book in *italic type*. In addition, words underlined twice (or more) in the original text are rendered in SMALL CAPITALS.

This book is dedicated to
Jane, Katharine and Robert

CONTENTS

FOREWORD by the late Sir Adrian Boult, CH   5

PREFACE   7

LIST OF PHOTOGRAPHS   13

ACKNOWLEDGEMENTS   17

INTRODUCTION   19

PART 1 1889–1899   23

First meeting and start of the friendship · *Froissart* · *Spanish Serenade* · *Black Knight* · *Sursum Corda* · Organ Sonata in G · *Bavarian Highlands* · *Light of Life* · *King Olaf* · Atkins' appointment to Worcester · Weekly meetings, and Atkins' first Three Choirs Festival as Worcester conductor · *Caractacus* · *Sea Pictures* · *Enigma Variations*

PART 2 1900–1903   49

Dream of Gerontius · Disappointment and triumph · *Pomp and Circumstance Marches* Nos 1 and 2 · *The Apostles* · the STP · Italy

PART 3 1904–1907   109

In the South · Elgar's knighthood · Move to Hereford · Birmingham professorship · *Pomp and Circumstance March* No 3 dedicated to Atkins · *Introduction and Allegro* · Elgar's first visit to America · Atkins' *Hymn of Faith* · Honorary Freedom of Worcester · Second visit to America · *The Kingdom* · Italy · Third visit to America · *Pomp and Circumstance March* No 4 · *Wand of Youth Suite* No 1

PART 4 1908–1911   167

Italy · *Wand of Youth Suite* No 2 · Death of Jaeger · First Symphony · Violin Concerto · Kreisler · The silver-topped stick · Second Symphony · Elgar–Atkins edition of Bach's *St Matthew Passion* · Worcester Festival · Tower music · The Flight from Worcester

PART 5 1912–1919 235

Hampstead · *The Crown of India Masque* · *The Music Makers* · *Falstaff* · *The Apostles* Part 3 · World War I · · Worcester Festival abandoned · Elgar's Special Constabulary duties in Hampstead · *Carillon* · *The Starlight Express* · *For the Fallen* in Worcester Cathedral · *The Sanguine Fan* · *The Fringes of the Fleet* · *The Spirit of England* · Brinkwells · Sonata in E minor · String Quartet · Quintet · Cello Concerto · Atkins takes preliminary steps for revival of Three Choirs Festival at Worcester in 1920

PART 6 1920–1922 299

Death of Lady Elgar · Discussions on programme, artists and orchestra for festival · Programme includes *Sursum Corda, Gerontius, For the Fallen, The Music Makers, Introduction and Allegro*, conducted by Elgar · Bach's *St Matthew Passion* · Memorial music for Parry, Lloyd and Sinclair · Festival success · Atkins' Oxford doctorate and knighthood · Elgar orchestrates Bach's Organ Fugue in C minor · Hull's first Hereford Festival as conductor · Elgar leaves 'Severn House' and moves to St James's Place · Carice's wedding · Rebuilding of Worcester Cathedral organ · Parry memorial organ book · Brewer's Gloucester Festival programme includes *The Apostles* and *The Kingdom* in consecutive performances · Bacon-sniffing expeditions · Another walking-stick · *The Wallet of Kai Lung*

PART 7 1923–1929 357

Elgar's return to Worcestershire · Napleton Grange · Battenhall Manor · Tiddington House (Stratford-upon-Avon) · Marl Bank · Elgar orchestrates Purcell and Battishill motets and Handel's Overture in D minor for the Worcester Festival · Amazon cruise · British Empire Exhibition · Master of the King's Musick · Marco · Reopening of Worcester Cathedral organ with Elgar's Fugue written in 1923 · Elgar in South Bank Nursing Home for three weeks · Discussions on 1926 Worcester Festival · *Apostles III* once more under consideration · HMV recordings · Mina · 'Giant onion' · Horse-racing · Elgar's seventieth birthday · *Civic Fanfare* · HMV recordings at Hereford Festival · KCVO · Boating on the Avon · *Beau Brummel* · Unsuccessful search for libretto for new Elgar work for Worcester Festival · Tertis' arrangement of Cello Concerto for Viola · Elgar rents Marl Bank for festival · Bach's *St John's Passion* · Bernard Shaw

PART 8 1930–1935   423

Elgar buys Marl Bank · Sunday suppers there · 'Turn the
volume   down—it's   awful!' · Autostop · *Enigma* · Test
records · Winifred   Barrows'   *Faery   Fantasy* · *Nursery
Suite* · Opening HMV new recording studios · *The Spanish
Lady* · *Severn   Suite* · Concert   Allegro · *Apostles   III* ·
· Severn   Bridge   parapet · Yehudi   Menuhin   plays   Violin
Concerto · Sketches   for   Third   Symphony · Restless
activity · Croydon Philharmonic *Apostles* · GCVO · Flight to
Paris · Visit to Delius · Hereford, Elgar's last festival · *The
Kingdom* · Illness · South Bank Nursing Home · Return to
Marl Bank · Elgar's telephone-line recording of Woodland
Interlude   from   *Caractacus* · Death · Funeral · Memorial
service · Three Choirs memorial performances · Dedication of
memorial window in Worcester Cathedral · *Gerontius*

EPILOGUE   469

APPENDIX 1   470

Reminiscences of early Worcester Festivals and of Elgar's childhood and youth

APPENDIX 2   481

Worcester Festivals and the Elgar family

APPENDIX 3   482

Some Worcester Festivals of special interest to Elgar and Atkins

BIOGRAPHICAL NOTES   490

INDEX   501

LIST OF PHOTOGRAPHS

Sir Edward Elgar and Sir Ivor Atkins, 1922   Frontispiece
The first two pages of the manuscript score of *Froissart*   33
Chorus rehearsal for the 1891 Festival at Hereford   33
Ivor Atkins at Ludlow in 1893   34
Elgar in Hereford, 1896   34
Percy Hull, Max Mossel, George Sinclair, Dan and Elgar in
    Sinclair's garden, 1896   34
Atkins, Sinclair and Herbert Brewer in Worcester, 1899   67
Alice and Edward Elgar outside Forli, Malvern Link   68
Birchwood Lodge in Herefordshire   68
Elgar finishing the score of *Gerontius*, August 1900   68
Elgar in Düsseldorf, May 1902   117
Four studies of Elgar at Craeg Lea, 1902   118
Portrait of Elgar by Dr Grindrod, 1903   119
Elgar on the Malvern Hills, 1903   120
Elgar at Craeg Lea, 1903: possibly a self-portrait?   137
Elgar about to take a drive, Plas Gwyn, 1904   138
Portrait of Elgar taken in 1904 for a postcard set of 'English
    Celebrities'   138
Elgar writing *Introduction and Allegro*, Hereford, 1905   138
S. S. Sanford and the Elgars on board SS *Kaiser Wilhelm der
    Gross*, 1905   171
Three Choirs Festival at Worcester, 1905   172
Elgar writing *The Kingdom*, 1906   172
Professor S. S. Sanford, Elgar and Sinclair in Hereford,
    1906   221
Elgar and Carice at Plas Gwyn, 1906   221
Elgar and S. S. Sanford outside the Green Dragon Hotel,
    Hereford   221
Alice in the drawing room at Plas Gwyn   222
Carice with Peter Rabbit   222
Elgar, Carice and Alice in Hereford, 1910   223

Atkins in his study, 1908   224
Elgar in 'The Ark' at Plas Gwyn   224
The author in 1911 with his silver-topped walking stick, a
   present from Elgar   257
Atkins at the time of the Elgar–Atkins Edition of Bach's *St
   Matthew Passion*, 1911   257
The Atkins family home at 8 College Yard, Worcester   257
Players before and during a performance of Bach's chorales
   for brass instruments; Gloucester, 1913   258
'The Flight from Worcester', September 1911: Elgar and C.
   Sanford Terry   259
Alice Elgar in 1912   260
Elgar at Severn House, Hampstead, in 1913   309
Atkins in the Worcester Cathedral Music Library, July
   1916   309
The author as a Cathedral chorister at Worcester, 1917   309
Revival of the Three Choirs Festival, Worcester, 1920:
   Elgar, Atkins and W. H. Reed outside the Cathedral   310
W. H. Reed at the Atkins' home   310
Gervase Elwes and W. H. Reed, Worcester, 1920   310
Atkins in his Oxford Doctor of Music robes, 1920   310
Brent-Smith, Edgar Day, Wulstan Atkins and Sir Ivor
   Atkins outside the Atkins's Festival house in Hereford,
   1921   343
Elgar returning from a 'bacon-sniffing' visit to the Atkins's
   Festival house in Gloucester, 1922   343
Portrait of Elgar in 1922   343
Elgar and a 'haltered' Billy Reed in College Yard, Worces-
   ter, 1923   344
Elgar and frightened hen at Napleton Grange, Kempsey,
   1923   344
Alexander Brent Smith, Wulstan Atkins, Sir Edward
   Elgar, Billy Reed, Dame Ethel Smyth, Lady Atkins,
   H. C. J. Shuttleworth-King, Dr Herbert Brewer, Sir
   Ivor Atkins and Dr Perry Hull outside the Atkins' house
   on 7 September 1926   344
Elgar in 1925   361
Atkins, Easter 1926   361
Elgar playing the piano at Napleton Grange, Kempsey   362
Elgar with Marco, Meg and Mina at Napleton Grange   362

Stanley Baldwin with Elgar and Atkins in August 1926   363

Elgar, Mina and Marco outside the Atkins's home   363

Atkins seeing Elgar into his car   363

Billy Reed and Elgar with the 'large onion'   364

Elgar with Mina and Meg in front of Napleton Grange   364

Elgar out rowing on the River Avon   364

Elgar's preliminary sketch for *Pomp and Circumstance March* No 5   381

Billy Reed, Atkins and Elgar in front of the Deanery drive, Worcester   381

Sir Barry Jackson's party at Lawnside, Great Malvern, 1929   381

Elgar arriving to take a rehearsal of the Croydon Philharmonic, November 1931   382

Yehudi Menuhin and Sir Edward Elgar at Abbey Road Recording Studios, 1932   382

Elgar working on sketches for the Third Symphony at Marl Bank, Worcester, 1932   382

Sir Ivor Atkins, Dr Percy Hull, Dr Herbert Sumsion and Sir Edward Elgar, Hereford, 1933   415

Sir Edward Elgar outside the West Porch of Hereford Cathedral, September 1933   416

ACKNOWLEDGEMENTS

This book has been in my mind for more than 25 years, and indeed much of the material for it was collected at that time. It was always my intention to write the book but other interests continually intervened. It is due to constant pressure from my family, ably supported by gentle insistence from the late Sir Adrian Boult and the late Dr Herbert Howells, that three years ago I began writing in earnest, and I should like to express my gratitude to them for their persistence. At Sir Adrian's request the first draft of each section was sent to him as it was written, and his helpful comments have been invaluable.

I should like to thank Anne Soden for her diligent search for, and provision of, photostatic copies of early programmes of the Hereford and Gloucester Meetings of the Three Choirs Festivals, and for details of various concerts given in Birmingham. In the latter connection I am also greatly indebted to Paul Wilson, the music librarian of the Birmingham University Music Library of the Barber Institute of Fine Arts, who also has provided photostats and other information especially about the 'Clef Club'.

I owe a special debt to Dr Jerrold Northrop Moore and to Paul Mathias, both of whom individually read every word of the first draft of the book and made valuable suggestions, many of which have been incorporated in this book.

I should like to thank Jack McKenzie, until recently Curator of the Elgar Birthplace, for his help in providing photostatic copies of some of Elgar's own early Festival programmes and for verifying certain information from the news-cuttings books. I am grateful to the present Curator, Jim Bennett, for looking up other information on my behalf and for arranging for me to receive copies of three photographs now in the Birthplace, and to the Trustees of the Birthplace for allowing me to reproduce them.

I am also indebted to the Elgar Will Trust, the holders of the copyright, for granting me permission to reproduce Elgar's letters to my father. If I have unwittingly infringed any other copyrights I would crave forgiveness.

I recall with pleasure and gratitude conversations with Alan Webb, a former Curator of the Birthplace, the late Edgar Day, the late Dr Alcock of Gloucester; with Lady Hull and Dr Herbert Sumsion, and with many others, mainly at Three Choirs Festivals, which have added to and amplified my general knowledge.

I cannot adequately express my gratitude to Alan Jackson, who has devoted his great skill and very many hours of hard work to producing the excellent prints used for illustrating this book, from my own badly scratched and neglected negatives, and from often faded and sometimes damaged photographs which are 50 and in some instances 90 years old.

All authors owe a great deal to their publishers, but my own debt is a large one. No author likes to have paragraphs to which he has devoted much time and thought cut out, but Mary Byrne and Tim Hall, the editors of this book, have by their interest and sympathetic understanding made this necessary operation as painless as possible, and even almost a pleasure. They have undoubtedly by their work improved the book for the general reader. I should like to express my appreciation also to David & Charles' Art department for the layout of the photographs and line drawings, and especially for their most effective jacket cover with its period photographs.

But my greatest debt is to my wife Jane who has devoted so much time and energy over the last three years to making this book possible. Her keen interest and knowledge as a professional musician have enabled many obscure allusions in the letters to be clarified. I have discussed with her at length each section before she typed it and her thoughtful and sometimes forceful criticism has resulted in many improvements. In addition to typing the book she has also undertaken the arduous task of preparing the comprehensive Index.

INTRODUCTION

Music in England today is very different from what it was at the end of the nineteenth century. London is now pre-eminently the centre of the English musical world, and indeed, in certain aspects of music, throughout the world. But in the eighteenth and early nineteenth centuries the great provincial music festivals took a very prominent place in English music, and as far as choral works were concerned offered composers almost the only opportunity of getting their works published.

The period covered by this book extends from 1889 to 1934, with some references to earlier and later years, and to appreciate many of the letters it is necessary to keep in mind the great changes that were occurring in the musical world over this period especially before and after World War I.

Let me try, therefore, to paint in a broad background of English music between the last quarter of the nineteenth century and 1914. It was the heyday of music festivals all over the country. The Three Choirs Festivals had run continuously from at least 1715 and were taking on a new lease of life. Three other festivals, dating from the late eighteenth century—Birmingham (1768), Norwich (1770) and Chester (1772)—had become regular triennial festivals. The Leeds Festival (1858), the Bristol Festival (1873), the North Staffordshire Music Festival at Hanley (1888), the Cardiff Festival (1892), and the Sheffield Festival (1895), were now also regular triennial festivals. Each had its own special character, but all had a strong choral background, and made the fullest use of local talent.

In the latter part of the nineteenth century the Leeds chorus, under Alfred Broughton, became so famous that for many years a contingent from Leeds augmented the local choral resources at the Three Choirs and almost every other festival. Early in this century, however, most of the local choruses were strong enough to stand on their own, and great was the competition between them.

Rivalry between the festivals was not, however, restricted to performances. It also extended to the commissioning of new works, the music committees of the Birmingham and Leeds Festivals making a very special feature of the encouragement financially of British composers. The great triennial music festivals were indeed between them to be responsible for many of the compositions of Parry, Stanford, Elgar, Bantock, Walford Davies, Holbrooke and Vaughan Williams, to name only a few.

The Hanley and Chester Festivals were to come to an end in 1899 and 1900, but all the other festivals continued until World War I, when they went into abeyance, most, alas, never to re-start.

What a wonderful time it was in English musical history in the Provinces! Never less than two great music festivals each year, and sometimes, as in 1896 and 1902, five. What excitement there was for young musicians like my father, who in his desire to hear all the music he could and add to his experience, rushed from festival to festival, and made visits abroad as often as he could.

Important as it is to understand the musical background of the period, it is also necessary to know something about the lives of Elgar and my father before they met in 1890, and as I learnt from listening to them reminiscing about their early days.

Edward William Elgar was born at Broadheath, 3 miles north-west of Worcester, on 2 June 1857. His father, William Henry, had an extensive and growing piano-tuning business. Anne, his country-bred wife, who wanted her family to be brought up in the countryside, had persuaded him to move to Broadheath in 1856. Pressure of business, however, forced a return, in 1860, to Worcester, where William and his younger brother, Henry, also a piano tuner, set up a music shop at 10, High Street. Anne continued, however, to take the children to Broadheath, where Edward spent his holidays on a farm until he was about 11. From there he could see the full range of the Malvern Hills which were to have such an influence on his life and music.

In 1866 the Elgars went to live above the shop, and Edward increasingly helped in it until 1879, when he went to live with his sister Pollie Grafton. On their leaving Worcester in 1883 he moved to his sister Lucy Pipe, and stayed there until his marriage to Caroline Alice Roberts in 1889. After their marriage the Elgars went to live in London but had little success there and returned to Worcestershire in 1891, settling in Malvern Link.

At an early age Edward began to show his genius as a composer.

His first 'sketch', 'Humoreske', was written in 1867 when he was only 10. In the 1870s, however, his parents had visions of Edward becoming a lawyer, and in 1872 he was articled to a local solicitor. This lasted for less than a year, and Edward then firmly took up music as his career. From then on a number of sketches appeared, and by this time he could play the violin, various other instruments and the organ, and deputised for his father who served as organist at St George's Church, Worcester. In 1885 he became organist there.

Elgar made his first public appearance as a violinist in Worcester in 1873, and from then on played in most of the local orchestras in the neighbourhood and was the leader in several. He also began teaching the violin and built up an extensive practice in and around Worcester.

The 1880s were to see Elgar's first published compositions, some of them written earlier: *Salve Regina* and others for St George's Church; *Rosemary*; *Serenade Mauresque*, which received its first performance in 1883 by W. C. Stockley's Birmingham Orchestra in which Elgar played; *Sevillana*; and *Salut d'Amour* (*Liebesgrüss*); to name but a few of his now well-known works. *Sevillana* was performed in London at the Crystal Palace in July 1884, conducted by August Manns, and was probably the only orchestral work of Elgar's which had at that time been heard outside the Midlands. He was therefore virtually unknown outside Worcestershire when my father first met him.

My father, Ivor Algernon, was born on the outskirts of the little city of Llandaff near Cardiff on 29 November 1869, the sixth of seven children. The Atkins family came from Gloucestershire, where my grandfather, Frederick Pyke, was born in 1830. At an early age he went to Llandaff, where he died in 1897, having spent all his working life there as a professional musician. He was for many years organist of St John's Church, Cardiff, and a leading light in the musical life of Wales. He was responsible for all the music in connection with the reopening ceremony in 1889 after the restoration of Llandaff Cathedral and was very involved in the Eisteddfod movement. My father's elder brother, Reginald Mozart, 9 years his senior, was also a church organist, and his elder sister Florence was a very fine pianist.

My father was therefore brought up with a strong musical background. From the age of 15 he increasingly helped his father at St John's Church, and at 17 he took his first professional appointment as organist of a church at Stonehaven in Scotland. In 1886, George Robertson Sinclair, who had become organist at Truro Cathedral in 1881, invited my father to become his assistant there, where they both remained until Sinclair brought him to Hereford on his acceptance of the appointment of cathedral organist in 1889.

PART 1
1889–1899

1889

Ivor Algernon Atkins became assistant to George Robertson Sinclair, the organist of Truro Cathedral, in 1886, when he was 17, and on Sinclair's appointment as organist of Hereford Cathedral in October 1889 he brought Atkins with him as his assistant.

1890

The Three Choirs Festival of 1890 was held in Worcester, and appropriately Atkins' first introduction to the Three Choirs was at Worcester, and this same festival was also to be his first introduction to Elgar.

Elgar, his father and his uncle were all playing in the Band, as it was called, Elgar at the fourth desk of the first violins, his father with the second violins and his uncle among the violas. Sinclair drew Atkins' attention to Elgar during the Monday rehearsal.

The first performance of Elgar's first important orchestral work, the *Froissart* Overture, which would be conducted by the composer, was to be given at the Wednesday evening concert in the Public Hall on the 10 September. My father has left his impressions of the occasion:

Never before had I heard such a wonderful combination of a first-rate Chorus and Orchestra. I was naturally specially interested in Elgar, knowing that he was to produce a new Overture whose very title attracted me, for I had just been reading Froissart's *Chronicles*. Sinclair pointed Elgar out to me. There he was, fiddling among the first violins, with his fine intellectual face, his heavy moustache, his dark hair, his nervous eyes, and his beautiful sensitive hands. The Wednesday evening came. I had no dress clothes with me, having come over from Hereford for the day, so I crept up the steps leading to the back of the Orchestra and peeped from behind those on the platform. The new Overture was placed at the end of the first half of the programme.

The great moment came, and I watched Elgar's shy entry on to the platform. From that moment my eyes did not leave him, and I listened to the Overture, hearing it in the exciting way one hears music when among the players. I heard the surge of the strings, the chatter of the wood wind, the sudden bursts from the horns, the battle call of the trumpets, the awesome beat of the drums and the thrill of cymbal clashes. I was conscious of all these and of the hundred and one other sounds from an orchestra that stir one's blood and send one's heart into one's mouth.

But there was something else I was conscious of—I knew that Elgar was the man for me, I knew that I completely understood his music, and that my heart and soul went with it.

Nearly forty years later I heard Elgar's account of their first meeting. It was on an evening early in 1930. In accordance with our normal practice my father and I were spending the Sunday evening with Elgar, and, the meal over, we were sitting in front of a blazing coal fire in the study at Marl Bank. Elgar was in his usual chair to the right of the fire, smoking a small-bowled pipe with a rack of similar fully charged pipes by his side. My father was sitting opposite to him smoking a cigarette, and I was sitting between them with the dogs at our feet. Some reference to the *Froissart* Overture must have been made, and Elgar turned to me and said:

No doubt you know that it was at the first performance of *Froissart* that I met your father. I well remember the occasion. After conducting it I retired to the artists' room below the platform, and I was alone there when suddenly the door opened and a tall young man with red hair came in and shook my hand. He was too nervous to speak and so was I. But the eager excited look in his eyes told me that at least one musician had fully understood my music and had made it his own. No word passed between us, but we both knew that a real friendship had begun.

Elgar was thirty-three and my father nearly twenty-one when they first met.

Atkins next saw Elgar playing at a concert of the Herefordshire Philharmonic Society in the Shirehall, Hereford, on 21 November, and afterwards was introduced to his uncle Henry, who had been playing the viola. William Henry Elgar, his father, and his uncle had been Musical Associates, as the Herefordshire Society rather charmingly described the players, since the 1860s. Elgar himself joined them in 1883 and was Leader of the Band from 1891 until 1895.

For my father 1890 was a very special year, and he often spoke of it as opening up for him a new and exciting musical world, with the wonderful experience of hearing for the first time so many choral and orchestral works performed in a cathedral with a large orchestra and chorus, and great artists like Madame Albani, Edward Lloyd and Plunket Greene. Most eventful of all, however, was his first meeting with Elgar.

1891

Elgar was again in Hereford for the Philharmonic concert on 3 April, when he led the Band for the first time. Naturally my father was present, and he told me many years later how he had spent some hours with Elgar after the concert. He remembered him speaking with enthusiasm about Sinclair's inclusion in his first Hereford Festival programme that year of Wagner's Prelude to *Parsifal*—the first time that it would be heard in an English cathedral—and how important it was to introduce modern orchestral music into the Three Choirs Festivals as well as new choral works. He recalled Elgar telling him that the opportunities of hearing music were greater in Worcester than in Hereford, mainly because in addition to amateur players there were a number of professional musicians living there. My father was delighted to hear this, since it was easy to get from Hereford to Worcester by train, and, encouraged by Sinclair, he was at that time very anxious to hear as much music, especially orchestral music, as possible. In common with many other young musicians at that time, he knew most of the classical repertoire mainly from piano arrangements.

The most exciting part of this conversation, however, was Elgar's news that he and his wife would be leaving London and returning to Worcestershire as soon as they could find a house in Malvern. The Elgars moved into 'Forli', Malvern Link, on 20 June.

In October Atkins attended his first Birmingham Triennial Festival and saw for the first time Antonin Dvořák and Hans Richter. His great admiration for Richter clearly dated from the performances at this festival. At that time he could not have foreseen the great part Richter played in introducing Elgar's music to the English music world. In later years I often heard Elgar and my father discussing Richter's conducting, and it was evident that in their minds in pre-war days only Arthur Nikisch, with his mesmeric control of orchestras, could compete with him.

Elgar was in poor health for the last three months of 1891, but he came to Hereford on 10 November to play as usual in the Hereford Philharmonic concert, which included his own *My Love dwelt in a Northern Land*. His wife Alice came with him and Sinclair and Atkins met them at tea at Canon Musgrave's house.

A fortnight later Atkins saw Elgar again briefly at the Worcester

27

Festival Choral Society's concert in the Public Hall, Worcester, on 24 November. Hugh Blair, assistant to Dr W. Done, the cathedral organist, was now the Society's conductor. Elgar was the leader of the Band, his father led the second violins, his uncle led the violas, and his brother Frank was the first oboe.

1892

During the first few months of 1892 Elgar was still in poor health, and it was not until the next Hereford Philharmonic concert on 22 April that they met again. Four days later they met in Worcester at the WFCS performance of Handel's *Israel in Egypt*.

The Three Choirs Festival in Gloucester in September gave Atkins further opportunities of hearing large forces perform in the largest of the three cathedrals. Of all the works performed, however, it was Parry's *Job*, conducted by the composer, with Plunket Greene, Edward Lloyd and Watkin Mills as soloists, which most impressed him. The Elgars had come to Gloucester specially to hear this performance.

Elgar was playing in Hereford on 8 November at the Hereford Philharmonic concert, and Alice had come over with him. After the concert they all met at tea at the Musgraves. This tea had now become a regular feature. My father remembered that the Elgars were full of *The Black Knight*, Elgar's new choral work, which was now complete and ready for orchestrating, and of their recent tour in Germany.

1893

This was a year of special interest for my father, for on 7 April he attended the Hereford Philharmonic Society's concert, in which the first performance of Elgar's newly completed composition *Spanish Serenade* for Chorus and Orchestra ('Stars of the Summer Night'), Op 23, was given and made a great impression. (W. H. Reed in his book, *Elgar*, states on page 39 that the HPS gave the first performance of the *Serenade for Strings*, Op 20, at this concert. An examination of the programme and of two press reviews after the concert confirms Atkins' memory that only

Elgar's *Spanish Serenade* was performed.)

On 18 April Atkins and Sinclair went over to Worcester to hear the first performance of *The Black Knight*, conducted by the composer. Elgar had dedicated this work to Hugh Blair, and it had an enthusiastic reception.

In 1893 the Three Choirs Festival was held in Worcester, and Hugh Blair was festival conductor for the first time. This festival was also the last one in which Elgar played in the Band.

My father left a note about his meetings with Elgar during the early years of the 1890s:

From Elgar's return to Worcestershire [Forli, Malvern Link] he became interested in me and would discuss his works with the greatest frankness and—what delighted me most, for I was doing some compositions myself—he used often to talk of his methods of composing, illustrating his remarks from works like 'The Black Knight'.

In October Atkins took up his new appointment as organist to the Collegiate Church of Ludlow, a post he was to hold until 1897.

1894–1895

Sinclair's friendship with Elgar—he was only five years younger than Elgar—developed quickly on Elgar's return to Worcestershire, and by 1894 he was playing regularly with Elgar and his friends in chamber music in Worcester and Malvern. Through Sinclair and Blair, Atkins kept in close touch with the Three Choirs Festivals, and the Worcester and Hereford concerts. These concerts were now the only times that Atkins met Elgar, since the Elgars did not at that time go to the Three Choirs Festivals, apart from Worcester, and both these years they spent their summers at Garmisch in Bavaria.

Ludlow duties allowed Atkins to attend concerts over a wide area, including Birmingham and the Midlands. He was able to be present when Hugh Blair gave the first performance of *Sursum Corda* in Worcester Cathedral on 8 April 1894, and of Elgar's Organ Sonata in G on 8 July 1895, also in the cathedral.

1896

On 21 April Atkins heard Elgar conduct the first performance of his *From the Bavarian Highlands*, now orchestrated, at the Worcester Festival Choral Society's concert in the Public Hall.

The Festival in 1896 was at Worcester, and on 10 September Atkins was in the cathedral when Elgar conducted *The Light of Life* (*Lux Christi*) which had been written specially for the festival. My father recalls how impressive was the orchestral introduction, 'Meditation', and the subtle effects in tone coloration which later were to be such a feature of all Elgar's great choral works.

On 30 October, he went up to Hanley for the first performance of *King Olaf* at the North Staffordshire Musical Festival. Elgar conducted, and my father was very impressed by the chorus and their splendid voices. 'It was a glorious performance', he wrote.

1897

In August 1897, Atkins was elected organist of Worcester Cathedral, in time for him to take part in the Hereford Festival. Elgar's first letter to Atkins was written when he learnt of the appointment and was sent to him while he was still in Ludlow.

Forli, Malvern
Augt. 2: 1897

Dear Mr. Atkins,
 Please accept my congratulations on your appointment: I am so very glad you are to succeed Blair at Worcester.
 Will you tell me if you are thinking about the Conductorship of the Choral Society. It is always understood that the Cathedral Organist has it. My reason for asking is this: I have conducted for some years—to help Blair—the orchestral branch & have for some time been wishing to give it up. This year I have resigned, thinking you wd. of course succeed to the whole thing—which is what I should wish: *but*, if by any chance you do not want to be bothered with the Society if you wd let me know I *might* apply—*solely* because I don't want an outsider to have it. You can always rely on my assistance, if I am here, at the Concerts, &c. I think there is great scope for the formation of a big society in W. if 'worked up'. Kind regards.

Believe me,
Sincerely yours,
Edward Elgar.

Atkins replied:

Old Street, Ludlow.
9. Aug. 1897.

Dear Mr. Elgar,

Many thanks for your kind letter which I have received on my return from the sea.

In the event of my being offered the Conductorship of the Choral Society I should decidedly accept. Now as to the Orchestral Branch, if I were merely to think of myself I should be inclined to undertake this also, *for the sake of the experience* it would give. But as I am very diffident about my ability to succeed you there and as I see that it would afford me so many opportunities of working and coming into contact with you, I would ask you to take the matter into your own hands, always remembering that there need be no question of an outsider. Please do not regard this as an idle act of courtesy, but weigh very carefully in your mind the musical welfare of Worcester. I think I shall be able to bring a fair proportion of energy and enthusiasm to my work—but this is not all that is wanted.

I should greatly like to see you and have a chat about Worcester, but no doubt you are very busy.

With kind regards to Mrs. Elgar and yourself.
Yours sincerely,
I. A. Atkins.

The Hereford Festival of 1897 was an eventful one, which was to herald a new era in the Three Choirs Festivals. Sinclair was conducting his third festival, and it was Herbert Brewer's and Atkins' first Three Choirs Festival in their capacities of cathedral organists. Elgar, at Sinclair's request, had written a *Te Deum* and *Benedictus* in F for the Grand Opening Service, which also included the second performance of his *Imperial March*.

From now on the Elgars were present at all the Three Choirs Festivals, and in every festival there were to be performances of Elgar works, usually conducted by him.

Reverting to Worcester music, Atkins decided to take over both the choral and orchestral branches of the Worcester Festival Choral Society's concerts. Elgar's place as leader was taken over by John W. Austin, a well-known Worcester professional musician. Elgar's decision to give up the honorary leadership of the Society was partly because he wanted to concentrate on his composing, but also since, under pressure from his friends, he was considering the formation of a separate society of which he would be conductor.

The inaugural meeting of Elgar's new society was held in Worcester on 30 October, and the Worcestershire Philharmonic Society was launched. Both Sinclair and Atkins were founder members and later vice-presidents.

Elgar started voice trials early in November, and one of the first singing members was Dora Butler, who in 1899 married my father.

With Atkins' arrival in Worcester he and Elgar began meeting regularly, and that Christmas he received the first of a number of Elgar's characteristic Christmas–New Year cards. This card included a reproduction of an old lithograph of Malvern Priory, and a carol of two verses *Grete Malverne on a rocke*, set by Elgar. The words were said to be traditional, but Elgar's own invention cannot be entirely ruled out.

1898

Atkins was conducting his first Worcester Festival Choral Society concert on 25 January, and he had included in the programme Elgar's part-song *My Love dwelt in a Northern Land*. Elgar was now a non-playing member and had not therefore attended any of the rehearsals. He had, however, offered to give Atkins all the assistance that he could, and Atkins had accordingly asked Elgar to call on him at the cathedral when he was next passing, no doubt to consult him upon some point regarding the part-song, and hence the following letter.

Forli, Malvern
Jan. 6 [1898]

Dear Atkins,
    I am sorry I could not stop yesterday p.m. I came into the Cathedral &

(*opposite above*) The first two pages (second page is inset) of the manuscript score of *Froissart*. It was at the first performance of this work at the Three Choirs Festival at Worcester in 1890 that Atkins first met Elgar. Some forty years later Elgar gave Atkins the manuscript as a memento of the meeting which started their friendship. The drawing is an excellent example of Elgar's artistic ability

(*opposite below*) Chorus rehearsal in the Shirehall for the 1891 Festival at Hereford. George Robertson Sinclair is at the rostrum and Ivor Atkins at the piano (*Courtesy Basil Butcher*)

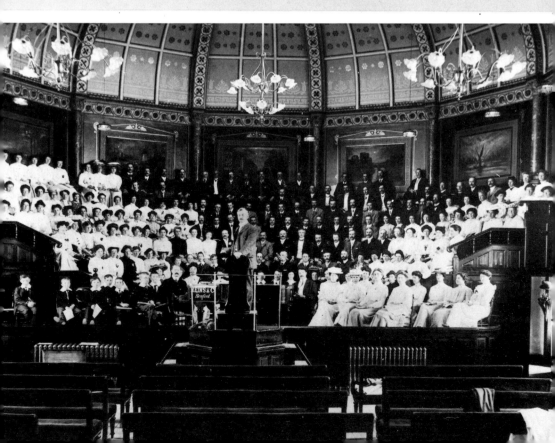

(*left*) Ivor Atkins at Ludlow in 1893 after his apppointment as organist to the Collegiate Church of St Lawrence, Ludlow; (*right*) Elgar in Hereford in 1896. This photograph was taken by Max Mossel, the violinist who was staying with George Sinclair, organist of Hereford Cathedral

Percy Hull (standing, left), Max Mossel (standing, right), George Sinclair (seated, left), Dan and Elgar photographed in Sinclair's garden in Hereford in 1896. Dan, the bulldog, who was more a bull terrier than the modern bulldog, was later to be the principal character in Variation XI of Elgar's *Enigma Variations* (*By permission of the Trustees of the Elgar Birthplace*)

remained as long as I could—but Mason [Atkins' assistant] will have told you this—if there's anything I can do let me hear.

Yours v. truly,

Ed. Elgar.

We go to London on Monday.

The new Worcestershire Philharmonic Society gave its first concert on 7 May, in the Public Hall, with Elgar conducting. The concert opened, as all the Philharmonic concerts were to do, with the chorus 'Wach auf!' from Wagner's *Die Meistersinger*, and the programme as might be expected was an ambitious one, including orchestral works by Beethoven, Tchaikovsky and Massenet, and choral works by Gounod, Humperdinck, Gluck, Liszt and a section from Elgar's *King Olaf*, 'And King Olaf heard the cry'. Among the second violins was Miss Rosa Burley, the proprietress of The Mount, a Malvern school where Elgar taught.

Mr and Mrs T. G. Hyde—he was one of Worcester's leading solicitors—gave receptions at their beautiful eighteenth-century house, 21, Foregate Street (which no longer exists) after each of these concerts. It was at these receptions, or in 'Forli', that Atkins first met Richard Arnold, William Meath Baker and Richard Baxter Townshend (two old friends of Alice Elgar's family), Isabel Fitton, Arthur Troyte Griffith, a Malvern architect, August J. Jaeger of Novello's, Basil Nevinson, Dora Penny (Dorabella), Hew David Steuart-Powell and Henry Ettling, a well-to-do amateur musician in Mainz and great admirer of Richter, who loved playing the drums whenever he could persuade Richter and others to let him. He represented a German wine house, but seemed able to attend concerts all over the country. He was a great practical joker and a very good amateur conjuror. The Elgars nicknamed him 'Uncle Klingsor'.

Atkins also met again at these receptions two old Hereford friends of his and Sinclair's, Miss Alice Underwood, a lady of great charm and dignity, known to all as 'The Duchess', and her friend Miss Lily Thomas. Many of these and others whom Atkins already knew became famous as Variations in Elgar's *Enigma Variations*.

In the summer of 1896, Elgar had found a small cottage, the lodge of a large house called Birchwood House, which he thought would make an ideal place in which to compose. In March 1898, the Elgars were able to rent Birchwood Lodge. It was a wonderful retreat for Elgar and they retained it until October 1903.

35

The next three letters relate to Birchwood Lodge.

Birchwood Lodge, Nr. Malvern
July 18 [1898]

Dear Atkins,

I have been so much occupied with my work for Leeds [*Caractacus*] that I have led the life of a recluse during the last six months & your call here [Forli] seems to have been ages ago—when will you come again? I am now orchestrating rabidly but have lucid intervals, mostly in the p.m. The greater portion of the week we are at our house in the woods. If you cycle wd you come up there? Tea? Let me hear where you are & I will send a map of the district. I hope to be at Gloucester & shall hope to see you at Leeds.

> Yours sincy,
> Edward Elgar.

Forli
July 20 [1898]

My dear Atkins,

I am so sorry but circumstances conspired to keep us here this week after all. We go to Birchwood on Monday for the week & wd be delighted to see you any p.m. If you cycle the best way is through Leigh Sinton keeping to the high road until you come to Birchwood drive gates—just a couple of hundred yards before *new* Storridge Church: we are a mile up the drive on your right—a little brown house on the edge of the wood.

If you walk, leave the high road just before the *tin Hospital* (turning on the right) & you follow the track up through the woods till you hit the house.

> Yours ever
> Edward Elgar.

P.S. If you should be engaged too fully next week I shall be *here* on Friday (the day you propose) & could give you a *bad* luncheon (our cook's away). Anyhow should be glad to see you.

Birchwood Lodge; Nr. Malvern.
Sunday [?14 August 1898]

Dear Atkins,

How very kind of you to unearth that Sonata: you will see we are away in the woods but shall be delighted to see you here if you can come so far. If you cycle the best way is this Leigh Sinton up as far as Storridge *new* church & then up—but I doubt if you will get so far!

If you come tomorrow the meet is near here & we might see some fun.

We can give you lunch or tea or both.

In great haste to catch post.

> Yours sincy,
> Ed. Elgar.

The reference to Gloucester in the 18 July letter was to the forthcoming Three Choirs Festival there in September. A. Herbert Brewer, who was to be the Festival Conductor for the first time, had asked Elgar to conduct the Meditation from *Lux Christi* in the opening service. The Elgars had been invited by William Meath Baker to stay for the festival week at Hasfield Court, and they expected to be at most of the performances.

On one of Atkins' visits to 'Forli' Elgar had talked about a Mendelssohn organ sonata which Blair had been fond of playing, and wondered if he had taken it with him or if it was still in the cathedral organ loft. Atkins could not recall it, but later, on reorganising the organ bookcase before his holiday, he found it and sent it to Elgar. Atkins had been hoping to get out to Birchwood Lodge before his holiday, but this had not been possible. Fridays were his free days, the cathedral services being unaccompanied, and from this time the Elgars extended an open invitation to him to visit them in 'Forli' or Birchwood on Fridays.

The great excitement of the year 1898, however, was the Leeds Festival, where, on Wednesday 5 October, an impressive first performance of Elgar's *Caractacus* was given to the enthusiastic delight of a number of Elgar's closest friends, including Atkins, who had travelled north specially. It was this festival which first made Elgar a public figure.

Ever since Atkins had heard the first performance of Elgar's Organ Sonata in G in July 1895, he had determined to play it himself on some occasion, and he included it in his cathedral organ recital on 17 November.

Birchwood Lodge
Nov. 18 [1898]

Dear Atkins,
   I send a hurried line to thank you for your performance of the Sonata: as you know I could not get over but my wife was present & was delighted with the rendering.
   I hope I may have the pleasure of hearing you play it some day on that mighty organ.

In haste
Sincerely Yours
Edward Elgar.

In late October Elgar began his sketches for the work which was to become the *Enigma Variations*, and he was working on them for the rest of the year. On Atkins' Friday visits Elgar played them to him.

My father told me that in his early drafting Elgar had considered making him the subject of one of the Variations, and indeed, on a 12-stave music paper sheet among the sketches now at the British Museum (Add MS 58003) the initials I.A.A. appear but are crossed out and G.R.S. (George Robertson Sinclair) placed on top, the G.R.S. initials in turn being crossed out. The initials of some of the other subjects also appear on the same sheet but not in their final order. This sheet is clearly a very early draft. G.R.S. and his bulldog Dan, mainly Dan, according to Elgar, became the subjects of Variation No XI. (A note in Elgar's handwriting, now in the Elgar Birthplace Archives, on Variation XI reads '. . . the variation has nothing to do with organs, Cathedrals or, except remotely, G.R.S. The first few bars were suggested by his great bull-dog "Dan" falling down the steep bank into the River Wye . . . G.R.S. said, "Set that to music." I did.')

Many years later I was to hear all about Dan's river exploits. In Hereford there is a popular walk from the cathedral across the old Wye Bridge, along the river bank to the footbridge and back through the Castle Green. This walk was a favourite one for Sinclair, his bulldog, Dan, my father and Elgar. During the Hereford Festivals of 1924, 1927 and 1930 I took this walk with Elgar and my father several times, and I heard on various occasions the story of Dan's rapid descent into the Wye after a stick, his paddling and triumphant return ashore. There was never any doubt about the point where Dan rushed down into the river, since there was an obvious place for this, but the point at which he re-emerged on the bank could never be agreed between them. Surprise has been expressed that Dan could swim, but as the photograph on page 34 shows, Dan was more like a modern bull terrier than today's heavy short-legged bulldog.

Even though my father did not in the end become a 'Variation', nevertheless his personality was to impress itself on Elgar musically, and Elgar did associate him with themes in the *Pomp and Circumstance March* No 3, dedicated to him, and in a passage in *The Kingdom*. (See pages 63 and 155.)

1899

In January Elgar was completing the *Variations*, and he then orchestrated them in the remarkably short time of a fortnight. On 24 February, he told Atkins that the score had been sent to Richter's manager, Nathaniel Vert. In a letter to Atkins postmarked 24 March Elgar writes, 'Richter is going to produce my Variations you will be glad to hear.' Some weeks later Elgar told Atkins that Richter's first rehearsal of the *Variations* would be held in the St James's Hall, which was on the present site of the Piccadilly Hotel, and invited him to be present.

Craeg Lea, Malvern
[Postmarked 2 June 1899, letter delivered in Worcester the same afternoon]

My dear Atkins,
 You asked me to let you have some old proofs [*Variations*]. I send 'em by this post—but if you *don't* want them keep them for me otherwise you are most welcome to them. The pf arrgt does not (as usual) at all represent the score.
 Kind regards & best hopes that all goes well with the festival & everything.
Sincy yours
Edward Elgar.

This letter was the start of a practice which was to continue throughout Elgar's and Atkins' friendship, namely the sending by Elgar of proofs of his compositions.
 On Monday 19 June, Atkins, with a large number of Elgar's friends, including many of the 'Variations', travelled to London for the first performance of the '*VARIATIONS for Full Orchestra (Op. 36)*', as it was named in the programme.
 The *Variations* ended the first part of the fifth concert of the thirty-second series of Richter concerts, which was held at St James's Hall.
 Atkins wrote that the work was an immediate success and that Richter and Elgar were delighted with the audience's enthusiastic reception of it. He noted that only Elgar, Jaeger and himself joined Richter in the artists' room, and although many musicians must have been present, none came to offer congratulations. 'Richter's deep toned voice and enthusiasm for the work made a great

impression upon my mind, but what Elgar's feelings at that moment were it would be impossible to say. I remember that he was singularly quiet.'

They soon, however, started discussing the work in detail, and Atkins recalled that Jaeger raised the point that the last Variation was too short and that the ending could be stronger. Jaeger appealed to Richter, who had already discussed one or two minor orchestral points, and Richter agreed that possibly as a concert piece the finale of the work could be further developed. Elgar disagreed. Shortly after this Richter left them. Jaeger continued pressing his point about the last Variation, and Atkins noted that Elgar was somewhat hurt and argued strongly that the ending was exactly as he wished it to be, and that any alteration would defeat his object.

Atkins had several discussions with Elgar over the succeeding weeks, and Elgar was clearly still very hurt about the matter, but he gradually accepted that further development might improve the final Variation, and by the time of the third performance, at the Worcester Festival Grand Concert in the Public Hall on 13 September, which was conducted by Elgar, some 100 bars had been added, so that the *Variations* were in their present form.

Reverting to March, there are two letters which refer to a hymn, *Lord of love and life and glory*, written by the Rev Henry Housman, later Rector of Bradley, Worcestershire, which Atkins afterwards set to music. (With the tune, *Worcester*, this hymn was to achieve success under the title *The Worcester Hymn*. In 1911 Novello's published a monograph about it with explanatory notes of the many references in it to the early history of the Worcester Diocese.)

Malvern
Tuesday p.m. [Postmarked 7 March 1899]

Dear Atkins,
   I saw Miss [Clemence] Houseman [*sic*] today & she will send you the Hymn with a request, I understand, that you will furnish a Tune.
   I told her my views as to the slight discrepancies in accents, but that matter will naturally fall to you to settle, i.e., if you write the Tune.
   I am glad you are pleased at my giving it up to you: don't forget (if anything shd prevent *your* doing it) that 'twill be 1000 pities that an outsider shd do it: You, as organist of the Cath. are the man.
Yours sincy
Edward Elgar.

College Yard, Worcester.
March 16th, 1899.

Dear Elgar,

I heard from Mr. Housman and have told him that it would give me great pleasure to write a tune for his hymn. Thank you very much for giving it up to me. I am afraid the immortality of the hymn and writer are sadly prejudiced. Who would have remembered Craigher but for Schubert's setting of Junge Nonne? But Mr. Housman had not that thought in his mind when he asked me.

Nothing shall prevent my doing it. Thank you very much.

Yours sincerely,
Ivor Atkins.

The 2nd and 3rd lines could never be brought to make sense in a musical setting. The point of rest is at the end of the 2nd line.

In 1899 the festival was at Worcester and was the first in which Atkins was the conductor and in charge of the programme. He was delighted that Elgar had promised to write a symphony—the *Gordon*—for this festival. Many of the letters this year therefore refer to festival matters and to the engagement of the individual players for the festival orchestra, which in those days was the personal responsibility of the conductor and was a very arduous one.

The story of Elgar's never written *Gordon* Symphony begins with a minute of the Worcester Festival's executive committee meeting on 29 December 1898. The conductor put before the committee the draft programme for the 1899 festival, which included the item 'Elgar—New Symphony'. It ends with a minute dated 18 May 1899:

The Conductor reported that Mr. Elgar found it impossible to carry out his promise to write a new Symphony, and the sub-committee decided instead to include in the programme Mr. Elgar's *Light of Life* [*Lux Christi*, written for the 1896 festival] . . .

Three of the following letters dealing with Worcester Festival matters are written from Basil G. Nevinson's home where the Elgars often stayed at this time when they were in London.

At 3, Tedworth Square, Chelsea, S.W.
March 19 [1899]

Dear Atkins:
   I hate to seem to interfere! but I saw Henderson (Timpani) at Q's Hall yesterday & he is most anxious to come to your Festival. You know what a good man he is.
   He said the engagements were out. I told him it was nothing to do with me but he asked me to send you a reminder.
Yours sincy
Ed. Elgar.

On 21 March the Elgars moved from 'Forli' to their new home, 'Craeg Lea' in Malvern Wells, and Elgar's first letter from this address, dated 24 March, and his earlier letter from Chelsea, refer to the fact that Atkins was at this time completing the separate engagement of each member of the festival orchestra.

Craeg Lea, Malvern
[Postmarked 24 March 1899]

My dear Atkins,
   If you haven't completed your *Contra Basso* list may I ask for Ch[arles] Winterbottom.
   He is *really* first-class.
   Richter is going to produce my Variations you will be glad to hear. We are settling in this new house & shall be glad to see you some time soon— it's rather *scrummagey* at present.
Yours sincy
Ed. Elgar.
P.S. Don't trouble to answer this: I get no end of letters asking me to plead for instrumentalists. I *only* bother you with those absolutely worthy!

Elgar's next letter refers to my father's marriage on 29 April to Katharine May Dorothea Butler. The remainder of this letter, and the following one, refer to the withdrawal by Elgar of the *Gordon* Symphony.

At 3, Tedworth Square, Chelsea, S.W.
May 9 [1899]

Dear Atkins:
   I am sorry we did not meet (I was away) before the auspicious day. All congratulations and good wishes for your future.
   Now—I am awfully sorry to tell you that I have had to write to Canon

42

Claughton as Chairman of the Music Committee to withdraw my new work from the scheme—the reason is merely the pecuniary one & this is unsurmountable. Its withdrawal need not be announced—just let it drop out of the scheme & no one will notice it.

I'm truly sorry—but it cannot be otherwise.

> Yours ever
> Edward Elgar.

On receipt of this letter, after a discussion with Canon Claughton, although it was not the practice of the festival committee to sponsor new works, Atkins wrote to Elgar offering to put forward at an early executive committee a proposal that they should consider making a payment which would ensure publication of the symphony, or perhaps pay a small fee.

3, Tedworth Square, Chelsea, S.W.
Sunday [Postmarked 15 May 1899]

My dear Atkins,
Very many thanks for your note which is most kind: I fear it is impossible to do anything about the Symphony—any publisher would *bring it out* but I cannot afford that—& I would not take a fee—if it were proposed—from your Committee, because there are plenty of composers who wd do 'something for nothing'.

> In much haste,
> Yours sincerely,
> Ed. Elgar.

This was not the full story, and it is most unlikely that the *Gordon* Symphony would have been written at this time even if a large commission had been forthcoming from another source, as some years later Elgar told Atkins that he had found that at this stage of his composition development he was not ready to write a symphony.

The next three letters refer to artists for the performance of *The Light of Life* (*Lux Christi*) in the forthcoming Worcester Festival.

Craeg Lea, Wells Road, Malvern.
June 6 [1899]

My dear Atkins:
I arrived home last night very hot. I saw Lloyd yesterday & he will willingly sing 'Lux Xti' instead of the 'Last Judgement' [Spohr] if it's in a programme for which he is already engaged.

Please do all you can to arrange this—it would *never do* to let anyone else do it at Wor[cester] as Lloyd produced it there.

I hope all else goes well.

In haste

Yours sincy

Ed. Elgar.

Let me know if there is any difficulty in arranging with L and I am most anxious to hear, (*before* the Committee announce anything), the rest of the proposed cast. Albani ought certainly to sing the Soprano, otherwise the thing will not draw, as is usual with the lesser works.

Atkins replied saying that he would look into the matter.

Craeg Lea, Wells Road, Malvern.
June 7 [1899]

Dear Atkins,

Many thanks for your note: please note that Lloyd will sing 'Lux' instead of 'Last Judgement' *only* if in a programme for which he is already engaged—I am not sure if I made it clear: it must not break into another day. I forget how the scheme goes so I could not tell him.

I hope it's all right. With many thanks for the rest of your note.

Yours ever,

Edward Elgar.

Craeg Lea, Wells Road, Malvern.
June 13 [1899]

Dear Atkins,

Many thanks for yours: if the cast you name can be managed it will do: the *festival manners* of the vocalists is beyond belief. Why they should look upon (for one week only) a $\frac{1}{2}$-programme work as a 'whole performance' is beyond me: as to any *favour*, it is of course out of the question to get Lloyd to do anything. I await your final decision—when you have heard from Vert—with breathless interest.

I have to go to Town for this Richter affair on Friday, [a preliminary discussion on the *Variations* score] so I cannot turn up at the Meeting on Saturday.

Yours sincy

Ed. Elgar.

In mighty haste.

Albani did not sing in *The Light of Life* and Esther Palliser took the soprano part, but Edward Lloyd sang his usual tenor part. The other artists were Marie Brema and Andrew Black.

Craeg Lea, Wells Road, Malvern.
July 23 [1899]

Dear Atkins,
  I am now home for a lucid interval after skirmishing in the North: we
are going to Birchwood Lodge to-morrow for a spell. How is the chorus
getting on? I hope well & should like to hear them sometime soon: the
Sheffield people are really splendid.
                              Yours sincy,
                              Edward Elgar.

  Elgar had been attending a rehearsal on 17 July when the
Sheffield Chorus were preparing his *King Olaf* for a performance
to be conducted by him on 11 October as part of the 1899 Sheffield
Festival.

Birchwood Lodge, near Malvern.
Augt. 25 [1899]

Dear Atkins,
  Do arrange for me a little earlier than 9 o'c so as to give time before the
people are tired.
  I shall be glad to hear also about London rehearsals also as soon as
possible: if you can avoid Wednesday morning (6th Sept.) please do as I
am wanted at Covent Garden but I am not sure if it is one of your days
but I suspect it is. Please give me a long time with the band!
                              Yours ever
                              Ed. Elgar.
  If you want a quiet afternoon bike up here & smoke in the woods—it's
no' bad.

  The first paragraph refers to the WFCS practice on Wednesday
30 August, when the *Light of Life* was to have been rehearsed last.
Atkins appreciated Elgar's point and rearranged the order of the
practice.
  The programme of Atkins' first Three Choirs Festival as
conductor, 10–15 September, followed the then standard practice
of opening with a 'Grand Service' and *Elijah*, and ending with the
Messiah and a closing 'Grand Service' on the Friday evening.
Coleridge-Taylor composed for the festival and conducted *Solemn
Prelude for Full Orchestra* Op 40, and Atkins had invited Horatio
Parker to conduct the first performance outside America of his
Hora Novissima. Elgar conducted his *Light of Life*, written for and
first performed at the 1896 festival, and at the Wednesday evening

concert his *Variations on an Original Theme*. This was the first performance of the *Variations* to include the last Variation in its extended form with the added coda, as we know it today. (The work was only performed twice in its original form.)

Horatio Parker was Professor of Music at Yale University, and his visit, with friends, was the start of regular visits to the Three Choirs Festivals of eminent American musicians. Many of them, Horatio Parker, George W. Chadwick, Samuel Simons Sanford and Thomas Whitney Surette, were to become close friends of Atkins and Elgar and will figure in this book.

It is of interest that the Band was for the first time at this festival called the Orchestra, and that it was the last time that the chorus included the Leeds contingent.

Among the principals at this festival were Madame Albani, Marie Brema, Ada Crossley, Muriel Foster, singing for the first time in the Three Choirs, Edward Lloyd, William Green and Plunket Greene. Atkins was very proud of having found Muriel Foster and of having started her on her great career.

The standing of artists like Madame Albani was very high. Atkins recalls how at this festival, when she stayed with the Dean, she brought her own carriage and pair and coachman with her, and always used it even to come down the short Deanery Drive to the cathedral. It had to be waiting outside the cathedral for her, and once when a rehearsal ended a few minutes early there was a great to-do until the carriage arrived.

On 5 October Atkins heard the first performance of Elgar's *Sea Pictures* at the Norwich Festival with Clara Butt as soloist, and on the 11th the Sheffield performance of *King Olaf*. Elgar's impression of the chorus was more than justified. My father often used to talk of the outstanding singing of the Sheffield choir, not only in *King Olaf*, but in Parry's *King Saul*, and in the *Messiah*.

Early in October Atkins decided to include the *Variations* in one of his regular cathedral organ recitals, and he invited Elgar to meet him in the cathedral on 26 October to try out various stop combinations.

[Postcard]
Tuesday [24 October 1899]

Dear Atkins,

Xqqq this card: we're just starting for B'wood. I'm your man on
Thursday: tell me, if you can conveniently, what time you want me 'cos
the trains are not nice. I'm sorry I've seen so little of you but I've been
awfully rushed. Do come over to the Cottage some day.

Yours ever
Ed Elgar.

They went through the work, Elgar adding to the score extra
notes for the organ, indications of scoring and suggestions for
organ registrations. The recital was given on 2 November, but as
the next letter shows, Elgar was unable to be present.

Craeg Lea, Wells Road, Malvern.
Nov 5 [1899]

My dear Atkins:

I was so sorry to miss your recital but I had to return early. I am sorry to
say my wife does not mend—I *think* she's a little better to-day but she has
been really unwell and I have felt tied.

I hope it all went well: if you have a moment give me your views as to
which of the things [*Variations*] are *arrangeable* for Organ in a not too
difficult way—there has been some talk of an (expurgated) edition for
organists' use—but it wd have to be for 3 manuals—I don't see how
anybody is to distil any spirit out of the Op. for two mans:

Your sincy
Edward Elgar.

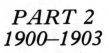

PART 2
1900–1903

1900

There are no letters between November 1899 and December 1900, no doubt because Atkins was now visiting the Elgars almost weekly.

The Birmingham Triennial Festival committee had commissioned Elgar in 1898 to write a choral work for the 1900 festival, and Elgar at first considered offering them a work about the Apostles on which he had been working intermittently for some years. He had also been working on sketches for *The Dream of Gerontius*. The scale of the scheme he was considering for the Apostles work, however, made him realise that he could not complete it in time for the 1900 festival, and he accordingly offered *The Dream of Gerontius*, which was accepted.

For most of the year Elgar was fully occupied with *Gerontius*, but he still found time for various concerts and for the Hereford Festival. He played over to Atkins during his Friday visits sections as they were written, and from April onwards gave him proofs as they were received.

My father told me about an incident that had occurred a few days before one of his visits in February. The back of 'Craeg Lea' was on the slopes of the Malvern Hills, with sheep grazing close to the house. The weather was very cold, and there had been a sudden and deep fall of snow. The shepherds appealed for help to rescue the buried sheep. Elgar broke off his writing and helped in the rescue of about five hundred sheep. On his return he continued his writing. He was working on his sketches for the 'Praise to the Holiest' section at the time, and six bars after 61 can be heard in the harp accompaniment the sound of the pattering of the rescued sheep on the frozen road surface.

During May there were two concerts in Worcester of particular interest to both of them. Atkins had invited Coleridge-Taylor to come down and conduct his *Hiawatha's Wedding Feast* and *Death of Minnehaha* at the WFCS concert on 3 May, and Elgar had included in his fifth Worcestershire Philharmonic Society concert, given on the afternoon of 5 May, Granville Bantock's orchestral scene, 'The Funeral', from his drama *Kehama*. The chorus for the Coleridge–Taylor concert, and Atkins' training of it, received warm praise in the *Musical Times*.

At the 1900 Hereford Festival in September, Elgar's *Te Deum*

51

and *Benedictus* in F were again played at the opening service, and he conducted Scene III from *Caractacus*.

The real excitement of 1900 was naturally *The Dream of Gerontius*, produced in the Birmingham Triennial Festival on 3 October. My father often talked about the events leading up to and the actual first performance, and among his papers I found some notes he wrote on the subject.

I travelled up for the final rehearsals with Elgar, cheerfully paying the excess upon my third-class ticket (a consideration to me in those days) in order to enjoy an hour's talk with him in the first class compartment in which he was travelling. At first *Gerontius* was entirely banished from the conversation, and we discussed far more important things—matters connected with the stage—its various conventions and so on. Eventually we got round to *Gerontius*. There were matters which I could see caused him anxiety. I remember him telling me to be prepared for disappointment in the semi-chorus. He said they did not reproduce what he had in mind, and the Demons' Chorus also had not gone well in the earlier rehearsal. The Chorus did not seem able to master it.

None the less, Elgar was in good form. Novellos, his publishers, had told him that Julius Buths, the Conductor of the Lower Rhine Festival, was coming to Birmingham, and that he and August Jaeger were to be quartered together at one of the hotels. He asked me to get in touch with both. Jaeger I already knew as a devoted Elgarite. In the musical world he is widely known today as the 'Nimrod' of the Ninth Variation. Jaeger was a man of very fine character, as may be judged from that variation—surely one of the noblest epitaphs ever written in music. Unfortunately, Jaeger was not well at Birmingham throughout the Festival, and Buths was thrown largely upon my hands. After the performance of *Gerontius* he and I met and compared notes. Notwithstanding the poor performance there was no mistaking his enthusiasm for the work. I well remember how impressed he was by its daring originality. His words tumbled over each other as he pointed out passage after passage, and lingered in admiration upon such master strokes of the imagination as that in the Angel's first entry, especially in the orchestration of the Allelujah, where the second violins and the double-basses double the melody at a distance of four octaves [full score fifth bar after No 11, Part 2].

During conversations with Elgar and my father some 25 years later, I asked Elgar how he set about fulfilling a commission for a new work, and whether he then had to think about a subject. Elgar explained that it was nothing like that, as far as *The Dream of Gerontius* was concerned, since he had been thinking about it for over 10 years and had indeed already prepared a large number of sketches. He then told me how it had all begun. Elgar had possessed a copy of the Newman poem for many years, and when Father Knight of St George's Church, Worcester, gave him, as a wedding present, another copy in which he had written in General Gordon's own notes, with the suggestion that he might consider setting it, Elgar had, as opportunity occurred, started working on it. He went on to say how delighted he was at the time of the commission that it had come from Birmingham, since Swinnerton Heap, who had been chorus master for the 1897 Birmingham Festival, was an old friend and a very accomplished musician, a solo pianist, a conductor and a promising composer, who understood his music thoroughly. But Heap's sudden death (11 June) had been a great shock and had altered everything. The festival committee was placed in a very difficult position, since there was not time to advertise for a new chorus master, and William Cole Stockley, who had been the chorus master from 1860 to 1896, had reluctantly agreed to take over training the chorus.

My father told me that it was in Stockley's Birmingham orchestra that Elgar had played as a first violin, and that Stockley had given the first performance of several of his early compositions. Elgar said that this was so, and he had in fact played in Stockley's orchestra from 1882 for about 6 years, and what a wonderful experience it had been for him at that time, playing in a large orchestra of professional players. The first performance of his *Sérénade Mauresque* was given by Stockley in 1883, and five years later he gave the first performance of an orchestral suite which later, in a revised form, became *Three Pieces for Orchestra*.

Elgar explained that though Stockley was a fine musician, he had been brought up in the old school, and in 1900 was in his seventies. He felt that Stockley would be unable to get the chorus, also brought up on the *Elijah* and the *Messiah*, to understand his new choral writing. Much rehearsal would be needed, and Elgar had hoped to be present at a number of these rehearsals. Rehearsals of the *Dream* were, in fact, very few, and Elgar was not invited to conduct the chorus until their final choral rehearsal on 12 September. At this rehearsal it was clear that the chorus were singing in a Handelian manner and did not understand the music or, for some of them, care for it. Elgar tried to explain, but felt that there was little that he could do.

My father asked Elgar whether he now felt he should have conducted the performance himself. Elgar replied:

I was at Richter's elbow for the orchestral and combined rehearsals, and if Richter, with all his great experience, could not get a good performance, I do not see how I could have done any better. The work had been under-rehearsed, and nothing could alter that.

This was indeed a year of disappointment for Elgar, not only because of the very poor Birmingham première of the *Dream*, but also because, largely due to this, August Manns on 4 October cancelled his Crystal Palace performance, which was to have taken place on 27 October, on the ground that he did not feel that it would be possible to train his chorus in time.

On 11 October Atkins gave an organ recital in the cathedral which included the Prelude to *Gerontius* and the *Enigma Variations*. Alice came to it, but Elgar, upset by the cancellation of the Crystal Palace performance, decided to go golfing.

Late in October Atkins, still disappointed by the withdrawal of the new Elgar work from the 1899 festival, sounded out Elgar for a new work for the Worcester festival in 1902, and Elgar said he would think about it. Atkins was also determined to include *Gerontius* in the Worcester programme, although he appreciated that a performance of it in an English cathedral would present difficulties. They had a discussion about *Gerontius*, but as no decision needed to be made about this until 1902 and Atkins desperately wanted a *new* Elgar work for Worcester, he concentrated all his efforts on trying to obtain Elgar's agreement to write one. On 10 November, thinking that a formal invitation might clinch the matter, he asked the festival committee to invite Elgar to write a new work for the 1902 Three Choirs Festival, the work to be in their hands by May 1902. Atkins' strategy, unfortunately, did not come off.

Langham Hotel, Portland Place, London, W.
Tuesday p.m. [Postmarked 11 December 1900]

My dear Atkins,
    I had a letter from the Secy of the Festival enquiring as to a new work. I had to decline but expressed a hope for 'Gerontius'.
    I also recommended strongly Walford Davies. I hope you approve of this & will back it up. I think he ought to have a chance; don't you?
    Kindest regards to Mrs. Atkins & yourself.
                    Yours ever
                    Edward Elgar.

Elgar's request that the committee should invite Henry Walford Davies, who was then virtually unknown as a composer, to write the 'new work' was characteristic of him and of his interest in encouraging young composers and artists.

Craeg Lea, Wells Road, Malvern.
Dec 18 [1900]

My dear Atkins,

Many thanks for your two letters. I am truly glad you like the Walford Davies idea. Will you thank your two Branches for their very kind congratulations which I appreciate very deeply. [Atkins had written, on behalf of both the choral and orchestral branches of the Worcester Festival Choral Society, to congratulate Elgar on the conferring on him of an honorary degree of Doctor of Music at Cambridge on 22 November.]

Now as to the conducting at your Concert; if YOU *really* wish it I'll come. I don't really think the Worcester people care two pins about me whom they call 'their *townsman*'—which I'm really not. But my goodwill to you is much, & I hate making a fuss, so if you'll have me I'll come. I daresay we shall meet before the time. So no more now.

Yours ever
Ed. Elgar.

1901

The concert referred to was a WFCS one on 14 January 1901, in which Elgar conducted his *My Love dwelt in a Northern Land*, Serenade for Strings, Op 20, and *Fly, Singing Bird, fly*. In the same concert C. Lee Williams conducted his choral song *Music*, and Atkins appeared, not only as conductor but also as an artist in a work now long forgotten, Benjamin Godard's Second Trio for Violin, Cello and Piano. The programme was an extensive one, containing also works by Brahms, Chaminade, Gounod, Percy Pitt, Purcell, Saint-Saëns, Sullivan, Tchaikovsky and Walthew.

Elgar's WPS concert on 17 January was largely devoted to English compositions, and included Stanford's *Last Post*, Parry's part-song *The Sea has many a thousand Sounds* and Walford Davies' *Hymn before Action*. Atkins was not well at this concert, which explains the following letter.

55

Craeg Lea, Wells Road, Malvern.
Jan 28 [1901]

My dear Atkins:
    I am anxious to know how you are—it seems a long age since the
Concert [17 January]. We do hope you are better: I should feel sure you
wd be by this time if the weather had been more suitable for out of doors.
    Look here, if you are not feeling fit you can turn me on any time for
your rehearsals—I'll always gladly do what I can.
    Kindest regards from us both to Mrs. Atkins & yourself.
                              Yours ever
                              Edward Elgar.

Elgar decided early in 1901 that, although it would not be
possible to give a complete performance of *The Dream of Gerontius*
at a Worcestershire Philharmonic Society concert, it would be
possible to give a 'Selection from the Dream of Gerontius' at their
9 May concert. The 'Selection' included the whole of Part 1, but
Part 2 was abridged. My father told me that he was amazed by the
results that Elgar obtained considering the limitations, especially
in the small orchestra. The performance was an excellent one and
showed clearly the value of adequate and painstaking rehearsals,
even with a chorus that already knew Elgar's music. Certainly this
performance gave great pleasure to those who had been present at
the Birmingham première.
    Included in the second half of the programme was *Sea Pictures*
and also an orchestral work, *Romance and Bolero*, by the leader,
John W. Austin, Junior, another example of Elgar's encouragement for local composers. John was later to become a personal
friend and to help Elgar in checking the orchestral parts in the
proofs. My father remembers how when Austin took the baton to
conduct his own work Elgar, who had quietly slipped into the
leader's seat, was awaiting his beat.

Malvern.
Sunday [2 June 1901]

My dear Atkins:
    I suppose you are home. Come over to tea tomorrow as is Whit
Monday. I want to hear your Brogue which I xpect is fine & strong.
    Jaeger is here until Tuesday. Orlando Howle is on hand & we are
festive.
                              Yours ever
                              Edward Elgar

Atkins had been adjudicating at the Feis Ceoil in Dublin. Orlando Howle was a character invented by Elgar and first used by him in a 'spoof' letter sent to 'A. Troyte Griffin, Esqre, Priory Gateway, Malvern', on 19 December 1900. Enclosed was a printed piece of sentimental verses which Elgar had cut out from some magazine. The letter signed 'Orlando Howle' said that Elgar had recommended him to send the lyric to Troyte as 'you can compose this sort of thing better than he can'. Troyte saw through the deception, and wrote to Elgar enclosing a letter from himself (Troyte) to Howle saying that he 'could not stand in the way of a brother artist. Dr Elgar undoubtedly has the prior claim.' The reference to Howle indicates that Troyte is with Elgar for his birthday.

On 3 June Elgar played over *Cockaigne* to Atkins and to Jaeger, and on 20 June Atkins attended the first performance at the Queen's Hall, London, which was conducted by the composer. 'A great success', he noted.

At the Gloucester Festival Elgar conducted the Prelude and Angel's Farewell from *Gerontius* in the opening service, and *Cockaigne* at the Wednesday evening concert, 11 September, and on the following evening Herbert Brewer conducted the first performance of *Emmaus*, which he had written specially for this festival. Earlier in the year there had been difficulties with the librettist, and Brewer had been ill. It had looked as if the performance would have to be postponed. Elgar, characteristically, on hearing of this, immediately offered to help with the orchestration, and so enabled the work to be ready for performance.

Professor Sanford had now become a close friend of both Atkins and Elgar and was a regular attender at Three Choirs Festivals. At Gloucester he had given Elgar a bag of American tobacco, and had promised on his return home to send further supplies. Sanford was still in England at this time and Atkins was going to see him.

Craeg Lea, Wells Road, Malvern.
Monday [Postmarked Worcester, 23 September 1901]

My dear Atkins:
We arrived home on Saturday night. I am distressed about the Gold Mine & have received no reports yet.
Will you tell Prof Sanford that I sat down in front of that Bag of

Tobacco & smoked solemnly for three days & am completely captured—I love it. I have given away remains of

    I   L[ambert] & B[utler]'s Bird's eye
    II   Craven Mix.
    III Evening Glow (Mix).
    IV A private Mixture of my own
    V   Sundry cigars
    VI   ,,   cigarettes

& now I've cleaned all my pipes (17) & am waiting with fevered eye, parched tongue, & a *box* of matches for MORE. I'm coming to see you as soon as I've 'cleared off' my accumulated letters. Howle has sent some more poems—fine!

Yours ever
Ed. Elgar

I cannot explain the 'Gold Mine' reference, which occurs also in later letters. I suspect, however, that it was one of Elgar's 'Japes', involving a small group of his friends of which my father was one and Alfred Kalisch another. It seems to have been a much smaller group than the STP Society, to which reference will be made later in the letters. The 'poems' supposedly sent by 'Howle' had possibly been sent by Troyte, but more probably Elgar had now found some more choice gems of doggerel to be jointly savoured.

Kalisch was a well-known critic on the Continent, and had championed Richard Strauss in the latter's early days. He was a close friend of Jaeger, who introduced him to Elgar and Atkins. He became a great friend of both, and also of Granville Bantock. He met them all frequently when reviewing English concerts. With a keen and mischievous sense of humour, he was always ready to enter into any of Elgar's lighthearted schemes.

On Atkins' visit on Friday evening, 25 October, Elgar and Alice were full of their visit to Rodewald in Liverpool, from which they had just returned, and of the tremendous reception Elgar had been given there after the first performance, on 19 October, of the *Pomp and Circumstance Marches* Nos 1 and 2. These had been given by the Liverpool Orchestral Society conducted by Rodewald, who by now had also become a friend of Atkins since he frequently visited the Elgars in Malvern.

Alfred E. Rodewald was of German extraction but had lived most of his life in England. He had built up a considerable fortune as a cotton broker, but his first love had always been music, and he became a very fine conductor, as well as being a double-bass player who often played for Richter. He lived in Liverpool, but had also a house in Saughall, Cheshire, and a cottage in Betws-y-Coed. The Elgars were always welcome guests, and stayed in all three houses from time to time. In 1884, when he was 23, Rodewald had founded in Liverpool the People's Orchestral Society, an entirely amateur group. In 1890 he reformed this into the Liverpool Orchestral Society, and, although there were still some amateur players, he added professional musicians, largely at his own expense, and enhanced the orchestra's reputation until it rivalled the long-established Liverpool Philharmonic Orchestra, who were still adhering to more conservative programmes. Rodewald had already performed many of Elgar's works, and in return for his great support Elgar dedicated the first *Pomp and Circumstance March* to him and to his orchestra. The second was dedicated to Granville Bantock.

Craeg Lea, Malvern
Thursday [? 31 October 1901]

My dear Atkins:
    Look at this HARD & send it back at once like an Angel.

Yours ever
Very ill
Edward

The note enclosed a first proof of the German vocal score of the *Dream of Gerontius*, a particularly fine example of Novello's beautiful engraving. Elgar at that time still had need of this proof, but subsequently he gave it to Atkins.

Craeg Lea, Wells Road, Malvern.
Nov 25 [1901]

My dear Atkins:
    I am so sorry I could not get in for you last Monday: owing to the awkward interdependence of things I rec'd your telegram late.
    Pray command me another time, & only if you can give me longer notice.

Yours ever
Ed. Elgar

Atkins had invited Elgar to be present at one of the Worcester Festival Choral Society's rehearsals.

On 12 December the ninth Worcestershire Philharmonic Society concert was held, and had a special interest for Atkins because Elgar was conducting the first performance in England of Philip Wolfrum's *Ein Weihnachts-Mysterium* (A Christmas Mystery). This work, now long forgotten, was first produced in Heidelberg in 1899, and had created a great impression in Germany in the many performances it had received there, because it had broken away from the normal oratorio form, and in consequence had greatly interested both Elgar and Atkins.

[Postcard of the Kunsthalle, Düsseldorf]
Düsseldorf. Dec. 23, 1901.

Best wishes to Mrs. Atkins & yourself for Xmas and always. Gerontius has been the most triumphant success.
Yours ever
Ed. Elgar.

This refers to the first, and less known, performance in Germany of *The Dream of Gerontius* in the German version prepared by Dr Julius Buths, which took place under his conductorship at Düsseldorf on 19 December. It was an outstanding success. Atkins had a number of discussions with Jaeger and Elgar about the first performance in Germany, and among his papers was this note about it:

The work was given in the Kaisersaal der Städtische Tonhalle, Düsseldorf, in the German version which had been made by Buths. A man of wide musical sympathies and high culture, he had been present at this production of 'Gerontius', and accepting it at once as a work of genius, he had marked it down for inclusion in the programme of the Lower Rhenish Festival of 1902. This 1901 performance, therefore, seems to have been intended as a try-out of the work in its German form, and a preparation for the performance at the larger 1902 Festival.

Elgar said that Wüllner was outstanding as Gerontius, and that at that time there was no singer in England to equal him for so completely entering into the part. He liked the bass, Metzmacher, as the Priest, but was disappointed in Antonie Beel as the Angel. Elgar was greatly impressed with the Chorus of 80 members of the Düsseldorf Choral Society and their round smooth tone, and very surprised by the very fine performance of the orchestra of 85, made up of the Town Band and members of the Band of the local Regiment.

Elgar was very interested in the effective placing of the small Semi-Chorus immediately behind the Soloists and in front of the Orchestra. He was particularly impressed also by Professor Franke's realisation of the Organ part. With a fine organ in the midst of the choral and orchestral forces, Franke had, in Elgar's words 'simply let himself go' fearlessly, giving the utmost support in just those places where Elgar had hoped for it.

The outstanding success of this performance of *The Dream of Gerontius* at Düsseldorf is clear from the reports in the German papers, which record that Elgar was repeatedly called to the platform and loudly applauded by the audience of over 2,500 who packed the hall. The chorus presented him with a large laurel wreath, and the orchestra greeted him with a special fanfare, both unusual honours.

1902

The year 1902 was a remarkable one for Elgar and his friends, especially for Atkins, for it not only saw three wonderful performances of *The Dream of Gerontius* (one at the Lower Rhenish Musical Festival at Düsseldorf, and the others, conducted by Elgar, at the Worcester meeting of the Three Choirs Festival and at the Sheffield Festival), but also the first performance of the *Coronation Ode* and the first serious start of the writing of *The Apostles*.

When Atkins went to Craeg Lea on 24 January, Elgar talked about his performance of the *Grania and Diarmid* music in the Queen's Hall concert on 18 January, and about the splendid reception that the *Pomp and Circumstance Marches* Nos 1 and 2 had been given in Birmingham the previous Tuesday. He also played over *Dream Children*, which he had recently finished.

Preparations for the performance of *Gerontius* at the forthcoming Three Choirs Festival were not only to occupy much of Atkins' and Elgar's time during the earlier months of 1902, but were also to be the principal item on many of the festival executive committee's agendas. At the festival committee on 5 February, Atkins had submitted a draft programme which showed the order of the music for the Thursday morning and afternoon, 11 September, to be: Bach's *The Lord is a Sun and Shield*; Elgar's *Gerontius*; and Brahms' Symphony in F. This had been approved.

There were, however, other musical events of interest to them both. On receiving Walford Davies' formal acceptance of the commission to write a new work, *The Temple*, for the festival, Atkins had felt that it would be a good idea to familiarise the chorus with some of his already published work, and accordingly the WFCS concert on 6 February contained Walford Davies' cantata *The Three Jovial Huntsmen*, conducted by the composer. Having recommended Walford Davies, Elgar was especially pleased, as was Atkins, at the fine performance of this happy work which was much enjoyed by the audience and performers alike.

On Friday 7 February, Atkins had spent the day, as usual, at Craeg Lea, and Elgar had played to him a tune which fascinated him and to which he lost his heart completely. Elgar immediately wrote it down and gave it to him. The sketch is entitled 'Pomp and Circumstance No 4. I. A. Atkins gewidmet', and signed and dated. 'Ed. E. Feb 7: 1902'. It eventually formed the trio of the third *Pomp and Circumstance March*, which he wrote in 1905 and dedicated to Atkins. The sketch is reproduced opposite.

Atkins had clearly been thinking again about the order of the music on the Thursday morning at the festival, as both of the following letters make reference to the Elgar tune.

8, College Yard, Worcester.
Feb. 8th, 1902.
My dear Elgar,
I have been turning over the order of Thursday's performance, Bach, Gerontius, Brahms; and when I recall the end of Gerontius it gives me rather a cold shudder to think of the jarring start of the Brahms. Unquestionably, from the poetic side, this is better:—Brahms, Gerontius, Bach. Then you have 'Bring us not, Lord, very low . . . Come back, O Lord . . . and be entreated for Thy servants. Praise to the Holiest.'

And then after the Gerontius the Chorus break into 'For the Lord our God is a sun and shield.'

Of course, against this arrangement you must put the fact of keeping the chorus 35 minutes. In point of time it works out all right: (. . .)

Now this is a point for you and for you alone, turn it over quietly and let me know on Tuesday.

I played *the* tune very proudly this afternoon to an attentive and a thrilled congregation, and I know that their deeds will now be valiant for they were woxen moche pale and leve of praysing and wakying, like Reynart.

Eh! but that is an insidious tune!
Yours ever,
Ivor Atkins.

The start of the Cantabile section. This P&C March was published as No 3.

In the last sentence of this letter Atkins drops into the language of Caxton's 1481 version of 'Reynard the Fox'. He had for some years possessed a copy of Edward Arber's admirable reprint of the Caxton version, and he had recently found a second copy which he had given to Elgar. They both loved literature and were in the habit of presenting each other with books which had pleased them. Atkins was fascinated by 'Reynard the Fox'. Its wit, its caustic satire, the vividness of its language and even its spelling were a deep joy to him. He felt sure that it would appeal to Elgar. It did. He completely fell for it.

Craeg Lea, Wells Road, Malvern
Sunday [Postmarked 9 February 1902]

My dear Atkins:
Very many thanks for thinking of the position of 'Gerontius'. I *fear* it will have to remain as it is—we'll talk & before talking I'll think again.
Yours ever
Ed. Elgar.

This appears on the back of the envelope of this letter.

A few weeks later the Thursday morning programme was, in fact, rearranged in a different order.

On 1 March it was announced at a festival committee that Elgar's *Dream of Gerontius* would be performed during the forthcoming Three Choirs Festival.

A postcard to Atkins written on the evening of 7 March is reproduced here. Atkins had been unable to go to Craeg Lea on the two previous Fridays, but before this card was posted Elgar had learnt that he was coming over that same afternoon (Saturday 8 March). He stayed to dinner and returned by the last train.

The dramatic fragment, 'Avenge the foul death of my father', appears to be a parody of George Tolhurst's style in his oratorio *Ruth*, a work my father told me had greatly amused them both—that 'fountain of joy', Elgar called it. When they were together at this time, he said, there was a serious danger that one or other of them would break out and declaim it in impassioned tones.

The next letter is unusual in that it is entirely written in a light-coloured green ink which Elgar kept for proof-correcting. The

WFCS weekly practice had been the previous evening and was devoted mainly to rehearsing *Gerontius*.

Thursday [13 March 1902]

My dear Atkins:
  This *is* ink!

I am a 〰 [worm] & no man—having a chill—better to-day but dubious about future. Hope you had a good Chorus meeting & all is going well as it leaves me *not* at present.
                    I am woxen moche pale
                        Yours ever
                          Ed. E.

Craeg Lea, Wells Road, Malvern
March 17 [1902]

            Firapeel:
My dear ~~Isambart~~
  I have been in euyll case—bad cold better now but wheezy. I hope to be out to-day for more than a short walk, which was all allowed me, for my synnes yesterday.
  Come over soon: it has been a dreary week & I can't think how I took this chill, certainly NOT in teachynge Dame Erswynd to fysshe.
                  What an awful Book it is!
                      Yours ever
                        Ed. Elgar.

This letter shows that Elgar was experimenting with a character for Atkins. His first idea of 'Isambart' appears to be a combination of Isegrim the Wolf and Grimbart the Badger. He finally chose Firapeel the Leopard, and he himself naturally was Reynart the Foxe.

With work on the *Coronation Ode* and preparations for the forthcoming performance of the *Dream* at the festival, both Elgar and Atkins had to put aside for some weeks the charms of Reynart the Foxe, and their letters continued in the old style.

8, College Yard, Worcester.
March 18th, 1902.

My dear Elgar,
  We are under way with 'Gerontius'. We tackled the Demons' Chorus with appropriate savagery and it was, I assure you, quite a realistic bit of

Atkins, Sinclair and Herbert Brewer photographed outside the cloister gate at
the Three Choirs Festival at Worcester in September, 1899. This was Atkins'
first Festival as conductor. Photograph by T. Bennett and Sons

(*left*) Alice and Edward Elgar outside their home Forli, Malvern Link. In 1897 Atkins became organist of Worcester Cathedral and began making regular visits to the Elgars; (*right*) Birchwood Lodge, a cottage set in woods near Storridge in Herefordshire, with a superb view to the north east of the valley of the river Severn and of Elgar's much-loved river Teme. Much of *Gerontius* was written in this favourite retreat

Elgar finishing the score of *Gerontius* on 3 August, 1900, photographed by his friend William Eller of Ledbury, who bicycled over to see him that afternoon

work. Enough to make some of them retrace their steps.

But the work is wonderfully beautiful and appeals to me in every bar. Dear old Elgar, it will be strange if we don't give it a fine performance. I shall put all the little I know into making it what it ought to be, and I can see that it's going to draw the best out of my chorus.

Just off to my boys [the cathedral choristers]. I hope to come and see you both Wed or Thursday.

Excuse this vile scrawl,

Yours ever,

I.A.

The Dream of Gerontius was the main subject of festival executive committee meetings during March and April. After the meeting was over Elgar went back to lunch with Atkins, who told him again how much the *Dream* appealed to him and how well the WFCS rehearsals were going. He also suggested that on his next Friday's visit they should bicycle together into Herefordshire and, to save time, that they should start from Colwall station, Atkins bringing his bicycle there by train. Elgar thought this would be a good idea. Unfortunately he was not well the next week, and hence the next letter.

Craeg Lea, Wells Road, Malvern.
Wednesday night [26 March 1902]

My dear Atkins,

I was beastly bad yesterday—better to-day, corrected proofs all the a.m. & went for a mild Bicycle ride with Claughton in the afternoon. [Alban Claughton, a son of Canon Claughton, was then organist of Malvern Priory.]

I should have written in time for ordinary post but callers, or rather *callesses* (new word) & one stayed to dinner: peace now, & chortling thereat & therefore.

Your Friday scheme is noble but no good *Bikily*: Look 'ere! If I *walk* to Colwall pushing the Bike over the hill I shall get $\frac{1}{4}$ mile ride—& have to push the Bike all the way back here. If the evenings were a *bit* longer we could have gone to the Holly Bush Pass to tea & 'so home' (Pepys). Do you come straight here & we'll jaw this time, & plan other raids into Herefordshire.

Thanks for *all* you say regarding my beloved work—I do hope they will *see* it & feel it—the Chorus, I mean. I am sure you will 'enthuse' them if anybody can and all thanks to you for so doing.

I look for a visit on Friday.

Yours ever

Edward Elgar.

When the decision was taken to include the *Dream of Gerontius* in the 1902 festival Atkins appreciated that there would be some doctrinal problems to be solved if the performance was to be, as planned, in the cathedral. The main difficulty would be that the Invocations to the Blessed Virgin Mary and to the saints in the poem, although in accordance with Roman Catholic doctrine, were contrary to the Thirty-nine Articles of the Church of England. Atkins therefore had informal discussions with Canon T. L. Claughton (the Chairman of the festival executive committee) and with the Dean, Dr R. W. Forrest. All were anxious for the performance to take place in the cathedral and for a solution to be found. It was clear that the Litany of the Saints would have to be omitted, and alterations or omissions made in the references to the Blessed Virgin Mary.

Atkins on his recent visits to Elgar had discussed the matter with him. Elgar saw the difficulty and said that he would be agreeable to any music changes that might be involved. He also appreciated that, when a suggested solution had been found, the consent of the copyright holder of the poem would have to be obtained. He said that he knew well Father Richard Bellasis, of the Birmingham Oratory, and agreed to approach through him Father William Neville, who had been a very old friend of Cardinal Newman and who was now his executor and the owner of the copyright. After further discussions between Atkins and Canon Claughton and further thoughts regarding the changes that seemed necessary, it was agreed that the matter must be put formally to the Lord Bishop of the Diocese (Bishop Gore), who would then write to the festival executive committee.

At the festival executive meeting on 12 April the letter from the Bishop, dated 10 April, was read stating that representations had been made to him pointing out that in *The Dream of Gerontius*, which was included in the festival programme, there were invocations to the Blessed Virgin Mary and to the saints and angels such as were not lawful in the Church of England. Canon Claughton (the Chairman) stated that he had seen Bishop Gore and had discussed with him the subject of his letter and he thought it would be advisable to postpone consideration of the subject for a short time. This suggestion was adopted, and an adjourned meeting of the committee was fixed for 26 April. On Atkins' next visit to Elgar on 19 April the Bishop's letter was further discussed between them. It was agreed that Elgar would now approach Father Bellasis to arrange a meeting with Father Neville.

The following postcard probably refers to some other matter discussed at the same visit. It is one of several other mysterious 'reports'.

[IA to EE, postcard, 21 April 1902]

Gold Recovery Works

Belated Inspector's Report

Great activity at works. Two men, two wheelbarrows, all in motion. Fear our ground being encroached upon by Sasparilla Pills. Matter needs investigation.

Atkins was unable to go over to Elgar the next Friday, and hence the following letter, which refers to *Dream of Gerontius* rehearsals and reminds Elgar of the urgency of contacting Father Neville.

8, College Yard, Worcester.
April 25th, 1902.

My dear Elgar,
    We want you (i.e. *I* want you)

	Wednesday 30th April	(Full)
7.30 p.m.	Monday, 5th May	(Full)
	and	
	Wednesday, 7th May	(S. and A.)

    Two practices are full and one is for the 'Hupper' voices. I attach great importance to the latter—if you would rather not take this one will you let me know by return. I have not tackled the problem of the 3 sopranos pp. 124, 125, so they have not touched these bits. I think the better way would be to give the *2nd* part to Gloucester and the others (1 and 3) to W. and H. It would save the complications of a division into 3.
    We rely on you to write to the owner of the copyright via Father B[ellasis].
    I love the sound of Diarmid [*Grania and Diarmid*, incidental music to words by Yeats and George Moore, 1901]. Its rarely beautiful and sehr innig—sehr innig! Ach Gott! how fayre the ideas be! My best anticipatory greetings to Dame E[rswynd]. Will you be smitten moche harte? Muste ye bend very lowe? Yours in sympathy when the time comes,

I.A.

Elgar had given Atkins proofs of *Grania and Diarmid*, and he had been studying them with a view to a possible performance.

At the adjourned meeting of the festival executive committee on 26 April, a second letter from Bishop Gore, dated 25 April, was read. This referred to certain alterations which it had been suggested might be made in the words of the *Dream of Gerontius*, and stating that if the work was thus modified his objections to it were gone. Canon Claughton explained the nature of the modifications, which at this stage were on the basis of omitting the Litany of the Saints, and of a general substitution of 'Jesus', 'Lord' or 'Saviour' for 'Mary'; of 'souls' for 'souls in purgatory'; and, in the Angel's Farewell, of 'prayers' for 'Masses', and he added that Dr Elgar fell in with the suggestions and had promised to apply for the assent of the representative of the author.

On 10 May Elgar conducted, as usual, the Worcestershire Philharmonic concert. Henry Ettling was staying with the Elgars and had brought his drums with him. The programme included Parry's cantata *The Lotos-Eaters*, Elgar's *Pomp and Circumstance Marches* Nos 1 and 2 and Schubert's Symphony No 5 in B flat. My father told me that Ettling's drum-playing, nobly supported by Alban Claughton on the cymbals and W. Austin on the triangle, was sensational, and that the audience went mad with excitement. At tea at the Hydes after the concert Ettling was again the life and soul of the party with his conjuring and sleight-of-hand tricks.

Elgar was very busy at this time with *Dream Children* (Op 43) proofs, orchestrating the *Coronation Ode* (Op 44) and with matters in connection with the forthcoming performance of the *Dream of Gerontius* at the Lower Rhine Festival.

By 16 May when the Elgars had to leave for Germany to attend rehearsals with Dr Julius Buths, Elgar had still not visited Father Bellasis, and the matter was now becoming urgent as printing of the Word Books for the festival was now in hand. Atkins accordingly had to prepare, for the copyright holder's approval, drafts of the suggested modification of the words of Newman's poem which would appear in the Book of Words. He prepared two sets of drafts, the first embodying the word modifications which had been approved by Bishop Gore, and the second prepared on Atkins' own plan of omissions only, which would be indicated by asterisks, and which he felt might be more acceptable. He then made his own arrangements to call upon Father Neville at the Birmingham Oratory. My father has left a note describing his interview from which I quote below:

I spoke of our love for the work and my own anxiety that a way should be found for its performance at Worcester. I spoke of my own feeling for the poem, and pointed out that no word would be changed. 'No', he said, 'there must be no alteration.' I then produced the proofs of the poem as it was to appear in the word books. He looked at the opening line where the word 'Maria' had been omitted and indicated by dotted lines—'Jesu, . . . I am near to death.' He went carefully through the poem, I at his side pointing out where omissions had been made (other than those made by Elgar when setting the work). At the end he put the proofs into my hands with the words, 'In that form I give my consent to the poem being printed. But remember—there must be no alterations.'

Elgar had already agreed with Atkins the omissions he himself wanted. The draft based on only those omissions approved by Father Neville was acceptable to Bishop Gore, and was now sent back to the printers to be inserted in Herbert Thompson's analytical notes.

With the Book of Words settled and WFCS rehearsals going well, Atkins' mind turned to Elgar and the Lower Rhine Festival performance of *The Dream of Gerontius*. Jaeger and Elgar had very much wanted him to go over to Düsseldorf, but with the rehearsals on the Saturday and Monday and the performance on Monday night, 19 May, it would have meant him being away not only for the weekend cathedral services, but also for his Monday evening WFCS rehearsal, which at this time was unthinkable. It was not until June that he was to hear detailed accounts of Elgar's visit to Düsseldorf, both from him and from Jaeger. To put events in the correct sequence, however, I give now an abbreviated account of the events at Düsseldorf taken from my father's notes.

Elgar and Alice had travelled out with Alfred Rodewald, who accompanied them throughout their whole tour. At Düsseldorf they were joined by Jaeger, Mr and Mrs Arthur Johnstone, Alfred Kalisch and Henry J. Wood. There were banquets each evening, and the English party were lavishly entertained, Strauss going out of his way with Buths to ensure their comfort.

For the performance of *The Dream of Gerontius* on 19 May, the organ was again played by Professor F. W. Franke of Cologne. There was an orchestra of 127 players: 3 harps, 42 violins, 16 violas, 12 cellos, 10 double basses, 6 flutes, 6 oboes, 4 clarinets, 4 bassoons, 8 horns, 6 trumpets, 4 trombones, 1 tuba, 1 kettle-drum, 3 percussion and organ. The chorus of 490 singers, which included members of the Düsseldorf Society who had sung the work in 1901 and were now thoroughly familiar with it, consisted of 169 sopranos, 160 altos, 56 tenors and 96 basses. The semi-chorus was again placed behind the soloists and in front of the orchestra. Dr Ludwig Wüllner repeated his 1901 success as Gerontius, and Johannes Messchaert of Wiesbaden rendered the parts of the Priest and the Angel of the Agony with great dignity and understanding, but it was Muriel Foster, with her impressive and moving performance as the Angel who was the great sensation at this festival. Buths directed a superb, brilliant and deeply moving performance, which was cheered to the echo, with Elgar once again making repeated appearances on the platform. Again he was presented with a large laurel wreath, which for long afterwards adorned a wall in his study.

The festival closed on the Tuesday night with a Grand Festival Supper in the town hall, attended by the soloists, the orchestra, the chorus and a number of eminent musicians including Richard Strauss. A number of toasts had been given, when, unexpectedly,

Richard Strauss suddenly rose and spoke with great enthusiasm of *The Dream of Gerontius* and of Elgar as a composer. He ended his speech with his now famous toast, 'I raise my glass to the welfare and success of the first English Progressivist, Meister Edward Elgar, and of the young progressive School of English composers.'

These generous words by Germany's most distinguished living musician were received with acclamation by the large assembly of musicians, and Strauss' enthusiasm focused the attention of the whole world upon the fact that a great English composer had arisen. Elgar's reputation abroad was made.

On Elgar's return the Düsseldorf performance of *Gerontius* naturally occupied much of the conversation between him and Atkins, and the positioning of the large forces and their effect on the performance was discussed at length. Elgar was again particularly enthusiastic about the placing of the semi-chorus behind the soloists and in front of the orchestra. They discussed the possibility of placing the semi-chorus in a similar position at Worcester, but reluctantly agreed that it was not practical because of the smaller chorus and lack of space in the orchestral area.

Elgar attended the WFCS rehearsal of *Gerontius* on 23 June, and presented Atkins with a copy of the full score of *God Save the King*, inscribed on the title page. I do not know if the gift had any special significance at this time, apart from the fact that it had only just been published, but it indicated in pencil alternative cuts that could be made.

Early in the year Elgar had been specially commissioned to write a *Coronation Ode*, to be performed at Covent Garden as part of the state ceremonies of coronation week. The work had been completed and a rehearsal had already taken place, when news came on 24 June of the King's illness and the postponement of the coronation, which was to have been on 26 June. Atkins, knowing what a great blow this must have been to Elgar, wrote the following letter:

8, College Yard, Worcester.
July 1st, 1902.

My dear Elgar,
    This postponement is a very great disappointment and I hope you are bearing as patiently as may be this derangement of your plans. Never

mind! when it does come off it will be with added zest and the wave of feeling that your music will call forth (let alone getting the King there at last!) will be simply enormous and overpowering.

It is a great personal disappointment to me, but your music will grow bigger in the meanwhile. Let me know you are well by a postcard and with my best love,

Yours ever,
I.A.A.

Malvern July 2:02

My dear Atkins,

Many thanks for your very kind letter. I have had too much experience of 'things' to worry at all, at all!

I have been Biking wildly—but not too well—during the last 10 days & playing Bach, who heals and pacifies all men & all things.

However it was good of you to write & I thank you.

I am now plotting GIGANTIC WORX of which more anon.

Kindest regards
Yours ever
Edward Elgar.

The words 'gigantic worx' are in very large block capitals, one word to a line. This is the first reference to the fact that Elgar had now begun planning in earnest for the new work recently commissioned by the committee for the 1903 Birmingham Festival, namely, *The Apostles*.

8, College Yard, Worcester.
July 3, 1902.

My dear Elgar,

I go to Hereford to-morrow. Could I, shall I, arrange with Sinclair to expect you on Monday or Friday next (July 7th or 11th), or failing these, Monday July 14th. Then about Gloucester, they also rehearse Mondays and Fridays, could you take a practice there?

Put clearly, the available dates are: (...)

I heard Gloucester do your work. They are very good and it's only a matter of *Tempi*.

Will you drop me an *immediate* line care of Sinclair or write to Sinclair direct (as you like)

Yours ever,
I. A. Atkins.

I am sorry to say that, owing to Blair's work not having come in, we were obliged to give it up. (The 2nd part of Walford Davies only came in time for last Monday's practice. It's too bad of composers.) This year the Festival is practically at the end of August. London Rehearsals begin Sep.2.

I am very sad about it, but it would never have done to have given a bad performance of it—and of course other works would have suffered too.

Massed Rehearsal Thurs. July 24th. When will you come on, before or after tea?

Malvern.
Wedy July 9.02

My dear Atkins:
The more I think of Blair's work the more distressed I feel. I know your judgement is good & there wd probably be difficulties in working up Hereford & Gloucester but I am sure Worcester wd attend any amt. of extra rehearsals for the purpose of making things smooth.

If there is any chance of its being reconsidered & the rehearsals shd interfere with your needed rest I would give up my Bayreuth trip & take any rehearsals necy. I can say no more.
In great haste
Yours ever
Ed. Elgar.
After all I shd not be away long & should have plenty of time.

Elgar had a special interest in Blair's *The Song of Deborah and Barak* since he had helped him with the scoring. Atkins was as anxious as Elgar that Blair's work should be performed at the festival, and fortunately shortly after this the parts arrived.

The following letter gives Elgar's suggestions for the orchestral concert of the Three Choirs Festival on 10 September. In the event, as will appear later, none of these suggestions were adopted.

Malvern
July 10 [1902]

My dear Atkins:
I've been thinking about the pieces.
Vorspiel 'Guntram'   Rd. Strauss
slow & serious
(I think this requires 3 each wood wind, but you might see the score)
Over. Rosamunde   Schubert
very cheerful
Symphonic Poem *Orpheus* Liszt.
slow & serious
this is lovely & wd suit you—wants 2 harps. Think of this well. I've a *score here*.
Huldigung's Marsch   Wagner

So here are two quiet things & two loud: the Orpheus is not difficult & you cd 'pull your soul out' in it.

Of course there are the Dvorak dances & the Liszt Rhapsodies, &c Tell me what you think.

Yours ever
Ed. Elgar.

In the meantime the rehearsals for *Gerontius* were going on steadily in the three cities. On 11 July Elgar was taking a practice in Hereford.

Herefordshire Club.
Saturday [12 July 1902]

My dear Atkins:

I arrived here in good case, per Bike: Sinclair & [Percy] Hull [assistant organist at Hereford Cathedral] met me & escorted me to Hereford.

I had a very good practice & all went well—a very friendly set of folk & so willing—the room is bad for sound but I was very pleased. I hope Gloucester will do as well.

I ride home tomorrow & on to G[loucester] on Monday.

I hope all is settling down & comfortable. I've been tasting Cider & have a head!

Yours ever
Reynart
(the guileless one)

This is the first letter signed 'Reynart'.

at 7, Palace Yard, Gloucester.
Tuesday [15 July 1902]

My dear Atkins:

I am really 'sun-stroked' & doddery, & too much to come over this a.m. You will have had my wire—I was not sure if you wd get it in time so I sent a fuller one to Southall [the festival secretary]. Brewer says they can do the whole thing here.

I had an excellent practice last night—the chorus is really a fine body of voices. I was going on to London to-day but fear my coup de soleil will prevent my further journeying.

Yours ever
Ed. Elgar.

The combined effect of sun and Herefordshire cider proved disastrous and occasioned Atkins anxiety as the first full chorus rehearsal, arranged for Thursday 24 July, drew nearer. *Gerontius* was down to start the rehearsal.

Langham Hotel, London.
Thursday p.m. [17 July 1902]

My dear Atkins:
I was extremely glad to receive your letter & that you say Deborah after all is not too *10d nailish* for the Chorus. I won't forget the Combined business on August 28th. Do, there's an angel, run thro' a bit of Gerontius for me on the 24th July—anything so as the Chorus may 'feel' a bit together—the Demons' Chorus & the 8-pt. 'Praise' for choice.
    I had a sunstroke on Sunday & was ill on Tuesday or I wd have come over.

I cross on Sunday night.
Yours ever
Ed. Elgar.

You can command me any time for rehearsals when I'm within reach. I *should* arrive home about the 30th, but I'll let you know.

Archibald Ramsden, a close friend of Elgar's father and a prosperous piano dealer, had offered to take Elgar to the Bayreuth Festival, an invitation too tempting for him to refuse. Atkins had, therefore, to take charge of the first massed rehearsal of *Gerontius* on 24 July. Elgar returned to Malvern on 29 July.

Craeg Lea, Wells Road, Malvern
Augt.1: 1902

My dear Atkins,
    I'm home & not very fit for things generally but anxious to hear how all goes on. I expect & hope you are having a rest just now. Tell me if I can do any semi-chorus practising any time. I shall be either here or at the Cottage [Birchwood] I think all the month, although there's a wild scheme to go to Cheshire [Rodewald's house in Saughall] for a space.
    I hope all goes smoothly now & that the Festival will be a pleasure to you & a great success.

Yours ever
Ed. Elgar.

My Bayreuth experiences are beyond the pen—so must keep for digestive loquacity when we next grub together.

    Atkins left for a holiday early on the same day, and Elgar's letter crossed his letter of 2 August.

24, Marina, St. Leonard's-on-Sea.
Aug.2. 1902.

My dear Elgar,
   I hear that you are back.
   Can you take a practice for me on Monday Aug.11th, 7.30 p.m.?
   I have asked them to bring
> 'Gerontius'
> 'Barak'
> and
> Williams in C.

They are well on with 'Barak' (& Deborah) and, in addition to that, ought to have a good 'go' at the last part of 'Gerontius' and no doubt you will manage to work in Lee Williams's service.
   We had a very good Combined Choir practice [24 July] and went through the Proficiscere, Demons' Chorus and eight-part chorus TWICE.
   How long shall you want on Aug 28th [the next combined chorus rehearsal]? Please answer this question.
   I can't get the Books of Words off my chest.
> Yours ever,
> I.A.A.

   Each morning and evening performance had its own Book of Words, and in those days it was the conductor's responsibility to ensure that the contents were correct. When Atkins went away the *final* proofs of some of the Word Books, including the *Gerontius* one, had not reached him.

24, Marina, St. Leonards-on-Sea.
Aug.3, 1902.

My dear Elgar,
   Thank you so much for your kind offer to relieve me of some of the work. I wrote a request yesterday. I'm so sorry to hear that you are not quite yourself.
   As to *Semi-Chorus*, we've had many grinds and they begin now to get at the spirit of the music. I hope you will be pleased with them; they're mortal (decidedly mortal) but very anxious to do well. I'm afraid the holidays will interfere with a big muster until Aug. 18th, but if you want them called together a p-card to Somerton (49, London Road) will do it. I should suggest 7 p.m. on Monday, Aug. 11th (the big practice being 7.30 p.m.)
   But perhaps you would rather wait until you can have 'em all. I think this would be best.
   They're divided into 2 1S, 3 2S, 3 1A, 2 2A, 4 Tenors and 4 Basses.

If we could get Sobrino and Muriel [Foster] I should feel happy, however.

We've ground Blair to something like a polish (with the exception of the last few pages), so please help the chorus with your closing pages.

The Massed Chorus made a fine sound in your work. How splendid it is!

Yours ever,
I.A.A.

Elgar telegraphed back that his plans had been changed and that he would be away on the 11th. He, Alice and their daughter Carice had decided to go on 8 August to stay with Alfred Rodewald and his sister at Saughall, Cheshire, and did not return to Malvern until 22 August.

Malvern   Tuesday [5 August 1902]

My dear Atkins:

I was so very much grieved to have to wire 'impossible'—we have arranged to skip bag & baggage to Cheshire & I can't possibly work in the rehearsal. I trust Williams [Lee Williams] is available? If it had been only my own convenience to consider I would have blown all my engagements to the further winds, but there is the whole household to consider.

Glad to hear of the Semi-chorus being progressive & fit, I thought we said

Sop.3^I 2^{II}
not 2^I 3^{II} as you say—but it may be a

seasideish holiday-mood-brinesque slip of your pen.

Get a good rest & turn up well.

Yours ever
Ed. Elgar.

On Friday address will be as over (. . .)

As to combined practice Augt.28. Can you give me 45 mins? I should like so much as the semi-ch. wd be in evidence for, I suppose, the first time.

The semi-chorus work had in fact already been rehearsed on 24 July, when Elgar was in Bayreuth.

While Atkins was on holiday at St Leonards he had been studying Strauss' *Tod und Verklärung*, and was fired with the idea of including it in the festival programme. He had written to Elgar, telling him what was in his mind.

Malvern   Thursday [7 August 1902]

My dear Atkins:

Your idea is noble but!—how about rehearsal time: Strauss complained to me that *he* only had *three* rehearsals & I fear you will find 'Tod &c' a handful with the limited time at your disposal. I would give anything in reason to see Strauss in the programme but I fear the want of time for preparation—the audience will be mystified &, in that small room, [the Public Hall] somewhat dazed with sound: you will gather from this that

I.   Sentimentally I would give anything for it to be done.

II.   Practically I see rocks ahead but you are the best judge of the time you can give to it.

I hope you are having a good rest: we start to-morrow.

Yours ever
Edward Elgar.

On receiving Elgar's letter Atkins weighed up the matter and decided to embark on the performance. He wrote to Elgar telling him of his decision.

The Cottage, Saughall.
Augt. 12 [1902]

My dear Atkins:

It *is* the real thing & should be done. Laus Deo! for plucK.

Now as to rehearsal won't *you* do 'Sursum Corda'—I will, if you really wish it, but I don't *like* (altho' I've done it before) conducting in the real service—I like to see one man go thro' the 'solemnity': but you decide.

As to Gerontius—give me as long as you can in London—in the a.m. for choice—we cd profitably spend the forenoon on it but I'm placable.

We are very jolly here but the weather is awful & I only hope it's better with you. Two or three (not more) friends want to come to the London Rehearsal. May I give 'em a card?

Yours ever
Ed. Elgar.

Elgar's *Sursum Corda*, Op 11, first performed by Hugh Blair on the Worcester Cathedral organ on 8 April 1894, and published by Schotts in 1899 for Strings, Brass and Organ, was included in the festival opening service. Atkins conducted it with the rest of the service.

8, College Yard, Worcester.
August 24, 1902.

Dear Guileful,
I hope to come and see you tomorrow morning if you can do with me (Monday).
I have ordered orchestral version of 'Sursum'.
Gerontius rehearsal fixed for Wednesday Morning Sept. 3rd. [Queen's Hall, London] if convenient to you (as I hope it will be). Other things we will talk over when I see you.
Expect me 10.30 a.m. (I should leave here 9.53)
Yours ever,
I.A.A.

The three letters that follow refer to a difficulty which arose over the approaching rehearsal of *Gerontius* in London. This had been fixed for 3 September. This date was given on the contract signed in March by the singer engaged for the part of Gerontius. Since then the singer concerned, William Green, had allowed himself to accept another engagement on this very day! The complications to which this gave rise are clearly shown.

The story begins in a letter to Elgar started by my mother.

Worcester. [Saturday] Aug. 30, 1902

Dear Dr. Elgar,
My husband has just received the following wire from William Green:
'Awful complications impossible to rehearse Wednesday could you arrange rehearsal Tuesday (Sept.2). Please do your best for me shall be Euston Hotel Monday night. W. Green'.
He does not like upsetting the rehearsal list, & there is a chance of course that he could not get Maria Brema and Plunket Greene on Tuesday—it is unlikely that he could. If you have any definite ideas on the subject, please wire to Ivor as early to-morrow as you can. He has put things well in train to find out if Coates is free for the two dates (rehearsal and performance).
[At this point my father came in and took up the pen and continued:]
You can wire between 9 and 10. These singers are businesslike over every detail *save rehearsal*, and I should do nothing that would in any way compromise the success of 'Gerontius', which ought to receive the fullest rehearsal. I have to learn also whether you are agreeable to rehearsing on Tuesday afternoon instead of Wednesday morning.
Yours ever,
I.A.A.
P.S. I should say 'No'. That's my notion.

The London orchestral and soloists' rehearsals started on Tuesday morning, 2 September, but Atkins had to travel up the previous afternoon. He had accordingly asked Elgar to take his normal chorus rehearsal in Worcester on the Monday evening, which he agreed to do.

Craeg Lea, Wells Road, Malvern.
Saturday [30 August 1902]

My dear Firapeel
Thanks for the admittance cards. I'll do all you tell me on Monday night.
It's sickening about W. Green! He has written to me (just received it) acknowledging the amendments in the words & says he's at the Preston Guild—I leave it to you. There's Coates—but then there may be awful difficulties.

Yours ever
In haste
Reynart.

Craeg Lea, Wells Road, Malvern.
Sunday [31 August 1902]

My dear Atkins:
I'm awfully sorry about all this bother! I fear you will end by hating me & everything connected with me.
Don't!
I will not say a word to W. Green—it is really absurd to think Gerontius can be whistled through like a well-known work. I recd the pt. II Temple & will try the fugal passages at least [at the chorus rehearsal which he was taking for Atkins next day]: but I don't know the tempo: anyhow it will familiarize the folk with it to amble thro' the counterpoint.
I hope you will have a good time in town & not work too hard. I hope my wife will be with me.

Yours ever
Ed. Elgar.

Atkins' difficulties regarding artists were not, however, over, since on his arrival in London he learnt that Marie Brema had fallen ill. Her place was taken by Muriel Foster. Green being definitely unable to rehearse with orchestra, he was fortunate in finding John Coates at his London home. By a lucky chance he was available for both rehearsal and performance. The final cast, therefore, was Muriel Foster, John Coates and Plunket Greene.

Craeg Lea, Wells Road, Malvern.
Monday Night [1 September 1902]

My dear Atkins:
   When you have all your orchestra nicely working please don't forget to
tell 'em how to divide in the following cases

Strings div: in 3 ⎫ these two perhaps in
    ,,   ,, in 4 ⎭ *desks*
3 soli *violas*
(name them)
3 soli *cellos*
(name them)

   I expect some of these sort of things will be wanted in other works & it
saves a lot of confusion if the Conductor settles it at *first*.
                              Yours ever
                              Ed. Elgar

   The following letter was written (on black-edged paper, as
Elgar's mother had died on 1 September) from the house in
College Green which the Elgars had taken for the festival week,
and was written after the Saturday rehearsal of the music for the
following day's opening service.

Castle House
Saturday [6 September 1902]

My dear Atkins:
   It sounded fine   Hooray!
   Take the *2nd pt* (G minor) in Sursum a good bit slower please.
   Can you give me two passes for Monday morning rehearsal.
                              Yours ever
                              Ed. Elgar
   Please drop the passes in the enclosed.

[On black-edged paper]
Castle House
Thursday p.m. [11 September 1902]

My dear Atkins:
   Will you very kindly convey to the Chorus & Orchestra my heartiest
thanks for their performance of Gerontius?
   I felt that everyone did his, or her best for my work & I am most
grateful to them; and to you, for the preparation of the work.
                        I send my brotherly love
                              Ever yours,
                              Edward Elgar.

[On black-edged paper]
[Castle House]
Friday a.m. [12 September 1902]

My dear Firapeel

I wanted to see you yesterday but this place was a howling desert—about 700 came whom I didn't know.

All thanks to you: 'it' came off after all—we will talk about it. Please thank the Chorus and Orchestra for me; Somerton [the chorus superintendent] wd with your permission stick up a notice.

One word more—it has been the GREATEST PLEASURE to me to hear praise of you & I hope you are happy over a good week. I think you ought to be, & I join in your praise ffff.

Ever thine,
Reynart ye Foxe
(in my cluse)

The festival orchestra included, at a back desk of the first violins, W. H. Reed, who had only shortly before been a student at the Royal Academy of Music, and who over the years was to become the intimate friend of Elgar and Atkins and the leader of the London Symphony Orchestra.

The programme had been an interesting one and had included a number of first performances and several works not previously heard at the Three Choirs. Elgar had conducted his *Cockaigne* and *The Dream of Gerontius*. This was the first time he had conducted *Gerontius* as a complete work in a cathedral and it had been a most moving experience for him and for the vast audience. (He had conducted the Prelude and Angel's Farewell in Gloucester Cathedral in the opening service of the 1901 festival.) From now on, with very few exceptions, *Gerontius* was to be performed at all the Three Choirs Festivals. Until Elgar's death in 1934 he conducted virtually all of these performances.

Some indication of the effect of the Worcester performance of *Gerontius* can be judged from this extract from a letter written by Granville Bantock to Ernest Newman on 11 September:

Never have I experienced such an impression before as I did on hearing Gerontius this morning in the Cathedral. If Elgar never writes another note of music I will still say that he is a giant, and overtops us all.

His music moved me profoundly. Believe me, although Elgar and I look at music through widely different spectacles, his 'Gerontius' is beyond all criticism or cavil. It is a great, great work, and the man who wrote it is a Master and a Leader.

We were all deeply affected and gave way to our feelings.

I want to hear nothing better.

Twice I have felt as if transfixed by a spike from the crown of my head to my feet. Once on hearing *Parsifal* at Bayreuth, when the dead swan is brought on, and to-day at the words 'Novissima Hora' (. . .)

I have been greatly moved by Elgar's and Rodewald's kind words to-day [after the performance of his *The Witch of Atlas*, the night before].

Elgar returns with Rodewald to Liverpool tomorrow. Go and see them, but give the watchword and countersign '*Skip the pavement*'.

Be sure not to forget this.

There is a magical import in these words. It is the Prelude to the downfall of the indigestible hard-boiled eggs, and opens the door for the new generation.

The 'indigestible hard-boiled eggs' referred to were the old school of traditional composers. Bantock had little sympathy with the old styles.

Jaeger and Rodewald had been staying with the Elgars for the festival, and Sanford, Horatio Parker and their American friends had been at the Star Hotel. Friendship between Atkins and Elgar and the American musicians had now become firmly established and was a feature of all the pre-war festivals. Granville Bantock had travelled over from Birmingham each day by train, lunching and dining with either the Atkins or with the Elgars. On one occasion when Atkins was visiting the Elgars, Bantock and Rodewald told him about a society which they had started in Liverpool called Skip the Pavement (STP). Bantock had started it with the very active support of Rodewald, and Elgar had quickly been enrolled, and not surprisingly soon made it his own. They invited Atkins to become a member, but said that in true secret society form it would be necessary for him to be formally initiated. While Bantock went into rather heavy explanations about the STP and how in addition to its lighter functions it was intended to provide encouragement for the younger school of English composers, Rodewald and Elgar were in much more frivolous mood, and Elgar, who had been scribbling, handed Atkins the sketch shown overleaf.

From this it is clear that it had, at least originally, started among a group of friends including music critics who had formed the habit after concerts of joining Rodewald and Bantock in the nearest hostelry for a quiet drink and smoke during which musical matters

S. T. P.

E.E. inv. et del.

were, no doubt, freely and critically discussed. Archibald Ramsden and Alfred Kalisch were early members, and Ernest Newman, T. Griffith and Charles F. Grindrod were enrolled later
this year.

Atkins took a holiday after the festival, and Elgar was away at
concerts in Liverpool, London, Bristol and Leeds during the last 3
months of 1902. They met in Sheffield on 2 October, where Elgar
conducted the delayed first performance of the *Coronation Ode*,
with Agnes Nicholls, Muriel Foster and John Coates, and another
performance of *Gerontius*, with the same soloists as in Worcester.

During the last three months of 1902 Atkins' Friday visits to
Elgar were not as regular as usual. On each of them Elgar was
absorbed in preparing his libretto for *The Apostles* and in playing
over the sketches he had made.

The STP initiation ceremony had had to be deferred until
Rodewald came to stay with the Elgars in Craeg Lea for Christmas.
Granville Bantock was coming over, and a grand ceremony was
arranged for Saturday, 27 December. At the last moment Bantock
could not attend, so the ceremony proceeded without him. After it
Atkins was given the legal-looking certificate shown opposite.

Elgar had earlier in the year acquired a typewriter. This fact, and
the phrasing, reminiscent of his time as a solicitor's clerk, leave no
doubt as to who prepared the document.

Skip the pavement Society   Dec: 27. 1902

founded by Bantock, Rodewald, and Elgar

DEcember 27,1902%

    T h e s e   are to give   N O T I C E   to all and   sundry &

that   the undersigned I v o r A l g e r n o n £ A t k i n s£

Is this day constituted a Full (paying) member of the S.-T.-B

       W i t n e s s e s :gg

A.E. Rodewald
principal Curse.book

Edward Elgar:
Secondary psalmist.

Signature of Member.

Ivor Algernon Atkins

1903

If 1902 might be called the year of the 'triumphant *Gerontius*', 2 years after its first performance and over 12 years since Elgar began thinking about it, then we may rightly consider 1903 as the year of *The Apostles*. Success in this case came at its première at the Birmingham Triennial Festival in October, and thirty-five years after the idea of one day composing a work about the Apostles first came into Elgar's mind.

Elgar, therefore, had been thinking about the composition of *The Apostles* for a far longer period than any of his other works. Its conception was unique for the time, as will appear. He wrote his own libretto, much of it arranged from the Scriptures and the apocryphal writings, as he did also for *The Kingdom*, which was planned and partly written at this time.

The Apostles was a favourite subject of conversation on our Sunday evening visits to Elgar in the mid-1920s. My father made a number of notes about the writing of the work which form the basis of much of this account.

Elgar told me how, in 1868, when he was a boy of 11 at school in Littleton House near Worcester, his headmaster, Francis Reeve, talking about Christ's Apostles, had said: 'The apostles were poor men, young men, at the time of their calling; perhaps before the descent of the Holy Ghost not cleverer than some of you here.' These words had impressed themselves deeply on him, and he then and there determined that some time he would create a work around the Apostles. He told me how, with this in mind, he had made sketches from about 1873 onwards. He started serious planning of *The Apostles* in July 1902, as was shown in his letter to my father dated 2 July: 'I am now plotting GIGANTIC WORX of which more anon.'

Little progress, however, had been made by 20 July, when Elgar went with Archibald Ramsden to Bayreuth, which he already knew, to hear the *Ring* and *Parsifal*. There is little doubt that this visit confirmed for Elgar the effectiveness of his proposed use of leitmotiv throughout the projected *Apostles* cycle. He returned to Malvern on 29 July, and began in earnest to collect material for the writing of his libretto. He also began consulting his clerical friends, both Roman Catholic and Anglican.

During the first 10 months of 1903 Atkins had spent even more time with Elgar than in previous years, sometimes visiting him twice a week. In this way he took a more active part in the writing of *The Apostles* than in any other Elgar composition except *The Kingdom*.

January 1903 was a very busy time. Jaeger came down and representatives from the Birmingham committee came over to finalise the terms and arrangements for the first performance in October. Richter also visited Craeg Lea to talk over the work and to hear those parts already written. By 21 January Elgar had completed the opening chorus, 'The Spirit of the Lord', and most of the first section, and on that day it was posted to Novello's.

It would be wrong, however, to suppose that Elgar was continuously in serious mood during his writing. He was still in the midst of his Skip the Pavement jape, as can be seen from the communication to Atkins shown overleaf, dated 21 January, and enclosing a fearsome-looking pin. This blood-curdling document was presumably posted at the same time as Elgar was sending his manuscript to Novello's. Clearly these japes provided him with the mental relaxation that he needed; manual relief also, it would seem, since he showed Atkins on his next visit a partly finished metal medallion which included the letters STP.

'Jape' was a favourite word of Elgar's and is sometimes thought to have been invented by him. In fact, the word is a Middle-English one, meaning a trick or a cheat, and it occurs a number of times in Arber's translation of 'Reynard the Fox'. Atkins could not recall Elgar using the word before 1902, and therefore it seems probable that he found the word in this book and immediately made it his own.

When Elgar dined with the Atkins on 16 February, he told them that he had now posted the whole of the first section of *The Apostles* to Novello's and that he expected to complete the first draft of the libretto within the next two or three days.

Elgar's writing of the libretto from the point of view of the contemporary onlooker was in complete contrast to the approach found in oratorios of the past, which had all been written on a historical basis, and the covering of a 3 day period consecutively but with constant change of scene, almost a modern film technique, was unique at the time.

Much of Atkins' visit on 20 February was devoted to going through the libretto and the first proofs which had arrived from

S.T.P.

Brother: put this into thy flesh.

Thu 21. 1903

Novello's a day or so earlier.

Let me try to portray Elgar's study at Craeg Lea as Atkins was to see it during the next few months. On a desk were Elgar's pipes, tobacco jar, two inkstands, one containing red ink, pens, knife-erasers, paper knife, paper, etc, and spread over everything, including the table, piano, piano stool, chairs, and often the floor as well, Bibles, Apocryphas, Cruden's Concordance, and other reference books; music sketch books, and those sections of *The Apostles* music written so far.

But dominating everything was a picture by a Russian painter, Kramskoi, entitled 'Christ in the Desert'. The picture shows Jesus sitting alone on some rocks with the desert stretching away to the horizon. The expression on Jesus' face is haunting, and draws one to him in a way that is beyond description. (In May at the Morecambe Competitive Festival Elgar met Canon C. V. Gorton, the rector and chairman of the festival, and saw at his house this picture which fascinated him and which Gorton gave him. Gorton was soon to become a close friend and was consulted frequently about the text of *The Apostles*.) Elgar had this picture of the 'Lonely Christ' constantly before him as he wrote *The Apostles*, and it influenced him considerably.

On 24 February Elgar conducted his *Coronation Ode* at the WFCS concert in the Public Hall. This concert also included Strauss' *Wanderers Sturmlied* conducted by Atkins. After the concert Elgar sent the following letter:

Malvern Feb 26 [1903]

My dear Firapeel:
   Hope you are well & festive after our gorjus evening. All thanks to you for looking after the Ode. I am sorry to say I shall be out tomorrow dentistring & shall not get in home until about 5.30. Come as soon as you can—but perhaps avoid tomorrow.
   In great haste, a lot of Apostles have just come [the proofs of the first section]. Sinclair to lunch en route home.
Yours ever
REYNART
the foxe.
If you meet the Chorus do give 'em my hearty thanks: they did sing like Kings & Queens!

Elgar was so impressed with the performance of *Wanderers Sturmlied* that he wrote to Strauss:

Malvern
March 4 [1903]

Dear Friend:

Last week at the Worcester Festival Choral Society I had the pleasure to hear your 'Sturmlied' (I was conducting the Coronation Ode at the same concert) & it was a real joy to me to hear an English chorus in a country town wrestling with your music: they sang *well* & had been well trained and interested in the work by Mr. Atkins.

I wish, if you have time, you would send me a postcard with just a little message to this chorus—not of thanks of course,—it is their *duty* to perform your works; but in this *Kapell meisterisch* & professorial land it is refreshing when the good people get interested in something, new noble & good.

So dear Richard Coeur de Lion send me, if you can a little word: Atkins conducted your work with affection & the right spirit.

Ever yours, with all greetings from my wife & myself.
Edward Elgar.

In due course Elgar received a congratulatory reply from Strauss, which Atkins read out to the chorus at their next rehearsal.

His first visit to Elgar in March was to be one of the most exciting ones, since not only were there more proofs to go through, but Elgar had also finished the second section, 'By the Wayside', and was working on the Mary Magdalene scene. There was therefore much to played through.

I have referred several times to my father's visits to Craeg Lea, and the following describes a typical day.

My father would take a train from Worcester soon after breakfast, sometimes—especially if they were going out to Birchwood—taking his bicycle with him. During the writing of *The Apostles* the proceedings were almost always the same. The mornings were spent discussing additions to the libretto and going through whatever music Elgar had composed since the last visit. Elgar would sit at the piano playing and explaining, and my father would struggle to keep the unruly pages in place, for the manuscript was all written on loose sheets. All would be going well, and then in some great moment when my father was too carried away to function properly in the double task of turning over and supplying a judicious supporting bass, he would fumble, and the loose sheets would scatter all over the place. Generally Elgar roared with laughter, and once the sheets had been sorted out they would carry on. Occasionally, if Elgar was worked up himself, he would slam the piano lid down, and light up a pipe and relax before returning to the piano.

When he had finished playing a section, he would stop and discuss various passages and replay some of them, perhaps with amendments. Then would always come the moment which my father half dreaded and half looked forward to. Elgar would jump up and demand that my father would play it over to him. He would start walking round the room, fill his pipe and start smoking, always on the move. From time to time he would take his pipe out to shout, 'Play that bit over again', 'Get more into it', 'Make more of the bass', and the like. My father said it was a somewhat harrowing experience, but Elgar loved to hear his music in this way, and no doubt it gave him 'distance'.

My father has written a description of Elgar's piano playing:

In his home it was always a delight to hear him play the piano, for though he had no considerable technique he had a beautiful touch, delicate and full of personality—ideally suited to bring out the sensitive qualities of his own music. He had a way of giving the chords some fascinating shades of colour which seemed almost impossible to recapture. I have noticed this again and again in trying to play for him, as he often asked me to do, something he had just played to me, and wished to hear for himself as he walked around the room.

For my father the mornings at Craeg Lea always passed too quickly. After lunch he and Elgar would drop down the hill to the golf links. Elgar would then play a round with some friend and my father would follow them round, supplying conversation and, when necessary, consolation. Elgar was at that time a keen golfer, but clearly they did not take the game as seriously as most do today. Back to Craeg Lea for tea, then more music, supper and a wild dash to the station.

In mid-March Elgar put *The Apostles* on one side to pay a visit to the Potteries to which he had been greatly looking forward. In October 1902, a deputation from Hanley had visited him and invited him to conduct there in March 1903, a performance of *The*

Dream of Gerontius. Elgar could choose his own soloists and the local orchestra would be augmented by additional players to be nominated by himself. He had conducted the North Staffordshire Festival Choir at the first performance of *King Olaf* in 1896, and he knew and greatly admired their singing, trained by their conductor, Swinnerton Heap. When Heap died suddenly in 1900, the North Staffordshire Triennial Festivals collapsed, as did the Festival Choir. The choral gap was, however, soon filled by the North Staffordshire District Choral Society, founded and trained by James Whewall, an ex-miner. This society very quickly built up a reputation as great as Heap's choir.

It was a most welcome invitation, and Elgar readily accepted it. He chose Muriel Foster, John Coates and David Ffrangcon-Davies, and added to the local twenty-six players forty-five players from the Hallé, led by Speelman. With his memories of the wonderful 1896 première of *King Olaf*, Atkins was determined to be at the concert, which was to be on Friday evening, 13 March, and having ascertained that he could be back in Worcester in the early hours of the Saturday, ready for the cathedral practices, he went to Hanley, where the first person he met was Henry Ettling, who was in his usual boisterous form.

Elgar was delighted, and my father told me that he would never have forgiven himself if he had missed this performance. It was one of the finest that he could remember.

By the end of March Elgar had finished the third section of *The Apostles* up to Jesus' forgiveness of Mary Magdalene, but without the final chorus. As originally written, this scene ended quietly, with Jesus' words, 'Go in Peace', but in May Elgar decided to add the final chorus, 'Turn you to the stronghold, ye prisoners of hope', which now ends Part 1.

In April Elgar started work on the second part, and most of the month was spent on the 'Betrayal' section. Elgar's unusual conception of the character of Judas colours the whole composition. He maintained that Judas was not by nature evil and a traitor, but being more of a man of the world than the other disciples, ambitious and something of a politician, he had followed Jesus believing that his Kingdom was to be of this world, and that he would share in his master's earthly triumph. It was only, therefore, when Judas understood that the Kingdom was to be a spiritual one that he betrayed Jesus in an attempt to force his hand

and make him show his power. Judas's remorse, when he realised what he had done, is one of the greatest moments of *The Apostles*. This scene, with Judas repenting in front of the temple, the temple choir singing inside, and at one point, the crowds passing behind the temple crying 'Crucify him, crucify him', is an excellent example of Elgar's novel technique.

The writing of this section caused Elgar more trouble than any other part of the work. I have on more than one occasion heard my father and Elgar reminiscing about one particular problem and its solution, which clearly gave them both pleasure. Fortunately my father wrote a description of the incident:

Some weeks there were passages which would not do as they stood, and they had to be altered. One was the Betrayal scene. Elgar played it to me and made me play it to him, but we both felt something lacking before the great Chorus entry at the words, 'Lord, how long shall the wicked triumph.'

It was not that the passage was not already strong. It was. But the more we heard it the more we both felt that something was still wanting which should prepare the mind of the listener for the great dramatic climax to which everything was leading. We tried it again before supper, but we were still dissatisfied when I had to run for my train.

The next Friday, when I arrived I found Elgar in a very gay mood, bubbling over with suppressed excitement. I could see that he was on edge about something which he was going to show me. After very carefully arranging the sheets of manuscript, those sheets which so often would fall off the piano desk at critical moments, he sat down and began to play over the Betrayal scene. When we got to the passage which had hung fire the week before, the alteration was so electrifying that I literally jumped out of my seat.

What had happened was that immediately after Judas' terrible cry, 'I have sinned, I have betrayed the innocent', Elgar had made the Chorus enter suddenly with a fortissimo shout on the word, 'SELAH'. You may tell me that no one knows what the word 'Selah' means—or that it means nothing. That may be true. But Elgar's great discovery was that it could be made to suggest something terrible and to give a sense of the inexorable fate which overhung Judas. It was a stroke of genius. My reaction to the passage gave Elgar just what he wanted. He was now sure that all was well. We both relaxed and indulged in exhibitions of wild joy. These ultimately brought Alice, and it all had to be played again.

On a visit about this time Elgar showed Atkins some photographs that Dr Grindrod, who lived in Malvern, had taken of him, which pleased the Elgars very much. He had spare copies of three of the photographs, which he gave to Atkins.

May and June were taken up with the correction of proofs and completing the remaining sections of the work—'Golgotha', 'At the Sepulchre' and 'The Ascension', but Elgar was also occupied with matters concerning the first performance in London of the *Dream of Gerontius*, which had been arranged for 6 June, in the as yet incomplete and unconsecrated Westminster Cathedral. Alice was particularly enthusiastic about it, since not only would it be the first performance in London, but also the first time that *Gerontius* would be heard in a Roman Catholic church.

The arrangements were in the hands of Jugo Görlitz, a well-known concert agent of the time, and, at Elgar's request, the North Staffordshire District Choral Society, who had given the fine performance in Hanley in March, were invited to be the chorus. Elgar suggested the same soloists—John Coates, Muriel Foster and David Ffrangcon-Davies. Görlitz, who was agent for Dr Ludwig Wüllner, wanted him to take the part of Gerontius, and Atkins recalls Elgar's ready agreement and his enthusiastic account of Wüllner's wonderful performances at Düsseldorf in 1901 and 1902. Elgar, of course, would be conducting.

The Amsterdam Orchestra was engaged, but late in April withdrew and was replaced by an orchestra made up of various London players. Atkins said that this was a great disappointment to Elgar, and remembered several discussions from which it was clear that Elgar was pressing for a large orchestra, but eventually had to accept fewer players than he wished.

As the performance was on a Saturday, Atkins could not be there, but on Elgar's return, and from the papers, he learnt that despite Alice's continual references to its great success, it had, in fact, been most unsatisfactory. The chorus and Muriel Foster and Ffrangcon-Davies had sung well, but Wüllner had been most disappointing, too dramatic and with very poor English, and the orchestra had missed many of the subtle points. Elgar did not like to say much, my father told me, in view of Alice's enthusiasm, but he was obviously very disappointed that the first London performance had been so unsatisfactory. Some 25 years later in a conversation at Marl Bank he admitted that it had been a mistake to have Wüllner for a performance in English, and that with the acoustics of Westminster Cathedral at that time it was impossible to do justice to the work.

Elgar had been planning *The Apostles* as the first of three works which would deal with the Apostles and Christ and his Church, and indeed some parts of what we now know as *The Kingdom*, but was then referred to as *Apostles II*, were already sketched out. He had intended to include some of this in the work to be performed at the Birmingham Festival. However, he had been suffering from severe headaches and his eyes had been giving him considerable trouble, so that slow progress had been made with the last section. In June Elgar decided that the work to be performed that year should be confined to what we now know as *The Apostles*. On Atkins' visit on 13 June Elgar played to him all the score except for the final chorus.

In the last week of June Elgar started orchestrating, and the final sheets of the full-score framework were ready by 3 July, when the Elgars left to stay with Rodewald at his cottage in Bettws-y-Coed, North Wales. Elgar completed the greater part of his orchestration while he was there, and returned to Malvern on 31 July.

Bettws-y-Coed
[30 July 1903]

My dear Firapeel:
How are you? I have been working like 10,000 smiths & we return home for Monday. I expect you are away but if not let me hear (at Malvern) wh day you are coming over. I hope the scoring is finished—if not let us talk it over an' it like you—I'm your man any time.
The weather has been truly awful but we have motored about & had much fun. No more now till I hear from you.
Yours ever
Reynart.

Atkins was orchestrating the *Magnificat* in A and *Nunc Dimittis* in D which he had composed for the opening service of the coming Hereford Festival, and Elgar had promised to help him with the scoring. He had already started a short holiday, but Elgar's letter was sent on to him.

Barrow Hall, Hull.
Aug. 2nd, 1903.

My dear Reynart,
A thousand thanks for your letter and kind offer of help. I've done the scoring, and knowing the deeds of glory you were engaged on [*The*

99

Apostles], I went over to old Bantock and showed it to him and got him to make his suggestions like the good fat old brick he is.

The day you wired to me from Chester I had a pathetic ride to Craeg Lea and to Birchwood. Craeg Lea I found padlocked, and my heart was heavy. Meeting your postman he told me that there were sounds of revelry the previous night at C.L. and I determined to ride to Birchwood—only to find it (apparently) untenanted. Dear man, I am longing to see you, longing to hear you play scales, longing to hear you snort in Edwardesque manner (where the brass come in), in fact longing for the sight and hearing of you. I return Saturday Aug 15 and unless you write to the contrary you must expect an early visit from me in the following week.

As to my score I dared not worry you before, but now that things are going well with you in point of time I would dearly like to show it to you.

I've been hard pressed, and am only now beginning to find time for the proofs you sent me. If all goes well expect to hear from me in glowing terms of ap- or disapproval of this new section. By Jove, it looks stunning. Being E's own I take it I may keep them until Friday next. I'm going to have a Festive time with it.

> My best love to you both,
> Yours ever,
> I.A.Atkins.

I am here until Saturday [8 August]

Craeg Lea, Wells Road, Malvern.
Augt 4 03

My dear Firapeel:

We're home. I'm so dreadfully sorry you had a lost journey—as far as we are concerned. Altho' the beauties of Birchwood shd have repaid you for much pedalling. I'm so glad you saw old Bantock, & I am ready to see you anytime—the sooner the better.

As to the proofs, keep 'em till you come. I think *most* corrections are made. We *may* go to Birchwood, but the weather is *not* promising— anyhow better send a p.c. *here*, allowing time for reply, & I'll let you know where we are.

> Much love
> Yours ever
> Edward (I forgot)
> Reynart
> ye foxe.

8, Melville Terrace, Filey.
[14 August 1903]

Dear Mrs. Elgar,

We leave here tomorrow 12.17 p.m.

May I come by 7.40 train (i.e. train arriving at that hour at Malvern Wells) tomorrow (Saturday) night and dine with you?

I'm saturated in 'The Apostles'.

It *is* wonderful music and music for *me* (I suppose we all feel that but I make it a personal matter). I can see a lot of you in the music. How delightful the simplicity is! I love such sections as 'Why seek ye the living?' Other parts one cries over, those wonderful pages 141 onwards.

No words can do justice to the wonderful scene in 'The Temple' the mingled emotions it calls up. It rends my heart.

Dear Mrs. Elgar, you must be very happy while our dear Meister is producing such music. I look upon him as one of the greatest teachers we have had. *It is great* to be able to do the work he is doing. I always feel so proud of him, but what must your feelings be!

Don't trouble to write or wire, but if a wire were necessary (in case you go out), c/o The Stationmaster, York will find me.

Yours sincerely,
I.A.Atkins.

Mrs Elgar wired 'Come Monday August 17th'. On Atkins' arrival he found that Elgar had completed the full score, and it was posted to Novello's that afternoon. Elgar played the whole score over, and Atkins stayed the night at Craeg Lea. A difficulty in his own scoring had arisen, and he left his score with Elgar.

Craeg Lea, Wells Road, Malvern.
Augt 18: 03

Dear Firapeel:

Here's the passage. It will make a good row. I've not critically examined every note for axidentals &c. I put the Cymbals for sheer cussedness, 'cos there's a line for them in the pieces of old score paper I used up. I think the harmony in the Horns, 3rd & 5th bars is what you meant—the chords there should be *quasi stacc*. so as not to obscure the strings.

Weather is better
Yours ever
Reynart
Foxe

The Elgars had taken a house in Hereford for the festival week (5–11 September), and Rodewald and Frank Schuster, a wealthy supporter of the Arts and friend of the Elgars, were staying with them. Atkins agreed to spend such time as he could with Elgar helping with proofs, etc. On Thursday the Elgars gave a large tea party to their many friends, including a number of members of the Gold Works and the STP. Among them were Bantock, Alfred Kalisch, Atkins and Ernest Newman. It was a wonderful reunion. On Friday after dinner the Atkins joined a few other friends, including John Coates and his wife for a private run through of the *Apostles* music, with Atkins and Elgar at the piano and Coates singing the part of John.

Elgar had decided very early on that he wanted David Ffrangcon-Davies to sing in *The Apostles*, and he had been engaged as early as March. By July Elgar had made up his mind that he should be Jesus, and proofs were sent to him in America, and in September Elgar sent him an autographed copy of Kramskoi's picture with the following letter:

Malvern Sep 14 03

My dear Ffrangcon,
   Please accept the poor photo of a fine picture: I know it will appeal to you, it is my ideal picture of the Lonely Christ as I have *tried* (and tried hard) to realize (musically for a few of us) the Character.
   It is by a Russian artist and there is a history to the picture which I will tell you. I hope to be in town soon and of course will let you know.

Yours ever
Edward Elgar.

On 19 September Atkins went over to Craeg Lea. They went through *The Apostles*, Atkins playing the piano and Elgar playing those violin proofs which had arrived.

For the remainder of September Elgar was finalising the last details for the *Apostles* performance. Richter was the festival conductor-in-chief, but Elgar had decided to conduct his own work.

In those days it was normal with commissioned works for the composer to have to provide at his own expense the individual orchestral parts required for the first performance, which was often conducted from the manuscript full score. Even when

Novello's were publishing the full score and parts in time for a first performance a great deal of checking still had to be done during the last few days. On 3 October Atkins went to Craeg Lea and spent nine hours helping Elgar and John Austin, who had done Elgar's copying for a number of years, check and correct the orchestral parts.

To express his appreciation Elgar sent Atkins a beautiful 1828 edition of *Lempriere's Classical Dictionary*, which he had bought in 1883 and which Atkins had greatly admired. The copy was a little weak in its binding and was inscribed, characteristically, 'now broken, baffled and bereft, given to Ivor Atkins by Edward Elgar (who is in like case)'.

The orchestral rehearsals were in Manchester on 6 and 7 October, with Richter in attendance, and Elgar was delighted with their playing. The first combined rehearsal of chorus and orchestra was to be in Birmingham on Friday 9 October, and Atkins, well aware that Elgar, with memories of the 1900 festival, was apprehensive and very conscious that this year all would depend on him himself, sent him the following letter:

8, College Yard, Worcester.
October 7th, 1903.

Meister mein, where art thou roaming? This is to send my love to you and my heartfelt wishes for the 'Apostles.' May it be all that you can wish. Everything promises well, and with your own dear old mystic self at the helm all should be right. Above all, I pray for poetic insight. Look lovingly at the chorus and they *must* give you their best. Never was there a work calculated to bring out more of their best than this. Scan them well, Edward, gleam poetry at them. Heavens, what a day it will be! but all too short.

Thank you for Lempriere. I shall value it muchly. I've always longed to have one but have never come across a copy in an old edition. This copy is quite near to Keats' time. Will you thank Mrs. Elgar for her kindness in despatching it.

Yours ever,
I.A.A.

Grand Hotel, Birmingham.
Saturday [10 October 1903]

My dear Firapeel:
 Where were you yesterday? I looked for you.
 Have you a ticket all right for Wednesday? Write *here* because *you* must be there.

Yours ever
Reynart.

8, College Yard, Worcester.
October 11th, 1903.

My dear Reynart,
 A 1000 thanks. I have tickets. Alas! I couldn't get over on Friday. I sat at home, gnashed my grinders and acted orchestra, soloists and chorus myself all the afternoon. After all, I got a good deal out of the combination. The orchestra was particularly good—technique of clarinet player perfect in scales. I had a fine Peter and the chorus wept—I never heard such intensity.
 I am hardening my hands for before the performance: after it I shall go away and not be seen of men for a little.
 We shall meet before that I hope.

Yours ever,
I.A.A.

The day of the first performance, 14 October, came. The soloists were Madame Albani as the Blessed Virgin and the Angel, Muriel Foster as Mary Magdalene, John Coates as John, Kennerley Rumford as Peter, Andrew Black as Judas and David Ffrangcon-Davies as Jesus. Atkins especially remembered Muriel Foster's singing of the Mary Magdalene part—she had a unique quality in her voice which had made her a wonderful Angel in *Gerontius*, and he was immensely impressed by Ffrangcon-Davies' interpretation of Jesus. Both singers were, in fact, to sing these parts in virtually every performance of the work over the next five years. The performance was a success, and wiped out all the disappointment of the ill-fated first performance of the *Dream* at the Birmingham Festival of 1900.

 On 23 October Atkins went to Craeg Lea as usual. Elgar was not well. All the exhilaration of his great success at Birmingham had gone and he was depressed and exhausted. He cheered up a little when they talked about the performance, and was looking forward to a visit from Ffrangcon-Davies the next day.

On 31 October they met again at the Imperial Hotel, Malvern. Some weeks earlier Elgar had founded the Malvern Concert Club, and had invited his old friends the Brodsky Quartet, and had asked Atkins to help entertain his guests. The concert went well, and Elgar, though still looking tired, was in good form. This was, in fact, the last time Atkins and Elgar met that year.

On 5 November Elgar sent Atkins a letter and an STP report:

Malvern Nov 5 [1903]

Perpend!
   In sending you the blood [STP] things communication in the other cover [these were some cabalistic wands, sent separately and packed with excessive care] I forgot Madresfield M[usical] C[ompetition]. I hear, Firapeel, that you will, under compulsion, select pieces for S.S.C. or S.C.C. and a *morceau* for Brass Band.
   So I retire from this scene to my earth.
I look for you daily
In haste
Reynart.
For heaven's sake do find something for these two classes. I *can't*. I am distraught.

New University Club,
St James' Street, S.W

Oct. 20. 1903 —

Nothing new to report from the 7.v.l. works —

a. k.

Heretic

Passed. Oct 22. 03

The letter refers to the new works composed for the Hereford Festival in September: Bantock's *The Wilderness*, Coleridge-Taylor's *The Atonement*, Cowen's *Indian Rhapsody* and Parry's *Voce clamantium*. These had been discussed by the S.T.P. members in Hereford and reviewed in the press. It is signed by A.K. (Alfred Kalisch) on his club's notepaper, endorsed in Birmingham by the Arch-Heretic G.B. (Granville Bantock), and 'passed', in Malvern, by Ahrimanes and countersigned Guido Faux in Elgar's handwriting. Bantock at this time was fascinated by Arabia and Persia and frequently made reference to Eastern names in his own letters. Why Elgar should have passed the document in the name of the Persian deity representing Evil is not clear, but probably he wished to outdo Bantock's Arch Heretic. The countersigning signature needs no explanation if the date is noted.

On 7 November news reached Atkins and Elgar that A. E. Rodewald had suddenly been taken very seriously ill. Atkins was shocked, but he knew that Elgar would be completely heart-broken.

8, College Yard,
Worcester.

Nov. 9th, 1903.

My dear Elgar,
    I too am bowled over by the news. I always envied poor old Rodewald his vigour and health.
    I hope for him, though even now the end may have come. It is too awful. Do let me know if any more hopeful news comes.
    My dear old boy, I am so sorry for the shock it must be to you.
                                        Thine,
                                        I.A.

Rodewald's death on 9 November was the last straw for Elgar. Utterly exhausted after his long preoccupation with *The Apostles*, his thoughts now turned to Italy. He came to say goodbye, but, alas, Atkins was busy rehearsing with Andrew Black for the WFCS concert that evening.

8, College Yard, Worcester.
Nov. 17, 1903.

My dear Firapeel
   I stole an hour between trains to say goodbye.
   I've been into the Cathedral, which I have known since I was four &
said 'farewell'—I wanted to see you. I am sad at heart & feel I shall never
return!
   My wife I think asked you to the station, forgetting it was a Concert
day. Best of luck to you now & always. My kindest regards to Mrs Atkins
& to you, Firapeel, much love.

Yours ever

Reynart

The year ended with two postcards from Italy, one on 30
November from Bordighera, and the other a Christmas/New Year
greeting from Alassio.

PART 3
1904—1907

1904

The year 1904 was one of honours for Elgar, for it was to bring him a second doctorate, this time from the University of Durham, a Covent Garden three-day festival entirely devoted to his compositions, including the Overture *In the South*, written largely when he was in Italy at Alassio, and a knighthood.

Elgar had left England in November 1903, completely exhausted and hoping that a few months in the warmth of Italy would restore not only his energy but his inspiration as well. He was still thinking of a symphony, though he was not sure that he was yet ready to write one. Italy turned out to be cold and wintry that autumn, and the Elgars did not enjoy their stay as much as they had anticipated, despite the good friends that they made there, including Dr Armitage Robinson, the Dean of Westminster. Inspiration was slow to return, as Atkins was to sense from the colour postcard which Elgar sent to him from Alassio where they had rented the Villa San Giovanni.

[Postmarked Alassio 19 January 1904]

Let's hear how you are sometime, Firapeel. I have rheumatism! I wolde fain be in my cluse. Yours ever Reynart.

Atkins had written expressing sympathy and encouragement, but the letter did not arrive in Alassio until after the Elgars had left. Elgar arrived in London on 1 February, bringing with him not a symphony but the nearly completed Overture *In the South*. Elgar had received a royal command to dine with King Edward VII on 3 February at Marlborough House, and afterwards attend a smoking concert of the Royal Amateur Orchestral Society, and conduct them in a performance of his *Pomp and Circumstance March* No 1. At their first meeting after his return from Italy Elgar gave Atkins a full account of this ceremonious and happy occasion. How much he enjoyed it is shown from the following letter written while the Elgars were staying at Frank Schuster's home, 22, Old Queen's Street, Westminster.

With Frank Schuster
& home one day soon (see below)
[5 February 1904]

Given at our Palace &c

Firapeel:
Your loving & friendly letter warms me & in return I will extend *two* fingers (royally) unto you.
These are the results of my recent frequentations!
Look here, old boy: I won't hear a word about conducting now.
My wife & Carice returned today to see if the house is fit for habitation—if it *is* I return tomorrow—if not I come on Monday. I'll let you know.
I'm awfully busy so I didn't answer your letter which reached me here this a.m. via Alassio.

Much love
Yours ever
Reynart
ye *royal* foxe!

Atkins had arranged for the Worcester Festival Choral Society's concert on 16 February to include Elgar's *King Olaf*, and he had in his letter invited him to conduct. The conducting reference in Elgar's letter of 5 February and in the next letter is to this concert.

Malvern Feb 9 1904

My dear Atkins:
I am woefully sorry &, if it was only conducting the Concert, I would come but I *cannot* possibly manage the rehearsals.
One other thing, much as I would like to meet my old friends in the Chorus I think YOU shd conduct my work because I gave up to another conductor on another occasion—& I can trust you to make old 'Olaf' swing:
If I can I will come in, but I am wearily busy & have miles to do.

Much love

Give my love to the chorus & wish them well from their old friend which is

Reynart

Mrs. Elgar is going to the concert anyway, & I'll come if I can.

Elgar was at this time working frantically to complete the Overture *In the South*. This went faster than he had expected, and he was able to be in Worcester on 16 February for the final rehearsal as well as for the concert. He insisted, however, on Atkins conducting *King Olaf* as well as the rest of the concert.

King Olaf received a splendid performance, according to Troyte Griffith who was present with Alice, and was given a great reception by the enthusiastic performers and audience. An amusing incident occurred at the end of the performance. The conductor retired with the soloists, and amid applause the soloists returned. There was then a short gap, and Atkins and Elgar, to the amusement of all, were seen struggling in friendly fashion across the platform as to who should appear first. In the end Elgar insisted on their taking the prolonged applause hand in hand.

On Atkins' visit to Elgar on 25 February Elgar told him that the last sheets of *In the South* had been posted to Novello's at the beginning of the week. Elgar and Alice also talked about their search, with Sinclair's help, for a new home in Hereford, which was then a quiet cathedral city with excellent rail facilities to London, via Gloucester as well as Worcester, and where apart from Sinclair they had many friends, as a result of Elgar's long association with the Hereford Philharmonic Society.

The Elgars were in London from early in March until 23 March. The Covent Garden Elgar Festival took place on 14, 15 and 16 March, and was attended by the King and Queen. His new Overture, *In the South*, was included in the last concert on 16 March and was conducted by him, the remainder of the programme being conducted by Hans Richter. My father was present at this concert and told me that the Overture was warmly welcomed, and that Elgar received tremendous and repeated applause, and was sent for by the Queen.

When Atkins visited Craeg Lea on 25 March the Elgars were full of the warm-hearted reception that they had received, not only at the concerts, but at the many suppers and parties which had been given in their honour during their stay in London. They also told him that they were leasing a house called 'Plas Gwyn', about a mile from the centre of Hereford on high ground with extensive views over the River Wye. 'A house of character', Alice said, where she was sure that Elgar would write great music. A prophetic remark indeed.

Atkins next visited Craeg Lea on 16 April. The main subject of conversation was the magnificent performance of *The Apostles* given in Birmingham by the Birmingham Festival Choral Society

113

two days before, conducted by Elgar. Atkins had been at it, and so also had Miss Burley, who was a fellow dinner guest. Alice spoke proudly of Elgar's election a few days earlier to the Athenaeum Club.

The Elgars were away for much of May in London and in Germany in connection with the Lower Rhine Festival in Cologne under the general conductorship of Dr Fritz Steinbach. The performance of *The Apostles* was on Sunday 22 May, and Jaeger reported to Atkins that it was 'immensely finer than any I have heard yet. The work had a *splendid* success.'

The Elgars, as they had done in 1902, stayed on after the festival, visiting a number of places, including Düsseldorf, where they stayed with Professor Buths. It was not, therefore, until 3 June that Atkins could next visit Craeg Lea.

Elgar was obviously delighted with Steinbach's performance, and the rare honour that had been given to him when he was called to the platform by performers and audience after Part 1 as well as at the end. Over 25 years later one evening at Marl Bank a reference was made to this performance, and I took the opportunity of asking Elgar all about it. He told me how impressed he had been with the study that Steinbach must have made of the music and of each soloist's part. He said that naturally he did not agree with every detail, and he could not in two rehearsals make some alterations which he would have liked to have done, given more time, but that these were of no real importance compared with a performance which had brought out the work generally as he had conceived it. He said that he could still hear in his mind the vivid orchestral colour, the velvet smoothness of the women singers and the sonority of the tenors and basses. I gained the impression that Elgar had enjoyed the 1904 Lower Rhine Festival even more than in 1902, perhaps, though he did not say so, because he had gone to it as an acknowledged European composer who this time was going to friends and colleagues. I remember then asking Elgar how the German chorus had compared with, say, a Three Choirs chorus or a Sheffield chorus. He told me that it was always difficult to compare choruses, but that the Rhinelanders lacked the North Country vigour and perhaps 'roughness' of Sheffield; they were more like a Three Choirs chorus, but being much larger were more sonorous and in some strange way more subtle and silkier. Choruses, he added, depended for their quality not only on training, but also on the places they sang in, the 'atmosphere' around them, and the relationship at the actual performance between them and the conductor.

On the following Friday, 10 June, Elgar had to be out all day, but he had received a letter from Professor S. S. Sanford, of Yale University, introducing Frank Damrosch, who had just received a Doctorate of Music at Yale. He was arriving in Malvern, on the Friday afternoon, and Elgar asked Atkins to go to Craeg Lea for dinner to meet him. Frank Damrosch was an elder brother of Walter Damrosch, the well-known conductor of the New York Philharmonic Orchestra, and also a conductor in his own right who specialised in choral music. He was conductor of the New York Oratorio Society and Director of the Institute of Musical Art in New York.

Atkins went over to Craeg Lea as usual on Friday 17 June, but Elgar had had to go out and his return was uncertain.

Craeg Lea, Wells Road, Malvern.
June 18, 1904.

My dear Firapeel:
I was so sorry to miss you yesterday but I got stuck out far away & arrived not at my 'cluse' till six. I go to Durham on Monday [to receive the honorary degree of D.Mus from the University] & hope to return on Wednesday: if so, I shall be in on Friday or round about the place somewhere.

Much love
Yours
Reynart
ye foxe.

Time was now running out as far as Craeg Lea was concerned, since the Elgars would begin moving out during the last week in June. Atkins was sad because of the forthcoming move, especially since it meant, at least for a time, the cessation of his weekly visits to Elgar.

Before the Friday arrived there had, however, been great news. Elgar had returned from Durham on the Wednesday to find a letter awaiting him to tell him that his name was included for a knighthood in the King's Birthday Honours list to be announced on 23 June. Elgar came over to Worcester on the Thursday to tell a few of his friends, including Atkins. There had been great rejoicing and congratulations.

On Friday 24 June, Atkins paid his last visit to Craeg Lea. He has left a note about this visit from which I quote:

... And now the Elgars were to leave Malvern for Plas Gwyn, Hereford. This meant that the Friday meetings which had been such a feature in my life were to cease. During the five years that Elgar had lived at Craeg Lea I had been in almost weekly touch with him, and as the weeks had passed, I had seen a steady succession of masterpieces unfold themselves before me. Now, all this was to come to an end, my last Friday visit was a sad one. As I rose to go, Elgar stopped me and slipped away to his desk and wrote:

'*Edward Elgar:*
June 24: 1904

Farewell to Craeg Lea & all good & fine associations[x]—no frequentations with Ivor (Firapeel)
[x]the associations will last.'

The Elgars moved in to Plas Gwyn on 1 July, and on the 4th went to London for the conferment of his knighthood. Towards the end of the month he wrote to Atkins.

Plas Gwyn, Hereford.
July 27th 1904

My dear Firapeel:
   How & where are you?
   After numerous jaunts, taken sorely against my will, I am now home & the house is beginning to wear a human aspect. Do come & see us soon.
   I have had a cheery letter from *S.S.S.* [S. S. Sanford] he arrives as you will already know in England on Augt. 6 & promises tobacco!
   This is quite a 'cluse' & retired from fearsome beasts.
                    Yours ever
                    Reynart.

Atkins went over on Friday 29 July. Elgar's niece, May Grafton, was now living with them and helping to look after Carice. It was a lovely day and Elgar and May were preparing to bicycle to Kilpeck Church, but Atkins had not brought his bicycle with him and they all walked down to the river instead.

Atkins was on holiday during August and they did not meet again until the full chorus rehearsal in Gloucester Cathedral on 25 August. Elgar was to conduct three works at the Gloucester

This photograph of Elgar was taken in Düsseldorf in connection with the second performance in German of *Gerontius* on 19 May 1902. It was at the Festival Supper after this performance at the Lower Rhine Festival that Richard Strauss gave his now famous toast, 'I raise my glass to the welfare and success of the first English progressivist, Meister Edward Elgar, and one of the young progressive school of English composers.' It was this speech which established Elgar's European reputation

A series of studies by May Grafton of Elgar at Craeg Lea in 1902: with part of his growing library, at his writing table, working on *The Apostles* in his study and at the piano, while working on *The Apostles*

In April, 1903, while Elgar was working on *The Apostles*, his friend Dr Grindrod, who was an unusually fine amateur portrait photographer, made three photographic studies of Elgar. This is one of them

Elgar on the Malvern Hills in 1903. In his cravat is an interesting diamond pin to which he was very attached. It was made from some of Alice's family jewellery, and the detachable setting for the diamond was specially designed so that the diamond could be used as a tie pin or alternatively as a dress stud

festival, the Prelude and Angel's Farewell from *Gerontius* at the opening service, which also included a *Magnificat and Nunc Dimittis in G* by Atkins, specially written for this festival, *In the South*, whose first performance had been in May, and *The Apostles*. Elgar was very much looking forward to this performance of *The Apostles*, since it would be the first time that he would conduct the work in a cathedral. (There had been a performance of *The Apostles* in York Minster by the Leeds Choral Union on 29 June, when Embleton, their financial backer, had anonymously met all the expenses. Elgar could not be present, and it had been conducted by Alfred Benton the organist of Leeds Parish Church, who was their regular conductor.)

Elgar was not disappointed. The performance on 8 September was for many people the highlight of the festival, and set the standard for the many performances of *The Apostles* which were to follow, not only at the Three Choirs, but all over the country.

In view of the tremendous success of *King Olaf* at the WFCS concert in February, Atkins had decided that the November concert should be devoted to *Caractacus*, and while they were in Gloucester he invited Elgar to conduct it. Immediately after the festival he sent him a formal invitation.

[Typed in purple by Elgar in double-spacing]
Plas Gwyn, Hereford.
September ye thirteenth 1904.

Firapeel! MARK!
Your scrawl received scant attention as Jaegerissimo was here and the subscriber could not think of dates: now I have looked into Doom-his-daye and find blanks as desired. *BUT* whom do you propose to present Caractacus? I see trouble here because there are not too many walking the earth who can satisfy me and you wont want me to put up with a second string, eh? Is Andrew [Black] impossible, and if he is who comes next? The soprano and tenor and likewise the second bass will be easily found: but, by'r lakin, a parlous fear have I over the protagonist. Resolve this and I'm your man, although it will take a weary lot of journeyings and time, and mark ye, Firapeel, I waxe olde & dulle & glumme & sourmooded, bilious, excursive and dispertinent.
                    Yours ever
                    REYNART ye FOXE.

Atkins wrote giving the cast proposed, namely, Madame Luise Sobrino, Herbert Grover, Charles Tree (Caractacus) and Frederick Lightowler, a Worcester Cathedral lay clerk whom Elgar knew. Elgar was pleased with the choice.

The Elgars, Granville Bantock and Atkins had been together for several mornings of the festival, and indeed the three of them had heard *The Apostles* from the triforium to which Atkins had taken them. Was it these meetings which had resulted in the strange grafting of the East on to Reynart's usual style?

[Typed in purple ink]
Plas Gwyn, Hereford.
September 18th, 1904.

O Firapeel! this is rare! The Singing Tree: have ye not read in ye Eastern book which is the Bible of Bantock, about it? I tell yow it is rare and rarely thought by yow. Is not the history of it and the Talking Bird and the Golden Water written in the books of The Thousand and One Nights and a Knight? But O Firapeel! forget not the Talkinge Bird: I wish for him as well as the Singinge Tree, and above all, Firapeel, in these parts we wail for the Golden Water: the waters hereabout are exceeding fayre and are makynge me moche holpen up in the matter of Makynge, but Firapeel, I have gotten a deadly thirst—nay a bitter lust for the Golden Water feigned, as ye wot, of ye Eastern maker to turn all to Gold.

Bethink ye, Firapeel, (in sorrow and much watching) of ye Bookes possible after a course of ye golden Water! Of ye Wines! ye Cigars! YE foode! but above and beyond all on this hitherside of ye promised land, ye bookes,—no mean volumes stitched in unseemly habits, but Bookes faire to handle, fayre to read and mighty fayre to possess.

Firapeel, I drop the Talking Byrde, whilk after all mighte talk ribaldry and lies and belike, by over-fayre speaking lead us away, but I charge you pursue sleuthly and fast, the Singing Tree and I feel all will spring welle with us, it Sweyven so mery: Yea, it ever sweyves mery: and God wot in its wake may walk the Golden Water: we have gotten a new cluse and the passage thereto has been a travail and, Firapeel, the subscriber would lave in the Golden Water,—O the Golden Water!!
Farewell,—be secret, silent, and syncere,
Thne ever aqva-auriferouslie,
Reynart.

Atkins, bemused by all the references to the Talking Bird, etc, sent the following letter to Elgar.

8, College Yard, Worcester.
Sep. 20th, 1904.

Reynart ye be ever subtyl, ye be ever sprynging newe meruaylles upon me. No, I know not the Talking Bird, I know not the Singing Tree nor yet ye Golden Water. But Bantock I know and I wolde have you beware of him. He is fat, sleek and of silken speeche and walks circumspectley; yet, withal his wondrous tayles I misdoubt me these are but lesyngis of the Golden Waters. I know of none, save it be by *conversion* an' it be these I tell you that one stream availeth as much as another and I yield not the virtue of the Severn to the Wye.

But the Talking Bird, the Singing Tree! here be meruaylles indeed! None of my lynage have heard aught of them. Goe ye to Cardiff? I go wentling there tomorrow or Thursday morning. I am leve of wakying for the Golden Water an' if you be travailing to Cardiff write me to

176 Llandaff Road
Cardiff

that we may meet.

But even as I rise from reading your last script of the T.B., of the S T and the Golden Waters I sigh for you and wonder whether ye be withinforth as ye seeme outward.

Thine generously and sanely
Firapeel.

Elgar wrote by return of post:

Plas Gwyn, Hereford.
Sept 21: 1904

Firapeel.
  Assoil ye.
    Yow be dense.
Ye Singing Tree is he whom ye have marked to present Caractacus. Follow by eye and eke by nose until he be found.

Yours
Reynart.

(Charles Tree was to sing the part of Caractacus.)

On Friday 23 September Atkins went over to Plas Gwyn in the afternoon and stayed the night. It was like old times at Craeg Lea. Elgar was again surrounded with liturgical books. Canon Gorton had been staying with the Elgars, and Elgar had started thinking about the libretto for *Apostles II*, as *The Kingdom* was then known. Some of this part had been written in 1903, and after dinner Elgar and Atkins played over some of the old sketches on the new

Steinway upright piano, a gift from Sanford, which had been delivered a few days earlier. They talked about the earlier writing of *The Apostles* and the recent Gloucester performance, and about Elgar's ideas for the next section still to be worked out.

Elgar also mentioned that he had ordered a telephone, indeed, its installation had started that morning.

Atkins did not go over to Hereford at all during October, but Frank Schuster, who had a motor car and was staying at Plas Gwyn, brought Elgar over to Malvern and Worcester on a series of visits, including one to my parents, about the middle of the month. The visit was necessarily a short one, but Elgar seemed in excellent form.

Atkins' next visit to Plas Gwyn was on 3 November. Elgar told him about a proposal to form a Chair of Music at Birmingham University, and how Bantock and others were encouraging him to consider becoming the first professor there. There was no doubt that he would be approached officially before long. He seemed very uncertain, and Atkins does not appear to have expressed any firm views. This would be understandable since he knew that Elgar's genius lay in composing, rather than teaching.

Work on *Apostles II* appeared temporarily to have been put on one side, and Elgar talked about putting into shape the *Pomp and Circumstance March* No 3. The sketch for the Trio of this had been given to Atkins in February 1902.

The WFCS performance of *Caractacus*, conducted by Elgar on 9 November, went well, and 'The Singing Tree' and the other artists met with Elgar's as well as the audience's approval. Elgar was well pleased.

Elgar told Atkins that there were to be performances of *The Apostles* at the end of November and early December in Mainz and Rotterdam, and that Steinbach was giving a performance of *In the South* in Cologne. Elgar went over with Frank Schuster, and was there for nearly a fortnight, and then stayed on in London with Schuster for a few days.

The Athenaeum, Pall Mall, S.W.
Dec 16: 1904

My dear Firapeel:
Many thanks: so glad to hear you are well & flourishing, all *three* of you

I hope. I am so very happy about the new arrival & envy you your *son*— alas! I receive in this world all that I never want or wish for.

Steinbach &c fine!

Au revoir

Yours ever

Reynart

ye Foxe.

This letter was in response to a letter from my father telling him of my birth on 24 November.

On 20 December Elgar, on the way home, stayed in Birmingham for the Halford Society Concert which was being conducted by Richard Strauss, and included his *Don Juan*, Op 20, *Tod und Verklärung*, Op 24, *Ein Heldenleben*, Op 40, and his Violin Concerto in D minor, Op 8, with Max Mossel as soloist.

Atkins and Sinclair had arranged to travel over together, and after the concert they were invited by George Halford, then the chief orchestral conductor in Birmingham, to go with Elgar and Richard Peyton, who had endowed the university music professorship, to the supper at the Clef Club, which was being given in honour of Strauss. This was a memorable evening with Elgar and Strauss as the principal speakers. It was Elgar's first public speech in Birmingham since he had accepted the chair of music.

The Birmingham Clef Club had been founded in the early 1880s, and was originally almost entirely composed of members from the music profession, the theatre and the arts. In its earlier days, especially when directed by Ebenezer Prout, it had given concerts of a very high order. Sir Arthur Sullivan had been a president, and Sir Henry Irving a distinguished member. By this time it had become more of a social club which prided itself on the support it gave to music in Birmingham, and on the special suppers which it gave after celebrity concerts.

Elgar reminded Atkins of an earlier occasion after a Richter concert when Ettling had been playing the drums and had been invited to join them at the Clef Club supper. During the reception Ettling had played his usual sleight-of-hand tricks, and when the host wanted to consult his watch to see if it was time to move in to supper, it was missing. When Ettling returned the watch the host, who was somewhat pompous, was not amused. Fortunately the onlookers were. It was the only time that Elgar could remember when 'Uncle Klingsor' was completely dumbfounded.

125

On Elgar's return to Plas Gwyn the next morning he found that the proofs of *Pomp and Circumstance March* No 3, which he had finished before going away and dedicated to Atkins, had arrived from Boosey's.

Plas Gwyn, Hereford.
Dec 21 1904

Firapeel!
    The score (proof) is here: & it looks well. Will you be able to look it thro' if I send it? Send a p.c. & say: you must not think of it if you are busy: but it is Noel, & over a pipe, look you, you might do much to amend the failings of
                        Yours ever
                            Reynart.
    will you come & see it? It is fayre.
        They have engraved
            'To my friend
                Ivor A.F. King'

Christmas is a very busy time for cathedral organists, and Atkins could only spare an odd hour or so. He accordingly went over the next morning, and after he had inspected the proof Elgar played over the whole March and then talked about his visit to the Continent. Volbach had given a fine performance of *The Apostles* in Mainz and this work had also been a great success in Rotterdam. Steinbach had given a great and warm interpretation of *In the South* in Cologne. Altogether it had been a wonderful holiday. In addition they had found time to visit Düsseldorf and had lunched with the Buths. Elgar had clearly been as much impressed with Steinbach as he had been in May, since he spoke also about Steinbach's concert in London on 15 December with the London Symphony Orchestra, which had included Beethoven's Violin Concerto with Zimmermann as soloist, and Brahms' Symphony No 4. Steinbach had been a close friend of Brahms and this performance, said Elgar, had absolutely thrilled him.
    The year ended with Elgar's usual Christmas card, this time a photograph of the sundial, a gift from Schuster, which Elgar had recently installed in the garden at Plas Gwyn.

1905

The year 1905 brought Elgar a fourth doctorate, namely, the Oxford D Mus, and saw the composition of the *Introduction and Allegro for Strings*, his appointment as the first professor of music at Birmingham University, his first visit to America, at the invitation of Professor S. S. Sanford, another doctorate, D Mus, Yale, and of him being made an honorary Freeman of the City and County of Worcester.

It was Worcester's turn to have the Three Choirs Festival, and Atkins had for some time been devoting his thoughts to the programme. On moving to Hereford Elgar had given up most of his Worcester committees, but Atkins was anxious to have him on the 1905 Worcester festival committee, or if possible, on the executive committee. He accordingly went over to Plas Gwyn on 14 January, and sounded Elgar out. Elgar was delighted to go on the main committee, but a little doubtful about the executive committee because of its more frequent meetings.

The weather was very cold, and Elgar who had a chill was staying indoors. He told Atkins that an artist, Talbot Hughes, had been staying with them but had left that morning. He was painting a portrait of Elgar, but it was a tedious business and likely to mean more sittings. He cheered up later, but was obviously not his usual self.

Atkins formally proposed Elgar for the executive committee, and hence the following letter.

Plas Gwyn, Hereford.
Jan 25. 1905.

Firapeel, my dear!
I have heard (scribendiously) from S. Southall [the festival secretary] saying I am on the Xecutive Committee; is this right and what you wish? I have said I will 'ack' thereon.
Now I want to be in Worcester for the week [festival week, 9–16 September] and
—Pirrivate
we should like a house. When we spoke to the people (I forget the name) whose house we had last time, soon after the event, they seemed inclined to be very peevish and the rent swelled absurdly. Now, don't mention my name but see if you can hear of an entertainable house; I would like the same one for convenience, or belike, the one next, but I don't want to be fleeced or cheeked. So keep your eyes open for a cluse for your
Reynart
& the family.

Elgar attended the next meeting of the executive committee on 31 January. At this Atkins was asked to write a sacred work for the forthcoming festival, and as he knew Elgar's skill in drawing up a libretto, he turned to him for help. It was immediately forthcoming.

Elgar was going to Oxford the following week to receive an honorary D Mus degree and to conduct the *Enigma Variations*. He was also in the midst of writing the *Introduction and Allegro for Strings*, but expected to finish it shortly after his return from Oxford. At the next executive committee meeting, on 14 February, he told Atkins that the work was now finished and had been sent to Novello's the previous day. He was hoping now to turn to a libretto for Atkins.

When Atkins went over to Plas Gwyn on 17 February, Elgar was full of an invitation which he had received from their mutual old friend, S. S. Sanford. He had asked them both to go over to

America for June and July, and was planning to include some concerts in which Elgar could conduct some of his works. Elgar had also had some thoughts about the *Hymn of Faith* libretto, which they discussed, and he hoped to send the first draft of this within the next few days.

Plas Gwyn, Hereford.
21 Feb 1905

Dear Firapeel:
   Here is the 'Faith' Hymn. If you don't use it be sure do not let anyone else have it. I want it myself. All good luck to you.
                         Yours
                         Reynart
The subject is most apposite to the time & is just the thing after all this correspondence & preaching about 'Do we believe?'

8, College Yard, Worcester.
Feb 22nd 1905

Dear Edward,
   Your libretto is simply fine. You are a Prince of the craft you really are a brilliant man: the best intellect I know—apart from the Art.* I'm in a glow over it and only hope I may do partial justice to it. You see I don't expect to by any means do what should be done to it.
   I've always admitted that you could write a good tune *under provocation* but Providence has dealt over-generously with you in all other intellectual directions and I am profoundly grateful.
   Dear old boy I am so proud to have a libretto of your drawing up to work at: Heaven grant that I may do some good work with it! I feel that is of your best and I leave you to imagine how grateful I am to you for giving yourself up so wholeheartedly to thinking it out. Bless you, Meister meisterin (new genitive).
   Williams [C. Lee Williams] is here and looks forward to seeing you to-morrow at the Stewards' meeting. Mind you come and back up Canon Claughton and Committee.
   My warmest thanks to Carice and all who have helped in any way.
                         Yours ever,
                         Ivor Atkins.
* On re-reading I find that this is distinctly good.

   Elgar came over the next day for the festival stewards' meeting, and after it Atkins was able to thank him again for the libretto.

POST CARD
Hfd. Feb 26: 1905

Many thanks for programme [of coming Three Choirs meeting at Worcester]. I will find ye a ticket for Mar 8 an ye be there wot ye well. *Now* get out a *good tune* for the banners.

Yours ever
E.E.

Programme A.1.

March 8 was the date of the forthcoming London Symphony Orchestra's concert in the Queen's Hall devoted to Elgar's compositions, to be conducted by him, which would include the first performance of the *Introduction and Allegro for Strings*, Op 47, and of *Pomp and Circumstance March* No 3.

The 'banners' is a reference to the *Hymn of Faith* in which the chorus' opening line is 'In the name of God we will set up our banners.' When preparing his libretto for *The Apostles* Elgar had studied deeply the Biblical and Apocryphal writings, and there is little doubt that his libretto for the *Hymn of Faith* was prepared at this time from the same sources, and, as his letter of 21 February showed, that he had considered setting it to music himself. It is an excellent example of his skill as a librettist.

Atkins wrote by return of post asking for the proffered ticket and telling Elgar that he was thinking of holding the London orchestral rehearsals for the festival in the St Andrew's Hall, Newman Street.

Plas Gwyn, Hereford
March 2. 1905

Firapeel:
Meek & humble as ever I answer ye on the day of your asking. Perpend: a ticket shall be yours, even at the box office under yr name, if not despatched before.

The Hall of the Scots Saint is useful but uninspiring: I think more correctable than in the *Hall of ye Queene*, & the men are under yr hand as it were. But it is stuffy & faded & depresseth me.

Peradventure it's cheap & to be commended. For *practical* use I wd advise its use, leaving poetry to come in the Worcester fane.

Off tomorrow
Yrs ever
Edward Elgar

alias

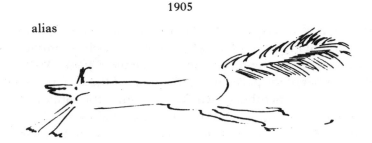

c/o L. F. Schuster Esq
22 Old Queen St
Westminster S.W.

Oil paint; no less
I'll do ye a landscape
some day.

On 8 March Atkins went up to London for the concert, which was part of the recently formed London Symphony Orchestra's first session of London concerts. The whole of the concert was devoted to Elgar works—*In the South*, the Funeral March from *Grania and Diarmid*, *Sea Pictures*, *Pomp and Circumstance March No 3*, *Cockaigne*, *Introduction and Allegro for Strings*, and the *Enigma Variations*, all conducted by Elgar. The *Introduction and Allegro*, dedicated to S. S. Sanford, and the *Pomp and Circumstance March* No 3, dedicated to Atkins, were receiving their first performances.

Atkins went straight to the morning rehearsal which went well, but Elgar did not seem to be up to his usual form. On the way to lunch with the Schusters he admitted to being unwell. At the concert, however, he seemed more like his usual self and obtained fine performances.

Atkins and the Elgar party were all going to the Albert Hall that evening to hear a performance of *The Apostles*, which was being given by the Royal Choral Society. After tea, however, it was clear that Elgar was too ill to go. Atkins therefore stayed with him, while the rest of the party, including Sinclair, went to *The Apostles*.

At this time Hereford and especially Gloucester had thriving music societies based on a broad shire basis, these in addition to their festival choral societies. Elgar's Worcestershire Philharmonic Society had provided a similar organisation for Worcester, but with Elgar's absences from Worcester and now his move to Hereford the Philharmonic had gone into a decline, and it gave its last concert, the seventeenth, on 8 December 1904. Atkins knew that a number of the performing members of the society, especially the orchestral members, would welcome the opportunity of continuing their music. A Worcester Festival year, when he was already very fully occupied, was not a good time to be considering the foundation of a new society, but he felt that the idea should be ventilated, and hence the next letter.

8, College Yard, Worcester.
March 13th, 1905.

My dear Reynart,
  I want you to tell me whether you do not think something ought to be done in the way of organising an Orchestral Society for the whole county. You know what Hereford and particularly Gloucester (on account of its organisation) are doing, and here it seems to me that with the great work you have already done there ought to be a very good chance of a first-rate Society. It is of course a busy time with me just now, but none the less I feel that some steps ought to be taken at once—at any rate to moot the question, the organising might go on quietly in the interval between now and next autumn.
  With the quite exceptional amateurs who could be raked up at a good many points of the compass, and with you associated with it, some good work might surely be done.
  Will you give me your counsel.
                                        Yours ever,
                                        Firapeel.

  Elgar agreed with him, but it was felt that no formal action could be taken until after the Worcester Festival.
  A few days earlier Atkins had received an invitation from Sir Oliver Lodge, the principal of Birmingham University, to a reception before Sir Edward Elgar's inaugural lecture as Professor of Music on 16 March. Atkins attended, and in his papers is the following note.

On March 16th, 1905, Elgar gave his Inaugural Lecture as Richard Peyton Professor of Music in the University of Birmingham. It was a noteworthy occasion, and the Principal, Sir Oliver Lodge, had included a certain number of Elgar's musical friends amongst those invited. In the hall I found myself seated next to Sinclair, who at that time, in addition to being Organist of Hereford Cathedral, was also conductor of the Birmingham Festival Choral Society.

The Lecture was a little discursive and largely taken up with an uncompromising survey of Music in England at that time. It was stirring enough, and as Elgar lashed out fiercely at musicians and critics alike, we both fidgeted in our seats, becoming more and more anxious as the lecture proceeded about the effect of his words in the musical world at large. I think we understood their drift and significance more than did others present. Certainly Lodge radiated a sphinx-like calm which nothing could disturb. It was in the course of this lecture that Elgar made the startling statement (delivered with suppressed quietness) that the 'centre of English music must now be looked for somewhere further North.'

In this lecture Elgar was undoubtedly referring to the great influence that Richter in Manchester with the Hallé, and elsewhere, was beginning to have on music all over England. The remark quoted was a paraphrase of what Elgar had written to Canon C. V. Gorton on 26 May 1903, about the Morecambe Competitive Festival: 'Some day the Press will awake to the fact, already known abroad and to some few of us in England, that the living centre of music in Great Britain is not London but somewhere further North.' This letter had been quoted in the *Musical Times* of July 1903.

Elgar was still unwell but had to go to London the following day, and was away in Hanley, Leeds and York until the middle of April. On 17 April Atkins went to Hereford and found Elgar making a hutch for a large white rabbit which they had bought for Carice. The rabbit was already a universal favourite. It was called Peter, and over the next year or so was to figure in Elgar's writing. May Grafton, Elgar's niece, was now spending most of her time in Hereford and would be looking after Carice while the Elgars were away in America.

Since the end of February Atkins had been working hard on the *Hymn of Faith*, and he had brought the manuscript with him for a 'play-over' with Elgar and to discuss certain points. They had not finished when he had to leave, and he left it with Elgar.

Plas Gwyn Ap 19: 1905

My dear Firapeel:

I have had another bad 'turn' or I should have promptly ret*d* your stuff with the addition.

N.B. Tobit is good: it refers to Jerusalem & can quite well be applied to a soul or souls which have temporarily lost the faith. it's A.1.

You might omit 2nd line 'and bless &c'.

ps 118.14 Is also A1.

I added v.15 *in case* you want more, but you can quite well omit it altogether: if you *do* use it say, preferably, 'dwellings' or 'tents' to avoid the literal meaning of tabernacle after we have used it figuratively above. v. 17 makes a good link 'but LIVE!!!'

wake up here

and declare the works of the Lord, for Faith shall flourish, &c &c. Now go ahead

I hope you will like the new lines.

Yours ever

Reynart

On 8 May Atkins was in Plas Gwyn again to go over the *Hymn of Faith*. After this Elgar was away in the North and Atkins did not see him again until 2 June, when he presented him with a signed full score of *Pomp and Circumstance March* No 3.

On 7 June Elgar came to Worcester and called on the Atkins to say good-bye and to collect their messages for Sanford. Among their fellow passengers on the voyage to New York was a Mrs Worthington, who was later to become a close friend of the Elgars and the Atkins. They were met in New York by Sanford, and on 28 June Yale University conferred upon Elgar the degree of Doctor of Music.

Towards the end of June Atkins received a somewhat mysterious coloured postcard from Elgar:

[Postmarked New Haven, Connecticut, 19 June 1905]

Firapeel: Hope all goes well. We sail July 11th. If you receive cable don't answer without consulting me.

Love Reynart.

No cable came, and the mystery remained until the Elgars' return home. Sanford had travelled over with them on the SS *Kaiser Wilhelm der Grosse*, but had gone straight to London. On 20 July Elgar came over to Worcester for the festival full-chorus rehearsal in the Public Hall, at which he was rehearsing *The Apostles*. He lunched with the Atkins and explained his mysterious card. He had, he said, been empowered by Frank Damrosch, who was then Director of the Institute of Musical Art, the principal

Conservatoire in New York, to offer Atkins the appointment of Professor in charge of the Organ Department. A formal confirmation of the offer would follow in a few weeks time. Elgar begged him to consider the offer carefully and talk it over again before he made his decision.

By a curious coincidence there had come, at the same time, another offer, the post of Organist and Director of Music at St Bartholomew's Church, New York. Both posts were very tempting financially, and the appointment at the Conservatoire offered very wide recital opportunities all over America. Fortunately there was no pressing urgency, since the autumn had been suggested for both appointments, and Atkins promised to give the matter very careful consideration.

On 21 July he went over to Plas Gwyn, and Elgar helped him with the orchestration of the *Hymn of Faith*, which was now otherwise complete. On the following Friday they worked again on the orchestration. On 1 August Atkins bicycled over to Hereford, and by lunchtime the orchestration was nearly complete. After lunch Elgar persuaded him to help mend and fill a large tub, repair a gate post, and, with May Grafton's help, put wire netting over the back gate to keep Peter the rabbit in. I suspect that my father was the labourer, for Elgar was a real craftsman in both wood and metal, and my father, apart from bicycle repairs, chains, punctures, etc, for which, like organ maintenance, removal of ciphers and so on, he had a gift, was no handyman. Sinclair joined them for supper, and the next day the orchestration of the *Hymn of Faith* was completed. After tea Atkins rode back to Worcester, with Elgar and May Grafton riding part of the way with him. The habit of riding out to meet your guest and of going part of the way back with him when he left was a ritual which had originated with Sinclair some years before Elgar took up bicycling.

When Sinclair first brought Atkins to Hereford in 1889 they hired and then bought bicycles, and both were very enthusiastic cyclists, always up to date with the latest freewheel, three-speed, oil-bath models. In those days it was quite normal to bicycle 40, 50 or more miles in a day, and to take your bicycle with you by train on holiday. When Atkins was at Ludlow, and he and Sinclair were both bachelors, they often cycled over to see each other, and this 'seeing off the guest' was not unknown to result in the 'host' becoming the 'guest' for the night, and a rushed train journey back the next morning. The Elgars only took up bicycling in the summer of 1900, when they were going frequently between Birchwood Lodge and Craeg Lea. Alice was never really keen, and gave up when they went to Hereford, but Elgar retained his love of cycling until they left Hereford for London in 1911, and indeed used it for much exploration of the countryside and for mental and physical relaxation. Many ideas came to him while pedalling along quiet lanes.

In August Atkins took his usual holiday, this year bicycling round Oban as a centre.

Plas Gwyn, Hereford.
Augt 20: 1905

My dear Firapeel.
    Glad to hear all progressed well.
    I did not bother you when away because you were better without.
    I trust your work [*Hymn of Faith*] has made you happy—your work here has been fully appreciated & it has rained practically ever since you filled the tub!
    Glad to hear the tickets [Festival] go.
    As to the paragraph: it will do *as amended*. Do cut out that about 'an English Cathedral organist' which makes it sound to the ordinary person that the anxiety was to secure 'an E.C. organist' at all costs, whereas the greatest & properest contempt is felt for the generality of such creatures e.g. Bridge. [Sir Frederick Bridge]. I suppose Edwards [F. G. Edwards, the editor of *Musical Times*] wrote the par: & he thinks you are all alike I believe!!
    I am not sure about next week yet. S.S.S. is on the way *theoretically*, but practically ???
Good luck to you
Yours ever
Reynart
    (More foxy than of yore!)
P.S. I may have to run up somewhere further north in a day or two, but shd. be home by Friday anyhow & S.S.S. might be here.
P.S.S. I have cut out Damrosch's name the *second* time: it *is* so clumsy to put it twice & in a newspaper par: draws attention away from the principal person, *you*. The man in the street reads it hurriedly & gets the (in this case) unimportant name *twice* & the important name *once* only. There is a great art (*understood by me*!!!) in writing this sort of thing & the M.T. has it not at all. Again all those capitals take attention away from the 'conservatory' &c &c & subject.

Atkins, having thought deeply during his holiday about the two

Elgar at Craeg Lea in 1903: self-portrait? In 1930 the author showed Elgar a
Kodak self-timer. He was interested, but said that in the early years of the century
he had designed and used an apparatus for the same purpose. He described how he
had set up a laboratory stand on a table adjacent to the camera. On the stand were
three beakers connected with flexible tubing with two taps. The middle beaker
was on a movable platform with an extension which rested lightly on the exposure
bulk of the camera. The top beaker was filled with water and the taps set to allow
time for Elgar to stand at a predetermined position in front of a door or window
and to give the necessary exposure time. This photograph is the only one of those
Elgar gave to Atkins which seems to fit the above description

appointments offered to him in America, had now decided to decline both and remain at Worcester. Now that his decision had been taken the *Musical Times* wished to make an announcement in an early issue and had sent Atkins a draft version. He did not like the wording as it stood and had sent it on to Elgar, who was very skilled in such matters, for advice.

Atkins went over to Hereford on Friday 25 August. Elgar was finishing a new part-song, *Evening Scene*, words by Coventry Patmore, which he played over. On 31 August, Sanford, who had come on the 29th, hired a motor car and brought the Elgars over to Worcester for the full chorus rehearsal in the cathedral.

The Elgars had again taken Castle House in College Green for the festival week, and their house party included Carice, May Grafton, Mrs Worthington, Frank Schuster, Jaeger, Canon Gorton and Mrs Gandy, another Morecambe Festival friend. On 12 September, the day started with a Guildhall ceremony in which Elgar was formally enrolled as an Honorary Freeman of the City and County of Worcester, and presented with an elaborate casket containing the legal Document. (This is now in the Elgar Birthplace at Broadheath.)

Elgar had brought back with him from America the magnificent brightly coloured Yale University Doctor of Music gown, which had been presented to him by Sanford, and with his keen sense of colour and pageantry he had decided to wear this for the ceremony and the procession to the cathedral afterwards. Perhaps his decision was also as a token of appreciation for the presence of Sanford and other American friends. The musical world was, naturally, very well represented, quite apart from the Three Choirs artists and conductors, both past and present, since C. Lee Williams and Hugh Blair were there. As the procession passed the

(*opposite above*) Plas Gwyn, Hereford, October 1904. Elgar about to take a drive in Frank Schuster's Fiat motor car. Lady Elgar and Elgar with Schuster, and by the car Barry, Schuster's secretary (*By permission of the Trustees of the Elgar Birthplace*)

(*below left*) This photograph of Elgar was taken in 1904 and reproduced as a post-card in an English Celebrities series. The sapphire tie pin, a present from Alice, was made out of one of several large star sapphires brought to England by Alice's father on his retirement from the Indian army

(*below right*) Elgar writing *Introduction and Allegro* at Plas Gwyn, Hereford, 1905. Photograph by May Grafton

music shop in the High Street Elgar bowed to his father who was sitting at an upper window. His father was now too frail to leave his room. The sun was shining brightly that day, and my mother recalled how it had picked out the colours in Elgar's gown.

At the cathedral Atkins conducted *Gerontius*, for which the text was the same as used at the 1902 festival. After lunch Part 2 began with Atkins conducting his *Hymn of Faith*, in which the soloist was Muriel Foster, followed by Brahms' Symphony No 4 in E minor, always a favourite of his.

On the Wednesday the morning started with Strauss' *Tod und Verklärung*. This had been the subject of much conversation between Atkins and Elgar. This time, in view of Atkins' success with the work in 1902, there were no doubts about the advisability of including it, and the sale of tickets showed that the public had now learnt to appreciate Strauss' style.

During the remainder of the festival Elgar conducted his *Introduction and Allegro* and *The Apostles*. As at Gloucester the previous year it was noted by Atkins and others how greatly enhanced the work was when performed in a cathedral.

The Atkins, as usual, entertained throughout the festival week. Mrs Worthington came over several times, and the Atkins, like all those who met her, were greatly taken by her vivacious charm, and it was the beginning of a long friendship.

Schuster had brought to Worcester an invitation from his friend Admiral Charles Beresford for Elgar and himself to go as his guests on a cruise in the Mediterranean. Elgar and Schuster went straight from the festival to Athens, where they joined the Admiral's party. After cruising around for some days the party went on to Turkey where they spent a few days in Constantinople. Elgar arrived back in Hereford on 14 October, after attending a rehearsal in Norwich on 12 October.

Plas Gwyn, Hereford.
Oct 18 1905
My dear Firapeel.

I arrd. home (via Norwich chorus) on Saturday night & (I tell you) I have had a weary time with epistles & worse—Friday I'm off again & there is small rest for months I see.

How are you? & when can I see you?

My love anyhow
Yours ever
Reynart.

N.B.
There be dogges a-mange in Stamboul.
Bugges also.
Likewise Ratons
& Cokeroaches.
Cattes but few;
but I suspect
ye pies.

The formation of a new orchestral society for Worcestershire was now becoming urgent, and Atkins was trying to arrange a public meeting at which he hoped that Elgar would take the chair.

Plas Gwyn, Hereford.
Monday a.m. [23 October 1905]

My dear Firapeel
   This in case I do not see you at Worcester in passing through. I was laid up with a bad eye all yesterday & today it's not much better.
   I might come over on Nov 2 or 3 or 4 in the p.m. but will you write & say what you really want of
Your devoted
Reynart.

8, College Yard, Worcester.
Oct. 27th, 1905.

My dear Reynart,
   A thousand thanks for your letter of Monday. Not knowing where to write to I have waited for your return. Of the dates you have given me I have chosen Saturday, Nov. 4th for the meeting which will be held at the Assembly Rooms, Guildhall, (lately connected with other gaieties) [Elgar's Freedom] at 2.30 p.m. I will post on to you to-night local papers containing a letter in which I set forth the facts.
   Now, I am delighted, dear old boy, that you are going to direct the formation of what I hope if properly worked may turn out a really useful Society, able to buy much music (performance is an after consideration).
   I see every chance of a good membership. There has been a very good response to the letter I wrote earlier in the year, and Miss Fitton sends me a list as long as my arm.
   I've seen Leicester, who has given me use of room, is much interested and will be at the meeting.
   Can you do with me on Thursday afternoon? I want to do lots of things: discuss ways and means, who are likely to be the best secs. (Ysobel for one, of course)—but more than all, there are so many musical things

owing to me. I'm musically stagnant. I must hear the 'Hans' theme, and I must have two hours of stimulus. I am ready to fire up over anything you've done. Moreover, it is not advisable for me to be going on any longer holding such capacities for enthusiasm un-used. By Jove, I expect I shall have a good time. You dear old thing, you've not shown me much this year—that wretched work of mine absorbed all our time.

Thine,
Firapeel.

The University, Birmingham [written from Plas Gwyn]
Oct 30 1905

The 'Hans' theme

My dear Firapeel

Why this forked tail?
Alas & alack I fear I cannot take my diversions this week or ever again in this weary world.

I'll turn up on Saturday & do what I can in the mean-time.

Your always
devoted
Ed
Reynart.

Elgar was overwhelmed at this time with outside distraction as far as composing was concerned. *Apostles II* had progressed, but his Mediterranean tour had put his writing schedule badly in arrears. Atkins asked Elgar to lunch on Saturday 4 November, before the meeting, but Elgar could not manage this.

Nov. 3 1905 Hfd.

My dear Firapeel.

I am so sorry but I really cannot get away until the corridor train arrg at S.Hill at 1.40. if you could meet me we could talk till 2.30—I am absolutely overwhelmed with work. Have a clearly written list of things to discuss.

Yrs ever
Reynart.

Elgar took the chair at the meeting in the Guildhall, and the
Worcestershire Orchestral Society came formally into existence.
He 'doodled' during the meeting, and his sketches are shown here.
After the meeting Atkins asked Elgar for suggestions for the music
to be studied. He promised to consider this and write, but would
not be able to do so for a week or so.

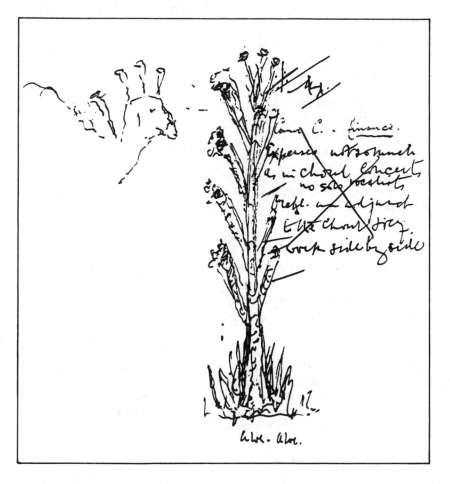

On 8 November Elgar gave his third professorial lecture in
Birmingham, which was devoted to Brahms' Third Symphony.
He illustrated this on the piano. Atkins greatly enjoyed this
lecture.

Elgar was away for much of November, and very worried about
the slow progress of *Apostles II*.

Plas Gwyn, Hereford.
Dec 2 1905

My dear Firapeel:

I am sorry times have been evyll. I fear to suggest a programme although it liketh me well to think. I really cannot think *what* you can do for a symphony: is Tschaikowsky No. 4 too much? Look at it.

I suppose you want trombones or it would be nice to do an untrombone programme.

> Egmont, or Coriolan
> Scotch Symphony
> Jeux d'Enfants—Bizet
>   &c
or Tschai[kowsky] No. 4.
> Schumann No. 3
> Overture 'Euryanthe'
> Struensee—Meyerbeer (You wd like this,
>   I think)
> Slavonic Dances—Dvorak. (any almost)

I don't know your strength & am quite at sea—but I think the Schumann wd really be a good beginning.

Do come & see me soon. I am wofully busy.

> Yours ever
> Reynart.

I think German's Welsh Rhapsody for a rousing *popular* thing wd do.

Atkins, availing himself of Elgar's suggestions, then drew up a rehearsal scheme which included:

Overture: Rienzi	Wagner
Symphony No 3. 'The Rhenish'	Schumann
Serenade in E minor (for strings)	Elgar
Slavonic Dances (1st set)	Dvořák
Rhapsody (Welsh)	German
March: 'Pomp and Circumstance' No. 1	Elgar

and sent it to Elgar before printing.

Plas Gwyn, Hereford.
Dec 9 1905

Dear Firapeel.

I think it doesn't look bad. Of course Schumann isn't quite the modern note you want to strike but then again it isn't too old-fashioned by any means & I think not difficult. I should put it *all* down—German &

Dvorak. You will want to practise a lot more stuff than you really play &
make folks happy.

For ord[inar]y filling-up practice-work, get some *Concerto* & ask one of
your lady friends to take the piano or one of your pupils, Beethoven C
minor or better, in G—only I did that one [in a WPS concert],
Mozart in D mi. Explain to them the delights & beauties of accompanying, &c &c & get a fresh pianist each time (Reynart) just for 20 mins:

Yours ever

Reynart.

Elgar was occupied with preparing two Birmingham lectures for
the first half of December. These lectures took up all his time and
put him off composing, but with the term over he started work
again on *Apostles II* during the last fortnight of the year, and
despite headaches, made real progress.

Plas Gwyn, Hereford.
Dec 30 1905

My dear Firapeel:

This is to wish you & yours all good things for the New Year.

I am seedy or should have sent for you to cheer me up on Friday. Belike
I am now beyond cheer. The work goes on [*Apostles II*, now known as
The Kingdom] & must be seen & heard. When will you come? I have not
much presentable yet.

I also want to hear of your work, & the new & old societies & your plans.
I am fixed here until April! This cluse is quiet & seemly, maugre feasts & a
certayn seasonable looseness among bond folks: so an ye come, come
sober & in grave apparel of a sub-fusc hue.

Thine

Reynart.

1906

This year saw the completion and first performance of *The
Kingdom*, and a second visit to America, in which Elgar conducted
some of his works at the Cincinnati Music Festival, including *The
Dream of Gerontius* and *The Apostles*, and the presentation of
another doctorate, the LL D, at Aberdeen University.

On 9 January Atkins went to Plas Gwyn to find Alfred Kalisch
had arrived that morning. He was staying the night, and after
dinner Elgar played over to them all of *Apostles II* that he had

written so far—some oddments, and the Prelude, which was virtually complete. The following morning they went over it again in their usual way, Elgar playing passages over first, and then getting Atkins to play them back to him. It was like old times at Craeg Lea, and they both enjoyed themselves.

Atkins went over on Saturday 20 January and found Elgar at work on the end of the first section, 'They gave forth the lots', and the chorus, 'O ye priests'. During the rest of January and early February Elgar made very slow progress. History was repeating itself. When Elgar had written to Atkins in July 1902, 'I am now plotting GIGANTIC WORX', he had in mind a 'whole-day' composition, and his initial drafting in 1903 had included much of the *Apostles II* he was now working on. Writing in 1903 had taken much longer than he had anticipated, and he had also suffered serious eye trouble, with the result that the work given in Birmingham in October 1903 had to be restricted to what we now know as *The Apostles*. When in September 1904, Elgar started planning *Apostles II* for the Birmingham Festival of 1906, he again intended his work to be a whole-day one, but time was now again running out, partly due to his visit to America, but mainly due to ill health in the form of prostrating headaches. After one of these attacks he was so depressed that he threatened to abandon the work altogether.

When Atkins went to Plas Gwyn on 14 February Elgar told him all about these difficulties which had arisen since they last met. He seemed contented, however, now that Novello's and the Birmingham committee had agreed to a morning-only work. He was now re-planning it, and was considering calling it *His Kingdom*. He said that some sketches would have to be put on one side, perhaps for a third work. Talk then turned to Atkins' concert in the Royal Albert Hall on the coming Sunday, when he was conducting the London Symphony Orchestra.

On his arrival at the Albert Hall on the Sunday morning for his rehearsal Atkins found a telegram of good wishes from Elgar. Atkins wrote to Elgar after the concert:

Hotel York, Berners Street, London W.1.
Feb. 18th, 1906.

Prologue.
  This pen is *damnable*.

My dear Reynart,
  Thank you for your telegram. I appreciated it more than I can say. It was most kind, most thoughtful. Bless you, dear old boy.
  And now as to 'Variations', Thank you for some of the greatest moments of a lifetime. Schuster was there and I hope will report to you. He came and saw me afterwards in the artists' room and appeared to be *delighted*—most enthusiastic. I, too, (Heaven forgive me for this new-found conceit) thought it a *fine* performance.
  But you know, Reynart I think I *do* understand and get down to the inner core of your music. It seems quite part of me—and always has. I think you would have been pleased. As to the band, well, they seem to open their hearts to you. It is simply amazing. Of course it is no light thing to conduct in such an awful place as the A. Hall, and I felt the magnitude of the task directly I tackled 'Egmont'. (It *is* badly scored), but directly we began the Variations it was quite another matter. I felt I could play upon the 'boys', and I felt that the whole thing was elastic and flowing. You ought to have been there. I made the folk strain their ears for the pp's—but it's all your music. We could not help ourselves.
  I don't think there was anything wrong, though I was more than once embarrassed by the unspeakable tenderness of the music. Reynart, take it from me—I KNOW—you are *the* master. God bless you and keep you for us all is the prayer of your devoted
Firapeel.
  Make Schuster report.

Plas Gwyn, Hereford.
Tuesday [20 February 1906]

My dear Firapeel:
  Leo [Schuster] hath reported sagely & warmly, not to say hotly & in admiration. He was *before* you by several posts. I am so glad it all went well, & hope you may go on & conduct that jolly lot again & again.
  Do come over soon. I *may* go to town on Friday, but there's Thursday & I want you to see some scraps.
Yours ever
Reynart.
I say: I thought I should see you. I want to talk to you about those songs of yours. Bring them with you when you come, & *don't* publish them until we've talked them over. I think I spy a spot or two which we can raise from 'ous' to 'ic' (chemical frase).

Atkins had orchestrated two of his songs, 'Too Late' and 'Thou art come', specially for the Hereford Festival. He had shown them to Elgar in manuscript, who had been thinking about the orchestration and some improvements he felt could be made before publication. By '"ous" to "ic"' Elgar was referring to the change from, for example, chlorous acid to chloric acid, the latter having a higher degree of oxidation (ie a purer form).

On Thursday 22 February, Atkins went to Plas Gwyn. Elgar was now writing hard. They played over what he had written since 20 January. Real progress had been made. Section 1 and Section 2, 'At the Beautiful Gate', were now complete, and a start had been made on Section 3, 'Pentecost'.

On 7 March Atkins found Frank Schuster staying with the Elgars. On this and the next day, Elgar played over all the music so far written. Most of the third section, 'Pentecost', was now written, but Elgar was still working on it. Schuster and Atkins were thrilled.

8, College Yard, Worcester.
March 8th, 1906.

My dear Reynart,
  Will this do? I've given one or two alternative versions out of which to make a decent rendition possible. Will you glance your wizard eye over it? I thought yesterday evening's new contribution simply magnificent. It is going to be greater than the first part by a good deal. You are getting very wise in that cluse of yours, but even I am amazed at some of that stuff. My eyes for all their tutoring get fairly opened now and then and those steadily built-up climaxes are going to be tremendous.
  I want you if you will (and Schuster hasn't grabbed it) to give me that single sheet that you copied twice.
                    Yours ever,
                    Firapeel.
I enjoyed myself immensely and we had a *great* evening.

Schuster had 'grabbed' it. I have no idea what section it contained.

On 23 March Atkins found that Elgar had completed Section 3 and most of Section 4, 'The Sign of Healing'. They played it all over, but had to break off as both had promised to go to tea with 'The Duchess' (Miss Underwood) and Miss Thomas, who were giving one of their special parties. Sinclair and many other old friends were there. As soon as they could they went back to Plas Gwyn and continued playing until supper, after which Atkins had to return to Worcester. He remembered being delighted with St Peter's solos, 'Look on us', and 'Ye men of Israel', to which Elgar was putting the final touches.

There were only a few days left before the Elgars left for America, but they asked Atkins to go over on 3 April. R. H. Wilson, the Birmingham chorus master, was coming over that day to go through the music so far written. On the morning of the 3rd, however, Atkins learnt by telegram that the household was too engrossed with preparations for departure to be able to put him up. A letter followed.

Plas Gwyn, Hereford.
April 3: 1906.

N.B. an F of considerable value [Elgar had drawn a huge F at the beginning of Firapeel].

My dear Firapeel:

I was bitterly sorry to have to send the telegram this a.m.—the rooms are impossible owing to packitis from which the whole household, save myself, is suffering acutely. Every room seems infested.

Can you come over on Thursday? in the day, I mean, leaving us in the evening. We might ride forth & raid a village.

Wilson is to be here soon for some hours talk & play over the work [*The Kingdom*]. I hoped you were coming early enough to join in the immolation of the innocent.

Do try for Thursday.
Yours ever

Atkins bicycled over on 5 April. Elgar rode out to meet him and they did 'raid a village' or so before lunch and again afterwards. 'The Duchess' and Miss Thomas came to a farewell tea. This time the Elgars were looking forward to their American visit.

On 6 April the Elgars left for Liverpool. They reached New York on 15 April, where they were met by Sanford, whom the Elgars had now nicknamed 'Gaffer'. That evening they met Walter and Frank Damrosch and Mrs Worthington, who was to go with them to the Cincinnati Music Festival and spend much time with them during the visit.

In the meantime, Atkins had conducted the eagerly awaited first concert of the newly formed Worcestershire Orchestral Society, on 26 April, in a programme largely modelled on Elgar's suggested list. The concert was an enormous success, and promised a great future for the Society. The only regret for many of those present was the unavoidable absence of Elgar.

From America, Elgar sent a postcard to Atkins:

Cincinnati April 27 1906.

Letter recd. no music yet. All well here but hot. Dreadfully busy [orchestrating *The Kingdom*]
Love Reynart.

The festival at Cincinnati was virtually an Elgar festival. He conducted *The Apostles*, *In the South*, *Introduction and Allegro* and *Gerontius*. This last was played to a huge audience which included nearly 800 people standing.

Atkins was not certain exactly when Elgar was returning, but when early in June he had not heard he telephoned to Plas Gwyn, and May Grafton, who was in charge of Carice and the house, explained that her uncle had returned at the end of May prostrated with headaches, and that Alice had, on doctor's advice, taken him to New Radnor for a rest.

On 5 July Atkins saw Elgar at the full-chorus rehearsal in Hereford, and heard that he had had a bad fall while at New Radnor. Elgar told Atkins that Mrs Worthington was coming to Hereford for the weekend, and that he was hard at work on *The Kingdom*.

Plas Gwyn, Hereford.
July 24 1906.

Dear Firapeel,

I was so very sorry to put you off the other day, but Sanford suddenly proposed himself & two others for dinner: the old dear fellow arrd. the evening *before* we expected him & I had to knock off work. Now I have finished except some scoring [*The Kingdom*].

I leave this on Thursday for a day or two's rest & then I shall hope to see you, & I want you to look the thing through. I would send on proofs if I had 'em but there are only old, uncorrected sheets which are worrying but I'll trouble you with it as soon as I can.

Yours ever
Reynart
ye
Foxe.

My father, however, started his own holiday a few days later. The whole family, including myself, had gone to St Laurence-on-Sea, near Ramsgate, where we were to spend our summer holidays for some years.

Hotel St. Cloud, St. Laurence-on-Sea, Ramsgate.
Aug. 12, 1906.

My dear Reynart,

Are you at home? I hope the work is now entirely off your hands. I want to see the new part muchly. We return this week (Thursday) and I want you to tell me whether you will be at home on the 20th if I came over.

Pray write of this. I hoped to have seen Sanford in town, on my way through, but I gather that fickle, elusive Paris has drawn him to herself. I shall try and see him when returning.

Sinclair reports a captive piano at Cox's [a piano shop in Cheltenham] and paints its charms in very gorgeous colours. (ALL THE SANCTACLAREAN GEESE—ARE THEY NOT SWANNES?)

Of course I'm frightfully jealous but bearing up. How does Lady Elgar with *her* scoring? Truly she is a valiant lady: who else would tackle the laying-on of such Leviathan scores? *Your* work seems light in comparison. There, if you like, is the power behind the throne!

Under our seal
Firapeel.

The piano at Cox's was a Steinway upright piano which Sanford had sent to Sinclair as a gift. Atkins' envy must have lasted for a very short time, since shortly afterwards Sanford gave him a very fine Steinway Grand. The words in capitals are an obvious reference to Sinclair's invariable optimism.

Plas Gwyn, Hereford.
Augt. 14: 1906

Firapeel:
 I wot well you are in merrie wise fallen on yr feste in Ram-hys-gate: albeit a fear, a parlous fear, holdes me, yr. true Friend, that you behave not altogether seemly in ye towne.
Perpend.
 I should have written ere this but moche penwork has befallen me & to-daye, being Carice's birthday, a jaunt, Gilpinwise *sans destrier*, was gotten up: Ye fayre town of Ludlow was our pointe,—& guided by a good fellowe—no churl he—yclept Charlton Palmer we raided ye churche, where yow pedalled, ye Castle, & both ripes of ye Teme: a goode daye & a restful. [Palmer had succeeded Atkins as the organist of Ludlow in 1897.]
 I am finishing scoring [*The Kingdom*] all right & expect to find proofs of the whole thing any day.
 Some of the *fullscore* is already here!
 I shall be home all the month so come when you can—with notice because I go out much.
 Yes, Sanford went to Paris & there *is* a piano at Cox's—destination unknown to me.
 Our love to you all, if you are all together.
 I finde ye annciente moode wearinge to ye penne, ye braine & to ye reader.
 But I will holde myselfe in olden wise that is now current.
 Subscribing myself yours, as *you demeane you*,
Reynart
ye Foxe.

Carice was 16 on 14 August, and according to my mother, rather thin and lanky at this time. She helped her father with odd jobs, and particularly with photography, in which Elgar was very interested. Shortly after they went to Plas Gwyn he had, with Grindrod's help, set up a dark-room in an upstairs bedroom. May Grafton had been introduced to the art some years earlier, and a number of her photographs appear in this book.

The above letter posted to Ramsgate arrived after Atkins had left, and was sent on to Worcester. In the meantime another letter had come from Elgar.

Plas Gwyn, Hereford.
Sunday [19 August 1906]

My dear Firapeel:
                    Come!
  I have some string parts. We will find you a bed and good gobbable
food.
  I must work in the a.m. till lunch so I can't meet you, but I'm ready for
legwise japing in the p.m.
                    Thine
                    Reynart.

  On 21 August Atkins went over in the afternoon and they walked
until tea. Then Elgar played over the new work. The soprano solo,
'The Sun goeth down', affected Atkins very deeply.
  After dinner they got down to the main purpose of the visit,
namely, the correcting of the proofs. Since Atkins' last visit Elgar,
finding a flow of visitors to Alice distracting when he was working
desperately to complete *The Kingdom*, had turned a bedroom next
to his dressing-room into an upstairs study. His main study on the
ground floor was adjacent to Alice's drawing-room, and by no
means sound-proof because of the French windows from both
rooms on to the veranda. Elgar gave over the upstairs study to
Atkins to check the vocal score, while he retired to his dressing-
room to deal with the string parts. They continued the next day
until Atkins had to leave to catch an afternoon train. There were
still a lot of proofs to be checked and Atkins returned to Hereford
after lunch on 24 August, and worked solidly until the early
evening, when Elgar took him for a long walk. Alice found them in
festive form on their return. They played over some of the sections
after dinner. The next day they worked again after breakfast and
finished the proof-checking in time for Atkins to return to
Worcester for evensong. Elgar, however, still had more orchestrating to complete.
  He was not at the massed rehearsal in Hereford on 30 August,
which included *The Apostles*, and thinking that he might be ill
again, Atkins called at Plas Gwyn to find him orchestrating
furiously. Jaeger had come down to discuss his 'Analysis' of *The
Kingdom*. He was unwell, and the Elgars had persuaded him to stay
on, which had slowed down the orchestration.
  The Elgars had some weeks earlier arranged a festival house-
party at Plas Gwyn. Elgar, however, was still frantically correcting

full-score and parts proofs. John Austin, 'Honest John', as the Elgars called him, was helping. Elgar was so busy that he was only able to conduct the Monday rehearsal and the performance at the Wednesday evening concert of his *Introduction and Allegro*, and even remained at home proof-correcting while Sinclair was conducting *Gerontius* and *The Apostles*.

September 19 and 20 were the full-chorus rehearsal dates for the Birmingham Festival performances of *The Apostles* and *The Kingdom*. Atkins was only able to go to the first, *The Kingdom*. It was the first time that he heard *The Kingdom* sung by a chorus. Wilson had trained them well, and though there was a certain amount of polishing still to be done, Atkins was most impressed. After the rehearsal Elgar told him that he was still under great pressure, as a number of proofs he had expected had not arrived, though they should be awaiting his return to Hereford. John Austin would be coming over on the Saturday. Atkins agreed to join them, and on 23 September the three of them worked all day on the proofs. They worked again after supper. The first orchestral rehearsal of *The Kingdom* was to be in Manchester on 25 September, and hence the frantic rush to complete the parts.

On 26 September the Elgars were going to Aberdeen where Elgar would receive an honorary LL D degree from the University. They had been invited to stay with the Professor of History, Charles Sanford Terry, who was soon to become a close friend of the Elgars and also of Atkins.

The combined chorus and orchestra rehearsals were in Birmingham on 28 and 29 September. Atkins went over on the 29th and found Mrs Worthington and Charlton Palmer with Alice, Carice and May. The rehearsal of *The Kingdom* was thrilling. The orchestral colour gave a new perspective to everything. Well though he now knew Elgar's orchestral genius Atkins was still amazed at the heightening of the tension and the depth of feeling which it added to the work.

The performance of *The Apostles* was on 3 October, and was very fine, but it was *The Kingdom* the next day which made the festival for Atkins. The great audience was deeply moved. There was a long silence before the hall re-echoed to the prolonged applause. Elgar was repeatedly recalled.

Elgar had presented Atkins with a bound inscribed vocal score immediately before the performance, and on the back of the title

My dear Prospect:

Oct. 3:13 86

Some themes you will my
friends: in my music they joes

with you: but it feels artistic
striving, educated (!) and
courteous only to a limited
degree: you are* "more than
all that" my dear friend.

Edward Elgar.

Birmingham.

LONDON:
NOVELLO AND COMPANY, LIMITED,
PRINTERS.

*more than all 'these' I should have
said like the lovers' melancholy.

page under the date, he had inscribed it as reproduced on the previous page. (The theme appears one bar after 157, where it is a linking passage in 'The Sun goeth down.')

After the performance the Elgars gave tea to their friends, and among the many guests Atkins spoke to were the Speyers, Frank Schuster, Mrs Worthington, now Julia to her friends, Sinclair, Wilson, Percy Pitt, Kalisch, S. Loeb and the Ernest Newmans. All were delighted with the first performance.

Elgar was away in London for a few days in the middle of October, and Atkins did not go over to Plas Gwyn until 24 October. Elgar was still very pleased about the Birmingham performance and its reception, but he was clearly worn out. His main interest appeared to be that Novello's were producing a German edition of *The Kingdom*. This had been one of the reasons for his London visit. He spoke about some chemical experiments he was making, and he was looking forward to the concert in Malvern on 3 November, at which his old friends from Hanley were to sing his part-songs.

On 3 November Atkins attended the concert in the Assembly Room, at which the Hanley Cauldron Chorus sang, among other part-songs, Elgar's 'My Love dwelt in a Northern Land', 'Evening Scene', 'Weary Wind of the West', and 'Feasting I Watch'. Atkins greatly enjoyed their singing. The vigour and almost 'roughness' of the singers gave an added strength to their forthright performance. Elgar had always had a 'soft spot' for the North Staffordshire singers, many of whom were potters, and was clearly delighted to have them in Malvern with him.

Atkins went over to Hereford on 10 November, and found Elgar very depressed. His Birmingham lecture had not gone well. It had been in a dark room, and his eyes were again giving him trouble. He was going to London the next week to conduct *In the South*, but was not looking forward to it. He also had another Birmingham lecture to give. After that he felt that they must get away as soon as they could to a warm place to rest, perhaps to Italy.

On 27 November, Atkins found Elgar, who had returned from London to Hereford that day, in a very poor state. His eyes were still troubling him and clearly he would not be well enough to come to Worcester the next day. This was a great disappointment to Atkins, since he was conducting his *Hymn of Faith* at the WFCS concert. Elgar told him that Birmingham University had given him sick leave and that he had already booked a passage to Naples on 28 December. The Elgars planned to stay in Italy for some weeks, in the South and then in Rome.

Atkins telephoned on 7 December, but learnt that Elgar's eyes were no better, and that he had gone to rest at Llandrindod Wells.

On 22 December Elgar wrote asking Atkins to go over.

Plas Gwyn, Hereford.
Dec. 22. 1906

My dear Firapeel:
Times is awry: & thus, my eyes are not well & get no better—not much better at any rate. I have been in evil case & fit for no good works.

I leave here (D.V.) via Southampton for ye East [ie Italy] on Saturday next. I know that owing to the ripeness of the year that Xtians wax gross in their food & religion, of whilk twain the first concerns you not, whilst the second may hold you fast to tickle silver into collection plates with warily selected tunes—such is the Xtian way.

But if you can, do come over one day & we can
walk
talk &
Balk the devil and all.

I am fairly well in my own self but the eyes. I cannot spring upon my quarry with the old certainty—& one who has pulled down harts of grease despises field mice, so I wait for amended vision.
Best wishes to you all,
Yours ever
Reynart
(ye Foxe)

Atkins wrote Elgar a long letter explaining the Christmas week's choral activities, but offering to go over on Boxing Day.

Plas Gwyn, Hereford.
Dec 25, 1906

My dear Firapeel:
I loved having your letter but alas! I fear I shall be gone to-morrow. I find it must be an early flit to get baggage on board. If I don't leave tomorrow by the corridor it must be early on Thursday. Our plans have been upset, revised, coddled, altered, married, rebuilt, rejuvenated, & a lot more. Now it is settled that Alice & I go on the *Orontes* on Friday. Love to you
Yours ever,
Edwd.
I propose to send a telegram if I pass through the city of W.

On 27 December Atkins saw them at Worcester Shrub Hill station for a brief farewell. Elgar, now that he was on the way to the warm South, was in much better form, but his eyes were still giving him trouble.

1907

The year 1907 was one of travelling for Elgar. He and Alice arrived in Naples on 6 January. They returned home to Hereford on 26 February. Atkins went over on 28 February. 'The Duchess' and Miss Thomas came to tea, and Elgar told them all about their Italian holiday. Naples had been disappointing, apart from Pompeii, but Capri was beautiful and they had greatly enjoyed their month there. Rome had been a great experience for them both. Elgar was in excellent form and looking forward to his American tour, he would be leaving on 2 March. Alice was not going with him.

The tour started with rehearsals and performances in New York of *The Apostles* and of *The Kingdom*, both concerts being conducted by Elgar. Sanford and Julia Worthington had met Elgar in New York and attended both performances, which had gone well. From New York Elgar went to Chicago, Cincinnati and Pittsburgh, at all of which he conducted various of his works. In Pittsburgh the performance of his *Enigma Variations* was followed by another degree ceremony, in which he was made an honorary LL D of the University of Pennsylvania. On 20 April he sailed for home from New York.

At the beginning of March the Worcester Festival Committee invited Atkins to write a new work for the 1908 festival. Atkins wrote at once to Elgar in America to give him the news. Elgar did not, however, receive this letter until late in March. He replied from 'The Wyoming', where he was staying with Julia Worthington at her New York home.

The Wyoming, 55th Street and Seventh Avenue, (New York)
Ap.2 1907

My dear Firapeel:
Your *most* welcome, welcome letter came here & I am just starting to Chicago so I send this card. Delighted to hear all your news but, I say, *you*

must try a secular work this time: never mind the Cathedral but go for the concert-room. I hope to have time for a letter in Chicago. The Italian post was awful. I had heaps of letters addressed only *Capri* which after all is no bigger than a decent ship! Love

Reynart.

Elgar arrived back in Hereford on 27 April, and then went on to the Morecambe Competitive Festival where he was adjudicating. He returned to Hereford again on 6 May.

Plas Gwyn, Hereford.
May 7: 1907.

My dear Firapeel:
I'm only just back & tired.
I fear there's some error: I only have met Lawson once & jawed. Ask your man, if it be possible to do so, to suggest that the Hon. Harry L.[awson] asks me. I may be in town very soon.
Oh! bless thee, I have reams to tell thee: moving incidents by flood & field. But they must wait until we meet.
I hope all prospers with you & the family: 'he' [the present author] must be growing apace. I must see him soon.
But when will ye come?
I think I *may* have to go to town tomorrow but I'll p.c.ˣ you.

Yours ever
Reynart

ˣa verb

Plas Gwyn, Hereford.
May 10: 1907

My dear Firapeel:
I wrote off very hurriedly (horridly) in answer to your note about the scrivener for the D.T. [*Daily Telegraph*] & had no time to say a word of ourselves. I am back & very well, except mine eyne which give out after an hour or two's work. I find millions of things to do & a tangled heap of letters to weary through.
I was going to suggest your coming over, but I must go away for a few days on Monday. After Whit-tide will ye no come? & if the weather holds fair couldn't we go out & marvel at churches & eat in the open air?
Think on this & hold me yours ever

Reynart
who hath a 'death-dealing tube' (Pope), otherwise an air rifle which is sport to us & death to nothing but bottles—ye same spent. Now you must come & drink to make targets.

When Atkins went to Plas Gwyn on 28 May, Elgar was relaxing after a bicycle ride. He said that Julia Worthington had only just left them after a short stay. Julia, with the Elgars' love of special names for their friends, had now become 'Pippa'. Elgar had recently been reading Longfellow and Browning, including 'Pippa Passes', and his new name for Julia was, according to my father, one of Elgar's finest inspirations, as it exactly fitted Julia's charm, kindness and ability to bring out the best in all her friends, and her light-hearted and even mischievous influence upon them.

Elgar very soon suggested a shooting match. He was now an expert with his air-rifle, and though Atkins could equal, if not surpass him, in the 'making of targets', he could not compete when it came to markmanship. Elgar then asked how he was getting on with finding a suitable text for his composition for the 1908 Worcester Festival. Atkins, who was exceptionally busy at the time, had not really begun thinking about it, and Elgar promised to keep his eyes open for a possible suitable text.

On 5 June Elgar stopped at Worcester on his way from Birmingham to Hereford. He went into the cathedral, as he very often did, and then stayed for tea. While in Birmingham he had heard of a possible libretto by Herbert Trench, and as he thought that he had a copy in Hereford he promised to hunt for it and send it to Atkins on his return from London, where he was going within the next few days. He was considering doing the journey in stages, by bicycle, if the weather continued fine.

He had been turning over in his mind ideas for a fourth *Pomp and Circumstance March*, which he said he would dedicate to Sinclair, and that he was now ready to start work on it. He also mentioned that for some time, 'off and on', he had been working on a Children's Overture, using old material dating back to the time when he had been 12 and had composed some music for a play which he and his brothers and sisters had written for their parents. Some of these old sketches had already been published as *Dream Children*, Op 43, which had received its first performance at Queen's Hall in September 1902. (Other material subsequently became the *Wand of Youth Suite*, Op 1A.)

Elgar went to Cambridge on 11 June to hear a performance of *The Kingdom* in King's College Chapel. Talking to Atkins later about this led to a discussion on the possibility of performing Stanford's *Stabat Mater* at the 1908 Worcester Festival. This was a new work which was to be produced at the Leeds Festival in October. They both agreed that it should be included, but felt that it might not be good 'box-office', and that it would take up valuable rehearsal time. The proposal would require considerable preparing of the ground if it was to be accepted by the committee.

The Athenaeum.
June 14: 1907

My dear Firapeel:

I had a look at 'The Festival' by Trench, but I did not post the volume as it's not mine I find.

I don't know if the thing wd be possible. It may be too leprously Eastern (the plague!). Haroun Alreschid-ish. You could perhaps easily see the volume in the Library in Worcester. If not I'll exhibit it to you.

I have been thinking over the Stanford work & feel with you that it ought to be done, [*Stabat Mater*] & I will do all I can to help it through & 'popularise', as it were, the idea.

In my ivy bush,
Yours ever

Events were conspiring to interrupt Atkins' regular visits to Plas Gwyn. Elgar was away a great deal at this time and Atkins' time was becoming very fully occupied.

They met in Gloucester on 4 July at the full-chorus rehearsal, where Elgar was conducting both *The Apostles* and *The Kingdom*. The rehearsal went well and Elgar seemed very pleased. He told Atkins that on 6 July he was going to Birmingham to have an honorary MA conferred upon him, and that on this occasion he was really looking forward to going to the University. No professorial lecture this time. He also said that the *Wand of Youth* was progressing well, that much was now ready to be played over, and he hoped to start work on sketches for a symphony and a violin concerto.

Alas! it proved impossible for Atkins to get over to Plas Gwyn, and hence the next letter.

Plas Gwyn, Hereford.
Saturday [10 August 1907]

My dear Firapeel:
  Thanx for your pixtures which make me long for a change. Why not when in Aberdeen call on Professor Sanford Terry (Cults), a good one.
  There is nothing doing save my little children's jape [*Wand of Youth Suite*] which you would not come to see & so must go unbenisoned to their inky doom (poetry).
  Good luck to your tour & your four-speed gear.

Much love,
Yours ever
Reynart

who hath taken (by wiles) four fysshes—& with a tender heart returned 'em all to the water: the poor beggars seemed so sad &, perpend, eke *small*.

  I do not know what the pictures were, but I suspect that they were travel brochures for Milan, Florence and Venice, since my father had contemplated, but rejected, a bicycling tour in Northern Italy with his new four-speed geared bicycle. Instead he had decided to tour the East Coast of Scotland. Elgar had stayed with Sanford Terry when Aberdeen University had conferred the LL D on him the previous year, and Atkins had been writing to Terry about Bach. (Terry was an acknowledged expert on Bach and his times.) Atkins stayed with him, and it started a series of reciprocal visits in which in later years I also was to participate. The note of regret in Elgar's letter was because the *Wand of Youth Suite* was the first large work for nearly 10 years in which Atkins had not been with him at various stages of its composition.
  The first performance of *Pomp and Circumstance March* No 4 was at the Queen's Hall on the evening of 4 September. It was conducted by Henry Wood, and Atkins and Sinclair, to whom it was dedicated, joined the Elgars' party, which included Pippa and Frank Schuster.
  At the Gloucester Festival Elgar conducted *The Apostles* on the Tuesday evening and *The Kingdom* on the Wednesday morning, and it was a wonderful occasion for all concerned. It was the first time that the two works had been performed one after the other, as Elgar wished them to be, and my father told me that the effect, greatly enhanced by the performances being in the cathedral, was completely overwhelming. The soloists for *The Apostles* were Madame Emily Squire, Marie Brema, Gervase Elwes, Dalton

Baker, Ffrangcon-Davies and Plunket Greene, and for *The Kingdom* Agnes Nicholls, Ada Crossley, John Coates and Ffrangcon-Davies.

The Elgars had invited Thomas Whitney Surette, the American music educationist, and his wife to stay with them in Hereford after the festival. The Surettes had been regular festival visitors since 1899, and they were now old friends of both Elgar and Atkins. The main reason for the present visit was to give Elgar an opportunity to discuss with Surette the lectures which he had invited him to give in Birmingham University in October as part of the professorial music course. He had decided earlier not to give the lectures himself because of his persistent eye trouble.

Elgar was also conducting *The Kingdom* at the Cardiff Triennial Musical Festival on 26 September. Atkins went to the performance but had to leave immediately after it without seeing Elgar. He told me later that his hurried visit had, however, been well worthwhile, for it had been a fine performance. What my father most remembered was the beautiful singing of the 280-strong chorus.

Plas Gwyn, Hereford.
Sep 29. 1907

My dear Firapeel:
   This is a sick house & all arrangements for last week were knocked on the Kopf. I was at the Castle for two days [St Fagan's] & fled home. We spoke of you a good deal & your work [*Hymn of Faith*] was recommended for performance by the President [the Earl of Plymouth] so you must have friends on the Committee who don't see eye to eye &c
   I am so sorry.
   Here is the rehearsal ticket for Leeds. Shall you go? I am glad to say that the patients [Alice had been ill and Carice had been badly stung] are mending, although Carice's sting has been a dreary enough business.
                    In spirit, Firapeel,
                         thine;
                    In body, Firapeel
                         calomel's
                    To the world
                         Reynart.

Atkins' *Hymn of Faith* had been considered for inclusion in the Cardiff Festival programme, but had been finally turned down by the committee in favour of a new work by a Welsh composer. It proved impossible for him to go to Leeds.

Plas Gwyn, Hereford.
Oct 6. 1907

My dear Firapeel:
I am truly sorry you will not be at Leeds—I shall miss you—this is complimentary, *verb. sap.*

Parry's work [*A Vision of Life*, first performed at Cardiff the previous month] is really fine & the poem A.1. Will it not do for Worcester? I don't know if the jarring creeds episode wd be grateful to a Dean & Chapter. Oh! ye priests!

I do want to see you.
Look here.

I am leaving with the lark tomorrow [for Leeds Festival where Elgar was conducting *The Kingdom*] & shall not be home until Wednesday or so in the following week. This house is 'let' for the winter & we go to Rome in the first week in Nov.r until April: so you must come after the 15th (say) or thereabouts.

Yours ever
Reynart.

Are you writing anything? Do go on.

Atkins had not so far found time even to decide the form his proposed composition was to take, let alone get down to writing it. On 17 October he telephoned Elgar, proposing to go over the next day and to bring with him a mutual old friend, Dr Ehrke, a fine amateur violinist who had played in Elgar's WPS and now played in and was a member of the committee of the Worcestershire Orchestral Society. This was not possible, however, because Elgar was taking the chair that day at Surette's last lecture at Birmingham University.

Plas Gwyn, Hereford.
Oct 20 1907

My dear Firapeel:
I was so sorry (& am now) that I had to be away.

This is my last week at home & I am more than busy. I *hope* I may see you but don't bring Ehrke just now, much as I would like to see him, but we are packing & storing things & are not really visible.

I shall be in W. soon & will call & will let you know.

In greatest haste
Yours ever
Reynart.

Atkins went to Hereford to wish them a wonderful 6 months in Italy. How different from 1906—this time they were all keenly looking forward to their stay in Italy, for Carice and May Grafton were going with them, and Elgar's creative inspiration was at a high level. He was taking his sketch books with him containing sections of a violin concerto and a symphony, and he had ideas for several part-songs. He clearly expected to spend much of his time composing. On 17 November Elgar wrote the following card from Rome:

Hope you are all well.
We are quite settled here now.
Don't forget Sgambati's Requiem.
      Love E.E.

Before Elgar left England he had drawn Atkins' attention to Giovanni Sgambati's *Messa da Requiem*, which had been composed in 1896. It was in use for all Italian royal funerals and had recently received two highly acclaimed performances in Germany. He suggested that it might be worth considering it for a WFCS concert, or possibly for the 1908 Worcester Festival. He expected to meet Sgambati in Rome and, if Atkins was interested, he felt sure that he could arrange for the orchestral parts to be available. Obtaining loan parts for Italian works was at that time difficult and expensive.

On 27 November Atkins conducted at the WFCS concert Grieg's *Recognition of Land* (*Landerkennung*), with William Higley as the soloist. Although now seldom heard, this work, written for baritone solo, male chorus and orchestra, is interesting as it deals with a different part of the story of Olaf Trygvason from that described in Elgar's *King Olaf*.

Atkins was going to the Queen's Hall on 4 December for the first performance of Elgar's *Wand of Youth Suite* No 1, Op 1A, which was being given by the Queen's Hall Orchestra conducted by Henry Wood, and Elgar arranged with Novello's to send him a full score. He was very much looking forward to this performance, the more so because although he had heard Elgar play over in 1902 some of the re-written sketches of the original music, he had not heard any of it in the final version.

The year ended with the usual Cathedral Christmas music. For Atkins and Elgar's other close friends, however, his absence so far away in Rome gave a tinge of sadness to their celebrations.

PART 4
1908–1911

1908

The year opened for Atkins with a visit to Hereford to hear the first performance of Elgar's *A Christmas Greeting*, to words by Alice and dedicated to 'Dr G. R. Sinclair and the Choristers of Hereford Cathedral'. This was given at the choristers' concert in the Town Hall on 1 January. Elgar had begun writing the work in Hereford and completed it in Rome.

The first news from him is contained in the following letter and refers to May Grafton's return to England. She had been part of the Elgar family since they went to Plas Gwyn and had been with them in Italy looking after Carice.

38, Via Gregoriana P.3, Roma.
Jan 17: 1908.

My dear Firapeel:
We have been deeply saddened by the death of my dear old comrade, May's father. She has left us for home & our little party is in sorrow.

Let me have news of you sometime soon. I hope all goes well. Here we have frosts but glorious sun all day—treacherous but seeming fair.

I have really nothing to tell you. I write a little & have furnished (good word) four part-songs, one whereof is in two keys at once! that is to say, the S.A. & right hand PF bear the signature of ♭♭♭ while simultaneously the T.B. & left hand PF are in ♯ . It will sound very remote & will please village choirs.

I am anxious as to the fate of Sgambati's Requiem, & hope it will be in.

I never go anywhere for music or see scarcely anyone except necessary ambassadorial visits, &c. I am sad.

Cheer me
I droop
Yours ever
Reynart.

The four part-songs referred to were Op 53: *There is sweet music*, dedicated to Canon Gorton (this is the one with the S & A and T & B in different keys); *Deep in my Soul*, dedicated to Julia H. Worthington; *O Wild West Wind*, dedicated to W. G. McNaught; and *Owls*, dedicated to Pietro d'Alba, Carice's white rabbit, Peter.

Early in February Atkins wrote to Elgar sending a 'first draft' of the programme for the Worcester Festival, which contained both *The Apostles* and *The Kingdom*, and explained that, with Stanford's *Stabat Mater* now approved by the festival committee he could not include Sgambati's Requiem. He had said that the committee was interested in Schubert's *Lazarus*, but only if it would be the first performance in England. He referred to a difficulty regarding the engagement of certain of the soloists, and he also told Elgar that he had included the *Wand of Youth Suite* (Op 1A) in the Worcestershire Orchestral Society's fourth concert, to be given on 2 May, and he hoped that, if he was back in England, Elgar would conduct it. Finally, he gave a very broad hint that the committee would greatly appreciate a new work from Elgar.

38, Via Gregoriana P.3, Roma.
Feb 24. 1908

My dear Firapeel:

I begin this now but I have only two minutes & hope to return 'a casa' shortly.

First: as to Lazarus being a 1st performance—I *think* I heard it at the Crystal Palace long ago, (not at a Saturday concert but on some Wednesday). I can (or *might*) tell from old programmes at the Palazzo Bianco (Herefordo). The rest of the programme seems good—yet it wants *something*—I can't tell what at the moment. I'm sorry I'm so far away & in consequence of no use. I should have written long ago (I sent a card) [it does not appear to have been received] had there been the remotest possibility of sending a word of interesting sense.

The orchestra here is the worst I ever heard & I have given up the concert arranged for me. The new huge concert hall is dreadfully bad acoustically & a death trap—only one narrow exit!

I hope the difficulties about soloists will be overcome. I don't understand the position quite but it must be *give* and take by all—& not all *take* on the other side. Surely this will be seen by the other side?

Are you hearing Sennis & Walter Hyde: I hear great things of the latter since the English Ring?

It has upset me very much seeing that advt. of poor dear Albani for pupils! distressing—a real good woman: if she had only been such as the others, Melba & the rest of the society—w——s, God would have blessed her infinitely! But she was good! How dreadful.

Now as to May 2nd. I fear we cannot get back in time but we shall hear of ships &c in a week or two & I will write. I greatly regret Sgambati's work.

A new work is what you want really, but I feel the position. As to myself I feel perhaps a ten minutes jape might come in for the concert, but do not depend upon me. You know I desired to give up all active interest in music, & never did I desire it more than now. 'I'm fair sick' of the art.

Love

Yours

Reynart.

S.S. Sanford   Edward Elgar

Alice and Edward Elgar   Alice, Elgar and Sanford

These photographs were taken on the SS *Kaiser Wilhelm der Gross* en route from New York to England, 11–17 July, 1905. On 28 June Yale University had conferred on Elgar the degree of Doctor of Music (*Photographs by courtesy of Henry Sanford, grandson of S.S. Sanford*)

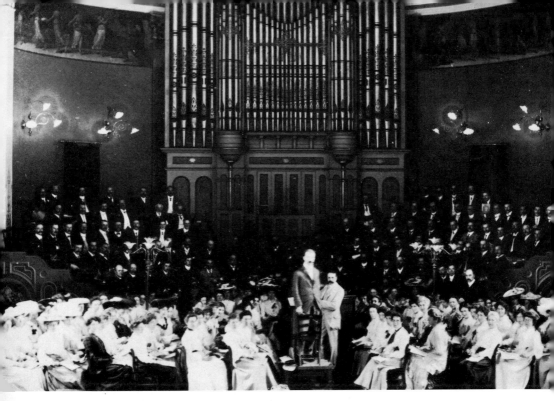

Three Choirs Festival at Worcester, 1905: first Combined Rehearsal in the Public Hall, 20 July. Atkins is on the rostrum with Elgar to the right. Atkins was conducting the *Dream of Gerontius* at this Festival and also his own *Hymn of Faith*, composed specially for the festival to a libretto written for him by Elgar. Photograph by W.W. Harris

Elgar photographed by May Grafton, in 1906: writing *The Kingdom*; at the piano with sketches of *The Kingdom*, Plas Gwyn, Hereford

There had been a further meeting of the festival committee since Atkins' letter, and on receipt of Elgar's letter he wrote again telling him that the committee had reconsidered their ideas of the Elgar works and did not want to leave out *Gerontius*. They did not feel, however, that all three choral works could be performed, and therefore they had decided to replace *The Apostles* in the draft programme with *Gerontius*. They had also abandoned the idea of Schubert's *Lazarus*, but were including Walford Davies' *Everyman*. Atkins told Elgar that he had not given up the idea of writing a work for the festival, but had still not found a suitable subject. He also enclosed a list of questions regarding Elgar's preferences for singers, and ended his letter with a direct request for a new orchestral work.

Rome Mar 3: 1908

My dear Reynart [*sic*]

I am truly glad you are going to produce something. I noticed the omission & should have mentioned it but, with more than Reynardian judgement I held my peace for fear there shd have been any arrangement on your part of which I did not know. Now I am glad & will think of a subject.

I cannot object to 'Gerontius' in place of 'Apostles' if it is really wished: of course with the Vigornian omissions I cannot conduct it—but you will [Atkins did]. Now I answer your numbered questions:

1) *I* don't want Hyde: [for *The Apostles*] I only feel that the interest in *singers* at these festivals must be kept up—I detest the Violin Concerto business in the Cathedral—& I thought perhaps you cd enliven your tenor department.

2) Failing Kirkby Lunn how about [Julia] Culp. Find out *how* she does at Q.'s Hall. I cannot think of anyone else in the contralto dept. I can't think that you wd be wrong in engaging J. Culp. I have heard so much of her & then there's Sennis Tenor. Do you want him?

3) Nicholls *only* for Kingdom—I cannot think of anyone that is to say. Perceval Allen did fairly well, but—try for Nicholls.

4) Elwes does not like to tackle the 'Kingdom', & *I* ought to ask for Coates—who has done so well—for 'Gerontius' & of course wd do so now, but I must not embarrass you. You must settle it, only I know Elwes will not or would not accept engagements for the 'Kingdom' from conscientious scruples (bless him) that he was not robust enough for it.

5) You must also settle about Higley. Of course if he's again all right we must have him. Failing him I think [Charles W.] Clark. I cannot tell about the orchl: work yet. It means the *whole* of the summer weather sacrificed, much expense at rehearsals &c & *never a penny* piece in return. It requires thought.

Set to work on your new thing at once. Don't wait for words.
                              Yours ever
                              Reynart.

    Some months earlier Elgar had suggested to Atkins that for the Worcester Festival he should try and add new blood to the well-known artists usually engaged for the Three Choirs Festivals, and Atkins had in his letter mentioned that he was thinking of engaging Walter Hyde and was looking out for other additional artists. At that time *The Apostles*, with its six soloists, was still in the draft programme. The Beethoven Violin Concerto was also included, and remained in the final programme, in spite of Elgar's obvious feeling at this time that a solo violinist would introduce a secular atmosphere. Walter Hyde was also engaged, but not for the Elgar works.

38 Via Gregoriana P.3, Roma.
March 9: 1908

My dear Firapeel:
    I have thought much 'for' your libretto:
    Here's an idea (probably impracticable), Solo Sop: or Contralto & Chorus. Look at Tennyson's 'Dream of Fair Women' (You won't *call* it that) anyhow.
    Begin to get an atmosphere, say—(but you must select the prologue yourself) line 2 stanza 4—'I saw, &c' & select further—certainly include 13 'All those sharp fancies Into the gulf of sleep'. Cut now to 'Slowly my sense undazzles' (omitting 31 stanzas). Go on with all this to the end of the section, scene, or whatever it is, ending either 'with the morning star', or 'the old year is dead'. You wd of course submit the 'words' to your Cathedral authorities. I think the idea *fine* & you could do it well.
    If however, you do not like it, or it is not approved by the Church, try something from Browning's 'Saul'.
    To return to Tennyson, you cd of course include any of the 'scenery'—
                    'The dim red morn' &c
                 & 'There was no motion,' &c
as the 'scenery' does not change with each vision. But you must end with the end of Jephtha's daughter. The end of the *poem* is not practical for your purpose.
                              Wade in
                              Love
                              Reynart.

Atkins replied thanking Elgar for his suggestions which he was following up. He would report progress. He also sent a formal invitation from the festival committee requesting Elgar to write a new work, preferable choral, for the festival, and followed this up with a telegram. An answering telegram from Elgar was amplified in the following letter of the same date.

Rome Ap 22: 1908

My dear Firapeel:
    We are just packing up & I am rather in a hurried mood. I have just recd your wire & have sent a reply. I am sorry about the new work but it is impossible, & has been impossible in this noisy place to settle down to any work of any length beyond the part-songs which you will soon see. I cannot afford a studio!
    I am truly sorry about your vocalist worries & cannot understand how it is possible for anyone to be so troublesome as the other conductor—I suppose you mean that—has been. I am glad to hear of the Koenen—but I know her not, some of the others you have named I may have heard but I remember nothing of them, P[hyllis] Lett, e.g. she may be an angel for all I know.
    I am sorry about the new work. Things do not pay, alas! I do not mind this for *myself* & wd gladly throw over the whole ghastly phase of respectability to be able to write my big things. But 'Gerontius' & the Apostles & the Variations, &c *nothing* in fact that is big pays for the paper it is written on. & I have MANY people to KEEP & FEED now. So I must write rot & drop all ambition. It is sickening, but it is so. God wills it & be damned to it.
                                        Yours ever
                                        E.E.

Atkins replied that he would report the position at the next festival committee meeting, and he explained that Tilly Koenen was a young Dutch contralto with a really marvellous voice whom he had heard recently. He was sure that when Elgar had heard her he would approve of her as the Angel in *Gerontius*.

Rome Ap 26 1908

My dear Firapeel:
    I was so glad to see your letter &c. I hope all went off well at your meeting & that your disagreeables are over.
    I fear I cannot *write* anything new. I make a suggestion with much fear & trembling & you must please decide whichever way you think . . I have

the *second Suite* UNHEARD from the '*Wand of Youth*'. If you think it wd be any sort of popular attraction I would conduct it at the Concert. I would write a few notes for the programme book. The Suite no.2 is about the same length as No.1. I fear it may be a little too *facile* for a Festival concert but it has a local interest, although our childish theatre is pulled down.

I hope you are going at your new work & that all goes well. I have tried for a thousand subjects for you but can strike none.

In greatest haste
Yours ever
Reynart.

Atkins was delighted with Elgar's suggestion that he should conduct the as yet unheard *Wand of Youth Suite* No 2, but with regard to his own composition he had still found no words to suit him, and had accordingly decided to drop the idea altogether, and told Elgar of his decision in the letter in which he sent him his final list of soloists for the festival.

Rome May 2::1908

My dear Firapeel

You *have* done nobly. I congratulate you on the list. It really looks fine & I am delighted. Glad you approve of the 2nd Suite which is nearly printed now.

As to your own work, don't worry: do the Hymn of Faith again [this was done] or a concert thing. Sorry I am no use for words: everything packed & we sail soon—arrive in London about May 22nd, I think. Good luck to you & congratulations.

Yours ever
Reynart.

The Elgars docked in Tilbury on 16 May, staying in London for a few days from where Elgar sent the following letter.

Langham Hotel, London.
May 23 1908

My dear Firapeel,

Here we are at last, We have really been here a week but have found so much to do patching teeth, clothes & generally setting up ourselves—I am anxious—*very*—to see you—the family go down on Monday & I follow soon. I'll let you know when: in the meantime I hope all goes well with you & yours. I have heard no news for weeks.

Ever yours
Reynart.

The orchestra at C. Garden under Richter plays more *wonderfully* than anything I have ever heard.

Elgar did not return to Hereford until the end of the month, and it was not until 12 June that Atkins went over to Plas Gwyn. He was staying the night and had suggested taking his bicycle with him, as he often had done, but Elgar told him that it was not worth while since 'biking' was no longer much fun these days owing to the motor cars which had increased greatly since he had been away. Walking by the river was better. He was in good form, and had his sketches for the symphony all over the table. Sinclair joined them and Elgar played all the part-songs and songs that he had recently written, including *In Memoriam—In Memory of a Seer*, which he had written only a few days earlier. This song was never published.

They planned to meet again the following week and for Elgar to come over to Worcester for a chorus rehearsal, which he was not able to do, however, since he was indisposed.

Plas Gwyn, Hereford
Thursday [25 June 1908]

My dear Firapeel:
I am so deadly sorry—I have been sick & ailing in the poitrine & *lower*: better now, but the doctor thinks I must potter about here a little.
All thanks for your letter. I am so glad 'Tillyvally lady' [Sir Toby, *Twelfth Night*, Act II, Scene 3] is so good [Tilly Koenen, whom Atkins had now been rehearsing with piano]. Thanks to you for your fraternal letter: shall see you tomorrow. *We* put out a feeler to G.R.S. *re* your coming here, but I think he wants you, so you must come here when you will.
The Symphony grows—a squalling child with teeth & hair, look you.
                        Yours ever
                        Reynart.

Atkins went over to Hereford on 26 June, stayed with Sinclair, attended a Hereford Chorus rehearsal that evening, at which Elgar did not appear, and the next afternoon went up to Plas Gwyn, where he found Elgar in bed with severe earache. They talked about Koenen, and Elgar told him that the symphony was now progressing fast.

On 10 July Atkins went to Hereford to conduct at a chorus rehearsal. He arrived at Plas Gwyn early in the afternoon. Elgar was working on the symphony, but stopped and took Atkins for a brisk walk, after which they played through all that he had written. They continued playing after the rehearsal.

Hereford. July 15: 1908

My dear Firapeel:
   You left your Baton here & it is Mine! It suits me, I love it, it hath a
dignified look, it is light; it can be waved fearsomely; it can float
gossamerrily on air; it is a divine thing! It is, as I said before—Mine, &
more pleasurably mine by reason of its once being yours. *Was it yours?*
Theft is not suggested—but—was it not preordained in the terrestrial
paradise that a tree should bloom in local meads & afford me a stick. I
think so: anyhow it's Mine.
   What severe assishness is afoot over free tickets—*who* is doing it, &
why, & where? I can ill afford to spend a day, or rather morning, over this
but I will try to come. The train arrives at 11.10, so play your fist till I
arrive. If I *cannot* come I will let you know. I see the Meeting [festival
committee] is at the Guildhall at 11.15 so I shd not be very late.
Yours ever
Reynart.
N.B. The stick is really Mine.

The following letter crossed posts with Elgar's.

8, College Yard, Worcester.
July 15 1908.

Dear Lady Elgar,
   Could you at a favourable moment get the dear Symphonist to let me
have his notes and musical illustrations to the Suite No. 2. I am anxious
for the sake of the printers to get the musical examples engraved.
   I very greatly enjoyed my visit last week and the Symphony is superb. I
am overjoyed that he could be writing it and under such conditions as to
inspiration.
   My verdict is that (being a symphony) it is absolute music (copyright).
With kindest regards,
Yours sincerely,
Ivor Atkins.

Elgar's programme notes for the *Wand of Youth Suite* No 2 are
reproduced opposite.
   On 16 July Elgar attended the festival committee in the
morning, and spoke out forcibly on the proposal to do away with
'free' tickets, especially for artists, composers, etc, when they were
not engaged for a particular performance. 'Free passes' issued
individually and signed had been, and still are, in use for soloists,
etc. They permit the holder to use any unoccupied seat.

Suite No. 2, "The Wand of Youth" (Op. 16).

EDWARD ELGAR.

(Music to a Child's Play).

  I. March.
 II. The Little Bells (Scherzino).
III. Moths and Butterflies.
 IV. Fountain Dance.
  V. The Tame Bear.
 VI. The Wild Bears.

These pieces are a second and final portion of the music intended to accompany an unacted play devised long ago. The "drama" was commenced in 1869, and the music underwent rearrangement and received additions for several years.

The circumstances, which gave rise to the little allegory set forth in the play, passed away, and with it the play also disappeared.

But the music remained; some numbers were completed (*e.g.*, No. 3 of the present suite), while others existed only in sketches. During the last year the orchestration has been revised and some of the movements re-written, but the main features remain as in the original.

During an enforced rest from larger and more complicated work it has been an amusement to reconstruct and rehabilitate these pieces which now obtain their first performance not far from the place of their inception.

(ξ۹)

Atkins had included the Bach Toccata in F arranged by Esser in the festival opening service, but was dissatisfied with its ending. He had, accordingly, persuaded Elgar to re-orchestrate the final section of the work.

Hereford July 19: 1908

My dear Firapeel:
Here is weather & joy attending. Also I send the climax of the Bach which will sound fine. I fear it will snuff out the earlier part somewhat, but anyhow it will be climactick & *final*. Do play it: it fires me to 'do' the E minor one: I *will* in time.
I am tired out with piety & a subsequent bicycle ride.
Ever thine
Reynart.

179

8, College Yard.
July 20, 1908.

My dear Reynart,
   The Bach additions look grand and ought to sound magnificent.
   You will now do the E minor, I am quite sure, and by Jove! won't it be a worthy tribute from Maestro to Maestro! There's a glow about those final pages that you have done for me that would please John highly. Let us hope he'll be there. I don't know how I shall snare you in—what form of decoy I may have to resort to—but come you must on the Sunday for the E minor depends on it. Your addition shall be copied, if with my own hands.
Thine,
Firapeel.
   You *are* a craftsman.

The 'E minor' is the Bach Prelude and Fugue in E minor ('The Wedge'). Elgar did not, in fact, orchestrate this.

   Atkins took a few days holiday at the beginning of August, and Elgar went over to Ostend in the middle of the month for performances of the *Enigma Variations*, *The Wand of Youth Suite No 1*, *In the South* and *Sea Pictures*, in which Tilly Koenen was the soloist. He sent the following postcard.

Ostende Aug 13 08

Fine Orchestra 125
Wish you were here
My concert is on Friday Night with Tilly.
Love Reynart.

   The Elgars were back in Hereford on 17 August, and on the 20th Atkins went over to meet Elgar's friends the Edward Speyers who were staying at Plas Gwyn. Elgar was working on the slow movement of the symphony, but it was not ready to be played. He told Atkins all about the concerts in Ostend, which had gone well, but he reported that, while greatly admiring her voice, he had been obliged to give Tilly Koenen extra piano rehearsals as she had not known her part in the *Sea Pictures* at the first orchestral rehearsal. He also said that he had definitely decided to resign his professorship at Birmingham University at the end of the month.
   On 27 August the second combined chorus rehearsal took place in Worcester Cathedral. Atkins had arranged for the fine 32ft pedal

open diapason to be connected up to the temporary festival organ at the west end, and he was looking forward to Elgar's comments, but he was not there. Alice, who was there with Carice, explained that he was finishing the Finale of the symphony. At the tea break Atkins wrote a note to Elgar about the 32ft. Later that evening he could not resist posting a second letter:

8, College Yard.
August 27, 1908.

To the
Dumb Oracle—

Sir,

In spite of your silence the 32 ft. effect is *immense*. Your silence, too shall not prevent me from drawing your attention to the fact that owing to the enormous success and consequent great demand upon my 32 ft. by composers who wish to supply bottom to their work—*where was no Bottom*—I have been compelled to charge 1/- per unit (bar) for use thereof. I shall be glad to know if you wish to solidify, unify or Bottomize your works. I may remark that my pipes have a singular welding and cohering power. It struck me that their use might give a fictitious 'depth' very desirable at all times.

Firapeel.

Plas Gwyn, Hereford.
Aug 28 1908

My dear Firapeel:

I am glad the 32 feet which after all is 1/3 of a centipede (environs), goes well. I did not know that the yesterday's rehearsal was to be in the Cathedral or I should have made an immense effort to come. Music in the fane pleaseth me & the disturbed dust of ancestors is good to my nostrils also.

Then there is Miserrimus & other things of my Xtreme youth's awe. Well! I missed something & regret.

I am (under submission) sending a line to Schröder [J. Schröder, the festival percussion player] to look at the percussion & 'jape' it for three or four of 'em.

1. Thanks for permission to introduce folks of good behaviour to the London rehearsals.

2. Thanks also for the passes for Lady Elgar & myself.

3. Thanks also for being *Mr.* Ivor Atkins. It does me good to see it, & may it remain.

4. Thanks

(Stop it)

I say, *do* provide some decent weather! I am glad you are sounding so flourishing.

Yours ever
Reynart.

P.S. Your second 32ft. epistle just arrived. Do you make any reduction on taking a large quantity—13 as 12 or something? I think your charge too high for such a cheap effect. I think I sold this idea at my annual festival rummage sale some 12 years ago! Yah!

The 'Miserrimus' was a small stone so inscribed in the floor outside the west door from the cathedral to the cloisters, which remains the pathetic memorial to Thomas Morris of Upton-upon-Severn, a Minor Canon of the cathedral and Vicar of Claines. He refused to take the oath of allegiance to King William III, and on being deprived of his livings died in great poverty. The 'other things' included the cross on the wall in the lane below Perry Wood Lane, Lark Hill, which used to be pointed out to Elgar, when a boy, as the place where Oliver Cromwell made his pact with the Devil. Elgar's point 3 refers to the fact that Atkins had declined an offer of a Canterbury honorary Doctorate of Music.

The London soloists and orchestra rehearsals were on 1, 2 and 3 September, with Atkins conducting *Gerontius* and Elgar *The Kingdom* and *Wand of Youth* no. 2. Tilly Koenen's voice drew admiration from all, but she clearly did not know her part in either *Gerontius* or *The Kingdom*. Atkins therefore asked Elgar, who was staying in London, if he would give her an additional piano rehearsal the following morning. Charles Clark, who was singing the Angel of the Agony, said that he would like to take this opportunity of an additional rehearsal. Atkins also arranged to send Koenen a telegram demanding another rehearsal with him in Worcester the same afternoon.

Langham   Friday [4 September 1908]

My dear Firapeel:
I hope you are easy in you mind now & not worried. I saw the terrible woman this a.m. & worked hard—but—she is impossible. She knows nothing & is unteachable I fear. I sent her off in good time & recapitulated your instructions & gave her your wire, which arrived safely, so I trust she got down to you & you have drilled the life out of her. I wish to goodness she wd give it all up—if we could get Phyllis Lett. I only had time to do my work [*The Kingdom*] over which she was duller than dull.

182

Clark came & sang like an angel. *Do* try the 'Angel of the Agony' song on Monday & get the opening a shade slower & the *orch* quieter. It is worth doing, I think, as Clark sings it as it has never been sung before. I arrive at four & hope to find all flourishing with you.

Bear up

Yours ever

Reynart.

Atkins spent a long time that Friday afternoon and evening rehearsing both works with Tilly Koenen, but sadly it became evident that she could not learn the parts in time, and a replacement would have to be found. Phyllis Lett was not available, but Alice Lakin took over both parts. Tilly Koenen withdrew because of 'throat trouble'.

This year the Elgars had taken for the festival week the King's School Headmaster's house.

The opening service on 6 September included Bach's Toccata in F, orchestrated by Esser, with Elgar's new ending. The Monday was, as usual, devoted to soloist, chorus and orchestral rehearsals, and brings my own first conscious memory of Elgar. My father was conducting his *Hymn of Faith* and Elgar's *Dream of Gerontius* that morning, and my mother wanted to hear the rehearsal of these works and took me in with her. I remember, even though I was barely 4, being greatly impressed by the crowds in the Cathedral and by all those people on a platform with my father waving a stick at them. I dimly remember him turning round and talking to Elgar who had gone up from a front seat. I fear, however, I disgraced myself because, shortly afterwards—and I remember this very clearly—I became bored and crawled under the seats to the far side of the row, causing a great commotion. I was mercilessly teased by Elgar years later about the incident, and according to him I disgraced myself even more on my recapture by my mother by saying in a loud voice during the rehearsal of *Gerontius*, 'Mummy, take me out. I can't stand this dreadful noise!'

That festival Elgar was conducting *The Kingdom* and his new orchestral work, *Wand of Youth Suite* No 2, which was being performed for the first time in the Wednesday night concert in the Public Hall. This had a great reception. The last two pieces, 'The Tame Bear' and 'The Wild Bears', brought the house down and had to be repeated. For the rest of the week these two tunes could be heard hummed or whistled all over the city.

Other works were Parry's *Beyond these Voices there is Peace*, specially written for the festival, and Bantock's *The Pierrot of the Minute*, another first performance. Both these were conducted by the composers, as was Stanford's *Stabat Mater*. Walford Davies' *Everyman*, Atkins' *Hymn of Faith* and Beethoven's Violin Concerto, with Mischa Elman as soloist, were also performed. Elgar told Atkins that the last two, both in the Cathedral, had sounded marvellous. If he still had any doubts about a violin concerto in a cathedral, this performance appears to have removed them.

After the festival Atkins went for a very short holiday in Scotland. He returned to conduct a concert in Tewkesbury Abbey.

The Athenaeum
Sep 29 1908.

My dear Firapeel:
I was glad to get your card & should have written but Scotland was vague. I saw later that you had been to Tewkesbury. I hope all went well. How I envy you conducting in that noble fane. We called there per motor on our way home from Worcester.
How long ago it all seems! & how pleasant to think over! I hope you are well & the boy & Mrs. Atkins after the exertion of the week. Home soon.
Yours ever
Reynart.

Elgar, who had been working almost continuously on the symphony since June, finished it at the end of September, and proofs began to come in during the last week in October. He had asked Atkins to come over and help, but unfortunately the latter was hopelessly tied up and could not get over. He sent a message explaining his position and adding that he had invited Sir Alexander Mackenzie to conduct a work of his at the WFCS concert in February 1909, and would like also to include the new symphony.

Plas Gwyn, Hereford.
Nov 11 1908

My dear Firapeel:
How are you? I have not seen you for ages, & not heard much—yes! you were at the apparently somewhat feeble IVtet concert. I have been and am wofully busy over those proofs. We have a private rehearsal on Nov.

23rd—just to run thro' it—&, Firapeel, it *is* good & would be better an ye were bodily assisting at the birth—not the baptism of the child.

Send news. I am so glad Mackenzie comes to you & if I am in England I'll come over.

Love to the family.

Yours ever

Reynart.

Atkins replied saying that he would get over some time within the next two or three days, but Fate was against him.

Plas Gwyn, Hereford.
Nov. 13 1908

My dear Firapeel:

I am so sorry: all the stuff has gone & I have only my skeleton proof of the score & this, alack & welladay! must accompany me on my sickening travels next week. I have to conduct on S. Coast watering places for needed bread & leave on Monday.

Now: the miniature score is to be ready on Dec. 2 before the first performance, also a piano arrgt. Newman is doing the analysis for Manchester & this will be ready a week before the concert. Further; with the London Symph. Orch. on Monday morning at eleven o'clock Nov. 23rd, at Queen's Hall, I have a private 'run through', all to myself! & I believe souls will be admitted. I am sorry I could not wire for you today but many things were fixed up.

I have invented a glass machine for making *H2S* & it is to be manufactured & brought out called the 'Elgar Sulp. Hy. Apparatus', designed by Sir Edward Elgar!!!!

Love from

Yours ever

Reynart

ye

Foxe

Elgar had promised Richter that he should conduct the first performance of the Symphony in Manchester. The 'glass machine' mentioned in the last paragraph became standard equipment in school laboratories and was in regular use in Herefordshire, Worcestershire and elsewhere for many years.

On 23 November Atkins attended the private run-through. He told me some years later that he had been overwhelmed by the symphony. Some of it he had heard played over on the piano, but he had seen none of it in its orchestrated final form. Elgar was delighted that he had come, and arranged with Novello's to post him a miniature score, which was only just off the printing press, and would not normally be released until the performance.

Hereford   Nov 29 1908

Firapeel.

I mislike this date—it smacketh of $\frac{1}{4}$ day, & is none of it either to pay or to receive—but still, I mislike the sound—the 29th—it is a mispickel. This letter is dated therefore a day hence or, as I may not prophesy—a day backward, anyway not on the 29th which is a sound I abhor as aforesaid & for reasons already said or sung.

Why won't Mrs. Atkins & you come over some doggy day between performances & stay the night?

I'm proud of this idea
Come
Yours ever
Reynart
ye Fo*xxx*e

(Note by Atkins: 'This insistence on the undesirability of November 29 as a date I suspect to be due to the fact that it was my birthday.')

The first performance of Elgar's symphony was given by the Hallé in the Free Trade Hall, Manchester, on 3 December, conducted by Richter. It was an absolute triumph. Elgar was called to the platform, and the whole orchestra and the audience stood up and applauded him. After the performance Atkins joined Elgar and Richter in the artists' room. Sinclair, Alice and Frank Schuster were there, and many others. All, including Richter, were excited and conscious of having taken part in a great experience.

On 7 December, on the occasion of the next performance of the symphony, in London, Elgar had a surprise waiting for Atkins, who had arranged to meet him and Richter in the artists' room before the concert. There Elgar gave him a beautifully bound copy of the miniature score of the symphony; on the title page he had inscribed 'Edward Elgar Dec 7 1908 to I.A.A.', and Hans Richter had countersigned and also dated it.

On Thursday, 17 December Atkins went over to Plas Gwyn and stayed the night. Elgar was working in 'The Ark', his chemical laboratory, when he arrived, and he was immediately given a demonstration of his sulphurated hydrogen machine, but most of the time was spent in talking about the two performances of the symphony, and of the great interest being shown by the general public. No work of Elgar's had so quickly captured the popular imagination, and performances were being arranged all over the country.

1909

The Elgars travelled to London on 1 January for Elgar to conduct his symphony for the first time at a public concert. Atkins could not be present then or on 7 January, when Elgar conducted it again, but he did go up to the Queen's Hall on 16 January, when Elgar conducted his symphony for the third time. My father told me that despite the effect the two earlier performances under Richter's baton had made upon him, and his careful study of the score, Elgar's own interpretation had shown the symphony in a new light and revealed many new points. In the artists' room afterwards he told Elgar that the slow movement could be arranged for organ, and he would like to do this. Elgar agreed to discuss it with Novello's who later published it.

Plas Gwyn, Hereford.
Jan 24 1909

My dear Firapeel:

I've just crept out of bed & write a few notes—first to you. I've a beastly cold & chest—going, I think & as soon as possible I start away.

Now: the question of the organ arrangement seems to resolve itself into one of the *difficulty* of the arrangement. I *know* your arrangement would be first class, but from a publisher's point of view is it *easy*? I was spoken to over the telephone last Monday when I was leaving town, but you had my message I've no doubt. I am writing to Messrs. N.[ovello] telling them they must decide about the arrangement: that your arrangement [is] sure to be A.1., &c. &c. but the actual settlement remains with them.

I shall not be well enough to start tomorrow, but as I said, I fly as soon as I can cease coughing &c.

Ever yours Reynart.

Atkins was worried about the despondency and ill health shown in Elgar's letter, but could not get over to Hereford for a few days.

He telephoned early in February to learn that Elgar had gone to Llandrindod Wells, where he expected to remain for about 10 days.

The WFCS concert in Worcester which contained Mackenzie's *The Dream of Jubal* and Elgar's symphony was on 23 February, and as Elgar had promised to conduct if he were free Atkins telephoned again. Elgar said that he was better, but not well enough to conduct, and that he would probably go over to Llandrindod for another few days holiday. A telegram of good wishes was sent on the 23rd from Llandrindod.

The concert went well. Worcester had been keenly looking forward to hearing the symphony, and it was received with tremendous enthusiasm, which was fortunate since its production had nearly wrecked the Society financially with the cost of all the additional orchestral players required. Atkins wired Elgar after the concert, sending best wishes for a speedy recovery.

Lld'd 24 II 09

My dear Firapeel
So glad to learn from your telegram that all went well—I wish *I* was busy as well
Yours ever
Reynart

Atkins then wrote sending Elgar a copy of the programme, and telling him how the symphony meant more to him with every hearing.

Llandrindod.
Feb. 27; 1909

My dear Firapeel
Many many thanks for your letter & book of the Concert: it is indeed refreshing to hear of your enthusiasm over the Symphony—what a pity you could not play it every night for a week it always seems such a long preparation for a short moment. I am glad the Vigornians liked it & am sorry I was not there to see the sight & hear the sound. I expect your *tempi* were *dead on*!—(vulgarism for perfect).

I feel no joy in my product. I am not well & dodging wintry ailments with no success & cannot afford to go away yet: so I rather feel that I wish I had never burdened the earth with any attempts at *good* work but had been a trifling commercial success with such rot as is beloved of that providence that shapes our ends: yes, I regret the serious work I have done—which is a sad saying.

Farewell: bless you & send you many good things.

Yours ever

E.E.

Elgar's stay in Llandrindod did not have the desired effect of improving his health. He returned to Hereford, and Sinclair, who had been to see him, told Atkins that he was listless and had spent several days in bed. Alice also seemed very unwell.

Atkins, who had been in Malvern, went over on 18 March. Elgar told him that earlier in the month he had gone to Exeter, but had returned home after two nights, and apart from walking and kite-flying when the sun was out (not so much fun as it used to be), he had spent most of his time indoors and in 'The Ark'. He was longing to get away to the South, but where? Perhaps Madeira, or Italy again. They had decided to let Plas Gwyn again for 3 months.

On 6 April Elgar paid a surprise visit to my parents, but my father was out. He explained to my mother that he was on his way to London, but had decided to break his journey in Worcester. His main news was that Pippa (Julia Worthington) had cabled them to say that she was taking a villa near Florence for a prolonged stay, and she had invited them all to go and stay with her. He was going to London for a few days and then to Paris, where Alice and Carice would join him *en route* for Italy.

Hôtel des Deux Mondes,
22, Avenue de l'Opéra, Paris.
Saturday [17 April 1909]

My dear Firapeel:

Truly the times have been out of joint & are not wholly fitting in their proper sockets now. I did want to see you before leaving but the amount of illness in the house has been daunting & interfered with everything. My wife is better & she & Carice join me today here & we travel ensemble to Italy next week.

I hear great things of your performance of the Symphony from many—last from C. Fry in London last week. I am sure you treated it as I.[zaak] Walton [in *The Compleat Angler*] counsels us to use the frog—'as if you loved him',—old brute, when the poor thing is being *threaded* for fishing, but you know all these nice bits & the Symphony was not on a barbed hook, & so it was easier to be gentle. Thank you.

I hope the arrgt of the Slow Movement progressed—I asked last week

& understood it was printing. I have no news. I have *done* nothing for months. I have plenty of thoughts but no inducements—pecuniary or ambitious—to help me to blacken paper: the commercial prospects of me are vile & I no longer take a proper pride in my artist life—if I ever did & so—& so—& so—

'Cut is the branch that might have grown full straight,
And burned is Apollo's Laurel bough
That sometime grew within this silly man.'

Do write & send news of you & your doings &c. I am not sure of any address except c/o T. Cook & Sons, Florence. This will find me for some time as we shall be somewhere within reach. Our plans are vague & will remain so until we see how health progresses, or rather promises for us: my wife has been *really* ill since mid. of January & I am not sure if change of climate is good or evil for her.

Love to you all,
Yours ever
Reynart.

The lines of poetry quoted in this letter are from Marlowe's *Doctor Faustus*, though the penultimate word has been altered (from 'learned').

On 28 April Atkins had conducted the Worcestershire Orchestral Society in a concert which included the *Pomp and Circumstance March* No 3 (dedicated to Atkins).

[Postcard, postmarked Florence, 8 May 1909]

Glad the concert was such a success
Tell us how you all are &c &c
Lovely here & wish you were here too
Reynart

Jaeger was very ill in 1909, and he died on 18 May.

Villa Silli, Careggi.
May 22, 1909.

My dear Firapeel:
My heart is heavy. I have just heard of poor dear Nimrod's death. I say no more now.
Your letter was a great joy & I was so glad that you are better & that the musical songs (various) have gone off so well. I send you this bit of real Florentine hand-made paper—I have bought some & will confound you

with it. When you see a whole sheet (this is a $\frac{1}{4}$) you will feel a pleasant illness all thro', of jealousy, &c &c.

We leave in two days & weary & wan—wasted wend we our way via venerable Verona & Venice to Vigornia [Worcester] & the Vaga [the Wye].

That's neat!
Love to you from us all,
Yours ever
Reynart.

The Elgars remained with Pippa at Careggi until 28 May. During this time they saw a great deal of Florence and made various excursions, but Elgar managed to spend many hours on his sketches. Pippa's keen interest and provision of the quiet background that he needed had enabled him to make some progress on the Violin Concerto.

Elgar had always greatly admired Italian paper, and he had found some handmade music paper which exactly suited him. He bought a large quantity of this paper, enough in fact, to enable him to present Atkins on his return home with a most generous supply and still keep enough himself to meet his own requirements for many years to come. The following note was written on a piece of this paper and posted from London.

Fayre Florentine
Handmade paper
for one (Firapeel)
who can appreciate
it really & truly
from
Reynart

June 16 1909

Just arrived in London
Love to you.

Elgar was back in Hereford on 22 June, and on 30 June Atkins spent a day with him. Elgar played over what he was then engaged on—sketches for the Violin Concerto and a new song, *Go Song of Mine*—a setting of Rossetti's translation of Guido Cavalcanti's poem.

8, College Yard, Worcester.
2nd July, 1909.

My dear Reynart,
Your 'Go, song of mine' still rings in my ears. It is good to hear anything with the *certainty* of that. As you go on your workmanship becomes more and more striking.

I write that down boldly as one of the VERY BEST things you have ever done, and I say too that you are a

Poet

seer

and that your insight is marvellous. I read that poem and failed to find it appeal to me at once, but now ———— ah well! it's different.

Bless you, go ahead. I do not know what Providence is going to let you do next.

My love to all,
Yours ever,
Firapeel.

The Elgars invited the Atkins to spend a night with them in Plas Gwyn on 23 July, but they could not get away.

Hereford   Sunday [Postmarked 25 July 1909]

My dear Firapeel:
We were so sorry you both could not come to us: is it possible *you* could come tomorrow (Monday) sometime, & belike dine & sleep?

I want to see you and if that is not inducement enough (if any) Mrs. Worthington is here. The weather is dreadful

Love,
Reynart.

P.S. We are out to luncheon but should be home at tea-time.
[Note in Mrs Worthington's handwriting]—Do come to see me & not them. J.H.W.
[Note in Alice's handwriting]—If you cd come, as we hope, wd you send a wire in the morning? So sorry not to see Mrs Atkins and you on Friday.

Fate was, however, against the reunion as Atkins was going on holiday to stay with Sanford Terry in Scotland. The Sanford Terrys lived in a beautiful house called Westerton of Pitfodels, near Cults, a village 4 miles south-west of Aberdeen.

Plas Gwyn, Hereford.
July 28 1909

My dear Firapeel:
How horrid of you to be in Cults when I am not—and I may pass through sometime.
In real professional language I have 'pencilled' your date (!!!) which is Aug.23 [a festival contingent rehearsal at Worcester of *The Apostles* and *Go, Song of Mine*, which were being done at the Hereford Festival] and I will *come if I can*.
Give my love to Terry: I wrote to him the other day. You can also say that Tupsley parish [in which he had been living] is holding its judgement. He will explain this. I don't know if you have started but yesterday, it is worth recording, was the worst wet day we have had. The powers that move the waters above evidently thought they had discovered a new trick & clapped into it roundly all day.
Think of me when you wield the tea-pot.

Yours ever,
Reynart.

Atkins returned from Scotland on 10 August, and the following letter and enclosure—an early draft of the First Symphony—was a delightful surprise for him. Elgar had shown this sketch to Atkins during the previous year, and he had at once laid claim to it when Elgar had finished with it. Unfortunately it was later mislaid, and Elgar had feared that it might have been accidentally destroyed.

Plas Gwyn, Hereford.
Aug. 13. 1909

My dear Firapeel:
Here is your sketch just found & sent as promised. 'Please note' that the slow movement is evolved from the quick, as already noted by correct historiographers.
Hope you have had a nice holiday.

Yours ever
Reynart
ye Foxe

First sketch for symphony.

On 23 August Elgar came over to Worcester to rehearse his *Go Song of Mine* with the Worcester contingent. He told Atkins that he had been working hard on the Violin Concerto and was planning a 'jape' for the festival.

When Atkins went over to the Massed Rehearsal in Hereford Cathedral on 26 August Elgar was worried about Carice who was very unwell. Although it was not known then, she was developing scarlet fever. Elgar went up to London on 30 August for the three days of soloist and orchestra rehearsals, and thus avoided quarantine. In the meantime Alice was in quarantine with Carice at Plas Gwyn, but by frantic efforts secured Harley House, Hereford, for their festival party. Pippa, Frank Schuster, the Kilburns and Sanford Terry were among those staying there, and there were the usual day visitors. The 'jape' proved to be an elaborate invitation to a party on the last night of the festival.

The Elgar works at the Hereford Festival were *Te Deum* in F, Op 34, and *The Apostles*, conducted by Sinclair. Elgar conducted *Cockaigne*, the Symphony in A flat, Op 55, and the Chorus for Voices, *Go, Song of Mine*, Op 57, which was receiving its first performance. The programme also included the first performance in England of Schubert's *Lazarus*, which had turned out never to have been performed in England. Atkins had meanwhile prepared an English edition which was now used.

At the end of the festival Elgar's friends, including the Atkins, Sinclair, Hull and the Brewers, forgathered at Harley House for the 'Harleyford Musical Festival, 1909'. Elgar had circulated handbills to his friends earlier in the week. It was, as might be expected, a hilarious evening, and Elgar was in his most carefree mood.

The Elgars went to the Birmingham Triennial Festival, in which the *Dream of Gerontius* and two new works, Rutland Boughton's *Midnight* and Bantock's *Omar Khayyám* Part 3 were the main items of interest. For most of October Elgar was away in the North, including the promised visit to Terry in Aberdeen, and during much of November he was in London.

The Elgars returned to Hereford on 20 November, but he had caught a chill and was in bed for a number of days. He was clearly not ready for a visit, and Atkins accordingly wrote enclosing a programme of the 17 November WFCS concert, which had included *Go, Song of Mine*. It contained some analytical notes

HARLEYFORD MUSICAL FESTIVAL, 1909.

Grand Culminating Cataclysmic

CONCERT & FIREWORK JERKATION

AT

HARLEY HOUSE, SEPT. 10th, 1909,

AT 8 P.M.

PROGRAMME (W.P.)

8-0.   Tympanocrashic Detonation of a Brass Bombardon 'an Delian Heckelphone.

    ☞ Beware of Pick-pockets !

8-5.   Overture   -   " I Diavoli deliriosi "   -   Sans-sens (Op. 2¼A.)

ORCHESTRA.

Strings - - - - - -	NONE
Wood Wind (the blooming lot) -	MR. L. F. SCHUSTER
Trumpet - - - -	SIR E. J. SOLOMON ELGAR ✳
Precarious Horn - - -	MR. C. S. TERRY
Percussion - MRS. WORTHINGTON and MR. N. KILBURN
Principal Solo Bagpipe - - -	MRS. N. KILBURN
At the Piano - - - - -	A CHAIR

Conductor: HERR DJETMANN. ✗

8-20.   Rhapsodie Ecossaise (unaccompanied)   -   -   Mac Havers
      MRS. KILBURN.

8-30.   Barley Water and Oat Cakes will be thrown to the Crowd.

8-45.   Lecture on " Tupsley Parish: or, Microbes I have met.   With some
      remarks on the Sewage Farm."   By Plas Gwyn of that Ilk.

9-30.   Grand Concluding Firework Display, including magnificent Set-piece,
      " Mrs. Worthington Discovering the North Pole."

☞ See Small Handbills and Ferpend.   Selah !

☞ The Programme is liable to alteration or cancellation on any and every (or thereby) ground.
    If the evening is wet, Aquatic Sports will be wielded on the extensive sward. Costumes
    on hire. Gents' medium at cut-throat prices.

☞ By order of the Lord Chamberlain the Bomb-proof Curtain will make frequent descents.

☞ Tickets from Concert-Direction Pietro Bunni and the usual old gents.

WILSON & PHILLIPS, PRINTERS, STATIONERS AND BOOKBINDERS, 11, HIGH STREET, HEREFORD.

✳ John Solomon was the well-known Principal Trumpet in the Festival
    Orchestra, and a great character.

✗ Probably Jakeman, of Jakeman and Carver, who was responsible for
    all the Festival ticket arrangements.

✝ Carice's Pet Rabbit.

written by his assistant, Alexander Brent-Smith, who was later to become a fine composer and writer.

[In pencil]
[Plas Gwyn, 7 December 1909]

Many thanks, dear Firapeel, for your letter & the programme—the notes were excellent but a *little* too adjectivy.

I'm a lost thing! Only out of bed for a few hours. I'll let you know if I ever get well enough to see anyone again.

Yours ever
Reynart.

I have had a *very sweet* & most touching letter from S.S.S.[anford]—a farewell, but I hope he lives still.

Atkins wrote again in an attempt to cheer Elgar up, but he likewise was greatly distressed by Sanford's illness.

Hereford   Dec 13 1909

My dear Firapeel:

It *has* been the most gloomy & desperate month! I only write to say I am passing over your last letter, clearing up ready for flight tomorrow. I am ordered away—should have been gone a month a go, & the result is a wreck. I am better now, but regret bitterly not seeing you during the past four weeks which were to have included much. Now the music is not fit to see or be seen. I have 'jerked' two little songs but nothing big. I'll write again soon.

In the meantime love to you,

Reynart.

I don't know at this moment *where* I am going!!

The two songs mentioned were *O soft was the Song*, to words by Gilbert Parker, and *The Torch*, with words adapted from an Eastern European folksong by 'Pietro d'Alba' (Elgar himself). Carice's white rabbit, Peter, was clearly a most accomplished linguist.

1910

The year started with sadness for both Elgar and Atkins.

Plas Gwyn, Hereford.
Jan 7: 1910

My dear Firapeel:
  I received a cable from Henry Sanford yesterday evening saying that our dear friend died at four o'clock yesterday morning: it is very, very sad & comes as a shock altho' we have expected it for a long time.
  I am home for a few days & wildly busy & *not well.* I fear I have nothing to show you but am hungering to see you: cd you come over tomorrow afternoon, or almost any time, say Monday. I leave home on Monday evening or Tuesday morning.

Do come,
Love
Yours ever
Reynart.

This letter was forwarded to Atkins who was staying for a few days in Bournemouth. He then went on to London and on 13 January called at the Langham Hotel in the hope of finding Elgar in.

Langham Hotel, London.
Thursday 1 p.m. [13 January 1910]

My dear Firapeel
  I was so very sorry to miss you. I am in town for some days & we must meet. I am fully engaged tonight. Give my love to the boy. Are you free tomorrow or wd you go to the theatre in the p.m.? Send word how you are fixed—I *may* remain here (in town) for a week or more.

Love,
Yrs ever
Reynart.

Elgar had taken a flat at Queen Anne's Mansions, and he invited Atkins, who was in London, to have dinner with him on 16 January. Elgar told him all about the Jaeger Memorial Concert, in which he was very much involved, with Muriel Foster, Plunket Greene and the LSO. The Alexandra Palace Male Voice Choir would take part. The date had now been fixed for 24 January, in the Queen's Hall. Richter was to be Conductor-in-chief, with

Parry, Elgar, Coleridge-Taylor and Walford Davies conducting their own works. Elgar was busy correcting the proofs of the recently orchestrated songs, Op 59, to words by Gilbert Parker, which would receive their first performance at this concert. On 24 January Atkins went to London for the Jaeger Memorial Concert, and he told me some 20 years later what an emotional occasion it had been. The hall was crowded, and with a few unavoidable exceptions all the well-known conductors, artists, orchestral players, music publishers and representatives of music societies were there to pay tribute to one who had done so much to promote English music and Elgar's in particular. Muriel Foster's singing of the new song cycle, especially *Twilight*, conducted by Elgar, and 'Nimrod' in the *Enigma Variations*, conducted by Richter, were deeply moving. Elgar had written a special note for the *Variations*, and I reproduce that part of it dealing with Variation IX, 'Nimrod'.

Something ardent and mercurial, in addition to the slow movement (No 9), would have been needful to portray the character and temperament of A. J. Jaeger (Nimrod). The Variation bearing this name is a record of a long summer evening talk, when my friend grew nobly eloquent (as only he could) on the grandeur of Beethoven and especially of his slow movements. A reference to the *Adagio* of the Pathétique Sonata is therefore seen in the opening bars of the *Nimrod* Variation.

On 7 February Atkins was in London and called at Queen Anne's Mansions on the chance of seeing Elgar. He was in, and persuaded Atkins to dine with him.

8, College Yard, Worcester.
Feb 8 1910.

My dear Reynart,
   It was a great joy to me to spend such a delightful evening with you and to find you in such magnificent form. We meet very rarely, but let me admit frankly that you are not replaceable. I am perfectly conscious of not having enjoyed any evening like that since we last met. And though I bring little to the feast, at least I bring a great love for you and a deep appreciation of, and great waves of sympathy for your noble music. And it was good to feel the old glow in listening to that Violin Concerto movement. It put me back longer than I care to think to the days of 'The Apostles' and more recently the Symphony. Well, you still go on, and the stream is as good as of yore—unless it be better, but my love for

199

various 'opera' is so great that I do not allow myself to institute comparisons.

Still, that Violin Concerto slow movement is *good*—I admit so much. Also it hath flavour—yea, I swear it, with the bow held at the proper angle it should produce some effect. Look well to it that the player be one well versed in sinuosity of phrase also that he be a man of a good herte. With these conditions fulfilled (and if you surreptitiously pass round a good bottle), 'you will see wonders'—as Brillat-Savarin [eighteenth-century gourmet] said of the Fondue.

Yours ever
Firapeel.

Elgar's letter of the 7th arrived in the afternoon.

British Empire Club, 12, St. James' Square, S.W.
Feb 7 [1910]

My dear Firapeel

I shall be home in a day or two & shall hope to see you. I asked Lady M[aud Warrender] & if dates, or rather a date—cd be found she would sing. Tell me (at Plas Gwyn) if you have afternoon performances & if certain days of the week, &c &c.

My love to you,
Reynart.

8, College Yard, Worcester.
Feb 8 1910.

My dear Reynart,

Thank you so much for your letter of yesterday. Yes, do let me try for an early meeting while I am still in touch with the V. Concerto.

As to Recitals I should like to fix a near Wednesday afternoon, if you think that would be a suitable day for Lady Maud. It certainly is the best day for our country folk. They turn up well of a Wednesday. Could she propose a couple of dates to make sure of suiting the Dean who is very kind and *keen* and by way of fathering the movement.

The R.A.M. have just made me an Hon. Member. It pleased me very much and even the Mayor (Allsop) wrote and congratulated me.

My love to you dear Reynart.

Firapeel.

Plas Gwyn, Hereford.
Feb 14 1910

My dear Firapeel.
   I am so delighted that you are an Hon.R.A.M. I see it in the papers and now dear Terry writes exuberantly thereupon. I wish he seemed better: a long time getting strong.
   I have no music here (MSS away) or I should press you to come but I hope I may see you.

Good luck from
Yours
Edward Elgar which is
Reynart familiarly.

   The Elgars had again let Plas Gwyn, thinking they might go to Italy, but when this fell through they decided to rent a flat in London.

Athenaeum   March 7 1910

My dear Firapeel:
   We have taken a flat for a few months here & so you'll understand if you don't see me in the Midland regions: but of course you will be up here & will find us out or preferably in at

58, New Cavendish St. W.
Telephone 3484 Mayfair (!)

I have no news but could talk somewhat wisely of things in general.

My love to you,
Yours ever
Reynart.

   The Elgars had only been in London for a few days before Frank Schuster suggested that Elgar should join him at Torquay where he was going for a holiday, and accompany him on a motor tour through Devon and Cornwall.
   The *Wand of Youth Suite* No 2 was to be included in the Worcestershire Orchestral Society's concert on 4 May, and Elgar had promised to conduct it if he was available.

[London, 12 April 1910]

My dear A Firapeel. (I nearly missed it)
   I am only this moment home. I really cannot come on the 4th, as although a long sojourn in Italy is impossible, a short one *is* possible &

201

imminent. We are here for a few weeks longer & I am going abroad for a space then Hereford. Good luck to you.

Yours ever
Reynart.

Atkins had for some time wanted to include Beethoven's *Choral Symphony* in a Worcester concert, but had put the idea on one side because of the difficulties for an amateur orchestra, and the heavy cost of the extra professional players who would be required. He now had two orchestras, and with the planning of the 1911 Worcester Festival, in which he hoped to include a performance of the symphony, now much in his thoughts, he determined to augment the WFCS orchestra with members from the WOS, and some outside professional players, and to include the work in the WFCS concert for 19 April. There had been a number of additional practices, and fine soloists had been engaged.

The opportunity of hearing this great work in Worcester was very much appreciated, and the hall was sold out well before the day of the concert. The performance exceeded Atkins' hopes and more than justified the experiment. Fortified by this result Atkins now decided to put Beethoven's Ninth Symphony in the 1911 festival programme.

King Edward's death on 6 May brought universal grief and special services at the Cathedral. The King's death was felt very deeply by Elgar, who had received much encouragement from him.

Elgar had been spending much of his time at Schuster's riverside cottage, 'The Hut', Bray. He had completed the Violin Concerto and also worked on his Second Symphony, but his anticipated short holiday in Italy had not materialised, and he attended rehearsals and concerts in different parts of the country.

The 3 months' lease of Plas Gwyn ended on 31 May, and on 4 June Elgar returned to Hereford, only to leave again on 7 June for Lincoln and London.

The Hut, Bray, Berks.
Friday [17 June 1910]

My dear Firapeel:
  Sometime tomorrow I travel home after much wandering with only two days at home since Febry!

202

Now the Concerto is printing & waxes big & you must see it. So I hope you will be able to come to us as of yore before the S. fever days—so long ago. I think you will like the stuff!

Beyond this I have no news & am working hard. I hope you are all 3 well.

My love to you,
Yours ever
Reynart
ye Foxe.

Atkins could not, however, go over immediately, and suggested a visit towards the end of the month.

Plas Gwyn, Hereford.
Saturday [25 June 1910]

Firapeel:

How does the subskevent plan segastruate?

W.H.Reed—a good man—cometh here on Thursday (morning I think—but the proceedings promise to be long & lively) to play thro' the Concerto & help me to 'bow' the same. Why should you not come & help? & cast an avuncular eye on the merry, vibrant gut?

Answer me that. Do come. We can put you up for the night in a *small* room—but there will be people here, all well-disposed to The Art.

Ever yours
Reynart.

If you answer wisely & fetisly I *could* send you some proofs. Shall I?

Atkins telephoned agreeing to go over on the Thursday, 30 March, and asking for a set of proofs so that he could study them before they met.

[Enclosing proofs of the Violin Concerto]
[Plas Gwyn]
June 27 1910

Firapeel:

For your own eye only! Treat it tenderly.

I *must* have them back first thing on Thursday—if Reed should be coming on *Wedy* evening I'll telegraph.

How's this?

I say—!!!!

Hereford
Tuesday [28 June 1910]

Dear Firapeel
    W. Reed comes at 12 o'c—arrives *here* I mean, & a pest!—leaves for
London the same evening (which is a Thursday) this is vexing as I hoped
he wd have stayed the night. Do come *early*, as soon as he does anyhow &
be sure let me have the proofs by 12 oc, an ye bring 'em not yourself.
    I have the joy of my life! a *pianola*.
                        Love
                        Reynart.

    Atkins and W. H. Reed had a wonderful afternoon and evening
at Plas Gwyn. The pianola referred to in Elgar's letter had been
installed by the Orchestrelle Company in the middle of June,
during his absence, as a result of a visit he had paid to the company
earlier in the year, when he had agreed that they should make a
pianola roll of the piano arrangement of the First Symphony. He
had visited their factory in April to settle the tempi for each section
and approve the roll.
    Atkins' private teaching practice had now built up to the point
that sadly he could not spare the time to go over to Hereford unless
it was vital and pre-arranged. They therefore now fell back on an
earlier practice. Elgar would tell Atkins on what day and train he

204

would next be travelling through Worcester to London, and if he could fit it in Atkins would catch the train at Henwick or Foregate Street and travel with Elgar to the Worcester main station, Shrub Hill, where the train remained for some minutes while the section from Wolverhampton was joined on. In this way they could be together for some 15–45 minutes according to trains, or longer if Elgar came in by an earlier train. From Hereford to the North of England also usually involved a change of trains at Worcester.

On one of these occasions, in July, I think, my father, probably at Elgar's request, decided to take me with him. Foregate Street is approached by a series of steps going up to the high-level platforms. I recall walking up these steps and going on to the platform. The train came in and Elgar was leaning out of the window looking for us. I remember clearly my excitement at getting into the train with him, his greeting and his chatting to me before he started talking to my father about music and other things. I remember our being turned out of the train, all too soon, at Shrub Hill station and watching the train depart and Elgar waving out of the window until it disappeared.

At the beginning of August, my parents, Sinclair and the two Miss Martleys went to Southern Germany and Austria, as they were to do in other years. They visited Munich, Garmisch, Innsbruck, Salzburg and Oberammergau for the Passion Play. It may well have been Oberammergau which crystallised Atkins' determination to prepare a special edition of Bach's *St Matthew Passion*.

During their stay in Garmisch Sinclair and Atkins visited the surrounding villages and towns, and were constantly reminded of the Elgars' vivid descriptions of the area when they went there in 1892, and how this had started them on continental touring.

Atkins next met Elgar in Gloucester for the full-chorus rehearsal in the cathedral on 25 August. Elgar told Atkins that since they had last met he had completed the orchestration of the whole Concerto and was now busy with proofs. As a relief he had started working on a setting of the 48th Psalm. The most interesting news, however, was that the Elgars were taking for the festival a large house near the cathedral, with a room which would make a fine music room, and that with W. H. Reed readily available he was considering giving a private performance of the concerto on the Sunday evening, with Reed playing the solo violin part and Elgar playing the orchestral part on the piano. He asked Atkins to help him with the orchestral colour by taking over the bass.

They met again in London on the last day of the orchestral rehearsals, when Elgar was conducting the symphony and *Gerontius*, and he told Atkins that Reed had agreed to play.

On the Sunday evening the room was packed, with the Elgar house-party—Frank, Pippa, Sanford Terry, Dorabella and Mrs W. H. Reed, known to her friends as 'James'. Leading musicians attending the festival included Harford Lloyd, C. Lee Williams and Herbert Howells, and there were a few music critics and other friends. This private play-through of the concerto made a wonderful start to the Gloucester Festival—and what a splendid festival it was.

The Tuesday evening began with Vaughan Williams' *Fantasia on a Theme of Thomas Tallis*, which had been written specially for the festival, and was conducted by the composer. This was followed by *Gerontius*, conducted by Elgar. Elgar's Symphony in A flat, which he conducted, was performed the next morning.

Elgar invited Atkins to come over after the Thursday evening performance. On his arrival he found that Kreisler was there, and later he and Elgar played some of the concerto. It was a wonderful experience to hear it as a listener, my father told me. Kreisler thrilled him, especially in the cadenza.

Towards the end of September Atkins and Elgar learned that their old friend Dr Grindrod was very seriously ill. Charles Grindrod was a fascinating and accomplished man, with artistic tastes and a love of literature and music, older than Elgar or Atkins and much loved by both of them.

Queen Anne's Mansions, S.W.
Oct, 17: 1910

My dear Firapeel

It *was* most dear of you to send that telegram [telling him of Grindrod's illness]. I thank you for it.

Here we are till Thursday, then home. I have *all* the orchl parts to do [Violin Concerto] & the good Austin comes to Plas Gwyn on Sunday by the 1 oc train & remains with me till 11.30 on Monday. I *did* want to work it in that the time might suit you—but I know this is hopeless. Belike I return on Thursday, or certainly Friday. Now could you be with us—join me in the corridor train for instance on Thursday at Shrub Hill (or on Friday as may be arranged) & stay the night or nights, & *we* might do a great deal to those parts by ourselves. Do not, dear Firapeel, *think* of giving anything up for this charitable business. You know I love to have you 'in it'—but at no cost of your engagements.

Kreisler was here on Saturday playing for three hours & comes again today. I wish you were here. It goes well.

Love

Reynart

ye Foxe.

Are you going to do the Passion [*St Matthew*] at your festival?

8, College Yard, Worcester.
Oct. 18, 1910.

My dear Reynart,

I did not follow up my telegram with a letter because there was some vague story of your having gone off with that Empire creature [Dr Charles Harris]—I didn't know how to interpret it but it was sufficiently disquieting to make one uncertain of your whereabouts. The Variations are greater than ever to me since I discovered that they will bear the impress of the Beast [Revelations 16 v2 and 19 v20] and yet remain unapproachably beautiful. For some reason the organ was not used in the Coda. I have no doubt that there was a very good reason for the omission, but I was expecting it and missed it.

Alas! Thursday I give an organ Recital in the Cathedral, and Friday I am teaching all day in Malvern. I shall be with you only in spirit, but should love to have come. If you have any voice in such matters, I should like to be there on the 10th, or should I write to the Philh: Secretary?

(Whisper it not abroad, but my heart goeth out to the 'Passion'—a work after your own heart. Have ye ony ideas, enue? Some day let us read it together. I yearn for a *subjective* rendering, with strength. I'm sure I'm right).

Thine,

Firapeel.

Harris was an impresario who fancied himself as a composer and conductor. He specialised in concerts with an Empire flavour, and a year or so earlier he had organised a concert for the LSO on condition that in it he conducted a *Coronation Mass—Edward VII*, which he had composed. He was at this time trying to get Elgar to go on an American–Canadian tour in 1911, which he was attempting to organise. It did not materialise. Atkins had recently heard a very indifferent performance of the *Variations*. Could the 'Beast' have been Harris?

Atkins wanted to be at the private rehearsal of the Violin

Concerto on 9 November as well as at the rehearsal and performance the next day. A special invitation was needed for this. Elgar's immediate reply was to post him a complete set of proofs of the concerto.

8, College Yard, Worcester.
Oct. 21st, 1910.

My dear Reynart,
It *was* kind of you to remember me in such a delightful way—and even to putting up the proofs with your own hands. I do appreciate it and them most warmly and thank you with a full heart for a precious gift.
I've been all day in Malvern, outwardly patient with foolish maidens but inwardly cursing full oft. I shall have a great 'go' with the Concerto tomorrow evening. The sight of it fills me with a desire for the night of the first note to arrive. And if it is so with me what must it be with you!
Much love to you all and again my deepest thanks.
Thine
Firapeel.

[Telegram]
Hereford 9.40 a.m. Oct. 22.10.
Atkins Cathedral Worcester

Busy all day with proofs so glad if you could come over even for an hour any time or stay night if possible.
Edward Elgar.

But Atkins was hopelessly booked up and had to wire that he could not get over.

Plas Gwyn, Hereford.
[25 October 1910]

My dear Firapeel:
I was sorry to trouble you with the telegram on Saturday, but I was sore pressed. Austin came on Sunday & we worked on did not go to bed till 1.20 a.m., beginning again on Monday at 9 oc. All the orch. stuff is returned. But if you are vagaring about do come over tomorrow, Wednesday & lunch or something. I am hard at the Symph II & welcome sane distraction—such as you can afford.
Yours ever
Reynart.
We shall be delighted if you can come & *stay the night* for choice or anything!

On 27 October, Atkins, having cancelled all his engagements, went over to Hereford in the morning and stayed until the last train. He found that Elgar had already put in many hours work on his Second Symphony, and after Elgar had played some of it over they decided after lunch to go for a long walk along the river to Mordiford and back. Mordiford is a village about 4 miles south-east of Hereford, where the River Lugg is crossed by a medieval bridge of nine arches. This was a favourite place where Elgar often fished and where he jotted down many of his musical ideas, and later a number of sketches for *The Music Makers*, on or near the bridge which he loved.

Plas Gwyn, Hereford.
Nov 7 1910

My dear Firapeel:
 Here is a card for *Thursday's* [10 November] rehearsal.
  Perpend!
No one is to be admitted on the *9th*.

but *your name* will be on a very attenuated list at the orch. door. Don't tell anybody this!
 Yours ever
 Reynart.

Atkins was thrilled by the rehearsal, after which Elgar handed him an invitation from Schuster to attend the special supper which he was giving in Elgar's honour after the concert.

The Philharmonic Society concert took place in the Queen's Hall. Elgar conducted, and in the first part his arrangement of the National Anthem was followed by Sterndale Bennett's Overture, *The Naiads*. Then came the Violin Concerto, with Kreisler giving the first performance. The second part consisted of the Symphony in A flat. The hall was crowded, and Elgar and Kreisler were repeatedly called back. The Symphony also received tremendous applause, and the audience would not let Elgar go.

22. OLD QUEEN STREET. S.W.

10th NOVEMBER. 1910.

Consommé à l'Indienne.

———

Filets de Sole à la Hut.

———

Culotte de Bœuf Braisée.

———

Poularde Farcie à la Kreisler.

———

Mousse Walkyrie.

After the concert they eventually found their way to 22, Old Queen Street. Reproduced here are the special menu, containing a quotation from the two opening bars of the concerto, and the 'E' table plan (overleaf).

Sir Adrian Boult, who was present at the supper, has kindly supplied the following information regarding some of his fellow guests. Sir Felix V. Schuster, always known as Bob, was a distant cousin of Frank Schuster, and his wife Lucy was an excellent amateur violinist, though she did not play at Frank's parties. Mrs Carl Derenburg, née Eibenschütz, a pianist, was a pupil of Brahms and of Clara Schumann. Enrique Fernandez Arbos, a violinist, had been a pupil of Joachim, and was now a well-known conductor. F. S. Kelly was a concert pianist, and Jacques Emile Blanche was a painter. Hugh Seymour Walpole was the writer of many novels, among them *The Cathedral*. Mrs Goetz was Muriel Foster before her marriage. Kennerley Rumford was Clara Butt's husband and accompanist.

Schuster had really thought of everything to please Elgar. The tables were laid out in the form of a large E, named after the three movements of the concerto and decorated with white heather.

210

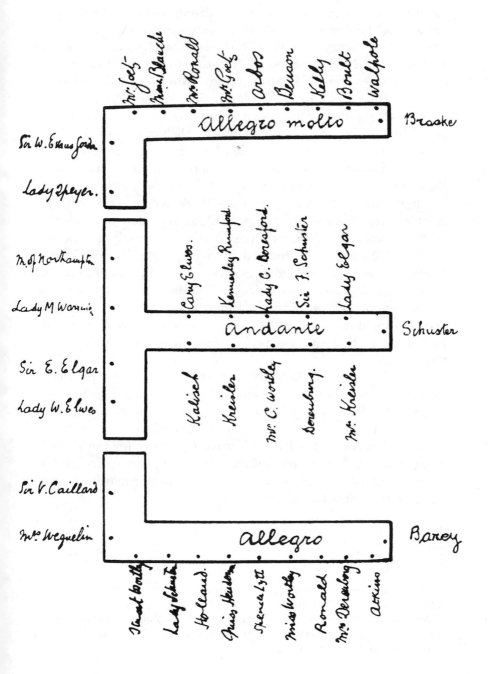

After the composer's health had been drunk, and that of Kreisler, a male voice choir appeared and sang the five part-songs comprising Op 45, *Part-Songs from the Greek Anthology*, which Elgar had written in 1902. This was not only a surprise for those assembled, but clearly also for the Elgars, and my father recalled the look of surprised pleasure on Elgar's face at that moment.

Atkins had for some time been wishing to discuss with Elgar the possibility of preparing jointly a new English edition of Bach's *St Matthew Passion*. On 24 November he went to stay at Plas Gwyn, and this visit was entirely devoted to a preliminary discussion on the work. Elgar stayed with my parents from 6 to 8 December, and much of 7 December was given up to work in connection with the *St Matthew Passion*. On the 8th Elgar attended the morning rehearsal and the afternoon concert of the recently augmented WOS, which had now changed its name to the Worcestershire Orchestral and Ladies Choral Society. The addition of voices to the orchestral players was welcome, because it greatly increased the repertoire for their concerts. Elgar, who was on the committee and had included a choral section in his earlier Worcestershire Philharmonic Society, was very interested in this new development.

Atkins had chosen a light but varied programme for the newly constituted society's first concert. This included Elgar's part-songs *Fly*, *Singing Bird* and *The Snow*, which Atkins had persuaded Elgar to conduct, to the delight of all.

On 13 December the Elgars left for Germany for the Krefeld Music Festival. Elgar was conducting his Symphony there, and on a later occasion told Atkins what a thrilling performance the large German orchestra had given.

[Plas Gwyn]
Dec 20 1910

My dear Firapeel:
    Just back—had a most triumphant time.
    Please thank Mrs. Atkins for her letter. The parcel for *E.W.I.A.* is a walking stick which is too long. I want you (if you think well) to open the parcel & get the stick cut down & the ferule replaced—not by your own inefficient hands but by an expert.
In haste,
Yours
Reynart.

8, College Yard, Worcester.
Dec 21st, 1910.

My dear Reynart,
    I will deal with the stick through some competent artificer. What joy it will give Wulstan. It was awfully kind of you to remember him. I hope the trip has done you a lot of good. Look out for me tomorrow, I am coming over [to Malvern] for the Troyte unveiling. I played the slow movement from the Vn Concerto on Saturday to a crowded Organ Recital congregation. (The place was thick with motors; really the town was *full* of them!) It went *finely*—I must throw modesty to the dogs as I am my own reporter—and sounded magnificent. People were enchanted and judging from the letters I have received and the things that have been said by word of mouth few things I have done have ever given so much pleasure. I wish you could have been there you would have approved.
With love to you both
Yours ever
I.A.A.

    I well remember Christmas, 1910, for I was given two presents which were to give me great pleasure for years to come. One was a large teddy bear, which joined the two smaller ones which had been given to me on the two previous Christmases. The other was the walking stick that Elgar had sent for me. I loved that stick, with its curved silver handle with my initials 'E.W.I.A. from E.E. 1910' engraved on it. I was always playing with it, and its silver handle bears many dents.

1911

The year started with great excitement for me, for on 2 January Elgar came to Worcester to visit my parents. Shortly after his arrival I was called down into the study to show Elgar the silver-topped stick that he had sent me as a Christmas present. I recall that he and my father and mother were there, and that I strutted round the room. I can see Elgar now, bending almost double to show me how to use the stick and how I should balance it so that I walked smoothly.
    On Friday 6 January, Atkins went over to Plas Gwyn in time for supper and stayed until the Monday.
    Elgar was hard at work on the first movement of the Second Symphony and Atkins was concentrating on the *St Matthew*

Passion. They had earlier agreed that Atkins would work on the revision of the words and Elgar on the music. After a long walk in the afternoon Elgar played over what he had so far written, and they then discussed the new edition of the *Passion*. On the Sunday Elgar was prostrated with one of his headaches during the morning but was more himself for the rest of the day. He was trying to complete the first movement before he had to go to London at the end of the week, where he was again conducting the Violin Concerto with Kreisler.

When Atkins saw him on 3 February, Elgar played over the first movement which was now complete. Atkins was thrilled. Elgar told him that he had finished it on 28 January, and played it over to Sinclair who had been wildly enthusiastic, the following day.

The next news from Elgar came in the following letter.

Plas Gwyn, Hereford.
[Written on 3 March]
March 4 1911

My dear Firapeel:
I am just leaving for London with the end of my work [Second Symphony]. I cannot tell you how really grieved I have been to have, perforce of circumstances, shut myself away from all friends for the last two months, & most of all from you but the work had to be done, or no roof over the heads of the family—alas! that my paynefulle purse so pryckylls me (spelling not guaranteed).
I hope to return from town on Monday or so & then to Bruxelles, & then the horrible U.S.A.tour. I *want* to see you very much indeed, & it is sad that the MS of the Symphony goes away without your words benedictory or maledictory.
It shan't happen again. Bless you.
Yours ever
E.E.
P.S. *Private* Carice is alas! ill in bed (rheumatism) with a nurse.

Elgar was going to Brussels to conduct his First Symphony on 12 March with the symphony orchestra which had been founded, and was managed, by Eugène Ysaÿe, the eminent Belgian violinist. Ysaÿe had taken the preceding rehearsals, and was so completely enthralled with the Symphony that he had decided to lead the orchestra himself, and after conducting an earlier item on the programme he brought in his violin and, to the amazement of the audience, took over the leader's position.

Elgar had been engaged for nearly a year to conduct six concerts in America and Canada, and now that the time had arrived was regretting this enforced absence from England. Atkins had made special efforts to have the *St Matthew Passion* text completed and ready for further discussion.

Plas Gwyn, Hereford.
Thursday [16 March 1911]

My dear Firapeel:
   Alas! I am at my wits' end. I cannot possibly come. I have an *awful chill* & am not allowed out at all. I doubt if I can go to America on Saturday it is too dreary & I cannot tell you how sorry I am to disappoint you after we had planned everything so well.
   The cold developed yesterday & I am an impossible wreck today—I *may* be well enough (as the wretched thing is at present confined to my *head*)—to leave on Saturday, but Canada hangs in the balance. I can say no more, only how desperately sorry I am to disappoint my friend.
Love
Reynart.
Private verb. sap. Muriel [Foster] is anxious to sing, I hear! Gerontius!

There was an important festival committee meeting the following week, and Atkins wrote to ask if Elgar could possibly attend; if not, would he express his views regarding certain possible alternative suggestions for the forthcoming programme.

[Plas Gwyn]
22 March 1911.

My dear Firapeel:
   I cannot possibly come over to the meeting, I wish I could. I am better & may start on Saturday (March 25th).
   I am allowed to get up now, so I try to scrawl a line in reply to yours—I would rather hear Verdi [*Requiem*] than Brahms, any day!
   Why not put the Symphony or Concerto in the Concert Hall & do Verdi?
   Also I wd prefer Mozart to either but there's the public. As to the Passion I don't see *how* my name is to come in unless I can do some expr. I return in May & shall be woefully busy till the end of June in London—with of course quiet days atwixt. I might even get a blank day (in town) in May & we cd do much—but that wd be too late I fear for anything. I am so

sorry to have been of so little use. Send me a line before Saturday an you can.

Yours ever

Reynart

I enclose a letter from Bax—a thing of his [*Festival Overture*] was done at the League.

Elgar was president of the Musical League, which had been formed to encourage and support performances of the works of contemporary British composers. Granville Bantock was largely responsible for its creation. Among the younger composers who had benefited were Arnold Bax, Havergal Brian, Balfour Gardiner, Joseph Holbrooke and Ralph Vaughan Williams.

Private   On Board the Cunard R.M.S. Mauretania.
        March 25 1911

My dear Atkins:

   I post this at Queenstown—it is understood that you agree to the terms proposed by Messrs. Novello for the performing fees of the Concerto & the Symphony. I agree to refund the amount of the performing fees—not, of course, their hiring fees, over which I have no control.

Yours ever,

Edwd. Elgar.

This is in reference to the Worcester Festival.

Elgar had generously made a private agreement with Atkins to forgo the performing fees for these compositions at the forthcoming festival, but it could only be done by Elgar refunding the fees, and hence this written confirmation.

With Elgar's preoccupation with the symphony and his visit to America Atkins had had to go ahead with the *Passion* on his own. It was progressing well and proofs were beginning to come in regularly, with corrections taking up much time. Knowing that Elgar was expected back early in May, Atkins had written telling him that the first proofs were ready for their joint inspection and required several decisions.

Hereford
12 May, 1911.

My dear Firapeel
  Yes! I am home & cannot breathe for work. So glad to get yours. I am here only until Sunday afternoon when I must go to town.
  Can you come over tomorrow afternoon, Saturday? & we could see the proofs.
                              In haste, yours ever,
                              Reynart.

  Atkins went over and found Elgar in the early stages of composing the *Coronation March*, Op 65. After playing over what he had written, they got down to the *St Matthew* proofs, and were able to settle the outstanding points.

  Coronation ceremonies and concerts would require frequent visits to London, and the Elgars had taken a lease on a house in Gloucester Place, Portman Square, from May to July. Elgar was planning to spend most of his time during this period in London. He was now rehearsing for the first performance of his Symphony No 2 in E flat, to be conducted by him on 24 May.

  Atkins went to London for the final rehearsal and the concert. He was deeply moved by the symphony, which received much applause, but he noted that, unlike the first performance of the First Symphony which had carried the whole audience with it, many people seemed to find the work difficult. He said that the performance of the symphony was excellent, but the ordinary music lover was not yet prepared for such a masterpiece.

  After the performance the Elgars gave a supper, and the guests included Sir Edgar and Lady Speyer, the Edward Speyers, the Stuart-Wortleys with their daughter Claire, Pippa, Sanford Terry, Atkins and Frank Schuster. It was a most delightful evening. The Elgars told Atkins all about a house in Netherhall Gardens, Hampstead, called 'Kelston', which Alice Stuart-Wortley had found. They said it was exactly what they had been looking for and that they were negotiating to buy it; this they did later and re-named it 'Severn House'.

  During early June more proofs of the *Passion* arrived and were corrected, and Atkins wrote to Elgar enclosing them and also referring to ideas for the Worcester Festival programme, especially regarding the Wednesday evening concert in the Public Hall. It had already been arranged that Elgar would conduct the

Second Symphony in the Cathedral on the Wednesday morning, and his Violin Concerto with Kreisler in the Cathedral on the Thursday evening, but Atkins now wanted Elgar, in addition, to conduct some work, possibly *Cockaigne*, in the Public Hall on the Wednesday evening.

75, Gloucester Place, Portman Square, W.
June 13 1911

My dear Firapeel:

I was glad to see your hand of write *and* the proof—I am woefully busy *to-day*—after this I hope for lucid moments. As to the evening concert, by *no* means put anything of mine in—there's no room & less reason!

I fear our projected party &c for my last festival must be abandoned. People cannot & will not come, alas! I shall probably come down alone for the day on which I am required.

I will have a good look at Bach as soon as possible & report thereon: at first sight it looks beautiful.

I hope all goes well with you—here we are either baked or frozen. I have been away for two Sundays & surrounding days—I ought to have said 'week-ends'. Now we are in the thick of coronation things & a free fight is on as I refused to go to the Abbey—I loathe a crowd even to crown a King. Apart from an orgy of dress, pageant & ball & court, London is very dull & things are anything but bright, I am sorry to say.

I must go now. More anon.

Yrs ever

Reynart.

75, Gloucester Place, Portman Square, W.
Sunday p.m. (and the first minute I have had)
[18 June 1911]

My dear Firapeel.

Alas! I am not helpful & fear I cannot be; but to-day I hope to read the Passion proof through.

I do not like your Concert programme at all! Why not do (yourself) Harty's 'Wild Geese', which is worth (surely) all the young stuff?

Do not do Cockaigne. Alice is writing to Mrs. Atkins about the house—it was too good of her to see about it—we cannot get together a party. I fear everybody seems to be going somewhere else. Mrs. Goetz [Muriel Foster] wd have sung for you.

I know of nothing new for orch which you wd thrill over but I may have missed possibilities—but I doubt it.

As to the markings in Bach. I detest brackets & so do you. Why not give a specimen of the types in yr. introduction & simply say,

𝄢   Bach's marking

𝄢   Editors' ,,   [Atkins   adopted   this course]. Then this does not account for

$\longleftarrow$ $\longrightarrow$ $>$ &c

so where are we? But anyone really interested can compare with the original.

Yours ever
Reynart.

I do not like (*Motet*)—what meaneth it really? But put it if you like. Chorus *is* dull and undescriptive you *have* bowels!

In the draft programme Elgar's *Go, Song of Mine*, Op 57, down for the Tuesday evening, to be conducted by Atkins, was described as a 'Motet for Six Voices'. Despite Elgar's objection the words appeared in the final programme, since Atkins could find no suitable alternative.

More proofs, including the title page of the *St Matthew*, had arrived, and Atkins sent a set to Elgar.

75, Gloucester Place, Portman Square, W.
June 20 1911

My dear Firapeel:
Certainly out with the prefix. [Omission of his title from the title page] I have had no moment yet to read the proof! Is it possible to work in town. I trow not.

Yrs ever
Reynart.

You will have seen the latest O.M. which will please you. [Elgar's OM was in the Honours List published on June 20.]
P.S. I fear the 28th & 29th are pretty deeply involved. I have a rehearsal at St. Paul's at 6 p.m. and the service is at 12 on the 29th. I'll see what I can do.

8, College Yard, Worcester.
June 22 1911

My dear Reynart,
Warmest congratulations on the O of M.
It *is* a great distinction and we all share to some extent in the honour.
I should like to come to your rehearsal at St. Paul's at 6 p.m. on Wednesday if it were possible. But perhaps you will be suggesting some other time.

Yours ever
I.A.A.

Atkins attended the rehearsal in St Paul's on Wednesday, 28 June, and was thrilled with the *Coronation March*. Elgar, who had Alice Stuart-Wortley with him, conducted but was clearly not well and complained of headaches.

On his return home Atkins found a letter from Novello's regarding cash or royalty payments on the *St Matthew Passion*. He sent this on to Elgar for his advice.

75, Gloucester Place, Portman Square, W.
Monday [3 July 1911]

My dear Firapeel:
I have been laid up since I saw you at St. Paul's (liver) better now &, just in, I find yr letter. I return Messrs. N's letter. I have done so little in the matter (& that little out of friendship for you!) that I cannot say much about figures. *I leave it to you.* I think a royalty for you wd be best but if my name was or is worth anything (which I gravely doubt) Messrs. N. might be disposed to give me something down, leaving the royalty to you.
In haste
Yrs ever
Reynart.
The above is only a suggestion. I hope to get down to Worcester for a day this week—perhaps.

Private
75, Gloucester Place, Portman Square, W.
July 11 1911

My dear Firapeel:
I am sorry that you shd not have known *first* about the house at Worcester, but we warned Terry, as he has been with us several times.

I have been unable to come down owing to several minor, teasing but necessary things & am still held here till—so far as I see now—to the end of next week.

We cannot possibly manage to take a house at Worcester. Terry is the only one of our party available & I cannot afford it. I have suddenly to make arrangements for the 'sustentation' of one of the family entirely (*probably a separate home with* NURSE). As it is I lose about one *hundred* pounds by coming at all! So I will do my best to come over for the performances & get through them with an extremely heavy heart. The whole question is one of finance, not necy to be entered upon here.
Ever yours
Reynart
You know that the festival was the one pleasure of the year I always looked forward to & you can guess how keenly I feel the situation.

(*above left*) Professor S.S. Sanford, Elgar and Sinclair in Sinclair's garden, Hereford, July 1906 (*By Courtesy of Henry Sanford*)

(*above right*) Elgar and Carice, Plas Gwyn, Hereford, July 1906

(*left*) Elgar and S.S. Sanford outside the Green Dragon Hotel, Hereford, July 1906 (see page 151)

Elgar's wife and daughter
photographed by May Grafton
in 1907: Alice in the drawing
room at Plas Gwyn. Note the
richly carved Indian table and
chair

Carice with Peter Rabbit

Elgar, Carice and Alice on the steps of Plas Gwyn, Hereford on 20 September 1910. Photographed by P.C. Hull

Atkins in his study, July 1908. The photograph was taken at the time of the Combined Rehearsals for the Three Choirs Festival at Worcester that year

Elgar's hobbies included photography and chemistry, and, characteristically, in both he reached professional standards. This photograph, taken by his niece, May Grafton, shows him in the laboratory he had created out of a shed at Plas Gwyn, which he called 'The Ark'. He patented an apparatus for making sulphurated hydrogen which was in use in school laboratories for many years

Elgar had evidently forgotten that he had already told Atkins about the house problem. He was unhappy at this time about his financial arrangements with Novello's, and he had written giving them a year's notice to terminate the existing agreement. His sister Dot, who was Mother Superior of a Dominican convent in Stroud, was very ill and was expecting to have an operation, after which constant nursing beyond the facilities at the convent might be necessary. Fortunately this contingency did not arise.

8, College Yard, Worcester.
July 14th, 1911.

My dear Reynart,
    I am truly sorry to hear of the reasons which make it impossible for you to stay here. It is a very great loss to us and throws a first shadow upon the Festival, but I know that you will sadly miss being amongst it all and I extract what comfort I can from the knowledge.
    We had a fine rehearsal of 'Go, song of mine'. That piece grows greater with every hearing. It must have been written in blood. We must certainly put it with your very greatest music. Tears are a poor tribute, but you exact them always with your best music, and all because you bring another world before one. You do see and hear wonderful things!
    Yes, the chorus sang it finely. I wish you had been there.
                        Yours ever,
                        I.A.A.
Tell me if you do not wish the addition I now make in addressing envelopes.

    Atkins had added 'OM' before Elgar's Mus Doc, LL D on the envelope, and was asking if he wished his name to be printed in the list of stewards in the festival programme with or without the degrees.
    On receipt of his letter Elgar had wired that they might be able to take the Worcester house after all. Was it still unlet? Atkins had wired back that it was but that others were interested, and he was trying to get a first refusal.

75, Gloucester Place, Portman Square, W.
July 17 1911

My dear Firapeel:
    Awful haste! Your wire has come & we wait anxiously your letter to say if the house is to be had still. We have wired to Terry, telling him to hold his hand regarding taking lodgings. Please keep the new address which is

quite correct, & *please* have O.M. put *first* in the list of Stewards. It is, of course, not used when I am a performer (Conductor). Worcester people (save you!) seem to have small notion of the glory of the O.M. I was marshalled correctly at Court & at the Investiture *above* the G.C.M.G. & G.C.V.O. (the highest Lord Beauchamp can go!)—next G.C.B. in fact. Such things as K.C.B.'s &c are *very cheap* it seems beside O.M. verb. sap.

I hope all will be arranged. Love,

Yours ever
Reynart.

The Elgars were able to rent 'Castle House', College Green, for the festival week.

Atkins was doubtful as to what Elgar meant about 'first' in the list of stewards. Did he, because of the OM, want to be placed out of alphabetical order as far as the Knights were concerned, or did he simply mean that 'OM' should come first after his name, as Atkins had intended?

75, Gloucester Place, Portman Square, W.
July 19 1911

My dear Firapeel:

Heavens! I only want O.M. put first after my name—don't alter the position of my name at all, at all.

As to the Concert. I don't see *what* there is to do. I can think of nothing suitable.

I think the new Coronation March will be available but it wd be best in the Cathedral—it wants organ of course—failing anything else, wd it do for the Concert—if ready?

In haste—packing up
Yrs ever
Reynart

Elgar returned to Plas Gwyn on 26 July, and on the 28th Atkins went over to Hereford in the morning with rough proofs of the Preface for the *Passion*.

It was this summer that my parents took me on my only visit to Plas Gwyn, and it most probably was on this occasion. We drove from the station to the house. I well remember being impressed by the stone steps from the drive up to the front door. Inside the hall we were met by the Elgars and taken into his study, where Elgar spent a little time talking to me and taking me out on to the veranda to see the sundial in the garden below. We left my father in the study with Elgar, and after spending a few minutes with Alice in the drawing room, where I was shown the richly carved Indian furniture, my mother took me through the fields and along the river bank to a house near the cathedral where we had lunch with 'The Duchess' and Miss Thomas. I was sent to rest for the afternoon, and we then went to tea with Sinclair and shortly afterwards caught a train back to Worcester.

My father and mother left for Southern Germany and Austria on 31 July for about a fortnight. The following letter awaited their return.

Plas Gwyn, Hereford.
Sunday [30 July 1911]

My dear Firapeel
I'm not well. selah. [heatwave] I have suggested some things. Parentheses must go generally—reserving them for (Ex. ____) &c. In *Libretto* section I opine that 'it' is correct, not the queried *them*.

The whole thing wants *closing up* the paragraphs must not be divided but *is* it to be *preface* & not *note* after the music.

Knock out all the capitals you can.
Love
Welcome back
from Reynart
who is ill.

While Atkins was in Germany he had visited the walled town of Rothenburg-on-Tauber, and had been in the Town Square at noon, where, after the *Rathaus* clock had finished striking, a brass band had played a hymn from the top of the church tower. This had given him an idea for introducing the first performance of the Elgar—Atkins edition of the *St Matthew Passion*, by playing before each part a Bach chorale from the top of the cathedral tower. The more he thought about it the better the idea seemed, and he was convinced that Elgar would instantly see its possibilities and agree to orchestrate the chorales for brass instruments. The chorales he had in mind were 'O Man bemoan thy grievous sin', and 'O Sacred Head Surrounded'. He accordingly sent a letter to Plas Gwyn to await Elgar's return.

Hereford
Sep 4 [1911]

My dear Firapeel:

By'r lakin a fine idea—but will the men play?—I trow not. They will expect a holiday. Let me know if you really mean to do it. The 'score' is not easy without Horns.

I travel up on Wednesday.

Yrs ever
Reynart

This letter was sent to Atkins in London, where he was staying for rehearsals in the St Andrew's Hall. On receipt of Elgar's letter Atkins discussed his idea of the tower music with the brass players, and inspired them with his own enthusiasm. On Elgar's arrival in the hall he was able to tell him that the players had agreed, and after the rehearsal Elgar made the necessary score, and parts were ready for try-out at the Worcester rehearsals. The front page of the manuscript score with Elgar's notes is reproduced here.

The Elgars moved into 'Castle House' on 9 September. Elgar was in his usual festival mood, and had prepared another jape, this time in the form of a handbill entitled 'Side Shows', which he circulated widely among his friends on the opening day. The allusions were to well-known public figures, festival personalities and members of the Elgars' house party. Most of them will be obvious, but perhaps a few need explanation.

'Burning of Heretics' refers indirectly to Granville Bantock, who was conducting his new work, *Overture to a Greek Tragedy* at the festival. Bantock was a co-founder of the STP Society, and signed himself the 'Arch Heretic' in their initiation ceremonies.

'Dr Elizabeth Pastoral' was Dr Herbert Brewer, the organist of Gloucester Cathedral, whose *Two Pastorals*, dealing with Elizabethan times, were being performed.

There had been a recent railway strike, with an orderly procession of banners and marching round 'Pitchcroft', a local open space by the river.

Canon J. M. Wilson, the cathedral librarian and a great authority on the architecture and history of the cathedral, had recently written an article about the probable origins of a stone coffin found during the cathedral restorations.

The local papers had reported the story of a fisherman who had caught a perch, which on being cleaned was found to have swallowed a gold ring.

St Kentigern, better known as St Mungo, lived about 518 to 603, and had ascribed to him a number of miracles, including the resuscitation of St Serf's favourite robin after it had been cooked in a pie, but, alas, with no golden treasure.

A town house in Worcester had recently been bought for the Bishop, whose main residence was Hartlebury Castle, which was some miles outside the city.

'Bearpit in College Yard'—archaeological excavations were in progress outside the north side of the cathedral.

Worcester was gayer than ever before, with coronation decorations adding to the usual festival flags. The city and the county houses were full of guests, including royalty, and there was a festive mood over everything.

The tower music had been well publicised, and the idea had captured the public imagination. The 1911 Three Choirs Festival was generally recognised to be the finest Worcester meeting to

WORCESTER FESTIVAL, 1911.

SIDE SHOWS

(By permission of Mr. Queer Hardie, M.P., and in Contemptuous Defiance of the Dean and Chapter).

Monday, 12th September, LECTURE in the Commandery by the O.M., entitled:

"Dyspeptic Hagiology Biologically Considered and Quantitatively Analysed."

Lie-m-Light Illustrations.

"Advertising Quartets" by the Beecham Guinea Orchestra of Coloured Specialists and the Holloway Knockabouts.

Tuesday, 13th September. Popular Day.

BURNING OF HERETICS

(Supply not guaranteed; every endeavour will be made to procure fresh imitations).

FREQUENT PARACHUTE DESCENTS

from the Cathedral Tower by Mrs. Worthington and the Trombones of the Orchestra.

SUMMER SPORTS in the Close (conducted by DR. ELIZABETH PASTORAL).

STRIKE MEETING of Composers for a Four-hours' Day and a British Pitch.

MOONLIGHT ASSAULT on the Elgar Tower by the Blacklegs of the Close.

Thereafter minions will raise "L" to the B(d)gar Statue.

Wednesday, 13th September.

GREAT ARSON ACT.

Firing of a Nunnery previously selected by a Committee of blinded Early Perp. Experts. The O.M. will fire the first faggot at Curfew.

Thursday, 14th September.

MIRACULOUS INTERLUDE

MISS GRAFTON (from Italy, where she has been studying the Science) will sail in a stone coffin (courteously provided by Canon Wilson, who will later on perish at the stake) from the Bridge to the Ferry. *En route* she will jerk a miracle selected by the Commissary of Oaths from a richly-assorted and old-landed parcel. The O.M., dibbling from the stern of the cist with a pig-tailed worm will repeatedly hook poly-carp, laughing daces, and gold-ring-containing perch, thereby administering a considerable slosh in the jaw to St. Mungo, who is expected to be present and make a few remarks for publication (or otherwise).

Friday, 15th September.

GRAND CONCLUDING ECCLESIASTICAL SCENA.

The Bishop of the Diocese, seizing the opportunity to procure a residence in the City, will (preceded by his Examining Chaplain) enter a newly-excavated Bear Pit in College Yard. Buns will be retailed by the Dean and Members of the Chapter at an easy rate.

CONCLUDING FIREWORK DISPLAY by the Minor Canons, Composers, and Prophets.

LEICESTER, TYP., WORCESTER.

date, and what a feast of music it was. The programme naturally had a strong coronation flavour. Parry conducted his *Coronation Te Deum*, Elgar his new *Coronation March*, and Wagner's *Kaisermarsch* was included in the opening service. Works specially written for the festival and conducted by their composers included Granville Bantock's *Overture to a Greek Tragedy*, Walford Davies' *Sayings of Christ*, W. H. Reed's *Variations for String Orchestra* and Vaughan Williams' *Five Mystical Songs*.

Elgar conducted his Symphony in E flat and the Violin Concerto, with Fritz Kreisler as soloist.

The playing of Elgar's orchestration of the two Bach chorales from the Cathedral tower was the sensation of the festival, and for many years they introduced the performances of the *St Matthew Passion* at Three Choirs Festivals. The great achievement of the brass players and the physical effort of climbing to the top of the Cathedral tower before they played was fully appreciated by all concerned and, at Elgar's suggestion, a special letter bearing the signatures of many prominent musicians was sent to them.

My own recollections of this festival were naturally of a more trivial nature—Elgar and Billy Reed playing trains with me and helping me to fly a captive clockwork aeroplane which they had given me. I say 'helping me' fly the aeroplane, but in fact they were so thrilled with it themselves that I was soon only a spectator. They both had a genius for making children happy.

Other memories I have from that festival are of Kreisler playing the Violin Concerto at a rehearsal, and of him at one of the lunches which my parents used to give in a tent in our garden. I can still hear my mother asking him if he would like some more, and his turning round and saying, '*Nein, nein*, I am vull, vull—I cannot!'

During the week I had heard great excitement among our house-party about some event to take place on the Cathedral tower, and could it and would it come off? Everybody was far too busy to explain it to me, but Billy, who was staying with us, told me on the day to be at the window of my nursery which was on the third floor, and listen. I heard a brass band playing from the top of the Cathedral tower, and I saw crowds of people, and saw the smiles of joy on the faces of Elgar and my father. It *had* come off!

The festival over, the house parties were breaking up and everybody was getting ready to go away. Sanford Terry had been with the Elgars at 'Castle House' and was going back to stay at Plas

Gwyn. Elgar had planned a final 'jape' with him, a 'Flight from Worcester'. They were full of it, and Elgar told my father that they planned to leave the train at Great Malvern, hire a donkey and a small horse (Terry was far too heavy for a donkey), which were always available on the lower slopes of the Worcestershire Beacon, and ride the whole length of the Malvern Hills, including the Herefordshire Beacon. They would then rejoin a later train to Hereford from either Malvern Wells or Colwall. The route hardly coincided with Charles II's flight after the Battle of Worcester, but Elgar could not resist the title for their journey. My parents took me to Church Stretton for a short holiday immediately after the festival, and while we were there Sanford Terry wrote with a full account of their joyful and amusing journey, adding that Elgar had a photograph which my father must insist on seeing (see p. 259).

Hereford Oct 4 1911

My dear Firapeel:
   I hope you are now thoroughly rested & happy in the retrospect—it *was* good at Worcester, but since the Exodus—on ass & horse—I had an awful chill, since when troubles innumerable. I have recd no acct of the fees & do not know how things stand regarding our private arrgt [letter of 25 March]. Have Novellos been paid yet?
   I have to go to town on Saturday: send a line here—the LAST to this address.
Yrs ever
E.E.
I am not sure if the photo (Terry says you want one) is reproducible. I have *one* and am enquiring for further copies.

   Elgar left Plas Gwyn on 7 October for London, and did not return to it. Alice remained clearing up and joined him later. There were difficulties in getting into 'Severn House', but up to Christmas London was Elgar's main base. He had a number of conducting engagements, however, with the London Symphony Orchestra and others, all over the country, as well as two concerts in Turin.

Langham Hotel
Nov 14 1911

My dear Firapeel:
   Will you let me know at once what you want done about those performing fees at the festival.

I wrote to Novellos enquiring, as I had heard nothing from anyone about it: now I learn (this morning) that the bill has been sent in to Worcester & paid—I do not know how much was charged—N. did not tell me. I can of course find out—they do not render an account of their stewardship frequently & that is how the matter has dropped *pro. tem.*

Let me hear how & to whom I am indebted.

In haste (I wrote yesterday),
Yrs ever
Reynart

The Worcester Festival had been a financial as well as an artistic success, and Atkins, despite their private agreement, had arranged that Elgar was *not* to forgo his performing fees.

Address   Langham
Nov 16 1911

My dear Firapeel

Glad to hear of you: all right about the fees: I only wanted to carry out our private plot agreeably to our understanding. Selah!

As to our move: it still hangs fire & will not take place just yet: delighted to hear your news & will let you know if anything happens worthy of chronicle.

The L.S.O. is in fine form. I am wofully busy. Love to you & I hope that Mrs. Atkins & the boy are well.

Ever yours
Reynart.

Atkins wrote with Worcester news and wishing the Elgars great happiness in their new home.

The Athenaeum, Pall Mall, S.W.
Dec 14 1911

My dear Firapeel:

I was overjoyed to get your letter. I am not very well & my rambles about the earth are only moderately satisfactory. I should have written long ago but have been waiting day to day to be able to tell you we are 'in'—but we are not 'in' yet owing to all sorts of things.

My love to you all
Yours ever
Reynart.

PART 5
1912–1919

1912

On 1 January the Elgars moved into 'Severn House', the first house that they had bought. On a later occasion Elgar was to tell Atkins how much that day had meant to them both—a dream come true, a house of their very own. Admittedly, it was heavily mortgaged and was always to involve them in financial problems, but it was a new and wonderful experience. Elgar had lived with his parents in the rooms above his father's music shop, and then in the homes of his two older married sisters, one after the other, until he married. Since their marriage they had always been in rented houses.

Severn House, 42, Netherhall Gardens, Hampstead, N.W.
Jan 11 1912

My dear Firapeel:
   My love to you & yours after a long silence, at least it seems long to me. We are in 'roughly' now, & if you are in town wd love to see you—but we are not at all settled to receive company such as visitors & acquaintances, but an old friend wd forgive the vagaries of furniture, &c &c. It is very lovely here & *so quiet*—quieter at night (& by day also) than Hereford.
   I am fearfully busy & working well. [*Crown of India*, Op 66] I have been really very ill since Worcester Festival & am only beginning to eat again— I have quite given up smoking! No taste for it at all. These high matters must be discussed when you come—when are you coming?
                    Ever thine
                    Reynart.

This letter was forwarded to Westmorland, where we were all three staying with Henry Welch and his wife, Nellie, who was an old friend of my mother's. Leck Hall was to become our normal post-Christmas holiday.

The Palace Hotel, Edinburgh.
Sunday [4 February 1912].

Firapeel:
   In grim Edina I find your thoughtless note. To think that I walk from one kingdom to another & the ground shakes not in Vigorn! I am here, to be precise, with the [London] Sym. Orch.
   I shall be home on Thursday & will report. It is cold, belike it freezeth, but the deponent sitteth by ye fire in a coat which was once Isegrim's [The

Wolf in *Reynart the Foxe*] but which a connynge merchant disposed of as something sable & precious. Also I have the natural fur of
                                Reynart
and your affection which is also warmful.

The second sentence refers to the fact that after Richter, who had been the Principal Conductor of the London Symphony Orchestra for some years, had announced in January 1911 that he wished to retire at the end of the season, the members of the orchestra had unanimously invited Elgar to succeed him. The Edinburgh concert was the last but one of a series of six provincial concerts arranged by Percy Harrison which Elgar conducted with the LSO during the 1911–12 season. On his return to London he was fully occupied with the music *Crown of India* for the patriotic masque devised by Henry Hamilton which Oswald Stoll was putting on in the Coliseum in honour of the King's visit to India.

Atkins was rehearsing for the WFCS performance of *King Olaf*, to be given on 20 February, and had written reminding Elgar of the concert.

Severn House, 42, Netherhall Gardens, Hampstead, N.W.
Thursday [29 February 1912]

My dear Firapeel:
    I have been dreadfully overworked & no moment for anything. I wrote out a telegram for you on the 'Olaf' night but it got overlooked. So you had no word to my great regret. Navarro wrote to me about their enjoyment of it. [Navarro's wife was Mary Anderson, the actress.]
    I am hard at work at the Masque [*Crown of India*] which shapes well— do tell me if you are coming up any time. I have had no time to look at our house, but there is no reason you should not anyhow. My love to you,
                                Reynart.

The first performance of the *Crown of India* Masque took place on 11 March at the London Coliseum. There were two performances each day during the run, and Elgar conducted all of them.
    It was not until 21 April that Atkins was able to visit 'Severn House'. When he arrived he found May Grafton and Troyte Griffith there. Troyte was organising the fitting up of a library for Elgar, for which he was designing special bookcases. Elgar was having serious ear trouble and was rather depressed, but soon cheered up. They toured the house and garden, about which Alice

was most enthusiastic. Elgar had so far had very little time to give to detailed planning, but they both had many ideas for the future.

Since the Elgars had moved into 'Severn House' Elgar was again working at high level despite his ear trouble, and he hinted at a larger work to come. Was he already thinking about *Falstaff*, Op 68, not produced until 1913, or (more likely) The *Music Makers*, Op 69? Atkins was never clear on this point, but the next letter suggests strongly that it was the latter.

Severn House, 42, Netherhall Gardens, Hampstead, N.W.
June 23 1912

My dear Firapeel:
How are you & how goes everything? I am fearfully busy. I do not go out at all. The Ode [*Music Makers*] is finishing for the printer & alas! you have not seen it—which to me is sad & sorrowful. And the new Anthem [*Great is the Lord*, Op 67] with a real pedal part—this you shall see very soon.
Are you coming up? The new 'library' is finished & is soul-satisfying—austere & solid—'a cluse'. I want you to bless it soon.
Further than this I have no news & only want to know of you & your goings on—I hope they be all pleasant & successful.
My love to you
Reynart.

8, College Yard, Worcester.
July 7, 1912.

My dear Reynart,
Thank you immensely for the copy of the anthem. It *is* gorgeous. I played it over to my [choir] boys and they loved it and their keenness was good to see.
I made a sort of running transcription of it as I went along (with fine effect!) and it sounded great. When the Kings were assembled they really *were* amazed *and* dismayed. I'm longing to hear it done—we shall do it early next term (there is no time to get it up before the end of term).
It really is splendid music and some of the middle section fairly blazes, the pedal part cunning to a degree.
I do wish we could find excuse in our church for occasional big services.
With us a King must die, or a new one spring into life, before we allow ourselves to be stirred into a stirring service.
The 48th Psalm would have done grandly for a service such as we got together for the Coronation.
However we must content ourselves with a full choir performance.
The simple greatness of the end is you all over.

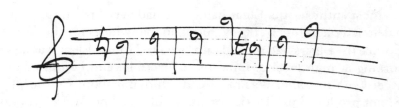

Where do you get these haunting phrases from?

Mind. I am to see an early copy of the ode [*Music Makers*] and I look for gorgeous music, self-asserting and daring.

Much love and once again thanks for the psalm.

Yours ever
I.A.A.

At the beginning of August all three of us had gone on holiday to St Leonards-on-Sea. Elgar had wired asking my father to help him with the proofs of the *Music Makers*, but the wire had not been sent on. My mother, shortly after our arrival, had gone down with pneumonia and was confined to bed. My father had written to Elgar telling him the news. The Elgars had themselves gone away for a few days and there was delay in forwarding my father's letter.

Little Langleys, Steep, Petersfield, Hants.
Tuesday [20 August 1912]

My dear Firapeel:

I am so sorry to hear that Mrs. Atkins is ill & grieved for your anxiety. I hope all will be well very soon. I thought you were away as I sent a telegram some time back, asking if you could look at proofs, but I had no reply, so the thing is so far advanced that copies will be ready soon & I will send. The orchestration also is concluded so I can rest. [This refers to the *Music Makers* full score.] I have been laid up with gout & the weather is depressing.

Write to Severn House & it will be sent on. I do not know what I shall do next. My movements depend on the weather.

Love & good wishes
Yours ever
Reynart.

Elgar's continued absence from London prevented him sending the proofs of the *Music Makers* to Atkins.

Severn House, 42, Netherhall Gardens, Hampstead, N.W.
Augt 24 1912

My dear Firapeel
    I am so very glad all goes well: best wishes. We are held up by the weather—intended to pass thro' London, but it is really of no use to go anywhere!
Love,
Reynart.
Sorry about the proofs—all printed now, alas!

    On 29 August Elgar went to Hereford for the Massed Rehearsal of *Gerontius*, which this year he was conducting, although it was being performed in the Anglican Church form as agreed between Atkins and Newman's executor, Father Neville, for the Worcester Festival of 1902. Up to now the 1902 performance had been the only one in this form which Elgar himself had conducted.

    The Elgars did not have a house-party this year but stayed at the Castle Pool Hotel. I remember this festival well, because my parents, at Sinclair's invitation, took me to some of the rehearsals, and I was very proud to be included in an official photograph of the cathedral organists, who that year had held their conference in Hereford so that they could attend the festival.

    On 1 October Atkins went over to Birmingham for the first performance of *The Music Makers*, which was conducted by Elgar with Muriel Foster as the soloist. She was in magnificent form, as were the chorus and orchestra, and my father told me that it was one of the best performances that he had heard at any Birmingham Triennial Festival. The concert was, however, made even more memorable for him, for in the second part Sibelius conducted the first performance of his Symphony No 4 in A minor, Op 63. My father told me that this performance started for him his intense interest in the Finnish composer's work, which was to remain with him all his life.

    Atkins' rehearsals for two Worcester concerts were going well. *The Music Makers* and Coleridge-Taylor's *Hiawatha's Wedding Feast* were the main items in the WFCS concert on 26 November, and Atkins thought that it would be worth trying to persuade Elgar to come down and conduct his work. He accordingly wrote early in November.

Severn House, 42, Netherhall Gardens, Hampstead, N.W.
Nov 10 1912

My dear Firapeel:
   I have been away & arrived home yesterday & find your letter. I fear it is
not possible for me to come, I am so much engaged but my heart & good
wishes are with you all the time.
   Are you ever coming up—I have no news as I have been having a sort of
holiday—which means resting from music & working harder than ever on
other things.

My love to you
Yours ever & ever
Edward Elgar
which is Reynart ye Foxe.

The Athenaeum, Pall Mall, S.W.
Nov 28 [1912]

My dear Firapeel
   I hope all went well on Tuesday [the WFCS performance of *Music
Makers*]. I had a wild thought that I wd run down & look at you—but it
could not be. I hope I may see you soon: if the weather is decent I may get
a day off before Christmas.

Love to you
Yours ever
Reynart

Severn House, Hampstead, N.W.
Dec 24 1912

My dear Firapeel:
   All good wishes for the New Year. I was just finding these sketches
when your song arrived. [*The Virgin's Lullaby*] It looks lovely.
   My love to you all. We shall be here & anxious to see you all any time.

Love
Reynart.

Elgar enclosed two pages from the sketch book he had used for *The
Music Makers*. The first gave the Nimrod theme from one bar after
figure 52 for eleven bars. The second was the ten bars starting at
No 15.

1.

Sent to me   Dec. 24. 1912

2.

1913

At the beginning of January my parents took me to London for our usual week of theatres and shopping. My father took the opportunity of visiting the Elgars at 'Severn House'. Elgar was not well, and hoped to go to stay with the Edward Speyers at Ridgehurst and at 'The Hut' for a change. He could not be far from London then, but he said that they hoped to go to Italy at the end of the month.

Elgar sent a postcard from Naples on 10 February and another from Rome on the 17th. He returned to 'Severn House' on 23 February, but was still unwell and restless. Soon after he went away to Llandrindod Wells and stayed there until mid-March.

Meanwhile Atkins was fully engaged in Worcester. In May he was going to adjudicate at a musical competitive festival in Aberdeen organised by Sanford Terry.

Severn House, Hampstead, N.W.
May 13 1913

My dear Firapeel:
It is ages since I have heard of you & yours. I have been ghastly unwell & am not much better now—but all things ceased with me. I have just recd from dear [Sanford] Terry his goodly book of the festival & you are going, I see, to help in it all. Give my love to him & let me know how you fare, and before this send me word how you are, & all news.
I have tried many things & much—Italy, Wales, Worcestershire & divers other environments but I am sped. Anyhow I love you.
Goodbye,
Yrs ever
Reynart.

Elgar continued in poor health and in a depressed state throughout the spring and summer, though he did rally from time to time when he went on with *Falstaff*. It was finished in August.

Early in June Atkins received news from him of Pippa's very serious illness, and later of her death (8 June). This was a tragedy for the Elgars and a great loss for the Atkins and her other friends.

This August was a memorable time for me, for my parents took me to Germany and Austria with them. I can see now the two onion-shaped towers on Munich Cathedral, and the outside timbered hotel in Garmisch-Partenkirchen, where we spent several days. I remember our breakfasts in the hot sunshine outside the dining-room, and how frightened I was with the wasps which settled on the cherry jam and on our food, and had to be shooed away for every mouthful. My father showed me some of the places associated with *From the Bavarian Highlands*, and I recall our walks through the woods, our visits to the Ettal monastery, the open charabanc trips to the lakes of Starnberg and other beauty spots, the railway journeys over the mountains into Innsbruck and Austria, and the villages with their brightly painted houses.

Elgar came on 3 September for the *St Matthew Passion* rehearsal in London. Sanford Terry was there. After the rehearsal Atkins dined at Severn House and played billiards with Elgar. Over the meal he learnt that the Elgars had stayed near Penmaenmawr on the North Wales coast, from 5 August until 1 September. They had not liked the place, but it had enabled Elgar to finish *Falstaff*, deal with the proofs, and write his masterly analysis of Falstaff's character which every listener should read if he is to understand fully the subtleties of Elgar's score. They told Atkins that this year they would be staying outside Gloucester for the festival, and Elgar said that he would miss being in the cathedral close atmosphere.

The highlight of the 1913 Gloucester Festival was the first performance of Saint-Saëns' new oratorio *The Promised Land*, conducted by the composer. Elgar was represented by *Gerontius* and the Second Symphony, which he conducted, and the 1911 *Coronation March* conducted by Brewer at the opening service.

Langham Hotel, London.
Tuesday [16 September 1913]

My dear Firapeel
I am flying thro' this wilderness—let me know if you can be in town next week [Leeds rehearsals] Falstaff, *Monday morning*, Sep 22. I'll send you a ticket—only let me know.
The Hut
Bray
BERKS
I hope you are all well & rested after your heavy week. My family is dispersed *pro.tem.* but we gather together again in a few days.
My love
Ever yours
Reynart.

The Hut
Thursday [18 September 1913]

My dear Firapeel:
   Here are two cards: bless you [of admission to *Falstaff* rehearsals]. I am asking Novellos to let you have a proof of min score if possible—I have nothing but what dire necessity requires or I wd shed leaves on you.
                    yours ever
                    Reynart.

September 1913 was to mark another starting point in my life, for I became a probationer-chorister at Worcester Cathedral, and a day boy at the choir school. Rehearsals and services were to be my background for the next 7 years. The experience gained as a chorister, where perfection must be the constant aim, was to influence my whole life.

The conducting at the 1913 Leeds Triennial Festival, 1–4 October, was shared between Nikisch, Elgar and Hugh Allen, and the new works were Elgar's *Falstaff*, Hamilton Harty's *Mystic Trumpeter*, Butterworth's *Shropshire Lad*, and Basil Harwood's *On a May Morning*. Atkins wanted to hear all these new works, and arranged to be at most of the festival. Elgar had gone to Leeds on 26 September, and from there on 29 September he posted to Atkins a copy of the miniature full score of *Falstaff*, inscribed and dated with a characteristic note.

The intention clearly was that Atkins would have time to study the score carefully before they met in Leeds. They must also have had an opportunity in Leeds of going through the score together before the performance, because a number of manuscript descriptions of Falstaff in varying moods and of other characters have been added against the bars concerned, with a note in Atkins' handwriting that the notes contain the substance of information given to him by Elgar at that time.

The programme for the 2 October concert, which was conducted by Elgar, included Bantock's *Dante and Beatrice*, Boito's Prologue to *Mefistofele*, Elgar's *Falstaff*, and ended with Harty's *Mystic Trumpeter*, conducted by the composer. The orchestra obviously liked *Falstaff*, which received much applause, but my father told me that, despite the excellent programme notes, it was evident that much of the subtle characterisation could not be taken in at first hearing.

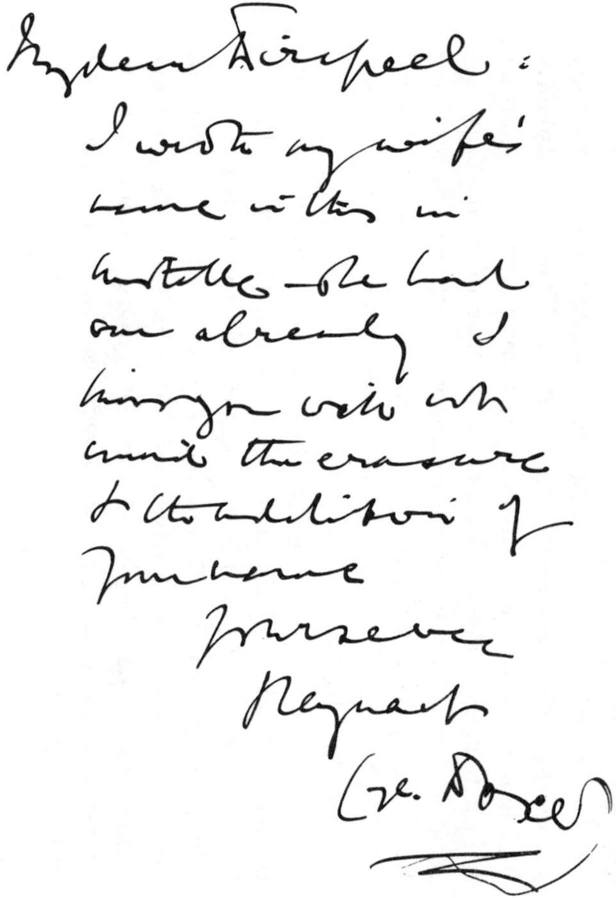
My dear Firapeel:
I wrote my wife's
name in this in
... — she had
one already &
bring you ...
... the erasure
& the addition of
your name
Yours ever
Reynart

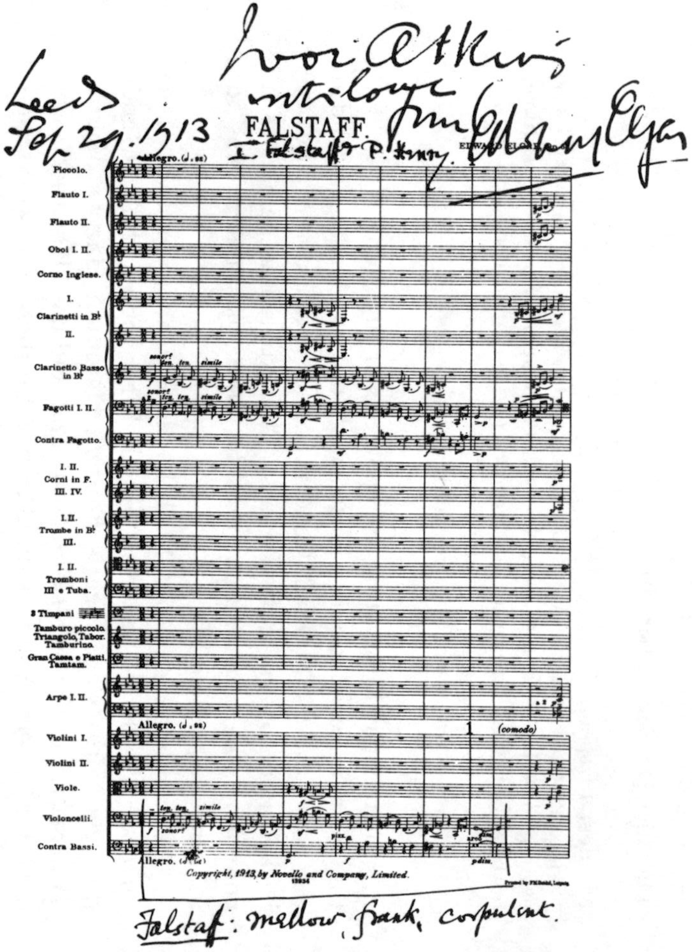

Ivor Atkins
with love from
Edward Elgar
Leeds
Sep 29. 1913
FALSTAFF.
I Falstaff & P. Henry
EDWARD ELGAR
Allegro.
Piccolo.
Flauto I.
Flauto II.
Oboi I. II.
Corno Inglese.
Clarinetti in B♭ I. II.
Clarinetto Basso in B♭
Fagotti I. II.
Contra Fagotto.
Corni in F. I. II. III. IV.
Trombe in B♭ I. II. III.
Tromboni I. II. III e Tuba.
3 Timpani
Tamburo piccolo. Triangolo, Tabor. Tamburino.
Gran Cassa e Piatti. Tamtam.
Arpe I. II.
Violini I.
Violini II.
Viole.
Violoncelli.
Contra Bassi.
(comodo)
Copyright, 1913, by Novello and Company, Limited.
Falstaff: mellow, frank, corpulent.

Hampstead, N.W.
Oct 6 1913

My dear Firapeel:
A copy of 'Jesu, priceless treasure' has come astray here—it is, of course welcome but not ours: it has been bound & removed from any cover it ever enjoyed: there are a few ink-markings in it which suggest a leopardic pen:—thine??
There are others, plumbagish which betray a heavier & a greasier paw—not thine??
If you claim the book it goes to you with love.
Ever thine
Reynart.

The copy was one Atkins had lent to Alice at the Leeds Festival.

8, College Yard, Worcester.
October 7th, 1913.

My dear Reynart,
The priceless treasure is mine, by every token, for (1) I wrested it from a wretched binding (the work of an amateur) on the day of my departure for Leeds, (2) I recognise the ink marking and (3) even the signs of the observant thumb are not unknown to me—I recorded their presence years ago after the book's absence on loan. To have it is better than to be without it, and perhaps a true cooper of books may make it comparatively presentable if much art be brought to the task—so I claim it.
I have done much work on 'Falstaff' since with the aid of some magnification of the sight, and truly it is gorgeous stuff and the workmanship is marvellous. In fact its skill likes me not—I fear there be some pact between you and the Dark One. Some factitious aid of the kind there must have been. It is great from so many points of view and I *do like* the picture it gives of Reynart the *English scholar*. This aspect seizes me greatly. Bless you, you are a cultured mortal!
Thine,
Firapeel.

Atkins was in the midst of planning the final programme for the 1914 Worcester Festival and had written to Elgar asking him to contribute a new work for Worcester.

Severn House, 42, Netherhall Gardens, Hampstead, N.W.
Oct 20 1913

My dear Firapeel:
Your most kind letter received: the matter requires most careful

consideration which I need not say it will receive with every possible favourable bias to your side. At this moment only thanks.

Yours ever

Reynart.

Silence indicated that Elgar was still considering this request, and thinking that it might help matters Atkins wrote again hinting at the possibility of a large choral work.

Hampstead.
Nov 6 1913

My dear Firapeel:

Alas! I can come to no conclusion for a few days—I am looking round & find it difficult to decide.

In haste

My love

Reynart.

The Elgars had been staying at Madresfield Court with Lord Beauchamp, and from there Elgar went on to stay with the Graftons at 'The Elms', Stoke Prior, on 10 November. He had to change trains in Worcester, and called on Atkins, when the possible 'new work' was discussed, and Atkins made a firm offer of a fee for Part 3 of *The Apostles*. Elgar left promising to consider this seriously, as he had already been thinking about it.

Hampstead Dec 2 1913

My dear Firapeel:

I have given the matter every consideration from every point of view & I do not see that it is possible to do a large work for Worcester; in the present state of things *no* big work is wanted. I longed to complete the *Apostles*, but you see the fee you offer wd be the *only* return for a whole year's work—we can only look forward to two or three performances of a 'sacred' work in these heathen days after the production. The same observation applies—without the religious side—to a large orchestral work—it will not pay, out of itself, for its printing. At the present moment the whole world is given over to short things—plays & music suffer most. I am very busy just now with trifles which must be done. If I can see my way to an orchestral work you shall have it but I dare not hold out any hopes. It is very sad that things should be so, but no one—comparatively—is interested in any religious work at all.

Please mention nothing of the following yet: I think it may do good reflectively on your Festival. [Henry C.] Embleton [a wealthy patron of music and supporter of Elgar] has arranged a huge performance of 'The Apostles' in Canterbury Cathedral, June 20, at 3 o'c & (this is the point) the Dean is going *to allow tickets to be sold*—proceeds for the restoration fund: this should show objectors that there is no crime in paying for a seat. I will let you hear further shortly.

Much love to you
Yours ever
Reynart.

Atkins did not know then that Embleton, when negotiating for the Canterbury Cathedral performance of *The Apostles*, had offered a very substantial fee if Elgar completed Part 3 and gave him the first performance. Elgar was still unhappy about not being able to offer a new work for the Worcester Festival.

Severn House, 42, Netherhall Gardens, Hampstead, N.W.
Dec 29 1913

My dear Firapeel:
    Christmas is no day to me but the New Year, the birth of it 'cannot be pretermitted to King or Cobbler', & I send you my love & best wishes. I have been wofully overwhelmed with busyness—quite a different thing from business—a tortured forced fervidity over necessary trifles which are more difficult to overcome than the big things—the performance of these last is denied me—the Lord desireth in these his days the pleasant degradation of Man (how foolish wd be an empty Hell to its maker!) & so— & so— & so—you understand.
    Well this sad year is going & I hope for all of us the presence, & later, the memory of 1914 may be of a better & wholesomer flavour than 1913. I am grieved & worry much over your offer & my refusal but I hope to be of some use to you still.

Again all good wishes
Yours ever
Reynart.

The 'King or Cobbler' reference is to an essay on 'New Year's Eve', written by Charles Lamb (1775–1834). It is a slight misquotation, the original being, 'The birth of a New Year is of an interest too wide to be pretermitted by king or cobbler.'

1914

We went to London as usual at the beginning of January, and my father spent much of his time with Elgar. Hampstead was an ideal centre for long walks over the Heath. We then went on to Leck Hall where my father walked miles every day over the Westmorland fells, while I went ferreting with our host, Henry Welch.

Severn House, Hampstead, N.W.
Monday Jany 19 1914

My dear Firapeel:
  I hope you have had a good rest & have been duly exercised in limbs & otherwise amused & set up—would that I had been so too—we have had afflicting colds, &c &c.
  I send Florent Schmitt (Psalm 47)—but the more I see of it the less I like it—it is an insult to the psalm to insist on *realising* the figurative 'Clap your hands'—so *uneducated*—but there you are—we have no critic who can say so & this is a great man, so they say. Do not return the stuff—I thought you might like to see it—it is *dans le mouvement*! alas!!
My love to you
Yrs ever
Reynart

  In the meantime replies to the invitation for stewards (guarantors) for the Worcester Festival had been coming in and about 200 acceptances had been received. It had been calculated, however, that there should be a minimum of 250 before firm commitments were made, and it was a matter of some concern whether that figure would be reached. By the end of January, however, acceptances from stewards had exceeded the minimum of 250 required, and active preparations were now proceeding.

Severn House, 42, Netherhall Gardens, Hampstead, N.W.
Feb 9: 1914

My dear Firapeel:
  I hear that you have your Stewards all right, & more than necessary for a start. I am so very glad.
  I knew you would not care for Florent Schmitt—I see he is coming to London as a guest—! so he is known.
  I am hoping I may find some new short thing for you if you may want it—but I cannot tell. I am really beyond words busy with necy things.

What about that Ps XLVIII?—I scored it last year, but if not possible for orch cd it be done at one of the services with organ?

Tell me some news of yourself & all of you & of the festl. I have written five choral songs of varying length & mood—they will reach you as soon as ready.

Love

Thine

Reynart

The songs were: Op 71 (1) *The Shower*, (2) *The Fountain*; Op 72, *Death on the Hills*; and Op 73, (1) *Love's Tempest*, (2) *Serenade*.

In his reply, Atkins mentioned various suggested works for the forthcoming Worcester Festival, and asked for Elgar's views, reminding him of the necessity to consider their box-office values.

Severn House, 42, Netherhall Gardens, Hampstead, N.W.
Feb 26 1914

My dear Firapeel:

I am so very glad to hear all is well & better than ever with the Stewards, & congratulate you, yourself, on the result; you must have worked tremendously hard & I hope you feel rewarded.

I have had a chill & have been going very slow but am alright again now. I quite agree as to Elijah—it is necessary. The Passion *ought* to be wanted by the public under these ideal conditions—but *is* it? You have the statistics of the three last festivals & can say. It was done at Gloucester in 1871 I think and at Worcester in (perhaps) '72 [correct].

Now you ask as to my bigger works: I cannot say what can be done. Gerontius seems to draw, but the others are uncertain. Naturally the Apostles wd be my choice, but I do not know if sufficient interest would be taken in it—if we only had some solo singers that people care to hear!

Let me hear if there is any news: if I can get through some absolutely necessary work I shall come down into the district for a night or two & shd. look for you.

Love

Yrs

Reynart

I wish you wd have done *at once* some slips something like the enclosed so that we could all enclose them in letters & hammer the [festival] *dates* in now.

P.S. As to the Executive Comm^ee—I don't see how I can possibly be of any use. I cannot come down on any particular date. I have however written to Mr. FitzClarence accepting.

PRELIMINARY NOTICE.

Canterbury Cathedral.

SIR EDWARD ELGAR will conduct a special performance of his Oratorio "THE APOSTLES" on FRIDAY, JUNE 19TH, at 3 p.m., in aid of the Restoration Fund.

Soloists :

MADAME AGNES NICHOLLS.

MISS MURIEL FOSTER,

MR. JOHN COATES,

MR. THORPE BATES,

MR. ROBERT RADFORD,

MR. HERBERT HEYNER.

The Chorus will consist of 250 members of the Leeds Choral Union (Conductor : DR. HENRY COWARD).

The new Symphony Orchestra (100 performers) has been engaged for the occasion, and a special organ will be erected.

Further particulars will be announced later.

Worcester Musical Festival,

September 6th, 8th, 9th, 10th and 11th, 1914.

THE 191st MEETING OF THE THREE CHOIRS OF WORCESTER, HEREFORD AND GLOUCESTER.

Principal Performers:

Madame NOORDEWIER-REDDINGIUS.
Miss DOROTHY SILK.
Miss CARRIE TUBB.
Miss RUTH VINCENT.
Madame KIRKBY LUNN.
Madame DE HAAN-MANIFARGES.
Miss SARA SILVERS.

Mr. JOHN COATES.
Mr. GERVASE ELWES.
Mr. STEUART WILSON.
Mr. HERBERT HEYNER.
Mr. CHARLES MOTT.
Mr. ROBERT RADFORD.

ORGAN, Mornings - - - Dr. A. H. BREWER.
„ Evenings - - - Dr. G. R. SINCLAIR.

Conductor: Mr. IVOR ATKINS.

IN THE CATHEDRAL.

Sunday, Sept. 6th, 3.30 p.m. GRAND OPENING SERVICE, WITH CHORUS AND ORCHESTRA.

Tuesday Morning -
Sept. 8th, 11.30 a.m.

Gerontius - - - - - - - *Elgar*
Three 8-part Motets for unaccompanied Chorus
    (Fest- und Gedenksprüche) - - - *Brahms*
Symphony in D Minor - - - - *Franck*

Tuesday Evening -
7.30 p.m.

Elijah - - - - - - - *Mendelssohn*

Wednesday Morning
Sept. 9th, 11.30 a.m.

Manzoni Requiem - - - - - *Verdi*
Fantasy (founded on passages in Dante's
    Divina Commedia) (New work) - *Walford Davies*
Blest Pair of Sirens - - - - *Parry*
Motet for unaccompanied Chorus - *Orlando di Lasso*
Symphonic Poem, "Tod und Verklärung" - *Strauss*

Thursday Morning -
Sept. 10th, 11.30 a.m.

Mass in B minor - - - - - - *Bach*

Thursday Evening -
7.30 p.m.

Symphony in G minor - - - - *Mozart*
New Work - - - - - *A. E. Brent Smith*
New Work - - - - *Vaughan Williams*
Creation, Part I - - - - - *Haydn*

Friday Morning - -
Sept. 11th, 11.30 a.m.

Messiah - - - - - - - *Handel*

Friday Evening, 6.0 p.m. Closing Service by the Three Choirs.

IN THE PUBLIC HALL.

Wednesday Evening
8 p.m.

Concert. "Till Eulenspiegel" - - - *Strauss*
    and new works by *Elgar*, *Sibelius*, etc.

Programmes with all information as to Tickets, etc., may be obtained from
Messrs. Deighton & Co. and Messrs. Spark & Co., Worcester.

CHORUS AND ORCHESTRA OF ABOUT 400 PERFORMERS.

Reduced Railway Fares from nearly all parts on production of Festival Ticket.

All Seats are Numbered and Reserved.   *Prices from 2/6 to 15/-*

255

1914

Important

Severn House, Hampstead, N.W.
March 16 1914

My dear Firapeel:
I have heard Charles Mott (Baritone) Royal Opera Covent Garden,
W.C., sing Köthner better than ever I have heard the part before. He has
been here singing to me & I should like him to sing in *Gerontius* if that
might be. I wish you might hear him as a possible Elijah—I think a little
new blood wd do good. He sang some of it to me finely, but these classics
are more in your hands. In any case do not decide before you have heard
him.

> In greatest haste
> Yrs ever
> Reynart.

Atkins subsequently heard Charles Mott himself and was
equally impressed. As a result he was engaged to sing the part of
the Priest in *Gerontius*. John Coates and Madame Kirkby Lunn
were to be the other artists.

Severn House, 42, Netherhall Gardens, Hampstead, N.W.
April 15 1914

My dear Firapeel:
I have been away & wofully overworked—now I am clear of
encumbrances & I am trying to do something for you. I will write in a few
days & see how it shapes.
Here is the new Anthem—it wd do well for your Sunday with full
orch—thunderstorms & drums.

> Love
> Reynart.

Enclosed was a copy of *Give unto the Lord*, Psalm 29, Op 74.

(*opposite above, left*) This photograph was taken in January 1911, at Elgar's
request and shows the author with the silver-topped walking stick which Elgar
had given him the previous Christmas (see page 213). Photography by Bushnell of
Malvern.

(*above right*) Atkins, July 1911. A photograph taken in connection with the Elgar-
Atkins Edition of Bach's *St Matthew Passion*, which was to receive its first
performance at the Three Choirs Festival at Worcester in September

(*below*) The Atkins family home at 8 College Yard, Worcester

To introduce the first performance of the Elgar-Atkins Edition of Bach's *St Matthew Passion* at the 1911 Worcester Festival, Elgar, at Atkins's request, arranged two Bach chorales for brass instruments to be played from the top of the cathedral tower before the performance. The playing of the chorales before the *St Matthew Passion* became a Three Choirs tradition. No photographs were taken in 1911, but these two photographs show the players before and during performance on the top of the South Porch of Gloucester Cathedral in 1913. The conductor on this occasion was Prof C. Sanford Terry who appears in the top photograph front right with Edgar Day, the Worcester assistant organist standing to his left

'The Flight from Worcester', 16 September, 1911. Elgar is on Short and C. Sanford Terry on Kate. (See page 233)

Alice Elgar, taken in 1912, when the Elgars were living at Severn House, Hampstead (*Photograph by Claude Harris, by permission of the Trustees of the Elgar Birthplace*)

Severn House, Hampstead, N.W.
Sunday [1 June 1914]

My dear Firapeel:
   I am, if possible, coming down on Tuesday or Wedy & shall hope to see you for a minute. I am to be present at the Freedom presentation to Mr. Leader & shall stay with the Mayor [his friend Hubert Leicester] but it is quite uncertain at the moment when I arrive or depart.
   I have just had the sketch programme which looks well. I suppose Kirkby Lunn will do Gerontius:: you did not tell me. What is Charles Mott doing? I hope you will like him. I heard him do (since Kothner) Gunther, & the Herald in Lohengrin, both good. Have you had the new anthem Ps.XXIX?
Yours ever
Reynart.

Benjamin Williams Leader was a Worcester-born popular landscape painter. Elgar did come to Worcester for the Freedom ceremony, but he had to leave again in the afternoon when Atkins was still in Evensong.

   Atkins wrote giving Elgar the rehearsal dates, with tentative rehearsal schedules, and asking if there was any chance of a new composition, even a small one. He told him also that he was considering the possibility of including *Psalm 29* in the opening service and *Falstaff* in the Wednesday evening concert in the Public Hall. He added that he had to go to London on 12 and 17 June, and proposed to call on Elgar to discuss these matters.

Severn House, 42, Netherhall Gardens, Hampstead, N.W.
June 11 1914

My dear Firapeel:
   Just home after much wandering & off again tomorrow. I was so sorry to miss you at Worcester but I left at 4 oc.
   Now as to all your news. I have found it quite impossible to write anything new—I need scarcely say that I am deeply sorry.
   1) July 9 will suit me for the chorus—& I will do all I can to be with you. If you *can* arrange it between trains—that is so that I can get back here it wd be well.
   2) London rehearsal
      Thursday Sep 3rd I have booked
   3) As to *Falstaff*—I do not think it will be good in that small Hall. I would prefer something quieter & I will see—we might do an A & B—using the new string piece Sospiri for one of them if it beliked you.

This week is gone & next week is Canterbury 18th & 19th so you see I am engaged then & could not find a minute—we leave on the 18th & return the following Monday so you must let me know when you come up again.

I am leaving tomorrow till Monday.

In greatest haste
Love
Yrs
Reynart

It was not possible for Atkins to go up to London again, and in the meantime he had to finalise the opening and closing services arrangements. Timing and balance in the opening service required an orchestral work after the sermon, and the *Coronation March* had taken the place of *Psalm 29*. *Psalm 48* was, however, included with organ accompaniment in the Friday evening closing service. He had sent a draft of the now finalised opening and closing services to Elgar, but, hoping to see him, had not explained the reasons for the omission of Psalm 29. Elgar had clearly counted on this work being included.

Severn House, 42, Netherhall Gardens, Hampstead, N.W.
July 2 1914

My dear Firapeel

I have been rushed to a great extent or I should have written at once to say I do not understand on what ground you have withdrawn the anthem at the opening service.

I have been wondering if I am really wanted at all, but I hesitate to withdraw entirely from the festival although there is no inducement for me to come: you see Gerontius 'goes' without me & it wd be quite a safe draw with you—the evening concert I am not keen about. So do not announce anything conducted by me for the present & I will see. I am not now sure about next week's choral rehearsal & I leave home today & *may* not be able to return in time but naturally it is useless coming to a choral rehearsal if I am [not] going to conduct.

I hope all goes well.

Yours ever
Reynart

Severn House, 42, Netherhall Gardens, Hampstead, N.W.
Wedy [8 July 1914]

My dear Firapeel
    I am leaving for Worcester via all sorts of places today & shall be at the Mayor's tonight.
    I may not be able to report myself before morning—but will you ring me up early & tell me when Gerontius comes on—I want to get away early.

Ever yours
Reynart.

Elgar was in Worcester on 9 July for the combined chorus rehearsal, but had to leave immediately after rehearsing *Gerontius*.

Severn House, 42, Netherhall Gardens, Hampstead, N.W.
July 11: 1914

My dear Firapeel
    I had no time yesterday & arrived home last night.
    The chorus sounded *fine* to me & better than ever. I am going away for six weeks—as at present arranged—& I hope you will get a good holiday.
    I am not keen on appearing at the evening *Concert* & I think you cd. do well without me—do *try* to cut me out of it. I *wish* to be free.

Yours ever
Reynart.

Elgar's reluctance at this time to conduct at the Wednesday evening concert was because he had now committed himself to Embleton to write Part 3 of *The Apostles*, and had already collected around him all the books, drafts, etc, which he had used in the original composition. He had decided not to go abroad this year, but to take a long holiday in Scotland before starting serious composition. He expected to be fully occupied on the work in September and therefore only to come to Worcester for the first part of the festival. During the next few days, however, Atkins must have persuaded him to remain in Worcester for the festival week, at least up to Thursday 10 September, since in the final programme, dated 16 July, Elgar is shown as conducting *Gerontius* on Tuesday morning and *Introduction and Allegro* on Wednesday evening.
    We also were preparing to go on holiday, this time to Switzerland and Italy. I was very excited. I remember we all

263

visited Worcester's leading optician and were fitted with special sunglasses with hinged metal side-pieces for use in the snow-clad mountains of the Alps; and my parents went through guide-books and maps with me so that I would be prepared for the places we were to visit.

Rumours of possible war were, however, in the air, and my parents decided to give up the first few days of our Continental holiday and stay in Dover instead until the position became clearer. I remember much of our Grand Fleet was at Dover, and how we took a boat excursion round the harbour to see the great ships, and how at night time they were all lit up—a wonderful sight. The days slipped by, waiting to take ship to France, and then on 4 August war was declared and we went home.

On our return home my father was involved in meetings to consider if the Worcester Festival could go on. At the executive meeting held on 8 August it was decided to postpone it. At that time it was generally considered that the war would not last more than a few months.

The Elgars had left London on 19 July for Glasgow, and had then travelled northwards. The declaration of war found them staying in Gairloch on the remote West Coast of Scotland, with the nearest railhead at Achnasheen on the Kyle of Lochalsh—Inverness line. News filtered slowly to the Elgars, and it was a few days before they decided to get back to London. Elgar returned to Severn House on 14 August.

When he wrote from Gairloch on 7 August he did not know that talks regarding the postponement of the Worcester Festival were already taking place.

The Gairloch Hotel, Ross-shire.
Augt. 7: 1914

My dear Firapeel

I fear this awful war is trying you more than a great many people with your festival coming on: I hope you are well & prepared for any anxieties which may occur—I suppose there is no thought of abandoning the festival. You will let me hear any news you can. We are in a way fixed here but can escape soon & shall return home when possible—I will not go into particulars all minor troubles are as nothing in the face of the future possibilities.

All good wishes to you all & much love
Yours ever
Reynart.

On his return to London Elgar gave up any idea of continuing with Part 3 of *The Apostles*. He put away all the books, and sketches, and, determined to help the war effort, on 17 August he went to Hampstead police station, where he was sworn in as a special constable. At the end of September the Worcester Festival executive committee formally decided to abandon the festival.

Severn House, 42, Netherhall Gardens, Hampstead, N.W.
Oct 15 1914

My dear Firapeel:
    How are you & how are things in general? I have not written since the postponement notice—it all seemed too sad & what *could* one say? Your disappointment must have been greater than ours—although you know the festival is the one thing I look forward to with real joy. I cannot be at the meeting next week, & I fear there is little but inevitable formal closing up to be done, with, I hope, a radiant eye to the future. Will Worcester come on *next* year, or what will be the idea?
    Everything musical is nearly at a standstill except what you see in the D.T. & of course the inevitable popular things.
    Dear old [Sanford] Terry is in town & I have had the greatest pleasure seeing him twice. I hope he does not leave for a few days longer. My love to you & yours.
                    Yours ever
                    Reynart

    Atkins replied telling him that the WFCS were now rehearsing for a performance of *The Messiah* to be given on 21 December in aid of the Belgians, and that cathedral services were continuing normally.

Special Constabulary, Hampstead S. Division.
Oct 26 1914

My dear Firapeel:
    I was so glad to get your letter & to hear of what is going on. Have you read Masefield's poem ['August'] in the *English Review*? *That* is the best thing written yet, & here I feel as if you in the country were doing something, but altho' I am busy from morning till night the *houses* seem to choke it all off. We are fighting for the *country* & I wish I could *see* it. I think the postponement of the Fest: was the only right thing.
    If it is sunshiny just go round to the W. end [of the cathedral] & look over the valley towards Malvern—bless my beloved country for me—& send me a p.c. saying you have done so.
                    & Bless you too
                    Love
                    Reynart.

265

On 12 November Elgar, who was staying with the Graftons at Stoke, came over to Worcester and spent much time in the cathedral with my father, who played to him many of his favourite works on the organ. They also visited the cathedral library which they both loved, and of which later my father was to become librarian. Elgar gave my parents all the news from London and explained that Alice, who was an excellent linguist, had been teaching French to the troops at Chelsea Barracks, but that the course had now been stopped and she would be looking for other war work where her languages would help. Elgar said that he would be staying in Stoke until after the weekend, and it was arranged that he would come over for another day in the cathedral (he was not in fact able to do so). I did not see him, as I was in bed at the time with tonsillitis which shortly after became acute, and I was taken to Birmingham for an operation which resulted in a long convalescence.

Stoke Sunday [15 November 1914]

My dear Firapeel:
    It was too dreadfully wet on Friday, & yesterday too cold—today not possible & tomorrow I go home. I am so drearily sorry to have missed a second Worcester day. I was so thoroughly happy with you in our Blessed shrine or fane—I want to write newspaperily somehow.
                        Bless you
                        Yrs ever
                        Reynart.
I hope the boy is better: do send me a line home to tell me.

On 15 November news came that Field Marshal Lord Roberts had died in France on a visit to our troops. Atkins arranged with the Dean that an organ recital planned for 19 November should become a memorial service, and Charles Mott, who would be singing, would include 'Proficiscere' from *Gerontius*. Atkins telephoned Elgar about the service, who said that he would like to be present.

Severn House, Hampstead, N.W.
Nov 21 1914

My dear Firapeel:
   I am so very sorry I could not get down to Worcester on Thursday. What an excellent choice—*proficiscere*, & Mott, I hope, sang well. Thank you.
   I wish you gave a better account of your boy: send me word as soon as you can; the weather is very trying just now for old & young.
   As to the *Carillon*: you shall see it as soon as possible—if you had a good 'declaimer' the orch version shd be available for concert purposes. All good wishes. Love to Wulstan.
                    Yours ever
                    Reynart

When Elgar was in Worcester he had told Atkins that he had almost finished a patriotic composition for orchestra, *Carillon*, Op 75, which included a poem by Emile Cammaerts in honour of the Belgian forces. Madame Tita Brand Cammaerts (daughter of Maria Brema) would recite the poem in French at the first performance, to be given in the Queen's Hall on 7 December. She was also translating the poem into English so that it could be recited at performances all over the country in aid of the Belgians.

1915

Everybody who could was now helping the War Cause in one way or another. My mother had joined the Women's Volunteer Reserve and the Red Cross, and was soon to be working in the Worcester Infirmary in the Massage Department. My father combined his musical activities, much of which were in aid of war charities, with clerical work in the War Agricultural Committee and in the local Ministry of Food offices.
   By the end of January the final financial position of the abandoned 1914 Worcester Festival was known, and Atkins wrote to Elgar enclosing an advance copy of the statement. In the same letter he told Elgar that the military had taken over the Public Hall, Worcester, and that he was transferring the WO & LC Society concert, to be given on 13 February, to the Assembly Rooms, Malvern. He enclosed the proposed programme and added that, as he had an excellent French reciter, he intended to include *Carillon*.

Hampstead   Saturday [6 February 1915]

My dear Firapeel:
  I sent you a wire: looking at your programme I see you have Symphony
II Beethoven—a very small score. I do not think you would get much
climax out of *Carillon* without some sort of a *battery*. If your reciter were a
giant (or giantess) you might pull it through, but it would be hard going.
My love to you all
Yrs ever
Reynart.

  Carillon was performed in the 13 February concert, Cammaert's
poem 'Chantons Belges, Chantons', being magnificently de-
claimed by Madame Paul Robinet. The orchestra was specially
strengthened for the occasion, and my father told me that 'the
battery was after Elgar's heart'.
  Elgar, who was again staying with the Graftons, came over to
Worcester on 25 March. He told Atkins that he was setting some
poems from Laurence Binyon's *The Winnowing Fan*. He was
working on 'To Women', and particularly wanted to set 'For the
Fallen'. Unfortunately Cyril Rootham of Cambridge was doing a
setting of the same poem, and Elgar felt that he might have to give
up *For the Fallen* because of this, and shortly afterwards did so.
(Some weeks later, however, pressed by Binyon and others, Elgar
returned to his sketches and worked on them for the rest of 1915,
completing the work the next year. *For the Fallen* received its first
performance in Leeds on 4 May 1916.) Atkins and Elgar also
talked about the difficulties of putting on concerts as more
orchestral players and singers joined the armed forces.
  In June Elgar stayed with the Graftons, and on the 18th he and
Hubert Leicester looked in briefly. Elgar told Atkins that he was
checking the parts of a new orchestral work, *Polonia*, which he had
written in aid of the Polish Relief Fund, and dedicated to
Paderewski. The first performance would be on 7 July. He also
said that he had recently joined the Hampstead Volunteer Reserve
and was enjoying his rifle practices at which he was now becoming
quite an expert.

Prince of Wales Hotel, Grasmere.
Sep 21: 1915

My dear Firapeel:
I want to know how & where you are, & what has been doing. I hope
you & all yours are well. Alice & I have been staying at Newcastle & are
wending our way home slowly via the Lakes. It is difficult to write about
anything just now in these very trying times: my one regret in the music
world is the cessation of the Festivals—that I feel more deeply than
anything. What lovely things they were and how little, comparatively,
appreciated & understood. Will anyone miss them as much as you & I?
We have been with the Stuart-Wortleys & talked much of you, incited
thereto by the edn of the Passion, & Wortley speaks with great joy of his
conversation with you at our supper in Gloucester Place. Send a line to
Hampstead. I shall be back in a few days now. Tomorrow we propose to
walk over the hills to Ullswater.
Ever yours
Reynart.

The Elgars had given a supper party on 24 May 1911, after the
first performance of the Second Symphony, at which the Stuart-
Wortleys and Atkins had been guests. The *St Matthew Passion* had
been very much in his mind at the time, and he had found Stuart-
Wortley a most discerning and knowledgeable companion.

Atkins had written a long letter telling Elgar how much the
Three Choirs Festivals had meant to him personally since his first
one, and his first meeting with Elgar, at the Worcester Festival of
1890. He was determined to revive the festivals once the War was
over.

Severn House, 42, Netherhall Gardens, Hampstead, N.W.
Oct 3 1915

My dear Firapeel:
I am so glad to have your letter & know all your feelings regarding the
festival—the memory of them is very sweet to me.
I have long wanted to send you *Bayle* [Dictionary]; it is meant for you
(& me). I have tried to get a decent copy for a long time. I am not sure if I
have secured one now but if it should arrive it's from
your devoted
Reynart.
Bayle is my solace & delight in low moments & winter's a-coming.

Severn House, 42, Netherhall Gardens, Hampstead, N.W.
Oct 5 1915

My dear Firapeel:
I hear from Birmingham that Bayle is sent to you. I *hope* it is a nice copy: I will call & verify it & inscribe it to you next time I am near.
Oh! I hope you will enjoy the peculiar & exquisite flavour. You must read it in real *peace* & quiet—a little at a time: go slowly—for a taste try Abimelech &c, belike, Sarah. After that browse as you please, but send me a p.c. sometimes when you find a morsel which particularly affects the palate.

Love
Yours ever
Reynart
(the complete Baylite)

Atkins had written to say how much he was enjoying Bayle, but that he was a little worried at the high price that Elgar must have given for the five-volume leather bound folio dictionary, including a life of the author. It was the second English edition, of 1732, of the *Historical and Critical Dictionary of Mr Peter Bayle*. The original dictionary had been published in French in 1697.

Hampstead   Oct 9 1915

My dear Firapeel:
I extend you a hearty welcome into the (non-existent) society of complete Baylists. I *am* so glad you like it, but please do not think of any commercial value—it is the cheapest book in the world. Yours is a better edition than mine, & I lack the 'Life'.
I direct you to read '*Lemnos*', & if you get through that with satisfaction (Oh! the notes) I leave you to run alone, desiring you to report progress from time to time.

Bless you
Yours ever
Reynart.

At this time, though Atkins was not to learn this until the beginning of January 1916, Elgar was occupied with writing the music for the *Starlight Express*, a play based loosely on Algernon Blackwood's novel *A Prisoner in Fairyland*, to be performed at the Kingsway Theatre.

[Hampstead]
Dec 29: 1915

My dear Firapeel:
   I have been so rushed that I have been unable to send or do anything about friends at all, but you have been much in our thoughts, & I have stolen a moment to send you all good wishes for the New Year.
   Poor dear Alice is quite laid up with a taxi accident—better now, but in bed & will be there for a long time I fear. She mercifully remembers nothing about the collision—a perfect blank.
Love
Reynart.

Accidents were rather frequent at this time as the result of the wartime darkened streets.

1916

We went to London at the beginning of January as usual, and my father went out to see the Elgars. Elgar told him that the *Starlight Express* was running at the Kingsway Theatre, and though he did not like the sets he was pleased with the music and especially the songs. Naturally we immediately booked seats. It was all very exciting, but for me a mixture of delights and disappointments. For some reason I had anticipated that Elgar would be conducting the theatre orchestra, and was surprised when a young man, Julius Harrison, appeared on the rostrum. My disappointment soon disappeared, however, when Elgar's fascinating overture began and when the Organ-Grinder, Charles Mott, appeared on the apron of the stage to sing his first song, 'O children, open your arms to me'. Soon I was completely absorbed in the play, eagerly following the dream-like Sprites, the Lamplighter, the Sweep, the Dustman, the Woman-in-the-Haystack, the Starlight Express itself, and the Stardust Cavern in the Mountains.
   Elgar was conducting the LSO in Birmingham on 28 February. Atkins could not attend, but he sent him a note. The second concert in the series was in Manchester.

Midland Hotel, Manchester.
Tuesday evening [29 February 1916]

My dear Firapeel:
I am so dreadfully sorry but I did not open your note until after the Concert. I asked the sweet youth if you were present. I did not know that he was from Worcester but thought he was of the Hall. I should have been so glad to have said a word to him. Please tell him how sorry I am.

Yes: I received your beautiful letter but I have had no time to write the acknowledgement it deserves—I have been *doing things* which you shall hear ; belike *conduct* (!) some day.

No more now
Yours ever
Reynart.

The Worcestershire Musical Competitive Festival was being held in April, and Atkins had arranged for it to terminate with a performance in the cathedral on 29 April of Handel's *Samson*. Elgar had a special interest in competitive festivals, and Atkins invited him to come down for it. He also told him about a scheme he was working on for converting a part of the cathedral treasury into a separate music library, in which he would assemble all the cathedral musical treasures and gradually build up collections of music by composers connected with the cathedral, with a special section devoted to all Elgar's works. He asked Elgar to give him a manuscript full score, perhaps *The Apostles*. No reply came, and it was not until later that he learnt that earlier in April Elgar had been taken ill in the train to Worcester, and had been in hospital in Oxford for several days.

In April Atkins received and wrote about proof copies of Elgar's latest writings, *To Women* and *For the Fallen*. The first performances of these works were given in Leeds on 4 May 1916, and were conducted by Elgar. After the concert Elgar sent him a specially inscribed copy of *For the Fallen*.

Severn House, Hampstead, N.W.
May 15 1916

My dear Firapeel:
I am so glad you like the new things.
I don't think I have ever clearly talk[ed to] you about your long (not in an invidious sense) letter about the [Music] Library. I know I wrote [no trace of letter], but there is much I wanted to say—& I have been really ill & this has twice prevented my undertaking the journey down westwards.

I love the idea—and wanted much to give you 'it', that is a MS full score, say 'The Apostles', but there are *prior liens* in the way & I don't want to send anything small. We will leave it at that just now & will talk over the library.

Love to you

Yrs ever

E.E.

Thanks for pointing out the grammatical errors on p. 14, etc.—I *now* see there are fifths—what ARE we to do?

Shortly after this letter Elgar telephoned in great excitement because he had found and bought some reputed relics of King John which he proposed to give to the cathedral. He was coming down to Stoke and would bring them over.

Severn House, Hampstead, N.W.
May 26 1916

My dear Firapeel:
Alas! once more my efforts to get away have been blasted & I am not well. I will not say that I hope to come soon—I have said it so often. I sent, instead of carrying, the K. John relics to the Dean—I wonder what you think? I *rescued* them on the chance of their being genuine & Canon Wilson & the Dean accept them.

Love

Reynart.

On 6 June Elgar, who was staying at Stoke, visited my parents and spent some time in the cathedral seeing the King John relics, and in the new Music Library, where my father showed him what had been done so far. On this occasion I saw Elgar for a short time and he seemed very tired.

By the beginning of July the Music Library was really taking shape. I had helped my father in arranging books and putting up pictures, including the photograph Grindrod had taken of Elgar while he was writing *The Apostles*. A number of photographs of the library were then taken for the archives.

Hampstead   July 5 1916

My dear Firapeel:
I don't know how to thank you for the photograph of the Library. I feel very much overcome by seeing the eminence my presentment has

273

attained. I *wish* you wd *take him down*! But I will come & see him first.

I am not well yet & want a real (country) rest, so if you see a spectre soon do recognise my wasted form without a start.

Bless you

Yrs ever

Reynart.

In the middle of July Elgar was again staying with the Graftons. He came over to Worcester on the 20th. He told the Atkins that he and Alice were going up to the Lakes for a few weeks.

In August Atkins went on a walking tour in Wales and wrote to Elgar from Llantwit Major, mentioning that he had seen Elgar's uncle Henry before he left Worcester.

Severn House, Hampstead, N.W.
Augt 26 1916

My dear Firapeel:

It is good to see your writing & to hear good accounts of you: I hope the holiday time is kind to you & yours. Wales always sounds of fine air & mountains—streams &, belike, fish.

I do not improve much. We are just back from the Lakes & I have had a little *throat* examination & it seems that some small trouble there affects me: this trouble is being 'eliminated'—by nauseous means—& in a few days I shall be all right: it is said so, but I await in impatience. I do not like Nitrate of silver internally & think 'Non quo sed quomodo', which is all the Latin left to me.

I am glad my uncle keeps fairly well: he was 87 this week!

Make a note of *Temple Bar, July 1876*-I do not send it to you as you will sometime easily get a sight of it; read '*The last of the grand school of Connoisseurs*' & bless me for years after for showing you a real bit of enjoyable reading—the best picaresque life I have ever read: roll this out tenderly under the tongue & extract its full flavour.

Yes, I wish we cd walk & talk as of yore—perhaps soon, who knows? If I am better I shall surely come down—the Severn draws me & I want to walk by it from Worcester to Upton once more—will you join? Your acct of the church [Llantwit Major] sounds fascinating, & Baedeker is illuminating on it—I want to see it with you.

We have read appeals for the Charity (festival) [Three Choirs] & are sadly reminded of the warm, fine, & glorious days: will they ever come again? I see the Bishop's name appears nowhere: I shd like to know where he stands—the Bp of Gloucester was at Ullswater & I had talks with him—he seems in favour of the festivals; then I fear a new Dean of Hereford may sometime not far distant have to be reckoned with. Where are we? Do not trouble to write, as we must meet & you can tell me.

I hope Mrs. Atkins & the boy are flourishing—when do you return?
I fear this is all dull—but I will write better when I am better. My love
to you.

Yours ever
Reynart.

Severn House, 42, Netherhall Gardens, Hampstead, N.W.
Sep 8 1916

My dear Firapeel:
I was turning out some of the things & found this reminiscence of
Garmisch: as it implicates two of your friends I did not destroy it at once
but leave that feat to you: as far as I can remember my good nature solely
consisted of playing accompaniments.
I hope to see you next week (perhaps).

Love
Reynart.

The enclosure was a photograph of Alice Elgar and Nellie Bell.
Nellie had been staying at Garmisch when the Elgars were there
some years earlier. She was an excellent amateur singer and had
probably sung at an English party out there. Since their meeting
Nellie had married Henry Welch of Leck Hall, where we stayed
every January.

The Elgars were coming down to stay with the Berkeleys at
Spetchley Park for about a fortnight, and Elgar was proposing to
wander about the park and fish for the first week, after which he
intended coming on to Worcester. The Berkeleys were the leading
Roman Catholic family in Worcestershire, and maintained a small
Roman Catholic school on the estate mainly for their own
community. In the early 1860s Elgar had attended this school for a
short time before going to Littleton House.

Severn House, 42, Netherhall Gardens, Hampstead, N.W.
Sep 19 1916

My dear Firapeel:
I am glad you liked the *memorial* or testimonial. I had to come back via
my sister's & am now home for a long time: we were at Spetchley for a few
days, renewing an acquaintance (with the village) which was begun more
than fifty years ago: we had a lovely time there, & I caught many fish. My
sister's boy is being operated upon in the Worcester Infirmary & she was,
& I fear is, somewhat anxious—so I fled to see what could be done. I shall
hope for a day or two in Worcestershire & have a great idea that you & I cd

walk (obese one, ponder!) down the river to Upton & return by train—on
an autumn day it wd. be divine.

> My love to you
> Yrs ever
> Reynart

Towards the end of December Elgar sent Atkins a parcel of
proofs along with the following postcard:

Severn House, Hampstead, N.W.

With love only came today. I sent some old proofs to try & amuse Canon
Gorton [after his retirement he lived in Hereford until his death in 1913]
that's how it was beseen of G.R.S.

> Yrs ever
> E.E.

1917

Ever since Elgar had sent the proofs of *For the Fallen* to Atkins in
May 1916, the latter had been considering how he could arrange a
performance in Worcester Cathedral. Clearly an orchestra was out
of the question, but many of the orchestral effects could be
provided on the organ. To find enough men for the chorus would
be very difficult. Atkins had already rearranged the chorus parts
for women's voices only, and at the end of the previous year had
given a trial performance with piano accompaniment at Lawnside
School, Malvern, where he taught singing and musical appreciation. This had whetted his appetite and made him determined to
go ahead with a cathedral performance. Men, and at least drums, to
augment the organ, would have to be found, the cathedral choir
and men from the voluntary choir and elsewhere could strengthen
the male section of the WFCS, and Lawnside girls would join the
women's sections. The cathedral King's School at this time had a
large Officers' Training Corps unit, complete with bugles and
drums, who were more than willing to take part. Towards the end
of January 1917, plans were sufficiently advanced to enable Atkins
to write to Elgar, putting forward his ideas and asking him to come
down to conduct *For the Fallen*.

Severn House, Hampstead, N.W.
28 Jan 1917

My dear Firapeel:

It was good to see your writing & to know that you are superior to the winter weather—beastly weather which has laid so many low & none lower than the subscriber. I have had a loathsome time—one day out & four in bed since about November.

Your letter is thrilling!! I must say at once that on March 7th I am in Leeds, so that makes the 8th in Worcester impossible. How about the 15th? The only difficulty ahead (& which, wretchlike you don't suggest) is the

SOPRANO SOLOIST

What is to be done? All else,—*you* (supreme) at the organ, chorus, (all old &) new friends, my (very own) Cathedral—all beside the Woman, seems perfect.

Perpend, oh Firapeel! and instruct. I *am* glad to hear Canon Wilson is abounding & sympathetic. Let me hear as soon as you can if the 15th (or even the 1st) March wd do for you all: also as to your notions of soloist. I should like to have heard the Malvern performance with the Ladies only [the Lawnside School one].

No news here; everything musical—except some spurious opera—is moribund—the conductors dance over some exhumed corpses & the poorer the music the more acrobatic are the (mis)interpreters.

I should like a talk, God wot!

Ever yours

Reynart.

Atkins replied saying that he would try to arrange for the performance to be on 15 March, and that he would investigate the soloist question, but could not Elgar also do likewise in London? Letters from Elgar had for some months been written on thin plain paper.

Severn House, 42, Netherhall Gardens, Hampstead, N.W.
Feby 2 1917

My dear Firapeel:

Observe the paper I write upon! When this appears it is a sign of joy & uplifting—(As I write a *dense* yellow fog envelops the house).

I really do not know of any singers—no doubt some are to be had—other than Agnes [Nicholls] or Carrie Tubb. Stick to March *15th*, please—it will suit me far better than the 1st—it would be Ide-le (!!)—better perhaps 'Ide-al', classic allusion—for me to give reasons for this.

(No, I did *not* wilfully lead up to this colossal pun).

Let me know how your quest of the Golden Girl goes, & in the meantime, I will explore, vicariously, the rat-squeaking purlieus of Hampstead, etc. for soprano notes at once high & epic.

In great haste (what a pun it was!)

Yours ever

Reynart.

P.S. By'r lakin! a parlous pun!

It was a bad time in the War, with heavy losses, and it was decided that *For the Fallen* should form the centrepiece of the largest memorial service yet held in the cathedral. Subscribers to the Worcester Festival Choral Society announced that they would provide all the expenses in connection with the service. This solved the difficulty regarding the soloist for *For the Fallen*, since a professional singer could now be approached, and Carrie Tubb was engaged to sing the soprano part.

It was my father's custom at this time to take long walks between the end of Evensong and supper, and I usually went with him. I greatly enjoyed these walks, during which my father would often tell me detective stories, whose hero was a Professor Lombroso, possibly based on some book he was reading at the time. On 8 February we started out as usual, but my father was stopped by a friend just opposite the window of the *Worcester Herald* offices near the Cross. While they talked I looked in the window, and after looking at some photographs I saw an item headed 'Well-known Cathedral Organist Dies'. It was a short announcement that George Robertson Sinclair had died the previous night in a hotel bedroom in Birmingham.

He was a special friend of ours, having brought my father with him as assistant when he came from Truro to Hereford in 1889. He had been with my parents on many holidays abroad, and I had known and loved him ever since I could remember.

[On thin, headed notepaper]
Severn House, 42, Netherhall Gardens, Hampstead, N.W.
Friday am [9 February 1917]

My dear Firapeel:

I have just opened the paper & seen the sad, sad, sad news of Sinclair. I am overwhelmed & sorrowful and quite unable to *see* things as they are, & alas! are to be! I have no news beyond the Telegraph, & am confined to my room with a severe cold, so I am in the greatest state of tension—do send me any (Birmingham?) papers with full accounts. Poor dear old fellow— he was here & dined with us only last week or just before & was full of projects & good will. I *grieve*!!

Now, as to our 'affair' in the Cathedral. I am glad you have Carrie Tubb—as to the organ part I *fear* I can't do it: I am very busy with a little piece I am doing for a charity show [*The Sanguine Fan*], & have to do much writing myself—so short are we of men. I'll send you a *full-score* & if *you* are too busy to pick at it I will endeavour to do so—but I wd rather you wd do it.

Love

Yours ever

Reynart.

A sad blow to any hopes of reviving the festivals alas!

P.S. On the envp I just see your hospitable message [Atkins had invited Elgar to stay] but I really think I had better bed at the Star. I shd be such a nuisance to Mrs. A & the house generally—being such a cold mortal. We'll see!

[Hampstead]
Saturday [10 February 1917]

My dear Atkins:
   It is too dreadfully sad.
   I cannot possibly come [to Sinclair's funeral] as I am still tied to my room with this awful cold. Please explain to the relatives and especially to the newspapers the reason for my absence.
   I cannot realise it. Oh dear.

Bless you

Edward.

P.S. I have asked Mrs. Underwood to do this but it may not be possible for her. So I ask you also.

On 23 February Atkins was in London and went to 'Severn House'. Elgar played over his *Sanguine Fan* music which pleased Atkins very much. He told me some years later how refreshing the music was against the sombre war conditions. They discussed certain details concerning the Worcester performance of *For the Fallen*, and Atkins again invited the Elgars to stay with them.

Severn House, 42, Netherhall Gardens, Hampstead, N.W.
March 1 1917

My dear Firapeel:
   It will be best for us to go to the hotel & I have decided to do so as I

should have been only a trouble to your household with my many small but imperative needs.

I go to Leeds on Monday & shall travel back to London instead of going straight to Worcester as I had thought & hoped,

Ever yours
Reynart.

Severn House, Hampstead, N.W.
March 4 1917

My dear Firapeel:

I *am* so sorry—the drum parts [*For the Fallen*] only arrived yesterday & I hasten to send 'em on. G.[ran] C.[assa] & Cymbals stand as printed. The side drums (as many as you like, only arrange for one to play *solo* if required) play as printed till 28—let them begin pp with the Timp: cue & keep the rhythm going until 29. I have pencilled in the alteration.

I have been unwell & frightfully busy. We go to Leeds tomorrow for Mr Embleton. Send a line to me at Queen's Hotel. Home (D.V.) on Thursday.

Yours ever
Reynart

Queen's Hotel, Leeds.
March 7 1917

My dear Firapeel:

All's well: you will, I trust have recd long before this the drum parts. The delay was not mine but for the whilk I am sorry.

No; no drums at 4th bar before $\boxed{4}$. Let 'em begin at $\boxed{28}$ as in copy: *re* the 5 beats at $\boxed{29}$, I am in doubt. I should like to try these five beats—would it not be easy to cut 'em out if we did *not* like 'em? Let 'em go in anyhow.

Do you read *O. Henry*? Splendid writing: I wish he had had our country to write about instead of U.S.A. only: he's to be had in 1/- vols now & made for you &

Your
Reynart.

All thanks to Canon Wilson for the constructive hospitality. I'm sorry.

[Hampstead]
Thursday evening [8 March 1917]

My dear Firapeel:

I am just home & found *your p.c. dated* the *2nd* just arrd. What times we live in. I sent on the stuff on my own. I hope it's all right.

Great performance last night [Elgar had conducted *To Women*, with

280

Agnes Nicholls as soloist in Leeds]. At your leisure send me a schedule of *times* of rehearsal etc. I fear my time will be very hurried as I must clear up my poor dear old uncle's affairs. He left no will. [Henry Elgar had died on 24 February.]

Yours ever
Reynart

On receiving this letter Atkins sent him a full rehearsal schedule.

Hampstead N.W.3
Monday [12 March 1917]

My dear Firapeel:
   Your letter just recd & I note the times. *But*, alas! I am in bed!! I got an awful chill in the unwarmed train & have been nursing ever since: the doctor is just coming and I am straining every nerve to get a decent report. I am coming to Worcester if I can stand. I *hope* it will be all right but you must prepare a substitute. I am in an agony lest anything shd interfere with my coming. I hope & trust all may be well—or well enough. I remained in bed all yesterday & have tried every medicament known to man. I send this off early & will write again.

Yrs ever
Reynart.

I have just telephoned
a telegram to you.   Severn House, Hampstead, N.W.3.
Tuesday a.m. [13 March 1917]

My dear Firapeel:
   The doctor came & will let me out! But I am a dessicated worm: we arrive at 4.40 [14 March] & go straight to the Star [Hotel]. I will be ready for your rehearsal. On Thursday I shall want some time for business (my uncle's affairs) & I float away early on Friday to be in time for rehearsals here [*Sanguine Fan*]

In haste
Yrs ever
Reynart.

   That evening the Elgars dined with my parents and I spent some time with them. I recall Alice as short and affable, but disconcerting to a boy because she would come very close when she talked to you, a habit to which I was not accustomed. Elgar talked quickly, often moving about, often with a twinkle in his eye which put me at once at ease.
   I was not old enough, perhaps, to appreciate what death in

thousands meant, but I had already taken part in many memorial services, and for us choristers the moment was poignant enough because Edgar Day, our assistant cathedral organist, whom we had seen off to the War with some envy, had been severely wounded, but was being given special leave from Epsom Hospital to be present, and he would be playing the organ for the National Anthem. I knew that the performance would be the most moving and thrilling experience I had ever had.

The 'Recital of Solemn Music—In memory of those who have given their lives in the service of their Country' began at 8 pm, and when the cathedral choir in their royal scarlet cassocks and surplices processed from the Chapter House to their places, with the chorus on the special platform built on the steps leading from the nave into the choir, they found the Cathedral packed. The city corporation were sitting in state at the east end of the nave, and though not known to us then, there were crowds outside in the north porch. As I write this 65 years have passed but the scene is still vividly before me.

After the opening prayers the music began with the cathedral choir singing unaccompanied Psalm 23, 'The Lord is my Shepherd'. Elgar stepped on to the rostrum and, after a silence, he lifted his baton and my father on the organ played the Solemn Prelude which opens *For the Fallen* and leads into the chorus, 'With proud thanksgiving, a mother for her children. England mourns for her dead across the sea.' The second stanza begins 'Solemn the Drums thrill', and I can still hear the roll of the King's School drums and feel again the shivers which went down my spine. It is impossible to convey the emotions which raced through my mind as that intensely moving performance proceeded, or to describe how avidly I followed Elgar's beat, but anyone who has been privileged to take part in a performance under Elgar's baton, when he himself was completely and absolutely carried away by his music, will know how he played upon his singers and how they gave him results which they had no idea they were capable of.

For the Fallen ends with the chorus singing very quietly 'To the end they remain', and the final chord dying away into space. Absorbed in this music I was completely unprepared for, and shattered by, after a short silence, the first notes of the 'Last Post', which came from the darkness of the distant Lady Chapel. Even now I cannot hear the 'Last Post' without recapturing some of the

Wulstan Atkins.

NOVELLO'S ORIGINAL OCTAVO EDITION.

March 15. 1917

THE SPIRIT OF ENGLAND

No. 3

from Edward Elgar.

FOR THE FALLEN

A POEM

after the Cathedral performance

LAURENCE BINYON

SET TO MUSIC FOR TENOR OR SOPRANO SOLO, CHORUS,
AND ORCHESTRA

BY

EDWARD ELGAR

Op. 80, No. 3.

PRICE ONE SHILLING.

LONDON: NOVELLO AND COMPANY, LIMITED.
NEW YORK: THE H. W. GRAY CO., SOLE AGENTS FOR THE U.S.A.

283

terror I felt at that utterly unnerving sound.

This was followed by the Russian Contakion of the Departed, a funeral anthem, set to the Kieff melody. My father then played the Prelude to the *Dream of Gerontius*, after which we sang unaccompanied Bach's *Jesu, Priceless Treasure*, and Carrie Tubb sang Handel's *I know that my Redeemer Liveth*. The whole cathedral echoed with the singing of that huge congregation in the hymn *O God, our help in ages past*, and the service ended with prayers and the singing of the National Anthem. Never before or since have I heard it sung with such fervour and intensity. After the performance I found Elgar at the house, deeply moved. He took a copy from me and wrote an inscription on the title page.

Severn House, Hampstead, N.W.
March 22 1917

My dear Firapeel:
    A week ago today! I am so sorry I have been unable to write before this but every second has been taken up—the worry of the *amateur* entertainer is endless. Now, how different from the well-devised & perfectly working ceremony at Worcester under your management.
    I send the 8vo copy [from which he had conducted] with best memories of the beautiful evening.
    Now: as to M.S.S. [for the Cathedral Music Library] there are difficulties at present: on my return diligent search was made for the little oratorio [*The Light of Life*] & for 'Froissart' [both first performed at Worcester Festivals]. Neither of them is here & I cannot think where they can be: enquiry is hot afoot & is proceeding.
    The Fan Ballet was lovely & you *must* see it—some of the entertainment was a disgrace—low & *vulgarly uneducated*.
                                    Love
                                Yrs ever
                                Reynart.

The first performance of the ballet *The Sanguine Fan* had been given on 20 March as one of a number of scenes in *Chelsea on Tiptoe* at the Chelsea Palace Theatre.

Severn House, 42, Netherhall Gardens, Hampstead, N.W.
April 14 1917

My dear Firapeel:
    I hope you & yours are well, especially I write to ask with good hope! that Mrs. Atkins' eye is all right again after the troublesome accident.

If you are seeing the Dean please tell him that '*Red House Hill*' is Rainbow Hill. The Red House still exists & is now called Marlbank. S.T. Dutton lived there; it is an old house (200 years) & now much built in: so the position of the churches, which troubled the Dean, is correct. If the old Red House (which has oak floors etc) had been more free from surrounding new buildings I wd have ended my days in it—it *is* for sale.

Let me hear of you

Yrs ever

Reynart.

Twelve years later Elgar bought 'Marl Bank' and lived there until his death.

Towards the end of April Elgar came down again to stay with the Graftons, and on 2 May he visited the Atkins and spent some hours playing over the proofs of *The Spirit of England* which he had brought with him. The first section, 'The Fourth of August', was new to Atkins. Elgar said that he was considering setting some poems by Rudyard Kipling. These later became *The Fringes of the Fleet*. He also told Atkins that they felt they must find a cottage in the country near London where he could retreat when he wanted to compose.

Later in the month Elgar sent Atkins a proof of 'The Fourth of August', with a request that he would check it for him.

Severn House, 42, Netherhall Gardens, Hampstead, N.W.3.
July 1: 1917

My dear Firapeel:

I have had a very pleasant letter from Clayton [Novello] & the firm will send to your Library the f[ull] s[core] of the '*Light of Life*', orig M.S. at my request they will send it direct to you, so no inscription will be thereon & something suitable to their generosity & my good feeling can be added when I come down. As to '*Froissart*': their (Messrs. N.) memd. *records* that the M.S. was sent to me in 1901 but I cannot find it! If it does turn up it shall fly to you at once.

I *wish* you cd hear & *see* the songs at the Coliseum, [*The Fringes of the Fleet*] it is a huge piece of honest jovial heroism & a great success.

I am posting a clean copy of *The Fourth of August* which you revised for me.

Bless you

Yrs ever

Reynart.

It was usual for the publisher to hold the manuscript scores.

On 19 July my father was in London and he went to the Coliseum to hear *The Fringes of the Fleet*. He found Elgar there and shared his box. He told me that he enjoyed the evening immensely. The songs were clearly very popular with the large audience which contained many members of the armed forces on leave.

Towards the end of 1917 HMV issued the records which they had made earlier in July of the five songs from *The Fringes of the Fleet*. These records were probably the first Elgar records I ever heard. They were played to me by a young officer friend, then on leave, on a portable Decca gramophone, which he was taking back to the trenches with him.

In the middle of November Elgar stayed again at Stoke, and on 14 November came over to Worcester. He told Atkins that they had now found a cottage ('Brinkwells'), which he thought would prove ideal, and that in its peace he would be able to write real music. Since they had last met he had travelled around, especially with *The Fringes of the Fleet*, which had been very popular in Chatham and elsewhere. The most important event, however, had been his conducting the first performance in Leeds of 'The Fourth of August' on 28 October, and two days later of the whole of *The Spirit of England*. He said that wartime London was a terrible strain for him and he always felt better when he was back in Worcestershire.

The last 3 months of 1917 seemed to me to be full of memorial and other special services. These and his wartime duties took up much of my father's time, and he was also researching and writing a book on the organists of the cathedral since the dissolution of the monastery.

The year ended with 'A Recital of Christmas Music', given in the College Hall on 29 December, in aid of the Red Cross Depots in Worcester, and preparations for it had been going on for weeks. The music was to have a seventeenth-century character, and the boys and men were to appear in crimson cassocks and Elizabethan ruffs, which had been specially made for the occasion. All the choristers were very excited. The programme was extensive, beginning with Corelli's Christmas Concerto for viola, and including Palestrina, Pearsall, Handel, fifteenth-century traditional carols, Cornelius, Giles Farnaby, Byrd and two sections of Bach's *Christmas Oratorio*. The only contemporary carols were

Elgar's *A Christmas Greeting*, my father's *The Virgin's Lullaby* and Stanford's *A Carol of Bells*. The concert was given by candlelight, and though I was singing I remember thinking that I had never felt the message of Christmas so vividly as at this recital.

1918

It was not until April that news came from Elgar.

[Typewritten by Elgar]
Severn House, 42, Netherhall Gardens, Hampstead, N.W.3.
FRIDAY, April 5 1918

My dear Firapeel,
    I want to know how you and yours are and many things of less import besides. I hope you are all well and that things are possible with you,—it does not seem the correct thing to wish more than that in these awful times.
    I have had a bad winter, one illness after another and the entertainment culminated in a throat operation (vilely painful) and a spell in a nursing home, which was not cheering. I have been home for more than a week now and things are settling down but I am not yet strong by a long way.
    Terry passed thro' town on his way from the front, where, as you know, he has been lecturing to the accpt of shot & shell. We were out when he called and so missed the refreshment of a cheery word—the whilk I want badly—from him.
    It is hoped that we shall get away to the cottage soon; are you coming up to town? I want to see you. Tell me if Perry Wood has quite departed, I fear I should miss it sadly.
My love to you E.E.
[Signed] Edward Elgar.

    Imported timber supplies were beginning to run short, and the government was cutting down trees all over the country. The local papers had reported that Perry Wood, much beloved by Elgar, Atkins and all the older inhabitants of Worcester, was to be cut down. Atkins was able to write back and say that the report was much exaggerated, and only a thinning operation was to be carried out.

[Typewritten]
Severn House, 42, Netherhall Gardens, Hampstead, N.W.
April 8th 1918

My dear Firapeel,

Thanks for yours which came as a cheering ray & I hasten to send a word at once as I may be 'onto the wing' tomorrow, or, belike, the day after.

I read with envy in the report of the Histl. Soc. that you were perpetrating that book about the cath. organists and look forward to receiving it in due course. I do hope it will be among the next issued publications.

The cottage is in Sussex—I'll send you the proper address when we arrive; it is a divine woodland place and remote from the spoor of man ['Brinkwells', near Fittleworth]. Perhaps you might come!

Love from the family, to whom I delivered your messages with joy to them and to me.

yours ever,
ReynRat ye FOXE

[Handwritten] error of the press

Alice had found the cottage the previous year, and indeed the Elgars had already stayed there for short periods, but now they had decided to shut up 'Severn House' and make 'Brinkwells' their home for at least the spring, summer and autumn. Carice would get accommodation in London nearer her work. On 2 May they moved to 'Brinkwells'. Elgar was still not well, but soon the peace and restful surroundings began to have their effect. He appeared to put music on one side, and walked, fished, cut down trees, made walking sticks, tables and oddments for the house, and erected a garden house and a run for the chickens. He loved using his hands and he was a fine wood and metal worker. Coal was unobtainable, but he soon built up a large pile of logs for the cold evenings.

Time passed quickly, and by August Elgar was again thinking of music. A piano was sent for and placed in the 'studio', a large timber shed near the cottage, erected by the previous owner who was an artist. Elgar's mind had turned to chamber music, which he had not written since his early days. Billy Reed told Atkins, when he saw him in September, that Elgar was working on a violin and piano sonata and on sketches for a piano quintet. Atkins was therefore prepared for the following letter.

Brinkwells, Fittleworth, Sussex.
Sep 23 1918

My dear Firapeel:
  I have been thinking of you more than usual just round the dear
Festival dates & I want to see you badly.
  After the operation on my throat we came to this cottage & have been
here ever since, & are likely to remain: it is *divine*, & I have bought $1\frac{1}{2}$ acres
of wood to cut down & want an axeman badly!
  I have also made a table & have written a Sonata for Vn & Pf on it, & the
latter (that is the piano part) requires much consideration & advice from
Firapeel. Reed, dear man, has run down from London twice, & we have
'done' the Sonata & by'r lakin I think you will like it—it's the best of me.
  Tell me how you are. I am much better after the awful winter, but I do
not *travel* much yet. Otherwise I am normal.
                    Love,
                    Yrs ever
                    Reynart.

  The Sonata in E minor, Op 82, was first played privately, with
W. H. Reed as violinist and Elgar at the piano, on 15 October in
Elgar's home. Among the guests were Frank Schuster and Sir
Landon Ronald, a concert pianist and now a conductor. Ronald
was so impressed that he begged Elgar to allow him to give the first
public performance of the work with Reed.
  About this time Atkins arranged for an advance copy of his book
Organists of Worcester Cathedral to be sent to Elgar direct from the
publishers. He had dedicated it to him with the words:

I dedicate this little record of Worcester Musicians to Sir Edward Elgar,
O.M., a friend with whom I have shared much which I value most in life,
and, not least, the love of other days.

Hampstead
Saturday Nov 9: 1918
  10 a.m.

My dear dear Firapeel
  Observe the *date & time* & know that only this moment have I had a
chance to open the advance copy of the records of the organists you sent
me: *what* a brute you must have thought me, but my heart bounded when
I read your very beautiful dedication & before reading further I seized
this paper & hasten to send deepest thanks for the sweet & affectionate
words you have placed in the front of your book.

We have been having disturbed times here: Alice's 'little' operation on her forehead turned out to be of more importance than we thought: she is all right now but of course is swathed in bandages: our plans have been altered again & again but it is now settled that we return to the cottage on Monday.

I have a lot of new stuff to show you & should send on proofs if I cd get them but (in this again) times are difficult: however you shall see everything as soon as possible: a Sonata for V. & Pf *ought* to find a responsive thrill in you—I hope it will, because if it does I know it's all right.

Our love to you
Ever yours
Reynart.

Early in November there were rumours of the impending surrender by the Germans, and a few days later the news was confirmed that an Armistice would be signed and hostilities terminated at 11am on Monday, 11 November. A special service was hastily arranged in the cathedral, and even now I can recapture the mad enthusiasm in the city, a packed cathedral and general festivities all day. The service itself was a wonderful blend of joyousness and thankfulness, coupled with an impressive memorial to those who had died in the War.

At the end of the week Atkins received direct from Novello's a rough proof of the Violin and Piano Sonata, and immediately wrote telling Elgar how thrilled he was with it. He added that he was longing to see the other 'new stuff', which he understood would be a piano quintet and a quartet. Billy Reed had told him something about the strange mysterious atmosphere of the quintet.

Brinkwells etc.   Nov 26 1918

My dear Firapeel:
Thanks a-many for your letter but of that mair anon. The present note is to ask you to read the encld card (Sir Sidney Colvin) & tell me if there is a centaur in the Cathedral, etc. etc. I am telling C. that I am asking you.
    Wulstan would know, belike.

Yrs ever in mighty haste
Reynart.

I well remember this request since I was confident that there was a centaur in the cathedral and that it was carved on one of the mediaeval misericord seats. My father tactfully suggested that before he replied we should have another look at it since he would have to describe it in detail. You can imagine my chagrin when a closer look showed that it was a man riding a lion, and not a centaur at all. We examined all the thirty-seven misericord seats, and the arcade carvings in the choir transepts and Lady Chapel, but no centaur could be found. We must have been blind; there is, in fact, a very fine centaur in the west wall arcading of the south choir transept.

With the signing of the Armistice the country's mood began slowly to change to thoughts of a less restricted life, although it would be many months before things could return to normal. Christmas 1918 was a happy one for all.

1919

Our usual visit to London at the beginning of the year brought a meeting with Elgar. We were invited to lunch with him at the Langham Hotel, and I remember that he told us about the burglary which had taken place at 'Severn House' about a fortnight earlier while they were in 'Brinkwells'. For most of the lunch, however, he was telling my father about the Sonata, the Quartet now finished, and about the Quintet and Cello Concerto, the last still in a very early stage. My clearest memory of the lunch was that we had to surrender meat coupons for the meal since rationing was still in force.

Elgar seemed in excellent form and was most enthusiastic about 'Brinkwells' and its woods and peaceful countryside. He intended to spend as much time down there as he could, but visits to London were once again becoming essential.

Severn House, Hampstead, N.W.3.
March 18th 1919

My dear Firapeel:
It has been a weary long time since we had a word & I have had a heavy time getting new works out without your uncley eye (I scorn to say *avuncular*). However the sonata is in print & the IVtet on its (slow) way. The big Vtet, the whilk is *most* intensely Firapeelish, will not be in print for a long time, but bless you! we have played it through & it runs gigantically in a large mood.
When are you coming up? I fear I cannot get down to Worcester for

some time but this note may be as an early swallow & it may be that next week, or belike the week after, I may be at my sister's, & then!
Send a soothing word
Love
Yrs ever

Elgar and Reed had tried out the Violin Sonata on 15 October 1918, and there were now three 'try-outs' of the Elgar chamber works. On 7 January the Quartet, the Sonata and the first movement of the Quintet had been played in the music room at 'Severn House' by Reed and his quartet, with Elgar at the piano; and on 19 January the works were played again, with this time two movements of the Quintet, in Lord Beresford's flat. The third play-through was at 'Severn House' on 7 March. Elgar invited Ernest Newman, to whom the Quintet is dedicated, but he was unable to be present. Writing to Newman later Elgar mentioned that George Bernard Shaw had been there. This time the whole of the Quintet was played, though the last movement was still not in its final form.

On 21 March, in a chamber music concert in the Aeolian Hall, Reed and Landon Ronald gave the first public performance of the Violin Sonata. Atkins had hoped to have been there, but had to write to Elgar to tell him that it would not be possible for him to get up to London in the near future. He mentioned that he had read a report of a speech given by Sir Frederick Bridge, in which he had referred to the failure of the 1878 Worcester Festival musically.

Inadvertently he had written the 1875 festival, which was the 'mock festival' of services only. The 1878 festival followed the normal pattern of oratorios, but the Dean and Chapter had refused to allow the usual staging to be erected at the west end, and had insisted on a low platform only on the choir steps. Elgar had played for the first time in the festival orchestra in 1878, and Atkins had asked if Bridge's statement was correct since it did not agree with what he had heard locally.

Severn House, 42, Netherhall Gardens, Hampstead, N.W.3.
March 27: 1919

My dear Firapeel,
  I saw Bridge's speech & am sorry he referred to the 'platform'.
  The festival of 1878 (*not 75 as you say*) was a failure acoustically but I do not like to write direct to the papers to say so. You may however, give my opinion if you like.
  Your cacoturient parsons always seem to think I want the festivals for my own *pecuniary* betterment! & it is impossible to make this sort of person believe that I am more out of pocket by them than anyone I know & I don't care to defend myself, which if I write, I shall have to do.
  I wish I cd see you & have a talk.
                    In haste
                    Yrs ever
                    Reynart.
which hath a chill in every epigastric region alas!

The word 'cacoturient' was coined by Elgar from the Greek *kakos* (bad), cf 'cacophony'.

  On 16 April Elgar finished the Quintet, and Schuster invited a number of Elgar's friends to attend a first private performance of the Quartet and Quintet in his London home. On this occasion William Murdoch played the piano.

  On 21 May, in the Wigmore Hall, Albert Sammons, W. H. Reed, Raymond Jeremy, Felix Salmond and William Murdoch gave the first public performance of the Quartet and the Quintet, and Albert Sammons and William Murdoch gave a second public performance of the Violin Sonata. Atkins was present, and came away entranced.

  The miniature scores of the Quartet were not ready in time for the concert, but on 30 May Elgar sent Atkins a copy in memory of the occasion.

Severn House, 42, Netherhall Gardens, Hampstead, N.W.3.
May 30 1919

My dear Firapeel:
    The little scores have this moment arrived & I send you one.
    West is arranging the 2nd movement for the organ but I think your busy fingers & mind will 'extract a cordial resemblance' to the piacevole on your mighty leviathan.
Love
R[eynart]

I first heard the Quintet at the 1921 Hereford Festival, but I did not hear the Quartet or the Violin Sonata until 1926, and then only on gramophone records. In my last year at Cambridge I had acquired an HMV portable gramophone, which for the next few years was to accompany me wherever I went, and I began to collect records covering the classical repertoire—Bach, Beethoven and Brahms, in whom I was particularly interested at this time. Naturally, Elgar records featured largely in the collection, and were at that time the only ones which I tried systematically to buy, or beg from Elgar, when he had spare records, as and when they were issued.

    I have clear memories of Elgar's remarks about the writing of the Quintet in 'Brinkwells', and of his description of the 'haunted trees', and the legend about them—a cluster of tall trees on their own on high ground near Flexham Park, which was a pleasant walk through the woods from 'Brinkwells'; gnarled trees with twisted bare branches swaying in the wind, and creaking; weird and stark against the sky. Elgar said that the legend ran that nearby there had once been a monastery of Spanish monks who had renounced their vows and taken to evil and impious rites, for which they had been turned into these dead trees. He implied that these trees and their ghostly appearance had been much in his mind when he was writing the Sonata, the Quartet, and in particular the first movement of the Quintet.

    We played another record, and before I could turn it over Elgar rather dreamily talked about visits that Algernon Blackwood had paid to them at 'Brinkwells', and what an ideal guest he was to have at a country cottage, a fine walker and talker, a keen athlete and a rare expert at pole-jumping. He told how he had cut a long pole for him, and how he had demonstrated his art by leaping on to the top of a tall barred gate, jumping over a hedge, and by long horizontal jumps. From the way he talked Elgar was obviously on close terms with 'Starlight', as he called him, and very familiar with his writing.

Nobody in the Fittleworth area appears to know or have ever heard of a legend about dead trees and Spanish monks, and there is no evidence that there ever was a settlement of Spanish monks anywhere in Sussex. I have often wondered if there was any significance in Elgar's talk about Algernon Blackwood coming immediately after the earlier talk about the legend. It is a surmise only, which cannot now be proved one way or another, but might it not have been Blackwood himself who, on their walk together to the gaunt, twisted, misshapen trees, wove the legend? Trees and the occult fascinated him, as we know from other stories of his, and Elgar would himself respond immediately to such a feat of imagination.

Between June and October Elgar was engrossed in writing the Cello Concerto, and alternated between 'Severn House' and 'Brinkwells', spending as much time as possible in Sussex where he could work without interruption in peaceful surroundings.

In 1920 the festival would have been at Worcester, and Atkins was determined to revive the 'Three Choirs' that year. He had already had discussions with a number of people and written innumerable letters, with somewhat mixed reception, but this did not daunt him. He wanted to talk over these revival plans with Elgar and in particular to persuade him to attend an informal festival meeting, and to speak at the first general meeting since the War of the WO&LC Society. Elgar agreed, provided the two events could be in one week, which would fit in with his long deferred promised visit to Stoke Prior. Early November was suggested.

Severn House, Hampstead, N.W.3.
Saturday [25 October 1919]

My dear Firapeel:
   This wd have been written more than a week ago had not domestic superfluities made things look impossible—cook ill, etc.
   You will have had a telegram,—this is to confess that the subscriber hath jerked a concerto for the bass-viol the which is a good tune & a merry & requires legitimate sponsorship on Monday night: the heart of its

parent yearned *to* (Elizⁿ. use) Firapeel & I hope he can come. But it's too much to hope after all—I would the invitation could have been sent long ago—anyhow I shall think of thee many times during the performance—at the right bits.

Ever yrs

Reynart.

Atkins, short though the notice had been, immediately put off his Worcester afternoon and evening engagements. He could not get to London in time for the rehearsal, but he was able to be at the Queen's Hall for the concert. Elgar was conducting the Cello Concerto, the orchestra was the LSO, and Felix Salmond the soloist. There had been the usual problem of shortage of time for rehearsals, but my father told me what a fine work it was and how Felix Salmond's playing had been a revelation to him. This was not perhaps surprising, since Elgar told him that he and Salmond had played through the work together a number of times from sketch form to the final version.

Elgar kept his promise to come to the Worcester meetings. On 4 November he attended the first general meeting of the Worcester Orchestral & Ladies' Choral Society since the War, and gave a speech of encouragement about the revival of provincial music and his faith in it. I give below an extract from the report of the meeting as published in *Berrows Worcester Journal*.

Sir Edward Elgar, in an inspiring speech, thanked the members of the society for their warm welcome and congratulated them upon making so successful a re-start. He was glad to notice that music showed signs of a great revival throughout England. Their Society had a great opportunity now of doing good work for music in the county. He had lived long enough to see a great change in the technical skill of amateurs, which was now much greater than it used to be. This society was very lucky in having Mr. Atkins as their conductor. He had known him very many years. Mr. Atkins possessed that rare quality of combining infinite painstaking with real insight and inspiration. The other word for that quality was genius. Sir Edward went on to say that the success of a society could not be ensured by the secretary or chairman, or even conductor. It was the individual enthusiasm of each member which would carry on the society. Each member must foster and encourage that enthusiasm, and they must be careful to see that it did not languish. It must grow in strength and all must do their utmost to interest new members. In conclusion, Sir Edward said that he had moved about a good deal since he left Worcestershire, and it was his experience that provincial musicians were in every way as good as those to be found anywhere. It was certainly unnecessary to go to London.

The next evening Elgar dined with us. He was most enthusiastic about the active signs of the revival of music throughout the country, but still seemed a little doubtful about the advisability financially of reviving the Three Choirs Festival the following year. For me, however, the meal had an underlying sadness, since my voice had begun to break, and would not survive the year. My long-hoped-for dream of singing in the Three Choirs Festival was over.

Another subject discussed over the meal was an invitation that my father had received from America to conduct the following year at the Worcester Massachusetts Music Festival, and to give a series of organ recitals on the East Coast. He had also heard from their mutual friend Thomas Whitney Surette, encouraging him to accept. My father seemed very half-hearted about the matter, and said that he did not see how he could be away from the cathedral for so long. Elgar, however, was very keen that he should go, though he advised a careful examination of any contract and said that he would on his return home write to the Dean about the offer.

On the following morning Atkins and Elgar attended an informal meeting regarding the revival of the festival in Worcester in 1920, and it was decided to send out a formal invitation for a meeting of the standing committee.

Hampstead   Nov 11 1919

My dear Firapeel:
    I started early on Friday & since my arrival have had two days of chill—all right now. However, I sent off a scrawl (for U.S.A.) to the Dean. I need not warn you, altho' it behoves Reynart to be ever foxy, that reciprocity in the United States man means always to his own advantage. I hope you will go to Worcester Mass. *but* for art's sake, be very wary as to what you let *them* do in return—they are a sickening lot as I know better than you. You have only seen the good side but_____beware.
    I did enjoy my visit & thank Mrs. Atkins & you for the pleasant & goodly things you did for a wanderer.
    I am overwhelmed with absurd busyness as distinct from useful business.
                        Thine ever
                        Reynart.

At the meeting of the festival standing committee on 26 November, it was resolved that the Three Choirs Festival should be held at Worcester in September 1920, conditional on there being at least 300 stewards, and Atkins had been writing to his many friends with some success. Elgar was unable to be at this meeting as he was in Brussels on his way home after conducting the First Symphony and the Violin Concerto in Amsterdam. Atkins' firm conviction and hard work had prevailed, but it was only the beginning, and the real labours lay ahead. Many of those at the meeting were still worried about the financial aspects of the decision taken, but the Mayor, the Bishop, and the Dean were all fully behind the revival.

The year ended with the usual Christmas services and festivities, but for me with very mixed feelings, since my voice had broken and I was now only a passenger.

PART 6
1920–1922

1920

The year 1920, which was to prove momentous for us all, started quietly. Elgar, who knew that I was going away to Shrewsbury had sent me as a Christmas present a beautiful leather wallet with a pencil and a renewable diary section. I was thrilled with his gift, but disappointed that he had not written in it. My father suggested that when writing to thank him I could return the wallet/diary with a request for him to write my name on the inside of the wallet.

Severn House, Hampstead, N.W.3.
Jan 2: 1920

My dear Wulstan:
  I am so glad you like the diary & I have endeavoured to carry out your behest but leather is not a good surface & I have spoilt the cover: on your head be it!
  Yes: I thought you were going to Shrewsbury & wish you a very happy & successful time there. I know several old boys—some older even than myself—& they are *all of the best sort* so you have not only the great school tradition to keep up—this I know you will do—but also a private (vicarious) tradition of my own.
  You will be very busy at school but you might send me a line or a card sometime to tell me how the games go.
With my love
Your affectionate friend
Edward Elgar.

  Though I did not realise it at the time, Elgar's gift of this diary was to prove far more important than such gifts usually are, for it started me in the habit of keeping a diary, without which this book would suffer from a lack of detail.
  On 5 January, as my mother and I were leaving for Leeds where we were to meet my father, who had been in Wales, and go on to Leck, a large envelope arrived in Alice's handwriting. When my father opened it he found a copy of the first issue of *Music and Letters*, a new quarterly publication. This contained a reproduction of a drawing of Elgar made in 1919 by William Rothenstein, and an article on Elgar by George Bernard Shaw, both commissioned by the publishers. In the following letter to Alice my father comments on the article and gives her the latest news.

Leck Hall, Kirkby Lonsdale, Westmorland.
Jan 13 1920

My dear Lady Elgar,

Do forgive me for not having thanked you for G.B.S.'s article upon Edward. I hope it gave *you* pleasure. For myself I thought it easily the finest thing that has ever been written about him. The article shows really startling insight at times. I was grateful to G.B.S. amongst other things, for giving 'Cockaigne' its proper place. In a general way I find myself a little annoyed with Bernard Shaw (perhaps the feeling is stronger than annoyance) for some of his attitudes, but all through his article he was easily sure of my strongest sympathy. And then of course he is an amazing writer and I hug myself over so many of the tit-bits!

The Festival is started, but it needs driving power at the top. However, the Mayor [John Stallard] writes to me that he has now found a Secretary in Paul Amphlett [Vicar of Powick], and has called a meeting for the 17th. So I hope we shall go ahead. It has been so cold up here that I almost fancy myself not unfitted for Arctic exploration. I weather it quite successfully.

The pocket diary has given the very greatest pleasure to Wulstan. It was very kind of dear Edward to think of him.

Everybody was enchanted with E.E.'s all-round fitness. He went about the place like a Grand Seigneur, dealing with everything and everybody with Royal sureness of touch. We lionised him so far as time and opportunity offered. You can hardly realise the joy his debonaire ways conferred upon us! Much love to you all,

Yours sincerely and affect^{ly},
I.A.A.

The end of the letter refers to Elgar's visit to Worcester the previous November, the intense pleasure it had given to all those he met, and the great encouragement he had given to those determined to revive the festival.

On 14 January we returned home, and the next morning my father received the following letter from Elgar.

Severn House, Hampstead, N.W.
Jan 14 1920

My dear Firapeel, I have recd. the Mayor's notice of the Festl. Comm[ittee]: I cannot come—will you make any notification (if any is necy) at the time.

I fear the commercial side is a grave difficulty—some of the rich folk ought to see it thro'—it seems wicked that Dyson Perrins, for instance, cd with a stroke of the pen start & support the thing!

In order to participate in the Ballot this Form should be filled up and posted immediately.

WORCESTER TRIENNIAL MUSICAL FESTIVAL,

September 5th, 7th, 8th, 9th and 10th, 1920.

Conditions of Stewardship.

Extract from Circular Letter to Stewards issued January 26th, 1920:

" The condition of Stewardship is the purchase of First Division Tickets to an amount of not less than £3 13s. 6d., with tax (if any), and of a limited liability of £1 11s. 6d. towards any expense incurred over and above receipts, instead of an unlimited sum as in previous Festivals.

The office of Steward does not necessarily involve any active duties at the Festival, unless a Steward is willing to help in seating those who attend."

To the Hon. Secretary, Worcester Festival,
Powick Vicarage, Worcester.

Sir,

    I accept the office of Steward for the above Festival subject to the conditions as stated above.

Yours faithfully,

(Name in full) *Edward Elgar*

(Postal Address) *Severn House*

May 28/5 20 *Hampstead*

Yours faithfully,

(Name in full) *Alice Elgar*

(Postal Address)

303

However I suppose the first thing is to have the prelimin^y meeting, & then—— we shall see.

I was delighted to hear from the boy & hope great things for him.

I hope you may be coming to town sometime. Let us know.

Alice has been really ill alas! She is better now & has been out once for ten minutes——the first time since Nov. 2nd.

Yrs ever
Reynart

Carice is in Switzerland

At the meeting of the standing committee on 17 January, the dates for the festival were fixed as 5–10 September inclusive, and Atkins was formally appointed conductor. Elgar and Alice completed their forms as stewards and posted them back by return. Lee Williams did the same, but in his letter to the secretary he expressed serious doubts on the financial side and suggested a reduction to three days only, including the elimination of the Sunday opening service.

Atkins, however, felt very strongly about reviving the Three Choirs Festivals on the same lines as the abandoned 1914 Worcester Festival, and for him the religious aspect, with its 'Grand Orchestral Opening Service' on the Sunday and the other services forming part of the festival, was one of the unique and most essential features, and indeed largely the justification for the festivals being held in the cathedrals. The decision had been taken at Worcester that Three Choirs Festivals were to continue in their traditional form, and Atkins had begun planning the programme and thinking about orchestral and choral arrangements.

Although in the past, by far the majority of the players had in fact been members of the London Symphony Orchestra, each of them was always given an individual contract. Atkins had been considering for 1920 the possibility of engaging an existing orchestra instead of individual players, and had indeed discussed the pros and cons of the idea with Elgar.

Severn House, Hampstead, N.W.
Feb 14 1920

My dear Firapeel:

I send on the enclosed as promised to the writer thereof. I see a prophetic announcement of a new work [by Elgar]. I fear under present circumstances that it is very unlikely that my pen will proceed to write anything new.

I hope to be down Worcester ways soon & will come & see you if I do travel.

Yrs ever
Reynart.

The enclosure was a letter from the secretary of the New Symphony Orchestra, referring to Elgar composing a special work for the Worcester Festival, and asking him to use his influence to obtain an engagement for the orchestra. There was no chance, however, of an engagement for that orchestra, since Atkins had always had the London Symphony Orchestra in mind, with so many players who had already played individually at Worcester.

Severn House, 42, Netherhall Gardens, Hampstead, N.W.3.
Feb 15 1920

My dear Firapeel,

I am not sure about coming down—there are so many things cropping up. I hope you may find room for the enclosed anthem—with big orch: you will see the reference to *peace* at the end—about as far as we can go under the circumstances.

Yrs ever
Reynart.

Enclosed was a copy of *Give unto the Lord* (Psalm 29), Op 74, which had been composed by Elgar for, and given its first performance at, the 'Festival of the Sons of the Clergy', held in St Paul's Cathedral on 30 April 1914. He had sent Atkins a copy of this on 15 April 1914, when he had hoped that it would be included in that year's festival. He was now offering it for the Worcester Festival instead of a new composition, but it was not possible to include it.

Negotiations with the London Symphony Orchestra were protracted since their first estimate was so high it could not be considered, and it was not until 24 July that the formal agreement was signed. Meanwhile, a real start had been made in the preparations for the Festival.

Severn House, 42, Netherhall Gardens, Hampstead, N.W.3.
March 29 1920

My dear Firapeel
    I hope all goes well.
    This is a sad little note to tell you that my poor dear Alice is really ill,
very ill, I fear.

Love
Yrs ever
R.

This letter came as a great shock to the Atkins, since although
Elgar had told them that Alice had hardly left the house since
November, they had no idea that she was now seriously ill.

Alice died on 7th April. Elgar was completely prostrated by her
death. Carice telephoned to tell Atkins that the funeral, which
would be private, was to take place at St Wulstan's Church, Little
Malvern, on 10 April. Many years earlier Alice had said that she
would like to be buried there. She had loved the Quartet, and
Carice and Schuster arranged with Billy Reed that Albert
Sammons, Billy, Raymond Jeremy and Felix Salmond would play
the slow movement at the funeral service.

Atkins, Landon Ronald, Sanford Terry, Troyte Griffith and
Hubert Leicester were among the very few present other than
the family. Sir Charles Stanford, who was convalescing in
Malvern, came into the back of the church but did not go to the
grave.

I had returned from Shrewsbury on 7 April, but neither my
mother nor I went to the funeral. My father brought back Sanford
Terry with him to stay with us. Carice and Elgar stayed for a few
days at Kirklands, the Church House adjacent to St Wulstan's,
and Elgar then went on to stay at Stoke Prior. Sanford Terry
stayed with us until 12 April, and surprised and delighted me by
presenting to me the previous night a beautiful full hunter gold
watch. My father was very pleased, and I have no doubt that the
watch was also a thank-you to him for all the help that he had given
Terry in writing his three-volume book *Bach's Chorales*. The first
volume, dedicated to my father, had appeared in 1915, the second
in 1917, and the final volume was at this time in preparation for the
press.

Atkins had by now prepared, and the executive committee had

approved, the draft festival programme apart from the artists. He accordingly sent a copy to Elgar with certain suggestions regarding possible singers. Although he really knew that there was no hope of a new work by Elgar, he thought that he might be interested to consider one, or to suggest some existing short composition to be included in the Tuesday evening programme, which would help to take his mind off his great loss. Atkins, under pressure from others, including Elgar, had put down his own *Hymn of Faith* for one of the items for this evening.

[On black-edged paper]
[Severn House]
May 6 1920

My dear Firapeel: you must forgive me—I am a weary & a much broken man.

It will not be possible for me to write anything new—you cannot fathom the loneliness & desolation of my life I fear.

Now as to singers: for Gerontius K[*irkby*] *Lunn*—of the two possible tenors [John Coates or Gervase Elwes] which you please. Elwes is I suppose the more accustomed & popular 'G'. Bass [Herbert] Heyner. I have not heard Astra Desmond.

Would *The Music Makers* do for the Cathedral? *words* I mean. I feel rather vague (on looking at it now) about *pt II Apostles* standing alone.

If you do it.   A[gnes] Nicholls
                             P[hyllis] Lett
                             Coates
                             (Peter)—not much to do except the important burst on p.143.
                             Jesus   Heyner certainly
                             Judas   Radford certainly

If you include a symphony of mine No.2 please: but I don't quite understand the position.

I really like the idea of the civic procession—& you could get all the doctors etc of music to wear robes & the military too—it would be splendid.

I should like the *Music Makers*—I spoke to the Dean in Nov: about words generally & I do not think he would raise any objection—the whole 'point' is raised in stanza 8—'Once *more God's future draws nigh*' etc.

I am sorry, sorry to be so unhelpful. *We* had been looking forward to the dear old festival & suddenly the whole thing is hurled away from me.

I am glad to see you have [Julius] Harrison & B[rent] Smith in the scheme.

I think the programme from a popular point of view excellent—I wish that *Elijah* could have given way to a mixed modern programme but that wd. be fatal I fear. The *Messiah* you know I love & am delighted it is in its old place.

love

Yours ever

Reynart

To avoid smashing the whole affair I am going for Embleton to Newcastle on Saturday. I *may* have to *un*rhumatise at Droitwich on the way home: if so I will surely let you know & we can meet. EE

At the festival finance committee on 29 May Atkins reported that he had discussed with the Bishop the possibility of having royal patronage for the Worcester Festival, as previous festivals had been so honoured, and that the Bishop was making the necessary approaches. At the beginning of June the Bishop told him that the King and Queen, the Prince of Wales and the Duke of Connaught had all agreed to honour the festival with their especial patronage.

The final programme was approved on 12 June, and as Atkins wanted to get Elgar's reaction and agreement to conduct before this was printed he wrote giving the details and saying that he had now decided on Coates for *Gerontius* and that Elwes would sing in the *St Matthew Passion*. He proposed Astra Desmond for *The Music Makers*.

[On black-edged paper]
Brinkwells, Fittleworth, Sussex.
June 26, 1920

My dear Firapeel:
  We are down at the Cottage & it is quiet & restful but very, very, very sad. I do not get on in health as we could wish but the shock has been too

---

(*opposite above*) Elgar at Severn House, Hampstead, in 1913. Note the small-bowled long-stemmed pipe and books on his table, and behind him one of the bookcases which had been designed by Troyte Griffith. Photograph by Reginald Haines

(*below left*) Atkins in the Worcester Cathedral Music Library in July 1916, shortly after he had, with Elgar's encouragement, formed this as a separate library in what had been in monastic times part of the Treasury

(*below right*) The author in 1917, when, as a Cathedral chorister, he sang in *For the Fallen* under Elgar's baton in the Recital of Solemn Music in Worcester Cathedral on 15 March

great & although I struggled hard & went through some conducting in Newcastle & S. Wales the inevitable crash came—I am really all right but tire too easily & can take no interest in any thing.

Now as to Worcester & your queries.

(1) I don't know anything of Miss A. Desmond—if you think well, so be it (Gerontius I believe is to be K. Lunn?)

(2) Let's do the String piece [*Introduction and Allegro*] at the Evening Concert. You will remember that it takes some time to re-arrange the 'sitting' of the orch. & we want the Quartet as far as possible away from the orch—they cannot (with any effect) play close in.

(3) If it is better for the book please put 'conducted by the subscriber'. If anything shd interfere with this it wd show that I wanted to be with you.

I wish you could see this place, but it is uncertain how long we remain: it is difficult to get service—servants out of the question. My love to you & to the Boy.

Yrs ever

Reynart.

P.S. Carice thanks you for your letter which I have answered as she is so busy with housekeeping—she does everything now & does it well & nobly!

Brinkwells, Fittleworth, Sussex.
Augt. 1 1920

My dear Firapeel:

I hope all goes well & that you are not overworked, do not add to your busyness by writing more than a pc: Carice & I hope to be very quietly

---

(*opposite above*) Revival of the Three Choirs Festival at Worcester in 1920, after the abandonment of the 1914 Worcester Festival as a result of the outbreak of World War I. Elgar, Atkins and W. H. Reed outside the North Porch of the Cathedral after the afternoon rehearsal on Saturday, 4 September. Elgar had earlier that day rehearsed *The Music Makers* (*The Times*)

(*below, left to right*) W. H. Reed, Leader of the LSO, at the Atkins' home; Gervase Elwes and W. H. Reed, Worcester, September 1920. Before and after World War I the two greatest interpreters of Gerontius were generally considered to be Gervase Elwes and John Coates. Elwes came from one of the great English Roman Catholic families and his interpretation made Gerontius a devout, almost saintly, figure. John Coates' Gerontius was on a more earthly level, a dying man who feared as well as longed for his judgement. Elgar greatly admired these two fine singers and appreciated both interpretations, but perhaps on the whole considered Coates' Gerontius to be nearer his own idea of the man; Dr Atkins wearing the Oxford Doctor of Music robes which were presented to him at a ceremony in the Chapter House on Christmas Eve, 1920 (see page 324)

311

and *invisibly* in the Precincts—my uncle's old rooms—but do not tell anyone of this, as I do not want to visit or be visited, alas!

I hope this may find you in holiday & resting mood: the weather looks a little better this morning but it has been a weary & suffocating time.

I hope you are all well: my love,

Yrs ever

Reynart.

P.S. Let me know about rehearsals—London & Worcester—I hope to arrive in Worcester on *Friday* evening before the Festival so as to have a fatherly eye on it all. I hope you have not been worried by any friends of mine about rooms & tickets—it is not my fault if you have—however, you can direct such impertinent enquiries, with your easy grace, into the proper channels very easily!

Atkins wrote from Llantwit Major, where he was on holiday, reminding Elgar about the full-chorus rehearsal in the cathedral on Thursday afternoon, 26 August, and hoping that he would be able to come. He also enclosed a copy of the London and Worcester rehearsals programme for 31 August–6 September.

Fittleworth

19 AUG 1920 [the date is stamped in red ink]

My dear Firapeel:

Thanks for your letter. I have kept it by me hoping I shd be able to come to the choral rehearsal on the 26th—but alas! it is really impossible for me to do it and I am grieved. I note the London rehearsals & hope to be with you.

I send this to Worcr. for I cannot decipher your Welsh. I hope you have had a good & sufficient rest & are ready for the fray.

Love

Yrs ever

Reynart.

The full-chorus rehearsal in the cathedral on the 26th was a special occasion for me, as I heard my father's *Hymn of Faith* for the first time.

Brinkwells

Augt 27 1920

My dear Firapeel:

I am hoping to be with you all right next week in London & the following week in Worcester. *But*—I am not well & think it only right to

tell you so that you may make any arrgts you like—I am *longing* to come &
hope I may be all right, but I am very shaky.

Love

E.E.

On 31 August, I went with my father to the Morley Hall,
Hanover Square, for the rehearsal. To his delight we had hardly
arrived before Carice and Elgar came in. There was no Elgar work
in the programme that day and my father had only half expected
that he would come. He seemed in fine form, and after chatting to
us for a moment or so he moved on to talk to Billy Reed and other
friends in the orchestra before he sat down in the body of the hall
with Carice. I sat down near him and soon became enthralled in the
rehearsal. It was the first time that I had heard a top professional
orchestra, and I began to try to sort out the different instruments,
turning my head as necessary. After a bit Elgar noticed what I was
doing and beckoned me to sit with them. During breaks he pointed
out to me the main sections of the orchestra—strings, wood wind,
brass and timpani—and the different instruments. It was my first
lesson in orchestral music. Elgar loved Berlioz, and the *Carnival
Romain* was ideal for the lesson.

Soon, however, he became interested in Julius Harrison's new
work *Worcestershire Suite*, and the lesson ceased. He wandered off
for the Rimsky-Korsakov *Scheherazade*, but returned to hear Brent-
Smith's *Rhapsody* and the César Franck Symphony. I did not see
him after lunch, though he may well have been there for some of
the rehearsal.

On the Wednesday Carice and Elgar again came early, but this
time he sat near my father who was rehearsing the *St Matthew
Passion*, and occasionally made suggestions. After the lunch break
Elgar conducted *Gerontius*, and later the *Introduction and Allegro*.
The positioning of the quartet players relative to the main
orchestra was important to him and there was some rearranging on
the platform. It was fascinating to watch him with the orchestra,
who obviously had played for him many times before and knew
exactly what he wanted.

The Thursday morning rehearsal was devoted to Walford
Davies' *Fantasy*. Elgar came for this and then disappeared until
later, when he came back for my father's *Hymn of Faith*. After
lunch Elgar conducted *The Music Makers* and *For the Fallen*. Once

313

again it was a revelation to me to see him conduct, and especially in *For the Fallen*. What a difference the orchestral colour made to the work.

I was longing for the Worcester rehearsals and the performances. Friday and Saturday morning were very busy days of preparation for all. The tent was erected in the garden and tables and chairs had to be arranged and set out for lunch on the Saturday. Messages had to be sent to the precentor and the choir school regarding the timetables for the boys and for those coming from Gloucester and Hereford. I seemed to be constantly on my feet, but it was exciting.

The rehearsal in the cathedral on Saturday afternoon seemed quiet by contrast, but how wonderful it was now that I was hearing the orchestra, the soloists and the large chorus. After an hour of the *St Matthew Passion* Elgar's arrangement of the National Anthem was like a clarion call. Brahms' *How lovely is thy Dwelling-place* with orchestra was deeply moving for an ex-chorister. It was a new world for me. What would the actual performances be like?

Elgar and Carice had come down on the Friday evening and were staying very quietly with Miss Allcott in his uncle Henry's old rooms in the Precincts. My father had warned me that they would wish to be left alone, and I had only once seen Elgar and then only on the rostrum when after the tea break on Saturday he had conducted the rehearsal of *The Music Makers*.

On Sunday the festival started with the 'Grand Opening Service'. This began with Elgar's *Sursum Corda* conducted by my father and was followed by a chant by Sinclair and the Magnificat and Nunc Dimittis in D, which was specially composed for this festival by Lee Williams. Brahms' *How lovely is thy Dwelling-place* was for me even more moving than at the previous day's rehearsal. But Sullivan's *In Memoriam*, played in memory of Sinclair, sent tears to my eyes, for I had known him as long as I could remember.

The Monday was given over to rehearsals, and I attended as much of them as I could, but with a large house-party and about a hundred people a day invited to lunch and supper, not to mention teas, my mother needed help.

Hospitality had always been a great feature of the Three Choirs Festivals, and my parents felt the social side to be very important. My mother especially considered that, apart from the great pleasure it gave them, this was the way in which she could best

Three Choirs Festival.

Worcester Meeting,

September 5th, 7th, 8th, 9th, and 10th, 1920.

THE 200th MEETING OF THE THREE CHOIRS OF WORCESTER, HEREFORD, AND GLOUCESTER.

Principal Performers:

Miss FIFINE DE LA COTE.
Madame AGNES NICHOLLS.
Miss CARRIE TUBB.
Miss ASTRA DESMOND.
Miss MARION EADIE-REED.
Miss PHYLLIS LETT.
Madame KIRKBY LUNN.

Mr. JOHN COATES.
Mr. GERVASE ELWES.
Mr. STEUART WILSON.
Mr. NORMAN ALLIN.
Capt. HERBERT HEYNER.
Mr. ROBERT RADFORD.
Mr. FREDERIC RANALOW.

LONDON SYMPHONY ORCHESTRA (Principal, 1st Violin, Mr. W. H. REED).

ORGAN, Mornings   -   -   -   Dr. A. H. BREWER.
,,   Evenings   -   -   -   Mr. P. C. HULL.

Conductor: Mr. IVOR ATKINS.

IN THE CATHEDRAL.

Sunday, Sept. 5th, 3.30 p.m. GRAND OPENING SERVICE WITH CHORUS AND ORCHESTRA.

Tuesday Morning - "Elijah" - - - - - - *Mendelssohn*
Sept. 7th, 11.30 a.m.

Tuesday Evening - "Hymn of Faith" - - - - *Ivor Atkins*
"The Music Makers" - - , - - - *Elgar*
7.30 p.m. "Hymn of Praise" - - - - *Mendelssohn*

"Gerontius" - - - - - - - *Elgar*
Motet for unaccompanied Chorus—"There is
Wednesday Morning - an old belief" - - - - *Hubert Parry*
Sept. 8th, 11.30 a.m. New Work—Fantasy for Tenor Solo, Chorus
and Orchestra (founded on Dante's
Divina Commedia) - - - *H. Walford Davies*
Symphony in D Minor - - - - *César Franck*

Thursday Morning - "St. Matthew" Passion - - - - - *Bach*
Sept. 9th, 11.30 a.m.

Thursday Evening - New Work—Four Hymns, for Tenor Solo
and String Orchestra - - *Vaughan Williams*
7.30 p.m. "For the Fallen" - - - - - *Elgar*
Requiem - - - - - - - *Verdi*

Friday Morning - "Messiah" - - - - - - - *Handel*
Sept. 10th, 11.30 a.m.

Friday Evening, 6 p.m. Closing Service by the Three Choirs.

IN THE PUBLIC HALL.

Wednesday Evening - New Work for Orchestra — Worcestershire
Rhapsody - - - - - *A. E. Brent Smith*
8 p.m. and Works by *Elgar, Julius Harrison*, etc.

*Programmes containing all information as to Tickets, etc., may be obtained about the end
of June from Messrs. Deighton & Co. and Messrs. Spark & Co.*

CHORUS AND ORCHESTRA OF ABOUT 400 PERFORMERS.

Serial Tickets (for Stewards ONLY) £3 13s. 6d. *plus* tax. Single Tickets, *inclusive of tax*—1st Division £1,
2nd Division 13s. 6d., 3rd Division 7s. 6d., 4th Division 5s., 5th Division 3s. 6d. ;
Public Hall Concert, 13s. 6d. and 7s. 6d.

contribute to Worcester meetings. Naturally musicians and the artists taking part were to the fore at my parents' lunches, teas and suppers. I spent as much time as I could helping my mother with guests, but my main duty after welcoming them at the door was to look after my father and Billy Reed, who were always given lunch by themselves in the study, which was carefully guarded and kept absolutely private. Their lunch over, they would generally then join the guests in the tent. What fun these meals were—a curious mixture of seriousness and gaiety, with many stories usually of dry infectious humour flying across the table. What is it about musicians that makes them such good company?

But there was one who was greatly missed by all—Elgar, who avoiding all hospitality remained quietly with Carice in his lodging. I had so far seen virtually nothing of him in Worcester, but on the Wednesday evening I saw him at the Public Hall in the artists' room during the interval, where he was preparing to conduct the *Introduction and Allegro* in the second part. He asked me how I had enjoyed the Berlioz *Carnival Romain* and Julius Harrison's *Worcestershire Suite*, and ended by inviting me to go over to see him after breakfast the next day.

On the Thursday morning I went over to the Precincts and found him alone, Carice having gone out shopping. He seemed more like his normal self and admitted that the festival had done him good. He told me that he had seen nobody in his lodging apart from my father and Billy Reed. He was evidently pleased with the performances of his own works. Clearly he was responding to the love and understanding of all his old friends, orchestra, chorus and audience. He alone, apart from Gervase Elwes, knew that my own feelings about the Festival were very mixed, my joy turning quickly to sadness when I remembered how much I had wanted to have been singing in this festival. How wonderfully understanding Elgar was! In his own great sorrow he could appreciate and try to help the disappointment of an ex-chorister. I left him happier than when I had gone to him, and brought back a message that he would slip in and see us sometime the next afternoon or evening.

The festivals at this time ended with the *Messiah* on the Friday morning and early afternoon, and, at 5pm, a 'Grand Closing Service', given by the Three Choirs. On the Thursday it occurred to my father that it would be appropriate immediately after the performance of the *Messiah* to have a programme of memorial music at the Cenotaph. The music would consist of extracts from the *Messiah*, 'Since by man came death', followed by the 'Hallelujah' Chorus, one verse of 'O God, our help in ages past', and the 'Last Post'.

All concerned agreed, and large posters were quickly printed and put up. All musicians present with their robes were invited to march in the procession of the three cathedral choirs and the clergy from the Chapter House to the Cenotaph outside the Cathedral. The chorus and orchestral players would assemble at the Cenotaph together with representatives of the military and civic authorities. It was a most impressive and moving occasion.

I have vivid recollections of this very special revived festival. I recall the opening service on the Sunday, with the pageantry of the processions, the Lord Lieutenants, the Mayors and Corporations from all over Worcestershire and from Gloucester and Hereford, complete with their mace-bearers and other officials, their chains of office glittering in the sunlight, representatives of the Forces in full uniform, and the long procession of the clergy, the cross, the choir, the representatives of the colleges of music and the music schools, of the universities, arrayed in their colourful degree robes, the honorary canons, the canons, the three deans and the three bishops each with his chaplain.

I remember especially the impressive *Elijah*, with Agnes Nicholls, Phyllis Lett, Gervase Elwes and Herbert Heyner, and the chorus singing in my father's *Hymn of Faith* and in Elgar's *The Music Makers*. I was enthralled by the loveliness of Elgar's enduring and inspiring music, unknown to me until this festival. *The Dream of Gerontius*, with Kirkby Lunn, John Coates and Herbert Heyner, the chorus and the orchestra in the cathedral completely overwhelmed me. Beethoven's *Three Equali for four Trombones*, played in memory of Parry, Lloyd and Sinclair, reduced me to tears, as did *There is an old belief*, for I had loved Parry and Sinclair, both of whom I had known since I was a very small boy.

Every performance brought me fresh wonders. If, however, I must choose a highlight it must be the performance of Bach's *St Matthew Passion*, heralded as it was by the playing, four times, one from each side of the cathedral tower, of Elgar's arrangement for brass of Bach's Chorale 'O Mensch bewein' before the morning performance, and 'O Sacred Head surrounded' in the afternoon.

The chorales sounded magnificent to me, since I heard them from the top of the tower after I had escorted the LSO players up there, to many complaints from them as we made the steep ascent.

Orchestral players are remarkable people. Within minutes of the climb these wind players were performing with absolutely perfect pitch and glorious clear ringing tone, no doubt encouraged by the sight of the beer waiting for them which I had previously and surreptitiously taken up to the top of the tower.

Elgar loved the *Messiah*, and he and Carice had stayed specially for it. He remained for the cenotaph service, came in with Carice for a quick cup of tea, and then went on to Spetchley Park to stay with the Berkeleys for a few days before moving on to Stoke Prior. The festival had evidently helped him enormously. He was almost his normal self, talking about all the performances, how well they had all gone, the splendid state of the chorus, the wonderful playing of the LSO once they had become accustomed to the acoustics of the cathedral. He teased Billy about how lost the players were in the first few minutes of their first rehearsal in the cathedral, and left us with warm congratulations to my father. The festival had undoubtedly been an artistic success, but what would the financial results be? My father was able to tell him that there had been 476 stewards and he was, not unnaturally, very proud of the fact that he had personally obtained 139 of them. Festival conductors' duties and responsibilities were in those days very wide and by no means restricted to music.

After this strenuous week, we went to stay in the restful atmosphere of Ludlow, but it was impossible to get away completely from the festival, for soon the letters of congratulation began to pour in. They came from eminent musicians, artists, the LSO, clergy, official bodies and many total strangers. The letters reflect in different ways the state of music after the War, the grave fears that financially the restoration of the great provincial festivals was impossible, the anxiety regarding Worcester's bold decision, and the general satisfaction that artistically the 'Three Choirs' was back on the musical map in all its splendour. For the moment this was all that mattered. It had now been shown that revival of festivals outside London was possible and could be justified.

The following letter from Elgar gave Atkins particular pleasure.

Stoke Priors (home on Monday)
Sept 18 1920

My dear Firapeel:
 I hope you have had a good rest after *the* week: you can look back with
the greatest pride and satisfaction to your part in the revival & I
congratulate you on the whole of your work—it is very gratifying that
Worc! shd have led the way.
 I had a day or two at Spetchley—caught $\frac{1}{2}$ doz. fish & came on to my
sister's. I shd have come over if the weather had been settled—I was
booked for the one fine day I have enjoyed.
 I shall be glad to hear any news of the festl. I have read no press notices
but, for the first time for twenty years, am anxious to know how the
reptiles viewed it all. I heard of no disagreeables, but my sources are
shallow as I went only to H[ubert] Leicester on Sunday evening—to the
Brewers' house & to you: when you were not to be talked to about
newspapers.
 I cannot tell you how I loved the week—the cathedral—the weather,
and all of it. Thank you for a mighty effort & bless you.
 As for me, I was sad at heart really, beyond words, & my life (to use
dear old Kilburn's words which he always used about compositions not
worth discussion)—'IT WON'T DO.' I am tired of it & have nothing to work
for now, alas!
Love,
E.E.

Castle Square, Ludlow.
Sept. 23, 1920

My dear Reynart,
 It is almost unforgivable but you *must* forgive my delay for I have been
under the mark with a chill and only fit for the abominable task of clearing
up Festival debris. Well, it was a great Festival and I am only thankful
that I had *you* to help in the grand revival. At a time when one missed so
many you were a very anchor to me. I was more than pleased to see the
wonderful way in which you got on both in London and later at
Worcester. I don't think I ever remember your giving off greater nervous
power and it seemed to me that you were very happy in it all. I now look
upon 'Gerontius' as the Festival stay in the years to come. Your works
have done much for the Three Choirs in our day but they will go on when
you and I are dust. You ought even in the most difficult moments to find
some rest and anchorage in the thought of your works and their heaven-
sent message. They are great, but what I like is your vigour. You are
about as lively as Vesuvius and equally disturbing. You must have been

319

bucked in London by your power of making *really* magnificent noises. Your noises indeed terrify me, and what annoys me is that you have the audacity to take them quietly and even to suggest by your coolness that you are superior to them. This 'won't do'.

Goodbye, Reynart: God be with you, sure. Take courage and go on (though I grieve for you).

Love to you both,
Thine,
Firapeel.

There was still a small but vocal clerical element who had reservations about the type of music which should be played in a cathedral, and about the charging for seats. Indeed, in 1919 the Dean and Chapter had said in the early discussions that they were in favour of reviving the festivals and wanted a fine musical festival in the cathedral, but they were not in favour of the erection of the elaborate large platform and the work which extended over several weeks. They had given way only because they had been assured that it was not possible to perform oratorios like *Elijah* and the *Messiah* without it. Bishop Pearce, who was very musical, and had made history by singing as a tenor in the chorus at the festival, had up to now preserved a neutral position. After the festival he wrote an article in the October Worcester Diocesan Gazette, which for most people ended a controversy that had continued to a greater or a lesser degree for 50 years. The essence of his article is contained in the extract given here.

Well, clearly you could not justify what is merely a 'concert', save that instead of being held in a public hall it takes place in the Cathedral. My experience of this Festival shows me that you need not defend yourselves on this score at all. You are saved from any such danger by the obviously religious aim which inspires the conduct of the rehearsals. The *baton* is in the hand of a man who insists that you are to bring out the spiritual purport of the words. You are saved from it at the actual performances— let us be honest and say services—by the simple and appropriate prayers, simply and appropriately said by the Precentor or the Sacrist, and responded to simply and heartily by the people.

But I should like to take the whole consideration a step further. I understand music to be a great and independent art, divinely ordained like any other. It seems to me to be entitled to organise such an act of worship as these September days have seen, and I see no impropriety in music's claim that the Cathedral should lend itself for the purpose. It means financial organisation, for music, by the nature of the case, cannot be offered without cost, and those who 'pay for seats' take their natural

320

part in this offering, they are helping to provide music's sacrifice of praise and thanksgiving.

The gross receipts of the festival were £5,868 4s, and the expenses £5,279 10s 11d, which included nearly £700 Entertainment Tax for which a repayment appeal had been made to the Commissioners of Customs & Excise, and £100 reserved for the preliminary expenses in connection with the 1923 Worcester Festival. There was therefore a balance of £588 13s 1d, in addition to the collection which had amounted to £845 13s 7d. This sum would be invested as in former years to provide income for the Charity for the Widows and Orphans of the Clergy. The festival had therefore proved a financial as well as an artistic success, and the future was now certain.

The occasion was an historic one and the importance of the achievement is shown by the following extracts from tributes made at a meeting of the festival stewards. One of the stewards said that:

. . . no one who had taken part in the organisation of the festival could help but be struck by the enormous energy and devotion which Mr Ivor Atkins had put into the work, not only in the selection of principals and in the securing of the orchestra, but also in the training of the choir and bringing the whole up to the pitch of excellence that he had achieved. That the festival had been a success was due principally to their Conductor.

The Dean thought that the festival was a great personal triumph for Mr Atkins. He did not mind at all being proved a false prophet. He never thought that it would be possible to carry the festival through and to pay all the expenses when the cost amounted to such a large sum, but Mr Atkins never failed in believing that it could be done, and he had put his whole heart and soul and energy into the work, and it was the enthusiasm that he had shown which had brought the satisfactory results they had before them that day. The festival was a remarkable triumph of Mr Atkins' musical ability.

The publication of the financial results of the festival brought many letters of congratulation to Atkins and in the national press.

The last 2 months of 1920 were to bring further excitements. Atkins was very proud of his Oxford BMus, which he had passed by examination in 1892, and had always intended to sit for his DMus, but since he was appointed to Worcester in 1897 he had been too occupied to do so. After the festival he wrote to Hugh Allen, who was Professor of Music at Oxford as well as being Director at the Royal College of Music, regarding his wish to sit for the examination, and to find out if his existing compositions could be accepted for the purpose of the examination or if he had to write some special work. Atkins' letter, although he did not know it until several weeks later, was embarrassing to Allen because he had already arranged to put Atkins' name forward for an honorary D Mus.

On 23 November Atkins sat for his examination, the examiners being H. P. Allen, Percy C. Buck and Ralph Vaughan Williams. On 25 November he was notified that he had been awarded his degree and that the formal presentation would take place on 17 December. Letters came in from all over the country. Bishop Pearce's postcard is worth recording:

Hartlebury. 26.11.20.

Delighted to hear it. There ought to be a chorale on the Cathedral tower at the time when you are taking it.
E.W.

Severn House, Hampstead, N.W.
Dec. 5 1920

My dear Doctor Firapeel:
I cannot tell you the delight it gives me to address this with the honourable prefix which I have desired for you for so long. I am glad you have the real Oxford honour and not an Hony one—such things will come later—you wd have had such 'an one' long ago but for the intolerable small jealousies of which the professors of our art are capable: however, this is not the moment to reckon up my *dis*appointments but to send only a full-hearted word of congratulations to Mrs. Atkins & to you.
Bless you!
I hope to see you soon.
Love,
Reynart.

On 17 December my father and mother went to Oxford for the formal presentation of his degree of Doctor of Music.

I came home on 21 December to find a strange sense of excitement, noticeably where my mother was concerned, but also, though more controlled, in my father. Over tea I asked how the ceremony had gone in Oxford, and soon heard all about it, and also that there was going to be another ceremony in the Chapter House on Christmas Eve. A number of my father's friends, including the Bishop, the Dean and Elgar, had purchased the full robes of a Doctor of Music at Oxford, comprising hood, gown and hat, and the Dean would, on their behalf, present them to him. It was hoped that Elgar would be at the ceremony. I sensed, however, that this was not the whole story, and over our evening meal, under seal of secrecy, my father told me that that morning he had received a letter, signed personally by the Prime Minister, David Lloyd George, informing him that the King had been pleased to approve that the honour of knighthood be conferred upon him. The official announcement would be published in the New Year's Honours List, and it was vital that the matter be kept absolutely confidential until then.

Elgar sent his next letter in a prepaid envelope sent by the WO&LCS to bring its members together after the war.

[Hampstead]
Dec: 21: 1920

My dear Firapeel:
You will forgive the drastic economy betrayed by the envelope. Why shd not I batten on the Socys long ago generosity & save 1½d? There is but one answer.

This is only to wish you three all good things for Christmas & the New Year. We go to my sister's tomorrow
The Elms
Stoke Prior
Bromsgrove.
and I charge you 'keep me informed'.

I feel very shy & *unfoxlike* but I have to tell you that I have a CAR & we drove down. I know this is a sad lapse—but how many laps go to a mile? Idiotic.

So I may 'drive' !!!!!!!! over to Worcester &—well, I shall get out of the car in the Liberties & walk the rest of the way 'within walls'. I am (dear Firapeel) dreadfully & thoroughly ashamed of it all—but *by'r lakin* it *is* nice. Having left my cluse—after confession as above—I want news, or 'noose' as the U.S.Atians pronounce it—alas! that they do not get what they want & deserve. I saw that a Meeting was held at H'ford [festival meeting] & all seems to go well. I hope so & wrote to Hull to that effect. I wonder if that depleted county will rise as you caused Worcestershire to rise.

I am not well—I have made my struggle to take up the threads of the old life—I have worked and played, but '*it won't do*', as old Kilburn used to say, & I give it up.

    Again our love & all good wishes,
                        Thine ever
                        Reynart.

now a shotten herring

At Stoke
Thursday [23 December 1920]

My dear Firapeel:
    I will do all I can to get over tomorrow for the robing—but I sent the car back to London as my man (I have bowels) hath a wife & a family & I had not the heart to keep him away at Christmas-time: he will bring the car back next week. So far continue my abject revelations.
    I was delighted to receive your letter & to know my defection is assoilized[x]. Yes, the *izzard* by all means. Be calm. I do not drive the machine *m.p.*—I ride on the whirlwind & direct the storm.
    More when we meet: till that hour I am thine, *as you demean yourself*!
                 Reynart
                 ye Foxe

x preferably 'assoilzied'—it hath a pleasant smack [Scottish legal term meaning absolved; 'izzard'—an old name for the letter z].

On Christmas Eve Elgar arrived in ample time for the ceremony, and we went into the Chapter House where we found a large assembly awaiting us. The press were there, and the papers gave full accounts of the many speeches given. Elgar began his speech by saying that it was very curious that years ago he was turned out of that room for making a noise, and now he was invited in to make one (see Appendix 1). He was happy to add his congratulations to Dr Atkins on having a real degree. He himself had had many degrees conferred upon him, but in his case they were honorary distinctions. He had never worked for them, and he was bound to say he did not like it so much as when it was earned. He was proud that his friend had 'proceeded', though he was sorry in one respect because he wanted Dr Atkins to wear the robes that were given to him (Elgar) 20 years ago when a similar presentation was made to him. He had intended his robes to descend to his friend, but he had come on too quick, and he himself had not disappeared quickly enough. Nobody could add distinction to the degree of Doctor of Music better than their friend Dr Atkins could. They very rightly extolled his work in the Cathedral which was supreme, but to people who lived away from their native town his work in resuscitating the festival and in making it an artistic and a commercial success was more gratifying.

Perhaps what impressed me most in my father's speech were his final remarks about the music we would be hearing on Christmas Day, some of which dated from the eleventh century, and hymn tunes which had been in use since the Cathedral was built. The music of these hymns was as fresh and as serenely beautiful as in the earliest days of its use. It came to us with the added beauty of the use of many generations. He loved his calling as an organist, able to keep in touch with his music forebears through the living voice of their works.

As we walked back from the Chapter House Elgar put his hand on my shoulder and said, 'You must be a very proud boy today.' Indeed I was. When we reached the house he gave me to throw away the short notes that he had jotted down as the basis of his speech. I could not throw them away. For me they were a treasured memento.

My father, suspecting that Elgar had had a hand in his knighthood, wrote to him in strict confidence, and the letter was forwarded to Stoke Prior.

After Christmas my father wrote to thank Elgar for all he had done and for his speech at the robes ceremony. He also confirmed the arrangements they had made for Elgar to come over before his return to London.

Stoke   Dec 28 1920

My dear Firapeel:

I find that we shall have to return to London without paying our visit to Worcester—hereat I weep.

Many thanks for your letter received this a.m. I fully delight in all you say but wd rather have spoken with you. One more thing which (in the hectic days to come early in Jan^y—congratulations, etc—) I want you to remember that technically you will not be '*Sir* Ivor' until you have been sworded. The papers will probably call you so, & of course your friends will write & telegraph to you & Lady A. BUT if anything official in the smallest way, either local or otherwise, requires your name let it be Dr. & Mrs. until you have been to Court. I remember going to a 'great' reception the day the O.M. was announced with Claude Phillips, that day proclaimed Knight. The *major domo* who announced our names knew us both as well as I know you but he said to Claude 'What name?' 'Mr. Claude P[hillips]' was the correct & unhesitating reply. It wd be a reynartish thing to put in the papers a few days after the event— something like this (if you think well). 'Dr. & Mrs. Ivor Atkins are very grateful for the many congratulatory letters & telegrams received; these are too numerous to be acknowledged individually at present', or something of the sort. This wd shew you know where you are and, belike

save a good

many written

acknowledgements to people who don't matter. Above all keep me informed of any developments. If I may have the pleasure I will be your mentor as to the Court business; I used to be accustomed to wander through gorgeosity in predicted apparel in the good days. In the days of my acute loneliness I want only to help others.

Thine

Reynart.

On 31 December shortly after 11pm we all went up the tower to the bell-ringing chamber to take part in the short service for the bell-ringers which closed the old year and saw the New Year in. I often attended this ceremony, but this year it seemed right that as a family we should be together for the end of that wonderful year in the cathedral which meant so much to us all. We then climbed up past the actual bell-chamber to the top of the tower, with the lights of the city far below us, to hear from there the triumphant peal which heralded the New Year of 1921.

1921

On Saturday 1 January the newspapers announced the New Year Honours, including my father's knighthood, and all day we seemed to be answering the telephone. An air of restless excitement hung around the house, which increased when the telegrams began to come and when the afternoon posts arrived. The same thing happened all Sunday and Monday until we left on our usual visit to Leck. Not surprisingly, one of the first letters my father wrote was to Elgar, sending him, as promised, copies of the local and Birmingham papers.

Severn House, Hampstead, N.W.
Jan 3 1921

My dear Firapeel:
    Having warned you what *not* to do I could not resist doing it myself & typed the envelope myself [addressed to Sir Ivor Atkins, Mus.D.] for the sheer pleasure of seeing how fine it looks.
    Thank you a thousand times for your letter & cuttings telling me of the 'moving' day; please keep me *informed*. I look for any news. It was right & proper that you shd accidentally be called upon to play both services— quite the right touch. I rejoice that the thing has made you, & I hope *Lady Atkins*, also, happy.
    You ask after me—do *not*—I am sad, sad, sad.
                    Let me hear again.
                        Yours as ever
                            Reynart.

My father had the previous day played at the 6pm nave service in addition to the regular morning and afternoon Sunday services. This letter was the first of further batches of mail forwarded to us at Leck.

My father's investiture had now been fixed for 11 February at Buckingham Palace. There were a number of details to be arranged, and Elgar insisted on taking an active part in the preparations. My father had decided, or more probably my mother had persuaded him, to buy a new morning suit for the occasion. Elgar strongly recommended his own court tailor, and the diary shows several day visits to London at the end of January and early February. Elgar still had his rented car and chauffeur, and he would meet my father at Paddington, go with him to the tailor, lunch at the Athenaeum or another of Elgar's clubs, then perhaps to 'Severn House' for tea.

On 10 February Elgar met him as usual at Paddington, and after a final fitting and lunch they went to 'Severn House', where my father was staying the night. The next morning Elgar took him to Buckingham Palace. After the ceremony they returned to 'Severn House' for lunch and spent the afternoon playing through the Cello Concerto until it was time for my father to catch the train to Worcester.

Carice was now looking after Elgar, who was living very much within himself and taking little interest in outside matters other than a few engagements which he could not give up. Fortunately, however, he had taken up very seriously a new hobby in which he was to remain interested for the rest of his life, the use of microscopes and the preparation of slides for them. All natural objects so treated provided him with a new and fascinating world. Soon he was, as usual, a professional student, obtaining, as opportunity occurred, a series of lenses to fit his eventual three microscopes.

In the winter of 1920 Atkins had taken over the conductorship of the Malvern Choral Society, and was then rehearsing them for a performance of Dvořák's *Stabat Mater* on 31 March in the Malvern Assembly Rooms. He was also giving a performance of *Caractacus* at the WFCS concert in the Public Hall, Worcester, on 19 April. He had asked Elgar to conduct, but understandably he declined. He said that he might come down for the performance, but Atkins was sure that he would not do so. There had for a long time been an understanding that he would keep Elgar up to date on Worcester and now on Three Choirs matters, and he had tried to do so about once a month.

Severn House, Hampstead, N.W.
Ap 26 1921

My dear Firapeel:
You are forgiven; I have missed your usual (monthly we'll say) notes—but I have been withdrawing myself from the world: there is nothing the matter with me but what oldfashioned people used to call a broken heart. I have been living through the dreary anniversary—& I liked it not & shall die. I am giving up all life & retiring into an (imaginary) 'cluse': everything is dead to me.
The account of 'Caractacus' is cheering—I wish I cd have come. I was thinking of you all.
Let us know in good time when you are likely to be in town—we are servantless & no coal! & I fear we cd not make you comfortable even if we are here—we *should* be away but disjuncted trains & the rest of the troubles make plans impossible.
All thoughts & good wishes from your desolated
Reynart.
alas!
To soothe your lacerated conscience I will admit that Caractacus IS pretty *strong*!

Atkins was spending a couple of nights near London at the end of May and had suggested that Elgar should have lunch with him, but had received no reply before he left Worcester.

Brinkwells, Fittleworth, Sussex.
June 5 1921

My dear Firapeel:

I am so sorry we are away during your visit in & near London. We came away a fortnight ago—it is lovely here but very, very sad. We return for a short time on Wednesday—I have business to see to. I sent a card saying we shd be away or rather I wrote it—but I am not sure if it went to post—this I shall not know till we return.

It wd have been lovely to have had lunch with you & to see you & hear you again. The last months have been too much charged with melancholy memories for me to be like a human being—I am not fit for the company of my kind.

I am so very glad to hear you are happy & that the prefix wears sunnily with you: I look back to the small achievement (my part of it that is) with the greatest satisfaction—one little point in my life when I was able to shew friendship:—well we are now old friends & I will say no more. I am delighted to learn your mother rejoices in 'it'—I hope your wife does also—I wanted her to like 'it' but I don't expect her to say so!—women do not say anything & naturally she knows you deserved 'it' & only got your desert—no favour about it—but is she satisfied? I trust the golden-sounding jingle of 'Lady' is good to her.

I have orchestrated a Bach fugue [Organ Fugue in C minor] *in modern way*— largish orchestra—you may not approve. I did want you to see it before printing but I had to send it to the engraver—however, many arrgts have been made of Bach on the 'pretty' scale & I wanted to shew how gorgeous & great & brilliant he would have made himself sound if he had had our means.

This is the one

& the climax is pretty brilliant—take my word for it.

Send me a line saying when you are coming up again or anything of that kind.

Our love
Yours ever
Reynart.

Now wile-less & tail-less.

Alas!

Hereford 1921 would be Percy Hull's first Festival as conductor, and all his friends were wishing 'PC', as he was known to all, a highly successful festival, not least Elgar, who knew him well, since he and Sinclair had been frequent guests when Elgar was at Plas Gwyn. He had agreed to conduct *The Apostles*, the Cello Concerto with Beatrice Harrison, and *The Dream of Gerontius*.

The first full-chorus rehearsal was held in Hereford on 7 July. Elgar came down to conduct *The Apostles*. He told my parents on that occasion that Carice had become engaged to a 'gentleman-farmer', as they were then called, Samuel Blake, who farmed at Chilworth near Guildford in Surrey, and that they hoped to get married late that year or early in January. He was planning to give up 'Severn House' and move into a flat in central London. They would also, very sadly, be giving up 'Brinkwells'.

Severn House, Hampstead, N.W.
Thursday 8 a.m. [21 July 1921]

My dear Firapeel
    Alas! we are this moment starting for the Cottage.
    I am so sorry to miss you.
                            In haste
                            Yrs ever
                                Reynart.
Brinkwells
    Fittleworth
        Sussex

Atkins had written suggesting that they lunch together that day.

When Atkins had been in London in July he had taken the opportunity while at Novello's to look at a rough proof of Elgar's orchestration of Bach's Organ Fugue in C minor.

Brinkwells   Friday [19 August 1921]

My dear Firapeel:
    Your more than welcome letter arrived this morning. I am truly glad you saw the fugue & saw through it also. It's a 'wild wark' though.
    I had a very kind invitation from Lady Atkins but I had already written to Mrs. Leicester—knowing you were away—& I must stay the night with them. But I shall see you much: as how?—marry thus! I arrive in Worcester (from Gloucester) on Tuesday (23rd) morning—I have the afternoon free, for certain. On Wed. (24th) I have to go to Hereford *in the*

afternoon so I hope you will have an hour or two to spare & belike give me a midday meal or something of the sort. I assume the rehearsal will be about 7.30 sort of thing in Worcr.

I have no copy of the fugue. You saw it weeks earlier than I did! but if it comes I'll bring it & you shall sit Rhadamanthus, on it.

Best regards
Yrs ever
Reynart.

In Greek mythology Rhadamanthus was one of the judges in the lower world, hence allusively, an inflexible judge.

Great Western Royal Hotel, Paddington, London, W.2.
Monday [22 August 1921]

My dear Firapeel:

I have rescued the proofs [fugue] & shall bring them along on Tuesday.

I hope you have had a good time in B. & H. It must have been lovely amongst the canals.

Love
Reynart.

Atkins had been giving organ recitals in Belgium and Holland.

On 23 August Elgar spent the afternoon with my father and conducted the Worcester chorus contingent in the evening. The following week he came over to see the cathedral Music Library, where additional bookcases had been installed since his last visit. I thought that he was looking much better than when I had last seen him, and in his customary way he was now showing keen interest in all that he saw. We saw him again at the London orchestral and soloists' rehearsals from 30 August to 1 September. These rehearsals meant a great deal to me at this time, with the opportunity they gave for meeting and listening to composers conducting their own works.

Highlights of the Hereford Festival that year included Vaughan Williams conducting his *Fantasia on a Theme of Tallis*, Holst conducting his *Hymn of Jesus*, Elgar's Cello Concerto, conducted by the composer with Beatrice Harrison as soloist, and a wonderful performance of *The Apostles*. Another performance of great interest was the Elgar piano quintet played by Henry G. Ley and the W. H. Reed quartet. I found the music very eerie and strangely haunting. I longed to hear it again, but I was not to do so until 1926, and even then only from gramophone records. (Ethel Hobday and Spencer Dyke Quartet N.G.S. NN/RR.)

It was a glorious festival, and a great and richly deserved success for P. C. Hull, his first festival as conductor.

Afterwards Carice and Elgar went to Stoke Prior for a few days before they returned to London to begin sorting out things ready for the sale of 'Severn House', and to start looking for a flat for Elgar.

Severn House, 42, Netherhall Gardens, Hampstead, N.W.
Sep 30 1921

My dear Firapeel:
It seems ages ago since Hereford & the heroic doings therein & thereabout. I hope you are all well & settling down for a good winter's work. We are clearing things up here alas!—I am sending a lot of old programmes in a day or two [Three Choirs Festivals]: do what you like with them: some may not be in the festival collection.

Why do not you—the literary one—begin to get together all the material to carry on the History of the Festivals—it wd be a good thing to have the abundant material you must have at hand put in something like shape—do think of it—you might fill in any spare hour.

I have no news but this house is adtd for sale & we are slowly sorting out things.

My love & Carice's
Yours ever
Reynart.

At this time a Supplement to C. Lee Williams and H. Godwin Chance's *Annals of the Three Choirs* was in the printers' hands. It ended with the 1921 Hereford Festival, and it was doubtful if their history would be continued. In fact, a further supplement ending with the 1930 Hereford Festival was subsequently published.

Early in October Elgar decided to take a flat in St James's Place.

The Athenaeum, Pall Mall, S.W.1.
Oct 24 1921

My dear Firapeel:
Consequent upon Carice's approaching marriage we have had to make all sorts of arrangements; amongst the first was to find a home for me, so I am installed in a small suite as per enclosed schedule [a 'Memorandum' giving his new address].

It is very comfortable & I am close to three of my clubs—*lonely* of course but I must face that.

You will let me hear if you are coming up.
I hope all goes well with you all three.
                    Mighty haste
                    Thine ever
                    Reynart

On receipt of this letter Atkins decided to go up to London by the mid-day train, stay the night and call on Elgar at his new flat early on 26 October. He did so, and found that Elgar was going to the Queen's Hall that morning to attend a rehearsal of his orchestral version of the Bach C minor Organ Fugue. He noted that they heard it rehearsed by Eugène Goossens, sitting together at the back of the hall. 'It sounded magnificent', and he and Goossens were delighted with the transcription. The first performance was to be the following evening. After listening to Bax's *Garden of Fand*, they lunched at the Athenaeum and then returned to the flat and spent a pleasant afternoon before Atkins had to return to Worcester.

The Athenaeum, Pall Mall, S.W.1.
Oct 26 1921

My dear Firapeel,
    I felt rather lonely after you left. I am glad you have seen and blessed the rooms.
    Do not forget to find out what you can about this infliction of letters . . .
It's all incomprehensible & incredibly foolish.
    Do come up again soon & hear another fugue. It was delightful having you with me for the first hearing.
                    Ever thine
                    Reynart.

Elgar had received several letters from a lady, a mutual acquaintance, who had recently suffered a mental breakdown which resulted in fantasies and incessant letter writing.
    During November Atkins was busy with orchestral and choral rehearsals for the WFCS concert to be given on 6 December. He wrote telling Elgar about the concert and hoped that he might come down for it.

37, St. James's Place, S.W.1.
Dec 1: 1921

My dear Firapeel:
   I shd have given you another envelope, my pen having travelled back 60 years & tried to write Precincts—economy prevails as you see.
   I have kept your letter, as a sort of beacon, hoping I could follow your good advice & travel down, but things do not shape that way—& however much I wish, Kreisler plays the Concerto on the afternoon of the 6th, at the whilk I must be present.
   It is, I declare, courageous of you to frighten your people into singing 'Death on the Hills'—I *should* like to hear it & I know you wd get every bit of drama out of it—my ears have never quivered to it yet.
   Yes, my love to you all—it seems ages—it *is* nearly 3 months—since Hereford when all the good, friendly and intelligent musical faces were thronging round us. Bless them!

My love
Yours ever
Reynart
(ye Foxe)

[8, College Yard, Worcester]
Dec. 8th, 1921

My dear Reynart,
   The part-songs were a great success. They sang them like poets, and in my treatment of 'My love dwelt in a Northern land' I atoned for a very imperfect performance I gave in your hearing about 21 years ago—or more—at a time when I loved it equally well but had not the power to impress that love upon my chorus. People insisted upon an encore and the choir sang it even better the second time. The finest piece of singing that has been ever heard in Worcester in my day was, however, that of the 'Death on the Hills'. It would have thrilled you by its heartrending qualities and the pp's in the latter pages were attenuated to a sort of shuddering breathlessness. It created a great sensation and everybody clamoured for a repetition but I had to be firm against that. The mood was too wonderfully realized and its effect upon people too right to allow of any repetition that night or indeed for a week. I made the basses sing their part as if Death were horrified at his share in the transaction. I suppose there might be other readings but I seemed to see you in that reading of it.
   Somehow or other I am not quite satisfied with its coming to an end with the chord of A minor. I should have been content to have left it for ever on the chord of the sixth. Toss me a p.c. and tell me whether you renounce me.

With much love, Master mine,
Yours ever,
Firapeel.

Elgar had told Atkins that he would probably be spending part of December with the Graftons at Stoke Prior, and Atkins had written telling him about his Malvern Choral Society concert on 19 December, in which Brahms' *Liebeslieder* were being performed. Billy Reed would be the soloist in Bach's Concerto in E major and in his own arrangement of Purcell's *Three Pieces for Violin Solo with String Orchestra.* Atkins invited Elgar to come over before or after Christmas.

The Athenaeum, Pall Mall, S.W.1.
Dec 26 1921

My dear Firapeel:
It was good of you to remember me in the midst of the Christmas rushing times. The book arrived & I find it on the good side—of which mair anon. I am staying on in London; my sister is not well enough for me to go there & as the arrangement was 'hanging on' I could make no other plans—however, I am quite happy. I feel very much like Beau Tibbs [a character in Goldsmith's *The Citizen of the World*] sometimes when I am making a sup of tea in a slipshod sort of costume.
As to Gloucester [programme for 1922 festival] I think it has a fair healthy look—I wish I could have been represented by one work *less*. I hope to have the Prelude or rather Fantasia to the Fugue finished but Novellos may not like it. Now as to your muscle—I hope that is all right— 'Your Lordship goes abroad by advice?' (Falstaff). Be careful about it; it is easier to 'rick' it than to get it back—but it shd give you no real trouble to do this & I hope, no pain.
All good wishes to you all. Twelve months ago I allowed a nice firework to drop in Worcester—nicht wahr?
Ever Yours
Reynart

In the preliminary programme for the 1922 Gloucester Festival Brewer had included *The Apostles*, *The Kingdom* and *For the Fallen*, all to be conducted by Elgar, and in addition his transcription for full orchestra of Bach's *Fantasia and Fugue in C minor*.

1922

We all went to Leck on 5 January, where for most of our visit we were kept indoors by heavy snow storms.

Elgar had told me about the 'Alphabet Game', for concentrating one's attention on dull speeches and sermons, and my father and I competed on the first Sunday in Leck. (In this game one listens for words in alphabetical order, attempting to get to the letter z.) He got to R and I to Q. On the following Sunday neither of us could get beyond K. I have often wondered if the rector knew what we were up to, and made it as difficult as possible!

On 16 January, while we were still in Westmorland, Carice was married very quietly in London to Samuel Blake in St James's Church, Spanish Place.

It was not until February that Elgar wrote to my father. The previous October, when they were lunching at the Athenaeum, Elgar had suggested that my father should allow his name to go forward for membership.

The Athenaeum, Pall Mall, S.W.1.
Feb 17th 1922

My dear Firapeel:
    I have only this week had an opportunity of seeing the Bp. [of Worcester—Pearce] & as a result he will second you [for membership of the Athenaeum]. So now appears in the Candidates' book

> Sir Ivor Algernon Atkins, Kt.,
> College Yard, Worcester,
> Mus.D.Oxon.
> Organist Worcester Cathedral,
> Conductor Three Choirs Festival.

> Proposer Edward Elgar
> Seconder ... to come.

You will receive notice of election which may not be for years & you can withdraw your name at any time without ignominy—many people do but I know you wd enjoy being a member.

I have Brooks's close to me & several other clubs, but of course *this* is the serious thing.

I hope you are well & Lady A. & the boy.
                    Ever yours
                    Reynart.

In those days the writing room of the Athenaeum provided wax and heavily embossed seals showing the head of Athena, and Elgar had sealed the envelope with a beautiful clear impression in red wax. He loved seals and was an absolute master at producing perfect impressions, perhaps a result of his short legal experience.

[8, College Yard, Worcester]
Feb 19th 1922

My dear Reynart,

It is good to see your handwriting again and good to see your seal-handiwork. Be it known to you that none of that craft is wasted upon me. You can affix a seal with any man and nothing is more effective and thrilling. The sense of expectancy created and the glow excited by the olden & more courtly ways of an earlier generation make the effect one *cheaply* purchased at the trouble involved. Yes, I love your seals.

I thrill, too, over the remote prospect of the Athenaeum and am most grateful to you for proposing me. Your letter arrived at mid-day and oddly enough the Bishop (who visits us none too frequently) turned up in the afternoon and gave me the latest news of you. I was able to return thanks to him in person. I am so glad you like him for he is a great asset to us—so very straightforward, amd music-loving into the bargain. I gather from him that you are in great form and I rejoice. In spite of strenuous days and comparatively virtuous living I fell a victim to influenza in a mild but sufficiently unpleasant form, and, for a time, found my shadow disquieting and all human effort vain; but I am now cheerful again and find it not unnatural that birds should sing. What a great blessing good health is! The coming of Spring always had found me responsive and I hope not to lose *that* sense. Your letter yesterday gave me the greatest pleasure. The sight of your handwriting alone is always disturbingly cheering to me and I find myself going over old times for some hours. Old Montaigne knew all there was to be known of friendship and I have long since recognized all the symptoms.

Your proposal, I'll be bound has a brave appearance in the Candidates' book. The thought of its existence there in that script of yours makes me very proud.

We are all very busy here upon the B minor Mass. I've never done it and had a great desire to leave it on record that it *had* been done by our W.F.C.S. (on the ground that a really good Choral Society should at some time try conclusions with it). I think it will beat me, but I mean to have a good try for it and am putting on extra practices. Fortunately the whole Society will back my every effort, for they love it—but J.S.B. has crammed a good deal in for the time at our disposal.

I spoke to A.H.B.[rewer] about the Prelude (to precede the C minor Bach) and he was very keen about it. No doubt you have it all arranged now.

My wife is in Shrewsbury with Wulstan. It seems incredible that he should soon be going up to Cambridge to sit for his 'little go', yet so it is. If he gets through I am hoping that he will be able to go up to King's in October. He is a splendid worker, and only too anxious to make the best use of his time there, so that I face any effort which the expense of the thing will involve quite cheerfully. At the same time I do wish we could get our Cathedral finances into proper shape. I have *not* the wages of a crossing-sweeper. I am reminded of the Malvern platform lavatory wit;—'The wages of Sin is death'—and the wages of the G.W.R. is STARVATION. This story (yours) always pleased me and now affords solace when I think of the Dean & Chapter!

However I complain not and all is well while one may work.

I must show your letter to Dora [my mother] when she comes back. Much love dear Reynart

Yours ever

Firapeel.

My father had entered me for the Queen's College, Oxford, his own college and my grandfather's, but I had always wanted to be an engineer and I had, with the encouragement of the senior physics master, helped found the Shrewsbury School Engineering Society, and become its first president, and was very busy preparing for my first lecture on 'The Development of the Locomotive', to be given on 4 March. At that time Cambridge, with its new engineering laboratories, was generally considered to be better for engineering and I was very keen to go there.

Brooks's, St. James's Street, S.W.1.
Feb 21 1922

My dear Firapeel:

I *am* glad you are pleased—it looks well & the writing of the entry—on VELLUM—is better than this.

I rejoice in seals also—not phocal, of course.

Yrs ever

Reynart.

Central Station Hotel, Newcastle-on-Tyne
Friday [10 March 1922]

My dear Firapeel:
    Alas! I am taking L. Ronald's place—as he's not well—on the *wilder* portion of the orchl tour [an LSO tour of England and Scotland]. I rise at 5.30 & pursue trains & conduct concerts—all of which is unseemly in my old age.

Love to you
Yrs ever
Reynart.

Brooks's, St. James's Street, S.W.1.
March 25 1922

My dear Reynart [*sic*]
    This is only to say that I *may* be somewhere near you next week, so do not be surprised if I turn up suddenly. I will try to let you know lest the shock should be great.

Love
Reynart.

Elgar came down the following week and stayed with his sister at Stoke Prior. On 30 March he came to Worcester for the day. My father was deep in specifications for the rebuilding of the cathedral organ. They spent most of the afternoon discussing them. Arthur Harrison, of Harrison & Harrison, the Durham organ builders, was coming to stay with my parents from 4 to 7 April to study matters in the cathedral before submitting a tender. Elgar had promised to try to come over and stay with us on the 4th to meet him and go to the WFCS performance of Bach's Mass in B minor that evening.

Brooks's, St. James's Street, S.W.1.
Thursday [6 April 1922]

My dear Firapeel:
    I *am* so sorry but I had a chill & cd not return to Worcr. I am better now but shall be away for a few days longer.

Yrs ever
Reynart

The organ was now completely out of use, and on 14 April I helped move into the north choir aisle the large Steinway concert grand piano which for many months was to accompany the choir. My father, after a few trials and much re-tuning, decided to put it 'through its paces' that night in the closed empty cathedral. The results were a complete revelation to me. I could not believe that a piano could sound so magnificent in such a large building.

Over the next few weeks my father was adjudicating at competitive festivals and giving organ recitals all over the country.

[8, College Yard, Worcester.]
June 4th, 1922.

My dear Reynart,

It is long since you had news of me and long since I had news of you, though as I have been moving up and down the country a good deal of late I have heard sundry accounts of the sprightliness of your form. People keep telling me in what splendid case you are and I delight to hear it.

We have been hard at it over Festival rehearsals for a long time and are prepared to give a good account of ourselves when you pay us a visit. Is there any chance of your coming down soon? A visit to your sister is surely overdue and my people would love to sing 'The Kingdom' to you. I cannot tell you what joy we have had in rehearsing it. It has brought back great memories, not only to me personally but to the older members. It has many hallowed moments and I find it very moving. We sing it intimately (when we are at ease) and all of us feel you very much in our midst. I don't quite know what it is about the work, but when I put it on for rehearsal we all feel a little different and as the music proceeds I grow tenderer towards them and they to me and we end up by being the better for the music. It is a good feeling.

Of course you grip from the first 'Seek first the Kingdom of God'—you cannot get away from that opening. Association may play some part—I can never forget what the Lord's Prayer [in *The Kingdom*] was to me at Worcester [1908] and indeed to everyone; the music and the rising of the people made just that conviction of the oneness of us all which is unforgettable—but it isn't association. To go back to the work today is only to confirm one's earlier impression. It will be a great moment in Gloucester when it comes on for rehearsal and when in performance we reach the Lord's Prayer I shall know myself at one of the great landmarks. And you, too, will, Reynart. It is quite impossible that I should be mistaken—it is all a great procession up to that point (The Breaking of Bread, 'We thank Thee', 'As this Broken Bread'—just think of all this music) but in the final culmination the heavens open.

Well there it is: it's just you. I suppose there is nothing more to be said.

Brewer tells me that the Fugue is to have its Prelude. [Fantasia and

Fugue in C minor] Well, I already knew that you had done it but it will be good to have it at Gloucester. A.H.B. has done well with the programme which is certainly very comprehensive.

I was at Morecambe in May. The best thing they did was the 'Reveille' which was sung by some magnificent choirs. One of them—I forget which—gave it in a thrilling way which brought down the whole place. Coward [Sir Henry Coward, conductor of the Sheffield Choral Union] was with me. At Bristol about a fortnight ago some of the Welsh choirs came across and sang in competition with Bristol choruses (and one from the North) two of the Greek Anthology pieces. 'Feasting, I watch' was finely done. Those Welsh singers certainly have the knack of plunging *in medias res*, which is what you want for 'Feasting'.

The rebuilding of the organ has been rather hung up by some of the Committee (who shall be nameless but whose identity need not necessarily escape you) being inclined to take the line of least resistance about expense and favouring the cheaper of the two estimates. I was adamant about it and held out because I felt that the best and only the best was our only course. It was rather an anxious time and in fact it preyed upon my mind but I am thankful to say that the opposition has now broken down and on Monday next the Sub-Comm^{ee} are to recommend the adoption of the more expensive scheme. After Tuesday I hope we shall go full steam ahead about raising the money. Until the builder had been decided upon it was impossible to go forward. I do not mind how much work lies ahead so long as the cause is a righteous one and certainly Harrisons give me entire satisfaction. My only anxiety is to clear all out of the way so as not to interfere with our Festival schemes which must be set on foot in October. About these we must confer. I am wondering if you have anything in your mind or whether you have been writing anything of late. But all this we could talk of when you come. When will you come? I fancy Canterbury is about due. Much love dear one.

Thine,
Firapeel.

I was very sick about J.M.Barrie.

Elgar had considered writing incidental music to one of Sir James Barrie's plays but the author had refused permission.

Brooks's, St. James's Street, S.W.1.
June 7: 1922

My dear Firapeel:
Your welcome letter just come and I send a very small scrap, not to answer it but just as an acknowledgement—this because I have very busy days before me & know I shall not touch a pen for a long time.

It is good to hear news, but I will not start on that now. Just go & wave a loving blessing from me one sunset time from below the W. window to

(*above left*) Three Choirs
Festival at Hereford 1921:
Brent-Smith, Edgar Day,
Wulstan Atkins and Sir Ivor
Atkins outside the Atkins's
Festival house

Three Choirs Festival at
Gloucester, 1922: (*Above right*)
Elgar striding away from a
'bacon-sniffing' visit to the
Atkins's Festival house. See
page 348

Elgar in 1922, photographed
by Herbert Lambert

the Severn valley across to the Malverns: how I long for it! See the last chapter 'John Inglesant' & also (a long way behind) Mrs. Hy Wood—it *is* a divine scene.

Love
Reynart.

Elgar was rehearsing the Leeds Choral Union for their performance there on 8 June of *The Apostles*, and again in Canterbury Cathedral the following day.

John Inglesant was a Romance written by J. Henry Shorthouse in 1880, about the England of Charles I and Charles II, in which there is an account of Worcester Cathedral at the time when Thomas Tomkins was organist, and a wonderful description of a walk along the river bank with the cathedral and the Malverns shining in the setting sun.

The Mrs Henry Wood book referred to is *The Channings*, a story of life in Worcester, called in the book Helstonleigh, in early Victorian times. The cathedral is a central feature of the book. Elgar had introduced me to both these books about this time. My father had, of course, known them for many years.

The first full-chorus rehearsal of the Three Choirs was to be in the Shirehall, Gloucester, on 7 July, and *The Kingdom*, *The Apostles* and *For the Fallen* were all included. Elgar was expected to conduct, and my father was looking forward to seeing him. For

(*opposite above left*) 'That's haltered him'. Elgar and Billy Reed in College Yard, Worcester, 5 September 1923. During Festival week a rope was always kept attached to the top of the corner post ready to be tied across the steps in the left foreground for temporary crowd control. Reed was unsuspectingly approaching the steps and Elgar could not resist throwing the rope over Reed's head. Elgar's hands can be seen holding the rope

(*opposite above right*) Elgar and hen at Napleton Grange, Kempsey, on 30 September 1923. On walking round the property with Elgar, his niece (Madge Grafton) and my father, the author inadvertently frightened the hens, one of which landed on Elgar's shoulder and remained there. Photograph by Madge Grafton

(*opposite below*) Outside the Atkins' house on 7 September 1926. (left to right) (Back row) Alexander Brent Smith, Wulstan Atkins, Sir Edward Elgar. (Middle row) Billy Reed, Dame Ethel Smyth, Lady Atkins. (Front row) H. C. J. Shuttleworth-King, Dr Herbert Brewer, Sir Ivor Atkins, Dr Percy Hull. Brent Smith was conducting his Suite *In the Cotswolds*, specially written for this Worcester Festival, and Dame Ethel Smyth was conducting her Overture *The Boatswain's Mate* and *A Canticle of Spring*

345

some months he had, in his letters, been encouraging Elgar to start writing Part 3 of *The Apostles*, and he knew that Elgar was considering it. He hoped that the meeting might provide another opportunity to further the matter.

37, St. James's Place SW.1.
July 6 1922

My dear Firapeel:
   I was so sorry to miss the rehearsal today. I had my things packed all ready, but I was not fit to travel & so there it was.
   I have never been able to write anything adequate in return for your last letter which was of goodly length and juicy. I have no news—I lead a desultory life & do nothing. See the Summer number of Punch—
   The Idle Shepherdess is lovely & should please the Dresden china side of your many-facetted mind—I love it.
   I don't see my way to come down yet.
   Do you remember I asked you about certain crazy MSS [26 October 1921]. How are things going on in the quarter from which these things emanate? During the last two or three months I have received *reams* of the wildest stuff: it is very sad. Is the husband alive?
   Selah!
   I hope her Ladyship is well & Wulstan, & of course you.
Yours ever
Reynart.
Observe the sealiness of the seal! (fortuitous).

   The reference 'The Idle Shepherdess' is to a china statuette which had recently been put on the market. Elgar had bought one, and so—he knew—had Dean Moore Ede. He had sealed the envelope with an exceptionally fine impression in red wax of a running fox. He may have had this made, but it is more likely that he had come across it in a shop and could not resist buying it.

[8, College Yard, Worcester]
July 10, 1922

My dear Reynart,
   Your letter was more than welcome. I missed you sorely at Gloucester. Apart from the joy of seeing you your presence gives an authority to our proceedings which they sadly lacked without you. We had a very good practice. Brewer went all through both works. 'The Apostles' went splendidly, 'The Kingdom' though good, will be better at the second rehearsal—*when you must do it*. We did 'For the Fallen' also, which they

sang magnificently. I am sorry to have to praise the work of the Three Choirs contingents so unrestrainedly (if also dispassionately) but they deserve it. On the Monday previous I went through the two larger works and our people *really do sing* them. I shall defer rehearsing the final section of the Apostles again for a time, for I am inclined to behave like an idiot. It moves me so much that the tears trickle down and I can only stare blankly at my copy, not daring to look at the Chorus. I am not safe *anywhere*, but the Alleluias and everything from 223 onwards are too much for me (what are these wounds?) They are proud enough tears, for when I cease to find this music almost unbearable I shall know that all is over with my soul—but it doesn't do for a man in charge of a chorus! However there you are! Some day I shall ask you how *you* feel.

But, to change the music. I have just written for the Festival a setting (song) of a poem of Mrs. Meynell's 'She walks—the lady of my delight'— a charming poem which I have always meant to set. I should like you to see it but am diffident. Shortly, I hope to appear in town for the day and if we could meet I should like your opinion. Of late the Muse has been violent in her attentions and I have compiled a Choral Prelude, for the Parry book. I think it good and have the audacity to like it but it is Bach-like in idiom which is probably against it.

I have no news from the Herefordshire side of the county but will enquire quietly.

'The idle Shepherdess' is great. I only saw it for a few moments in the Deanery but found it delightful. I shall return to it.

Lo! I have written too long a letter—vale, vale! Much love from us all.

Yours ever
Firapeel.

The chorus were very disappointed but they count on you for August.

It had been decided to compile a book of organ pieces in memory of Sir Hubert Parry. Atkins was among those asked, and when this letter was written he had just finished his contribution, a *Chorale Prelude* on the tune 'Worcester', attributed to Thomas Tomkins. (Tomkins was a former organist of Worcester Cathedral who died in 1656.)

The Beacon Hotel, Crowborough, Sussex.
[Postmarked 17 August 1922]

My dear Firapeel

By some grotesque mischance your letter dated Aug. 3 has turned up at Chilworth (Carice's) I go home today & travel to Gloucester on Monday.

You will have thought me very cold over your 'Muse'—I had not heard of this *MSS-ing*,—& am keen to know more—I always encouraged you to go on & you should have encouraged me by sending 'it' for inspection. Good luck.

In haste,

Ever yours

Reynart.

Elgar went to Gloucester on 21 August to attend a rehearsal of the Gloucester chorus that evening. The following afternoon he came to stay with us for a rehearsal at Worcester. He was in splendid form, and though naturally they were engrossed in festival matters, he found time to ask me about Shrewsbury and my Cambridge ambitions, and to tease me about a number of things I have now forgotten. On 23 August, which was a glorious day, I managed to take several photographs of my father and him together in front of our house. The next day we all went over to Gloucester for the full-chorus rehearsal in the cathedral, where Elgar conducted *The Apostles*, *The Kingdom* and *For the Fallen*. The London rehearsals were held the following week.

The 1922 Gloucester Festival saw the start of an Elgar habit which lasted for many years. He and Billy Reed were both staying with the Brewers, who breakfasted early. We, being 'off duty' as far as my father was concerned until the 11.30 morning performance, usually had breakfast from about 8.45 onwards. Elgar and Billy Reed—they were always together on these occasions—having time on their hands, would come across and have an extra cup of coffee with us. We loved it, and so clearly did they, and by the end of the week it had become a practice. Elgar called his visits 'bacon-sniffing expeditions', and the name stuck.

This festival was to show a new side of Elgar. The Brewers had two sons, the eldest of whom was a naval officer and a good pianist with a gift for playing from memory light music and tunes from musical comedies. Brewer had told his sons that while Elgar was staying with them they were only to play if they were certain that he was not in the house. One afternoon after a rehearsal Brewer asked my father and myself to come in for a few minutes, and we accordingly walked across to his house together.

When we were approaching the door loud strains of musical-comedy tunes could be heard coming from the upstairs music room. Brewer, saying 'Oh, confound those boys!', rushed up the stairs ahead of us. Opening the door he shouted out, 'Stop it! I told you not . . .' and his sentence died in mid air for, as we shortly saw,

348

there was Elgar playing with a son on each side of him. We all sat down and listened to a first-rate 'pop' concert, with Elgar promptly playing any popular tune that the boys asked for. He then continued playing and asking them to identify tunes, which they did very quickly, but presently they became silent. Elgar teased them and said, 'Come now, you experts, you must do better than this!' He played another tune, and then with a broad grin said, 'Well, you could not be expected to know the last three as I invented them as I went along.'

After that the boys played whenever they wished to, and Elgar was often with them.

A feature of the festival was the unveiling of the memorial tablet to Sir Hubert Parry by Lord Gladstone, followed by a performance of Parry's *Blest Pair of Sirens*, conducted by Sir Hugh Allen.

After the performance the Brewers invited a number of people including my parents and myself to tea to meet Lord Gladstone. This was the first time that Elgar and Stanford had met for some years, and much has been made of their handshake as a token of reconciliation. I have no personal knowledge of their so-called quarrel. Their personalities were so totally different that they might well not have 'hit it off' together, but I do know that Elgar had a great admiration for much of Stanford's work and it was Stanford who was responsible for Elgar's first honorary doctorate, that from Cambridge. I can vouch for it that on this occasion they were conversing together in a most amiable manner.

What a feast of music there was at Gloucester this year! There were no less than four new works specially written for the festival—Bantock's Prelude and First Part of *The Song of Songs*, Bliss's *Colour Symphony*, Eugène Goossens' Poem for Chorus and Orchestra, *Silence*, and Herbert Howells' Phantasy for Orchestra and Organ, *Sine Nomine*, all conducted by the composers. Edward German conducted his *Two Orchestral Pieces*, and Holst's *Two Psalms* and Scriabin's *Le Poème de l'Extase* were conducted by Brewer.

These were only some of the highlights in the programme. The Scriabin was too much for most of the audience, who seemed stunned by it. I remember complaining to my father after the performance that even after two rehearsals as well as the performance I still could not understand it and I did not like it. He said, 'Well, you are in good company. I heard it with Elgar from the choir and he muttered, "To think that Gloucester Cathedral should ever echo to such music. It is a wonder that the very gargoyles don't come tumbling down!"'

For many, including myself, it was the opportunity of hearing in consecutive performances, on Tuesday evening and Wednesday morning, *The Apostles* and *The Kingdom*, both conducted by Elgar, that made the Festival so memorable. This was the first time since the War that the two works had been so performed. To hear them, with Agnes Nicholls, Phyllis Lett, John Coates, Herbert Heyner, George Parker and Norman Allin in the setting and acoustics of a great cathedral was an experience that can never be forgotten. Each work is intensely moving, but one coming after the other made them completely overwhelming.

Gloucester had continued the great success of Worcester and Hereford, and the Three Choirs Festivals were now firmly re-established and had achieved a new greatness.

37, St. James's Place,
London, S.W.1.
Sep 17 1922

My dear Firapeel,
   I hope you have all settled down quietly & restfully after the splendid week, both weather & music.
   I feel rather flat after it all & my thoughts wander back to many incidents.
   Let me have the time-list of *The Kingdom* anytime but the sooner the better. I have some thoughts upon the subject & belike, its successor.

My love to you all
Ever yours
Reynart.

Elgar had asked my father just before going on to conduct the work at Gloucester to time each section carefully. My father never missed an opportunity of urging the completion of the *Apostles* cycle, and he and Elgar must have had serious discussion on the subject at Gloucester.

Elgar, who loved walking sticks, had sent me my first stick with a solid silver handle when I was 6, and about a fortnight after the festival he gave me a beautiful malacca stick with a silver band on it inscribed, 'W.E.I.A. from EDWARD ELGAR 1922'. Needless to say I was enormously proud of it, and I still treasure it.

8, College Yard, Worcester.
Sep. 23rd 1922.

Dear Sir Edward,

I do not know how to thank you enough for the walking stick. I have only just received it, and it is hanging up in front of me, as I write; I feel I must write at once to thank you for it.

It exactly suits my height, and is absolutely TOP-HOLE.

I am more grateful to you than I can say.

Do you remember the two snaps I took of you at Gloucester, they both came out, but neither are really good.

I enclose one of them, also the other two of you and Dad I took at Worcester. I have cut Dad out of one as he came out dreadfully.

I will send you the other I took later on, as I have not got, at the moment, a print of it.

We are already thinking about the Worcester Festival a meeting is to be called almost at once.

We must beat the record Gloucester put up.

The Gloucester Festival was A.1. but ours must be absolutely 'IT'. 'Floreat Vigornia'.

I wish we could have a Festival almost every week, the more I understand Music the more I feel I *live* for the Festivals.

Dad and Mother wish to send messages to you.

Dad says he will write to you sometime next week.

I feel I can not thank you enough for that glorious stick.

Love and many thank you's from
Wulstan.

[8, College Yard, Worcester]
Sept. 24, 1922.

My dear Reynart,

We are not losing any time over starting for 1923. I went and saw the Mayor and fixed up the date of the first meeting—Oct 7th. Everybody is very keen to have a great Festival next year.

I also secured our new Secretary, a man named Shuttleworth King. He is a son-in-law of Sam: Southall's and is Town Clerk this year. Of course he has yet to be appointed by the Committee. The appointment will be made on Oct 7th. I tried to get him for 1920 but owing to his career as a solicitor having been checked by the war (generally styled the Great War) he had examinations to pass before becoming fully-qualified as a solicitor. I thought it well to sound Southall (with whom he is in partnership) and Southall was evidently pleased at the idea of the Son-in-law taking on the Secretaryship and assured me that he would enter into the whole thing *con amore*. As he (Shuttleworth King) will have a former Secretary at his back (and a man of great position in the town) I feel very happy about our prospects of running the thing in tip-top manner. Shuttleworth King has a good staff of clerks at his command and runs all his work on the Card-Index plan, so hurrah for Worcester! 1923.

I shall shortly appear at No 37—or else we must forgather elsewhere—so that I may lay my head with yours over the production of a great scheme.

Another matter. It has been much on my mind that I did not tell you how very much Howells appreciated what you did for him at Gloucester. I met the young man at the Mayor's luncheon and he was evidently much touched by some words of heartening which you spoke to him as he was going on [to conduct his *Sine Nomine*]. They seem to have been a real help to him.

Everybody, as I said before is most keen about having a wonderful Festival—even the Dean glows.

Love from us all,

Yours ever

Firapeel.

P.S. This letter runs to inordinate length but I must tell you how very kind we both thought it of you to send Wulstan that jolly stick. The boy worships it and you.

Elgar had supported Brewer in his idea of inviting the then comparatively little known Herbert Howells to write a work for the festival, and it was characteristic that he should have been around and waiting to give Howells encouragement as he went on to conduct his work.

37, St. James's Place, S.W.1.
Oct 2. 1922

My dear Firapeel:

Your prose in print IS woundy [a seventeenth-century word—'extremely'] good. I read.

It is good news about the fest! prospects—Secy etc—I was going to write a letter but I have to leave this hurriedly for a few days (*workmen coming in*) so I send this scrawl to thank Wulstan & you for your letters & to lay homage at the feet of Her Ladyship & to remind you that such a creature as

Reynart

existeth

(and writeth much)

Be ye ware!

The last 3 months of 1922 were hectic ones for Atkins, for in addition to preliminary preparations for the 1923 festival he was in the throes of rehearsals for various concerts.

[8, College Yard, Worcester]
Dec 23 1922

My dear Reynart,

I have long been pining for that promised letter but I expect that you, like me, have been inundated with work. I always *do* work, but this term has been crowded in a way which is surely without parallel in the annals of working. On the 12th we gave a magnificent performance of 'King Olaf', and having said so much, I think I can spare you details. The Chorus were enthusiastic to the point of three rehearsals in the week in the latter stages and they sang flawlessly, (this is going it rather strong in the way of praise but hang it, I worked for it). The event is now so far a thing of the past that I can speak dispassionately about it all, albeit my detached criticisms are apt to lean over to the side of imperfect appreciation of my own efforts.

But the work itself! I believe it is 26 years old. Heavens! it seems impossible to believe it. You may truly say with Swift (writing in after years of The Tale of a Tub) 'Good God what a genius I had when I wrote *that*'. The parallel ceases there, for Swift added but trifles to that immortal book while you — The hall rocked with the music. The wraith of Odin carried me back to the far-off days of Forli where you first played the Ballad to me. Well, you may well feel proud: the whole thing came out as fresh as the day on which it was written. Everything was there—even to the frightening vitality of some of it. But I am afraid that it must be admitted that you were ever subtyl. But if one admits that you were born Reynartian, it does not explain why in 1896 you should have worked with such unerring certainty in your strokes. It is *all* there. I would not mind if one could point to anything experimental. When I revive other works of the same period I find adipocene already establishing itself and the sight of the cere-cloths makes me feel like a bodysnatcher;—and I seize an early opportunity of shriving myself and being assoiled! Matters are otherwise with Olaf. Ah! but Reynart, there is not much wrong with that opening? Isn't that just Romance itself! What an atmosphere it makes in its few pages. But you dear old Seer you don't escape me. I am with you every moment. You never felt the thunder of that magnificent *Heimskringle* entry more than I do when I ever see it on paper—or at any rate I will allow you but little more than myself.

Now you have been skimping me of late. Postcard me no more postcards—an you will, write.

Festival I must see you at an early date—*a very early date*. My engagements are [...] Otherwise I will run up at any time. But I want a long time with you. Now do you propose—

If you are to be with Mrs. Grafton do try to come over for Dec 30—a concert after your own heart. I am making Bishop Dean & Canonry appear in their best University attire. It will be a real *College* affair.

Much love to you dear one
Firapeel.

Elgar did get to his sister at Stoke Prior, and though he said that he was not well he agreed to motor over to Worcester for the Christmas Recital on 30 December.

The Recital, with the 'Children of the Songschool' and 'The Songmen' in Royal crimson cassocks and immaculate Elizabethan ruffs, had an even more elaborate programme than in 1917, but by special request Elgar's *A Christmas Greeting* and my father's *The Virgin's Lullaby* were included. The programme was beautifully printed on extra sized paper with red rubrics, and was most impressive. The College Hall was again packed out and there was much applause.

For my father, myself and many others, however, there was sadness, for no Elgar appeared.

B'grove
Dec 30 1922

My dear Firapeel:
It is tragic that I cannot get to Worcester—I managed to get a car for an hour & rushed (not well in myself) to see the various invalids, but had no single moment: since then I have had a cold.

I shall be glad if you will thank Wulstan for his letter & photo which came this evng.

As to your letter I shd like to write at length. I *am* glad you 'see' Olaf & thank you heartily—wholeheartedly for putting all you feel into it: it always sweeps me off my feet: it seems strange that the strong (it is that) characteristic stuff shd have been conceived & written (by a poor wretch teaching all day) with a splitting headache after dinner & at odd, snatched moments—but the spirit & will was there in spite of the malevolence of the Creator of all things. Then the refusal of the publishers to have anything to do with such stuff etc. etc. It makes one smile now to think of the horrors piled on by the aforesaid beneficent fiend: but thro' it all shines the radiant mind & soul of my dearest departed one: she travelled to London (I was grinding at the High School) & became bound for one hundred pounds so that my work might be printed—bless her! You who like some of my works, must thank HER for all. *I* shd have destroyed it all & joined Job's wife in the congenial task of cursing God.

Those days passed & better things came & better feelings, but forgetfulness never. Well, well, I hear you made a mighty show of it & your letter delights me: it seems strange that London has never heard the work & of course never will.

As to the festival I cannot say. I feel I am out of it & I wish you cd do without me altogether: cannot this be so? Do not write: we will talk.

I leave this on Monday & shall be at Shrub Hill about 1.25, leaving at two o'c for Paddington—if you have the time do come up.

I fear this is a disjointed scrawl, but I have reams to write—senseless padding & musicopic prose which must be done.

Love

E.E.

which remains

Reynart

I hope to send 'The Wallet of Kai Lung' which is *ours* through and through.

The Wallet of Kai Lung was the first of Ernest Bramah's satirical books based on the adventures of an itinerant Chinese storyteller. They were to become a constant pleasure to us all and to provide many quotations over the coming years.

PART 7
1923–1929

1923

The year 1923 was to be a special one for me because Elgar returned to Worcestershire at Easter, the Three Choirs Festival was in Worcester, and I went to Cambridge in October.

The year began well, for on 1 January, my father and I went to Shrub Hill station to meet Elgar and spend half an hour with him before he went on to London. He did not look well, but soon brightened up, and after a general conversation most of the time was spent in talking about the forthcoming festival. Elgar was adamant that he would write nothing new, but he agreed to conduct as usual. He mentioned that Laurence Binyon had persuaded him to write the incidental music for his play, *King Arthur*, and that he would have to work on it as the first performance was to be on 12 March.

The most exciting part of the conversation, however, came last, when Elgar had settled himself comfortably in the London train and we were sitting in the compartment with the door open awaiting its departure. He then said that while he would keep his flat on for London visits, he had now definitely made up his mind that he wanted to rent a house near Worcester, and would my parents begin looking for a suitable house with a small garden not too far from Worcester, but in the country.

Early in February my mother heard that the Dudley-Smiths were going away and would be wanting to lease Napleton Grange, near Kempsey for a year or perhaps longer from March or April. My parents telephoned Elgar and invited him to come down and inspect the house. Elgar did so, and began negotiations to lease it.

Brooks's, St. James's Street, S.W.1.
Friday [16 February 1923]

My dear Firapeel:
    One line to say that there is a *splendid* notice of your recital in the D.T. [*Daily Telegraph*]—I hope you have it & that the Worc! papers will print it.

Haste
Love
Reynart
ye Foxe

37, St. James's Place, S.W.1.
March 27 1923

My dear Firapeel,
I rec'd the enclosed from [Sir Henry] Hadow & to save a lot of writing—I am very busy—send it on to you.
I have signed the agreement (yesterday) for Kempsey & should be down in a fortnight if all goes well. I can scarce believe it.
My love to you all
Yrs ever
Reynart
ye Foxe

I have no knowledge of what Hadow's letter contained, but it was probably a suggestion for the festival.

Brooks's, St. James's Street, S.W.1.
Saturday March 31 [1923]

My dear Firapeel:
I am just off. One line to say that at the earliest I do not arrive till *Saturday evening, but* it is not certain that I can get to K[empsey] on that day. I will let you hear further when things settle.
Ever yours
Reynart.

Napleton Kempsey
Ap 8 1923

My dear Firapeel:
We are here safely, my niece Madge Grafton & I.
I *fear* I cannot get into Wor. tomorrow—but if you cd come *here* in the afternoon we shd be charmed to see you—is not there a bus which wd serve? I will leave it at that because it is very doubtful as to my being able to get away—& if I did manage it I might run the risk of missing you if we leave it open about your coming: so come you here, an you will, 3,4,5 o'clock tea.
Yrs ever in haste
Reynart.

My father went out on 9 April and found Elgar and Madge Grafton busy settling in. From then on he paid frequent visits, usually in the evenings or at the weekend. Later the visits were to include regular Sunday evenings with Elgar. My father told him that I was now back home, and he sent a message inviting me to go

Elgar in 1925. Elgar sent the author a signed and framed copy of this photograph to hang in his college rooms in Cambridge, into which he had moved from 'digs' in the town. Photograph by Histed

Atkins, Easter 1926. Photograph taken by Swaine in connection with the Three Choirs Festival at Worcester that September

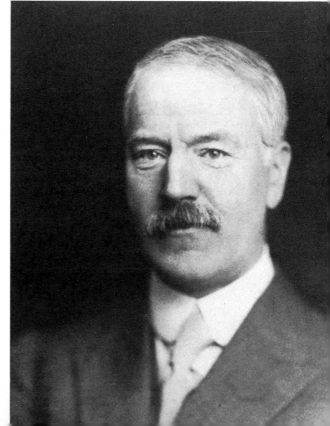

Elgar photographed by May Grafton at Napleton Grange, Kempsey, during the summer of 1925: (*above*) playing the piano. Inside the window can be seen one of Elgar's three microscopes; (*below*) with Marco, Meg and Mina

17 August 1926: (*left*) the Prime Minister, Stanley Baldwin, with Elgar and Atkins outside Worcester Cathedral; (*right*) Elgar, Mina and Marco leaving the Atkins's home

Atkins seeing Elgar into his Lea Francis car

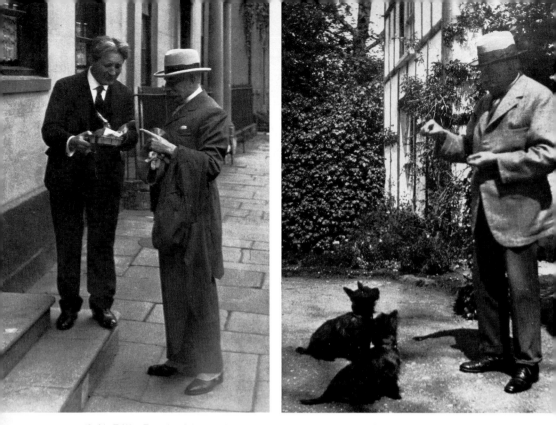

(*left*) Billy Reed with the 'large onion' and Elgar on the steps to the Atkins's home, 10 September, 1926. See p 395; (*right and below*) Two domestic portraits of Elgar again taken by May Grafton with Mina and Meg in front of Napleton Grange, Kempsey and at Tiddington House, Stratford-upon-Avon where the garden fronted the river Avon with a private boathouse. This was an added attraction for Elgar since he liked rowing and fishing

out with my father the next Sunday and spend the evening with him. This visit was to be the first of many wonderful Sunday evenings with Elgar, since later he gave me an open invitation to accompany my father on his Sunday visits whenever I was in Worcester.

I well remember that first visit and how excited I was. My father had recently given me a Sunbeam bicycle to match his own. Napleton Grange was about 5 miles out of Worcester and I recall spending the afternoon, quite unnecessarily, cleaning up the bicycles and trimming the lamps. It was a lovely spring evening for our bicycle ride, through the narrow winding lanes to Napleton Grange. As we turned into the drive of this delightful small house we were welcomed by Elgar and the Aberdeen terrier, Meg. Marco, the spaniel, did not come until 1924, and he bought Mina, the cairn, in 1926.

I recall Elgar and Meg taking us all over the estate, including the garage and the hen-house where Meg caused quite an uproar among the hens. On our return I helped Elgar unpack the latest batch of records from HMV. We then had supper and afterwards settled down for the evening.

Elgar sat smoking his small-bowled pipe and talked about the success of his incidental music which he had recently written for Binyon's *King Arthur*. This evening was the first of many visits for me. Elgar and my father always began by discussing the latest news, and then some reference would be made to past events and compositions, and this was my chance to ply them with questions and try to stir their memories.

Kempsey   Ap 24 [1923]

My dear Firapeel:
    I couldnt possibly get away on Monday—I had so much come by post. I hope you got back safely on Saturday night. By the way is 'For the Fallen' shelved—I thought that was going in? I trust the meeting went off well.
    What a wasted life mine is—now twelve o'c and I have been seeing to useless letters since *eight*.
                                    Yrs ever
                                    Reynart.

Elgar had been invited to the festival committee meeting, and had noticed that inadvertently *For the Fallen* had not appeared on the provisional list of works for performance.

May was a particularly busy time for my father, and he could not drop in casually on Elgar as much as he had been doing.

[8, College Yard, Worcester]
May 17, 1923.

My dear Reynart,
I toil so, might I come out to you on Saturday and stay perchance to dinner? It would be lovely.

I was thrilled at the sight of the scores—how fayre they be! Anyhow they will sound. I had an evening, or part of one to myself over the 'Kingdom'. You know, it *is* wonderful. I am going to give you more double basses but I am troubled about the organ. I want to tell you all my dispositions.

Yours ever
Firapeel

With the cathedral organ out of use during its reconstruction, my father was worried that the small festival organ would be inadequate for *The Kingdom*. The manuscript scores referred to were Elgar's orchestral scoring of two motets, Battishill's *O Lord look down from Heaven* and Wesley's *Let us lift up our heart*, and Handel's Overture in D minor. My father had persuaded Elgar some weeks earlier to orchestrate these three works specially for the coming Worcester Festival, and on an earlier Sunday Elgar had, to our great delight, played them over to us on the grand piano he had installed at Napleton. This was the first occasion, I think, that I realised that Elgar invariably played far more than appeared on his manuscript sheet, and what a remarkable pianist he was, with his gift of conveying orchestral colour.

Kempsey   May 27 1923

My dear Firapeel:
I saw Clayton: Novellos will take the Battishill as they publish it in $8^{vo.}$—the Wesley is under consideration: I told C. what you said about editing it, but they have some hesitation about committing themselves to publish in $8^{vo.}$ apparently because you are using Bayley & F[erguson]'s) ed^n for the Chorus [edited by Bairstow]. So I shall hear in a few days.

I am sending the Overture for them to *see*. I wish you cd lend me the *folio* edⁿ of Wesley because I had a glance at it in Wardour Street [Novello's] & I don't think I like the *added phrasing* in the Bayley & F.edn & wd revise my score before it is copied—so leave it out for me in case I can send in for it—belike it is embedded in a goodly tome.

It is too cold to think of any plans to get to Worcr.

I got here last night
Yrs ever
Reynart.

Kempsey   May 29 1923

My dear Firapeel:

Here is Novello's letter which is disappointing as regards Wesley. The two scores referred to are Battishill & the Handel Overture.

I shall send you the sc[ore] of Wesley & also return the folio Handel vol & the 8vo anthems in a day or so.

As Novello's have turned down the Wesley I shall not require the folio edn. which you say I can have.

It is *bitterly* cold & windy alas.

Ever yours
Reynart.

In the meantime Atkins had been in touch with Bayley & Ferguson and they had agreed in principle to take over the Elgar orchestration of the Wesley motet, and it was arranged that they would write direct to Elgar.

Kempsey   June 7 1923

My dear Firapeel:

Thanks: I think you might send a line to B. & F. whose letter is enclosed, saying that you believe '*Sir E.E. does not wish to make anything out of it & that possibly they might think well to offer him a comparatively small sum for the score*': if they do so, well & good:: if they do not I shall of course let you have it, as agreed, for nothing.

If they ask you what sum they ought to offer, say '£15.15.0, or something like that'.

In great haste
Yrs ever
Reynart.

I have heard nothing of the Handel Overture.

Kempsey, June 15 [1923]

My dear Firapeel:
I have heard from Messrs Novello & they will 'do' the Handel Overture. I have said it is required, & is to be free of charge for the Worcester Festival.
My daughter is with me & we saw you whirled by last night. Let me know what happens about the Wesley.
Yours ever
Reynart.
I am to be away for some time. London & Aberystwyth.

The Wesley motet was eventually bought by Bayley & Ferguson.

[8, College Yard, Worcester.]
June 20 1923

My dear Reynart
Just a hurried line to thank you for your letter telling me that all is well so far as the Wesley parts are concerned. It is most generous of you to part with that glorious piece of craftsmanship for that ridiculously nominal amount.
I will forward the score so that they may get on with the parts.
I should like to see or hear their recitation. Good luck to your Welsh music making.
Yours ever
I.A.A.

For some months Elgar had been trying to persuade Atkins to write a new work for performance at the festival, but Atkins said that he was far too busy with other matters to consider composing. Elgar accepted the position, but influenced the festival committee to insist that one of Atkins' existing compositions should be in the programme, and his anthem *Abide with me* was included in the opening service. He withdrew it later on the grounds that for the opening service the work would need to be orchestrated. Elgar tackled him again about it at the first combined rehearsal on 5 July, and told him that if he could not find time to orchestrate it he would do it himself.

[Kempsey, postcard postmarked 12 July 1923]

I have nearly finished scoring your anthem! I thought I had better make a shot at it.
Reynart.

Kempsey   Tuesday [24 July 1923]

My dear Firapeel:
This in case I do not see you. By all means ride over on Sunday [29 July] an'it likes you. I quite thought that you were leaving for the sea *to-day*—a week or so out—so I shall expect you weather etc permitting.
                    Ever yrs
                    Reynart.

My father and I went over to see Elgar on 29 July. He had shortly before finished two part-songs for male voices, *The Wanderer*, with piano accompaniment, and *Zut! Zut! Zut!* which was unaccompanied. It is described on the score as a marching song by Richard Marden, who was Elgar himself. He played over *The Wanderer* to us, and afterwards, very badly, we attempted to sing *Zut! Zut! Zut!* I remember this was very exciting, with much footwork.

What a house-party it was at Worcester that year! Billy and Elgar on their own were full of fun at festivals, but together in one house you could not hold them—it was 'japes' all the time, and they were great raconteurs, each capping the other's stories. And if Herbert Thompson was there, the stories went on until late in the night. He was not staying with us but was frequently in the house for meals, or after he had sent his 'copy' to the *Yorkshire Post*.

All our guests lent a hand in the mornings in shopping, taking messages, etc. Billy and Elgar, however, were seldom asked to shop, because my mother could never be certain what they would get or when they would come back. If they went alone you could be sure that all would be well, but together anything might happen. On one occasion they were asked to bring back enough tomatoes for lunch and apples for two large pies, and they came back in great glee with 12lb tomatoes and 2lb apples! We were eating tomatoes all the week, in salads and soups. The 'japes' were too numerous to record, but one I will mention since I took a photograph of it.

Our house, adjacent to the cathedral, stood on a high pavement, some 5ft above the level of the road leading to the north porch, and there are a number of wide steps leading from it down to the road. These are safe enough under normal circumstances, but could be dangerous for the large crowds attending the cathedral. At festival times, therefore, a stout rope was left hanging from one of the railings at the top of these steps, and this rope was when necessary tied across the steps to keep the crowds down at road level. On Wednesday morning Billy had gone out to the Sidbury Post Office, and Elgar and I were standing at the top of the steps watching him return across the churchyard. I had my camera with me as I was intending to take a photograph of both of them outside the north porch. Elgar suddenly noticed the loose rope, and beckoning Billy to go to the steps he threw it round Billy's neck, and before he could struggle out of it I managed to take a photograph. Elgar was delighted and said that it was the only time that he had been able to capture Billy. 'That's haltered him', he said.

When the prints came out I sent one to each of them, and Elgar inscribed his copy 'Billy haltered', and it stood on the mantelpiece at Napleton for some weeks.

The Worcester Festival of 1920 had provided a marvellous programme, but, as I had always hoped, 1923 was even finer. There were four Elgar works conducted by him, *For the Fallen*, *The Kingdom*, *Gerontius* and the Cello Concerto with Beatrice Harrison, four works specially transcribed or orchestrated by Elgar for this festival (Handel's Overture in D minor, Battishill's *O Lord, look down from Heaven*, Wesley's *Let us lift up our heart*, and my father's *Abide with me*) and in addition there was Elgar's arrangement of the National Anthem and orchestration of Parry's *Jerusalem*. New works specially composed for the festival included pieces by Bax, Alexander Brent-Smith and Malcolm Davidson.

A special feature of this festival was the unveiling by Elgar of the cloister window erected by John Randall and dedicated to the memory of five organists of the cathedral buried in the cloisters.

On Sunday 30 September, we went to Napleton and spent as usual a delightful evening. It was, I believe, on this visit that on our walk round the property my father and I as strangers disturbed the hens, one of which flew on to Elgar's shoulder and was 'snapped' by Madge Grafton, who was fortunately carrying a camera.

Thomas Whitney Surette and his wife Elizabeth from Concord, Massachusetts, stayed with us on 2 October, and as they had a car we all went out in the afternoon to see Elgar, who had also known them for many years.

A week later I went to Cambridge.

During one of my father's visits about this time Elgar reminded him that his lease on Napleton Grange was shortly coming to an end, and as he could not stand the cold of the winter he was considering leaving England in November for some weeks, in search of the sun. He had made no definite plans, but might take a sea trip. At this stage he wanted his plans to be confidential. My father was naturally sad that he would be away for some weeks, but also perturbed that this might make him put on one side any idea of proceeding with Part 3 of *The Apostles*, in which Elgar had been showing renewed interest.

Shortly after this visit Elgar returned to London.

The Athenaeum, Pall Mall, S.W.1.
Oct 26 1923.

My dear Reynart [*sic*]
First, many thanks for the festal cheque, the rect. of which is gratefully ackd. I have been much occupied with all sorts of silly businesses & so did not know of the Sympy! The only thing that at all reconciles me to leaving Kempsey is the awful weather. I shd have drowned at K. but I miss it awfully & it was good to see you always. As to the future—I can't tell but I am not going to give up the idea yet [of leasing Napleton Grange again].
PRIVATE. I do not want any newspaper pars: *yet*—I leave England on Nov. —th for a long time! I'll tell you later where, what & when.
Carici [*sic*] was up very radiant for the day on Wednesday & we talked over the festl & all the lovely time.
The organ looks wonderful [the new console had just arrived, but would not be in use for some months]—those couplers & accessories generally ravish me, but what a machine!
I am glad your many societies are active & I shd like to hear one or two things. 'Death on the hills' I have never heard! Your Cambridge news is good & it is a great happiness to know that W is well established there. When will the organ be opened—are you going to 'recite'? What about a new *Sonata* for the occasion—eh? Let me hear.

Love to you all 3
Yrs ever
Reynart
ye Foxe

The reconstruction of the organ took longer than originally anticipated, and at the official reopening recital in April 1925, as part of the organists' conference held in Worcester, Atkins played a fugue dated 'Napleton, June 29th, 1923'. Elgar had written this at the time when the organ was being rebuilt, and he may have intended it to be played at the opening service of the 1923 festival, but then realised that it would be unsuitable for the small Nicholson festival organ, and put it on one side. He appears to have forgotten all about this fugue when he wrote to my father on 26 October, unless he had in mind to use it as part of an organ sonata for the reopening ceremony. If so, he must have dropped the idea, and only had the fugue to give to him in 1925.

Elgar had decided to take a sea trip to South America, and had booked his passage on a small cargo-passenger ship which would be sailing 1,000 miles up the Amazon. He left in the middle of November, and expected to be back at the end of December, or at latest early January, the actual date being somewhat dependent on the cargoes available out there. It was not until the next year that we had any news of the actual cruise. It had been rough, but Elgar was an excellent sailor. He had a wonderful trip and strongly recommended it to all his friends.

1924

The year started with our usual holiday at Leck. This year there was no snow and we were able to explore further afield the wonderful country surrounding Leck, including Ingleborough, and to visit J. A. Fuller-Maitland, the music critic of *The Times* and editor of the then current second edition of Grove. He was an old friend of my father and had a very beautiful property nearby.

On the way my father told me a story about Fuller-Maitland, who tended to dress and speak in a somewhat old-fashioned way. At the house of a mutual friend he was introduced to a young married lady, who clearly had no idea who he was. During a conversation on a current topic she exclaimed 'Oh, but you are behind the times!'

'Yes Madam', he replied, 'I am indeed, and in more senses than you realise,' and smiling gently, passed on.

Back at Cambridge for the new term, I found the engineering laboratories full of the wonders of the forthcoming Wembley Exhibition. Later, my father wrote to tell me that Elgar had now returned to his flat in London and was writing a new 'Empire March', which he was to conduct at the official opening of the exhibition on 23 April. (Elgar did not, in fact, conduct his new march at the opening, since the King insisted on his conducting his *Land of Hope and Glory* instead. The first performance of the

Empire March was at Wembley on 21 July 1924, but was conducted by Henry Jaxon.)

On 2 March my father came to Cambridge to spend a week with me. We attended King's College Evensong, and sat in the organ loft with Dr Mann—'Daddy Mann' to his friends—and afterwards had tea with him. The next day my father introduced me to Alan Gray and to Cyril Rootham, the organists of Trinity and St John's. I received much kindness from both, and I spent almost every Sunday in Daddy Mann's organ loft for the whole 3 years that I was in Cambridge.

Unfortunately my father had to curtail his visit owing to the sudden illness of his mother in Cardiff.

8, College Yard, Worcester.
March 5—1924.

My dear Reynart,

Thank you so much for your telegram. I should have written earlier but have spent some anxious days of late and had to cut short a visit to Wulstan at Cambridge in order to see my dear mother for the last time. I got to her in time for her to recognize me, but I could do little more than hold her hand (she had such beautiful *young* hands to the end) and she had strength enough to press mine. Sweet soul, she passed away to-day.

Olaf came well into its own at Malvern. The Chorus and orchestra were splendid. I passed your message around the orchestra and everybody seemed to be trying to bring home its association with Malvern. It was a moving performance and got the best out of us all. I have never been so moved by 'as torrents'. It is so beautifully introduced and the following G major section and the end sounded noble. Your music went to our hearts—as it came from yours. That is why you never fail us. I *love* the work.

Is there any hope of your returning to us. I do trust you may.

Much love, dear one

Thine
Firapeel.

[37, St James's Place]
March 7: 1924

My dear Firapeel:

All sympathy—there is nothing one can say at these times—they come & you are one of the few who know how to bear the inevitable. *R.I.P.* But it is sad, sad, sad.

I am glad to hear of '*Olaf*—*1896*, 28 years ago & the thing is alive; of all 'lucky accidents' the PLACING of 'As torrents' was worthy of all praise—but it's a good libretto for the concert room. I don't suppose Acworth [who arranged and in part wrote the libretto] was there but he should have been. Thank *you*. I am wofully busy.

Love
Reynart

I returned to Worcester on 17 March, just in time for the rehearsal for the WFCS concert next day. I was interested in the two Elgar part-songs for female voices with accompaniment for two violins and piano, *Fly, Singing Bird, Fly*, and *The Snow*, to words by Alice. These had been included in memory of the much loved Mrs E. B. Fitton, who had recently died in her ninetieth year. She was the mother of Isabel Fitton, a viola player [Ysobel, Variation No VI]. Elgar had dedicated both part-songs to Mrs Fitton when he wrote them in 1894. They were superbly sung, and I was captivated by their beauty.

The first 3 months of 1924 were sad ones for Elgar and my father. Nicholas Kilburn had died at the end of 1923, Mrs Fitton early in the year, and Sir Frederick Bridge, a Worcestershire man, Sir Walter Parratt and Sir Charles Stanford all died in March. Elgar's brother Frank was also very ill, though happily he recovered, and though a sick man, lived until 1928.

37, St. James's Place, S.W.1.
Wedy [2 April 1924]

My dear Firapeel:

I am making a hurried flight to Worcester—I am going to the Leicesters for the night & on to Gloucester & Leeds. I shall try to get a glimpse of you but I am really going to do what I can for my brother, this will take up time, alas!

Yrs ever
Reynart.

On the way back from Gloucester Elgar's car broke down, and he stayed on with his sister Pollie at their new home.

Perryfield [Bromsgrove]
en route Leeds
Sunday [6 April 1924]

My dear Firapeel:

It *was* rather fun after all; our breakdown added to the excitement & I paced the road thinking of the coach accident on the same spot to Francois Cramer & the festival band years ago [in 1830, when the London coach was upset and A.W.Bennett, organist of New College, who was to have taken part in the Worcester Festival, was killed].

I liked seeing the people but I *remember* only a few alas!

My love to the III.

Yrs ever
Reynart.

The British Empire Exhibition opened in Wembley in April and during the next few months I made a number of visits to it, often at short notice. If I had time I usually called on Elgar at St James's Place on chance, but only twice was I lucky enough to find him in.

When I first went up to Christ's in 1923, I got to know Douglas Clarke, the organ scholar there, and Bernhard Ord, known to his friends as Boris, the organ scholar of Corpus Christi, who had recently become a Fellow of King's and assistant to 'Daddy Mann'. They introduced me to the famous Mrs Granville Gordon, known to all as 'Mrs G.'. Between the three of them I met all the other organ scholars and I was soon very much involved in the Cambridge musical world. Bernard Howells, an ex-chorister, had introduced me to Philip Dore, the organ scholar of Queens'. He was rather older than most of us and already a very fine organist. He conceived the wonderful idea of giving a series of Bach recitals in which he would play all the Choral Preludes and other works. He asked Bernard and myself to help by turning over and arranging stop registrations. We readily agreed, and when Bernard went down, for he was older than I was, I carried on.

It was a marvellous experience, and finding the right stop combinations on such varied organs to suit Dore, who was a perfectionist, was always fascinating, if at times extremely frustrating. My father and Elgar were most interested and, where organ specifications were available I had to try to recall the various combinations which had been used. This I found very difficult since I did not have the marked organ scores which we had used.

I have mentioned 'Mrs G.', who for some years was to become as well known at Three Choirs Festivals as in Cambridge, where she did so much for undergraduate music lovers. She was a well-to-do widow who had a large house in which she installed an E. M. Ginn gramophone with large external horn, and had built up a huge collection of classical records, which were continuously kept up to date, in a specially designed and well-catalogued library. She gave small intimate luncheons during the week, and large dinner parties on most Sundays of term. After dinner additional guests were invited to the musical evenings. Her home was open to all those genuinely interested in music, though naturally as numbers increased the visits had to be by special invitation. I suggested to her that she might consider renting a house for the 1925 festival, and for many years she took a house at each festival and brought with her a number of undergraduates, many of whom became regular festival visitors. Mrs G.'s festival houses were always open to all, and one could be sure over the week to meet most musicians there, including Billy and Elgar.

In May it was announced that Elgar had been made Master of the King's Musick.

[8, College Yard, Worcester.]
May 11, 1924.

My dear Reynart,

It is great to have you as Master of the King's Music. It means so much for Music and for the office itself. H.M. has shown great wisdom and I hope we shall now hear of a real revival of Court Music. You are bound to make things move. We are all overjoyed.

Patersons of Glasgow are very anxious to get a song from you and are, of course, prepared for anything you may ask. I promised Diacre, who runs their publishing department, to put in a word for them. They seem very go ahead and ought to be in a good position to make use of what they get. Whether you are likely to break into other outlets for your music I do not know, but another firm, Bayley and Ferguson, are most anxious to secure a part-song. They, too, would go to great lengths to attain this object. It is a fine firm and I like what I have seen of the partners. What did you do with that wonderful p.song I saw at Kempsey? So far as I know it has not yet made its appearance and yet it was one of the most thrilling things you have done. When it does come out it ought to make a great stir.

I was with Terry for a few days in Aberdeen at the end of April. He has given up the Secretaryship of the Competition Festival there but was tremendously occupied with all his irons. He works harder than most men. He really is the most restlessly energetic man I know. We were to have made expeditions with his motor, but of course the thing got nervous when it heard of my coming and so got into the hands of the motor-mechanics. I believe that they were putting in something new and wonderful the fruits of which others were to reap; But that is the way of motors: they are always holding out such promise.

I go to Ireland the week after next.

Love from us all

Yours ever

Firapeel.

My father was going to adjudicate at the Dublin Feis, and the part-song which he heard at Kempsey was *The Herald*.

At the Hereford Festival that year, Elgar's *Empire March*, originally intended for the Wembley Exhibition, was played at the opening service. He conducted *Gerontius*, *The Kingdom*, *Introduction and Allegro* and the Cello Concerto. New works conducted by their composers were my father's *There be none of Beauty's Daughters* and *The Year at the Spring*, Edgar Bainton's *The Tower*, Brent-Smith's *Introduction and Rondo*, Brewer's *Millers Green*, and Reed's *Aesop's Fables*. The other works which stand out in my memory were Bach's Mass in B minor, a marvellous work which I was now getting to know and fully appreciate, and Brahms' *Requiem* and Symphony No 4.

The real excitement for me at this festival was Elgar telling us in confidence that he was negotiating to return to Napleton Grange that October. He wrote to my mother.

37, St. James's Place, S.W.1.
Oct 4 1924

My dear Dora:

I hasten to tell you that unless something unexpected happens I shall be at (your house in) Kempsey on the 11th Oct for two years!

Please give my love to the family & say I hope to see them soon.

In the meantime although it is sure to leak out I do not want it talked about—I always hope that reticence may save me letters. Of course my family know.

Always sincerely yours

Edward Elgar.

The Athenaeum, Pall Mall, S.W.1.
Oct 11: 1924

My dear Ivor:
   The enclosed notice of your possible election [as a member of the Athenaeum] has arrived sooner than I expected. Will you read it & let me have it back anytime? You will see what the expense is & how it may be paid. In these narrow times the Committee have endeavoured to meet the wishes of new members. You may have changed your mind about being a member, &, if so, there is nothing in club life to prevent your withdrawing (many people do so) 'without a stain on your character.' Do not hurry over it but let me know your views as soon as you can. If you are feeling that this is an expensive time I should rather advise you to give up the club & buy a car!
In haste
Yours ever
E.E.

37, St. James's Place, S.W.1.
Oct 16 1924

My dear Firapeel:
   This is only to say that I do not come to Worcr. until *Monday* & therefore shall not be able to avail myself of Dora's very kind invitation— it was so good of her to propose my coming to you during the move.
   I shall be some time settling in but hope to see you soon.
Yrs ever
Reynart.

Moving in to Napleton, this time with his piano and larger possessions, books, etc, took longer than Elgar had anticipated, and he returned to his flat in London on 22 October.

The next four letters refer to my father's application for the Athenaeum.

Kempsey, Worcester.
Oct 21 1924

Dear Firapeel:
   Thanks for your note but I want you to say about your musical writings also, & the correct way to put your Cathedral appointment organist & are you Master of the Choristers or anything—just put *all* your official things correctly worded. The list is filed. I will select the necy—the vital points!
   I got down here yesterday but return to London tomorrow. I shall hope to be settled shortly.
Yrs ever
Reynart.

Napleton Grange, Kempsey, Worcester.
Oct 24 1924

My dear Firapeel:
Thanks for the list which is A.1.—but haven't you forgotten the Wr. Historical thing about the Organists? tell me of that. I don't think you need fear: that the list is not important enough—they keep a record & put the *salients* with exhibited card. I will see to that.
I am so sorry I cannot ask you here *yet* as amongst the colossal stupidities of the carriers none of my things has arrived yet! The confusion is trying. I will see about election day—in Westminster we have no contest—or there was to be none when I left London.
Yrs ever
Reynart.

Kempsey, Worcester.
25 Oct 1924

My dear Firapeel:
I *am* so sorry. I have now found your Historical Socy 'paper'. Your list now runs:—
'Author of The Early Organists, etc. of the Cathl Church (Worc. Hist. Soc.) Many musical studies (Art of Bach, etc etc) Hymn of Faith (Chos & orch) Services and organ compositions Songs &c.&c.'
So that's all right
Yrs ever
Reynart.

Kempsey   Oct 28 1924

My dear Firapeel:
Here you are: it's all right so far: it IS rather odd to have a *number*—it's long to call you 10,989 however every day.
My 'things' have at last arrived & seven mortal & hugeous packages are being undone this (& succeeding) days—after this the piano & then you.
I have had a welcome letter from Wulstan.
Yrs ever
Reynart

The great news from Worcester in November was that Elgar had bought a car and was delighted with it, and that he had also acquired another dog, Marco, a spaniel.

379

Napleton   Dec 2nd 1924

My dear Firapeel:

    I have had to go away etc.etc.

    I see the advt. of the Concert on the 9th, Festival Choral. I fear I cannot get to the Concert but I ought to be a subscriber to the Socy—nicht wahr? Will you enter my name & tell the secy to send all particulars to Napleton—

    I have to go to London again tomorrow but shall be back soon & I hope for a long stay & also to see you both.

Ever yrs

Reynart.

On Elgar's return he invited me out to Napleton with my father on Sunday 21 December. On arrival we were greeted by Elgar and the dogs, Meg and the new spaniel, Marco, who had already become his inseparable companion. We walked round the property and inspected the new car, but my father and Elgar were both tired, and the rest of the evening passed quietly. I can recall nothing else except the crackling of the fire and that drowsy complete contentment which comes when close friends are together and silence is as companionable as talking.

We saw much of Elgar over that Christmas, since he was frequently in Worcester now that he had his car.

(*left*) The main theme of what was to become Elgar's *Pomp and Circumstance March* No 5 occurred to him while he was out walking the dogs. He had no paper but jotted it down on the back of an ordnance map he had in the car. The sketch is dated 27 June, 1929. The *March* received its first performance in the Queen's Hall on 20 September, 1930. Elgar later gave the map to his doctor, William E. Moore Ede, and in 1982 his family presented it to the Elgar Birthplace. See p 417. (*By permission of the Trustees of the Elgar Birthplace*); (*right*) Billy Reed, Atkins and Elgar in front of the Deanery drive. Three Choirs Festival at Worcester, September, 1929; (*below*) Sir Barry Jackson's party at Lawnside, Great Malvern, on 17 August, 1929, for the opening performance of Bernard Shaw's play *The Apple Cart*

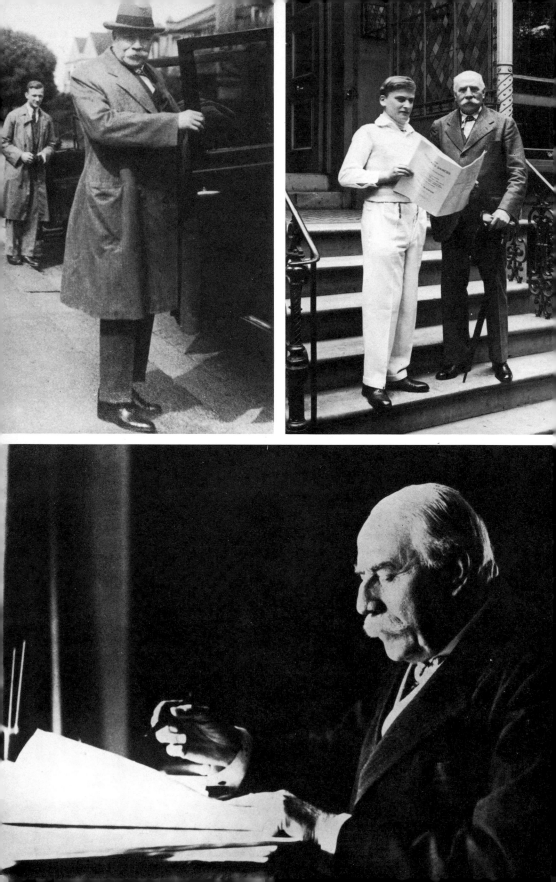

1925

When we returned from Leck, my father found the following letter waiting for him.

Napleton Grange, Kempsey, Worcester.
January 9th 1925

My dear Firapeel:
I hope you & Lady Atkins are having a good rest.
I am sorry to worry you with unagreeable things, but there is a question arising about the Athenaeum; I have taken my name off the list; my action is regretted by the Committee, but they admitted a person whom I think unfitted for membership & my action was short, sharp & decisive. Now the Secretary asks if I will provide, or rather suggest, a proposer for you. What about Sanford Terry or Hugh Allen? I will write to either if you like.

In haste
Yours ever
Edward Elgar
unofficially Reynart.

The committee of the Athenaeum had elected J. Ramsay MacDonald. Sanford Terry had himself only been elected a few months earlier, and my father mentioned the matter to Hugh Allen, who at once said that he would like to become his proposer, which he did, with the Bishop of Worcester as seconder, and my father was elected at the next meeting.

On 14 January I returned to Cambridge without having an opportunity to see Elgar. He was, however, now well settled in at Napleton and my father was going out there regularly. Elgar was greatly enjoying his car and the dogs. Dick Mountford, his

(*opposite above, left*) Elgar arriving at the Croydon 'Baths Hall' to take a rehearsal of the Croydon Philharmonic on 10 November 1931 (*By courtesy of the Croydon Philharmonic Society*)

(*above right*) Yehudi Menuhin and Sir Edward Elgar on the steps of the Abbey Road Recording Studios, St John's Wood, on 14 July 1932, at the time the Violin Concerto was being recorded. See page 445 (*EMI*)

(*below*) Elgar working on sketches for the Third Symphony in his study at Marl Bank, Worcester, in 1932. Photograph by Herbert Lambert

chauffeur-gardener-handyman, usually drove him into Worcester, but at this time Elgar liked driving himself when in the country. Dick's wife did the cooking and Elgar usually had his niece May Grafton with him, and sometimes her sister Madge. Mary Clifford acted as his secretary and helped to run the house. Carice also made frequent visits. On 12 February my father went out for lunch with them and found May Grafton and Mary Clifford there. Elgar had recently discovered the pleasures of crossword-puzzle solving, the latest craze, at which he later became highly proficient.

March and April were busy months for my father, with organ recitals in various parts of the country and three main concerts, in the last of which Elgar conducted his *Spanish Serenade* and the *Wand of Youth Suite* No 2. April also brought the organists' conference at Worcester and the official ceremonies in connection with the reopening of the cathedral organ, which had been rebuilt by Harrison & Harrison of Durham and 'voiced' in the cathedral by Arthur Harrison.

The rebuilt organ was first used for the cathedral services on 12 April, at which my father played the fugue which Elgar had written specially for the organ, dated 'Napleton, 29th June, 1923'. In 1932, in a different key and with a coda written by my father, this became the fugue movement of the Organ Sonata No 2, which he arranged from the *Severn Suite* with Elgar's approval.

At the end of April, E. Godfrey Brown, the Director of Music for the BBC in Belfast stayed with my parents and this led to a number of broadcasts by my father from Belfast, and an organ recital from Worcester Cathedral by land-line to Belfast.

On 28 May I had a delightful surprise. Elgar sent me a beautifully framed recent photograph of himself, which he had signed and dedicated to me.

Christ's College, Cambridge.
29.5.25.

Dear Sir Edward,
    I do not know how I can thank you for remembering me.
    Your delightful present came at a most opportune moment. I had been in all the afternoon trying to grind up some Heat Engine Work, and was just going out very 'out of sorts' when the photograph arrived.
    I need not tell you how my mood changed in an instant to joy.
    I look forward to thanking you in person as soon as I return home as no letter can express my joy and gratitude.

How are the dogs—especially dear Marco?

I am sure they are as wonderful as ever.

Please forgive this very short letter as with my forthcoming Examinations I must try and get my nose back to the grindstone.

Yours sincerely,

Wulstan Atkins.

I did not see Elgar again until the London rehearsals for the Gloucester Festival. At the festival Elgar was in his usual fine form. He conducted *The Apostles*, *For the Fallen* and the Symphony in A flat. There were new works by Basil Harwood, Holst, Howells, J. B. McEwen, Walford Davies and Charles Wood.

My father continued to visit Elgar regularly, and Carice was at Napleton during October. Elgar was not well that winter, and the death of his sister Lucy on 23 October depressed him.

Brooks's, St. James's Street, S.W.1.

Sunday Nov 15th 1925

My dear Firapeel:

I have been mending slowly but have not done much in way of going out before I made the grand plunge here on Tuesday. I am getting on. I hope to see you soon. The Philharmonic Concert is on Thursday 19th: if anything should be bringing you to London, do let me know at 37, St. James's Place. There is a supper after the Concert; it wd be splendid if you cd be there.

Love to you all,

Yours ever

Reynart.

Elgar had gone up to London early in November but did not go out much prior to 10 November, when he took a rehearsal for the broadcast performance of *For the Fallen* which he was conducting the next day—the 'grand plunge' referred to.

My father went up specially for the concert on the 19th, at which Sir Henry Wood presented Elgar with the Gold Medal of the Philharmonic Society, but was unable to stay for the supper. It was a wonderful occasion, with Elgar receiving tremendous applause from audience, chorus and orchestra, and this clearly cheered him up enormously.

The WFCS performed *Elijah* on 8 December, and Elgar, who loved the work, came and thoroughly enjoyed the evening.

On 11 December there was a broadcast from Belfast which included *Polonia*, *Carillon* and the *Sea Pictures*. Reception suffered some interference, but it was still a good broadcast with earphones.

Unfortunately, Elgar's ill health persisted, and on 23 December he had to go into the South Bank Nursing Home in Worcester for a small operation which left him in considerable pain for some days. He remained at South Bank until 14 January.

1926

At the beginning of January we went to London. On our return, my father went to the nursing home and found Elgar recovering well from his operation. He had been out for an hour or so and hoped to return to Napleton on Thursday. I did not see him for some weeks, however, as I returned to Cambridge that day.

Elgar's recovery was slow, and on his return to Napleton he had a slight relapse and was not well enough to have my father out until Sunday 24 January, when they discussed the plans for the Worcester Festival. He told my father that if he was well enough he had to go up to London at the end of the month.

Brooks's, St. James's Street, S.W.1.
Feb 2nd 1926

My dear Firapeel:
Here I am; as a trial trip it is more or less of a success but I get tired too easily.

I have been thinking over the 'scheme' [Worcester Festival programme] & my brains do not envisage any 'draw' amongst the classics. I *wish* you cd get some *decent* Bach instead of the infernally dull (some of them) cantatas; if we had anyone to sing them! it wd be different, but the miserable *yowling* we get wearies me.

Do not forget Mozart, Schubert (if necy). However, you know what is best & what is possible. How about the evening concert or concer*ts*? Shall you have the small orch: again in the Coll: Hall? I hope so & *do* knock out that awful woman who mis-sang with pianoforte!

This after all, is only to say how glad I was to see you the other night & that you did not object to my darling dogs.

I shall return either tomorrow or Thursday.

     Yrs ever
     Reynart.

On Elgar's return to Napleton much time was given up to further discussions about the draft festival programme.

Private
Kempsey   25 Feb 1926

My dear Firapeel:

I have had a letter from H.M.V. (the very charming Mr. Montgomery Beck whom you must meet one day) expressing a wish to make records of the performances at the Festival *in the Cathedral*. I have asked him not to write to anyone until I have consulted you: there wd be the Dean & Chapter's consent, etc.—delicate matter, altho under the new methods nobody would know that records were being made. From a business publicity point of view I shd strongly advocate the making of records. If we could meet & if you felt, after consideration, that the thing might be done, I would invite Mr. Beck down. (He could see you, the Cathedral & the organ, which you might exhibit.) It wd be a fine thing, for instance, if *you* cd make a few organ solo records on your new instrument. I do not see why all the 'advertising' people who play shd have it all their own way! So just consider—send me a word & we'll go on.

In haste

Yours ever

Reynart.

P.S. From the above letter & all it connotes you will gather that the surgeons in exploring & cutting the nameless regions did not remove the seat of fox-like wisdom—the brush.

My father, the Dean and the executive committee had fears that the making of records of performances might not do the festival justice, and also might, if known, reduce the size of the audience for a recorded performance, and therefore the collection for the charity. He and Elgar discussed it but reached no conclusion.

Brooks's, St. James's Street, S.W.1.
March 2nd 1926

My dear Firapeel:
Here is a letter from the Infliction [someone who wished to be engaged at the forthcoming Three Choirs Festival]. I have said in effect I have no influence but that I am sending the letter to Worcester: so here it is.
As to the records—I have no views—I do not see that they cd be in any way derogatory to the III Choirs—Broadcasting is quite another matter: but the records need not be issued if you did not think them satisfactory—which makes some difference in feeling: but you must decide.

In haste
Yrs ever
Reynart.

On 20 March, the WO&LCS concert included Holst's second group of *Choral Hymns from the Rig Veda*, Vaughan Williams' Overture *The Wasps* and the *Enigma Variations*, which Elgar himself conducted. This was received with prolonged applause and repeated appearances. He was evidently very affected by his reception. At lunch he had looked wan and seemed still to be recovering from the aftermath of his operation, but after the performance he was resilient and entirely his usual self. In Worcester, surrounded by his friends, especially when he was conducting his own works, he was always entirely at home and his performances had a serenity and a perfection which was deeply satisfying.

The next day being a Sunday, I went with my father to supper at Napleton. Carice was there, but was leaving on the Tuesday. We had a quick walk round the property with Marco and Meg, and after supper conversation turned to the previous night's concert. The real excitement of the evening came, however, just before we left when Elgar, to our great delight, suddenly said that after Carice had gone he would make a real attempt to write *Apostles III*.

On our visit the next Sunday we found the room littered with Bibles, reference books and music sketch books. After supper Elgar and my father retired to the piano and played over some of the sketches, but whether they were new or old drafts of 1903 not then used, I have no idea. A great deal of reminiscing went on, and on their return to the fireside I persuaded them to tell me more about the writing of *The Apostles*, which they did.

When we went to Napleton on 4 April the room was if anything more cluttered up with papers than before, and the procedure was as on the previous Sunday. The scene was, in fact, to be the same on the next two Sundays, and it was as a result of these Sundays in March and April that I was able to reconstruct a picture of the original writing of *The Apostles* already given for 1903.

On 20 April I returned to Cambridge, and my father told me later that Elgar had continued work on *Apostles III* for another week or so, but sadly his interest dropped, and gradually all the material was put away again. This may partly have been because Elgar was then discussing with HMV making records of his *Cockaigne*, *Enigma Variations*, the *Pomp and Circumstance Marches*, and his orchestral arrangement of Bach's *Fantasia and Fugue* in C minor, and was also conducting in London on 26 April, and making the records with HMV on the next day and on 28 April.

On Sunday 2 May, Elgar was in splendid form, and told my father about the recording sessions with Billy Reed, and how, to his surprise, they had proved far less tiring than he had anticipated. The new electrical recording system was not only technically an amazing advance, but for the first time allowed the use of a large orchestra in a concert hall instead of the special recording studio. *Cockaigne*, for example, had been recorded in the Queen's Hall with the full Royal Albert Hall orchestra and organ. Elgar was absorbed by his new experience in recording and most enthusiastic about it. It was still necessary to record in short sections, even with the two recording turntables, but it was wonderful to be able to record orchestral music as it had been written, instead of in a specially prepared form for the small number of instruments previously possible.

All this must have contributed to much of Elgar's buoyant condition, but another reason for his happiness was undoubtedly Mina, the cairn, which he had bought while he was in London and brought back with him.

The question of the possible making of records in the cathedral at the festival came up again. No firm decision had been taken, though both my father and the Dean had great reservations. A difficulty now arose from the HMV side. The LSO was engaged as an orchestra and not as individual players. The orchestra at that time were under contract to Columbia, and negotiating a special arrangement for the week of the festival might not be possible and might also raise difficulties regarding the festival authorities' own contract with the LSO. This really settled the matter, and to Elgar's disappointment, though he was too tactful to stress this, it was decided to let the matter rest.

The excitement at my father's next visit was a message from HMV that negotiations for recording Kreisler playing the Violin Concerto were going well, and that he was expected to be in London in June. Unfortunately these plans went awry, and Kreisler never recorded the work.

With my father now visiting Elgar virtually every Sunday and Elgar often calling on my parents during the week, letters between them became fewer, and were generally in connection with festival matters.

My father and the festival committee naturally always hoped for a new Elgar work for Worcester, and some months earlier, to their great satisfaction, he had agreed to write an orchestral suite, *King Arthur*, and to conduct its first performance at the festival. It would have been a relatively simple matter for Elgar to have used the actual music already written and performed for Binyon's play in 1923, but presumably at this time he was contemplating a larger suite which would have included new material. The suite was included in the draft programme and printed in the proof of the first edition of the finished programme. My father hoped that Elgar might be writing it, though as no reference was made to it during his many visits he began to suspect that all was not well. Now at this stage it was essential to know if the work would be ready for the festival, and my father therefore sent Elgar early in June an uncorrected proof copy of the programme with a request for comments.

Kempsey. June 8th 1926

My dear Firapeel:
I am just off to town & must return you your pretty proofling with dismal marks & remarks. The day (week, month, year, era, age, eon) is past for ever.

Yrs ever
Reynart.

Friday Evening, Sept. 10th, at 8 p.m.

IN THE COLLEGE HALL,

CONCERT (WITH SMALL ORCHESTRA).

PART I.

1. SYMPHONY in C major "Jupiter" ....*Mozart.*

2. SONGS............

MISS OLGA HALEY.

3. PAVANE POUR UNE INFANTE DEFUNTE.........*Ravel.*

4. SIEGFRIED IDYLL..*Wagner.*

PART II.

1. SUITE.................."King Arthur".............*Edward Elgar.*
First performance.
(Conducted by the Composer).

1. BRANDENBURG CONCERTO in F major.
(For Violin, Flute, Oboe, Trumpet and Strings).

2. SONGS............

MISS OLGA HALEY.

3. LES INDES GALANTES ....*Rameau-Dukas.*
(Airs de Ballet).

    1. Marche.
    2. Menuet.
    3. Danse des Sauvages (*Rondeau*).
    4. Chaconne.

391

Elgar had for a long time promised that sometime he would visit me in Cambridge. Time was now beginning to run short as I was in my last term.

Christ's College, Cambridge.
9.VI.26.

Dear Sir Edward,
I have always hoped that you would come up to Cambridge during my time up here.
Now alas my time is rapidly drawing to an end. I was wondering if you could (and would) honour me by coming up perhaps for Degree Day (June 26th). My people will be coming up on the 25th and if you would come up also, it would give me more pleasure than I can say.
I know that unless it is essential you hate leaving Napleton, Marco and Meg, and now Mina—I am longing to meet Mina—but I would like to have my Godfather as well as my parents on this special occasion. If you are kind enough to grant my request, I can get you a room, or rather I believe my people have an extra room already booked for my Godmother [Mrs Claughton, widow of Canon Claughton] who cannot come.
I should have asked you long ago only I could not screw up courage enough.
Please forgive this scrappy letter but as my Exams start tomorrow I can not pen a better one.
I do hope you will be able to come.
Yours very sincerely,
Wulstan Atkins.

[London]
June 11th 1926.

My dear Wulstan:
Thank you for your letter & invitation: I fear it will be impossible for me to be present on the great occasion; there is one remote chance left & that is that I may have to be in London, if this happens I could get to C. for the day. I hope this may be so. With all good wishes
I am
Yours very sincey,
Edward Elgar.

I returned to Worcester on 2 July, and on the Sunday began again my weekly visits with my father to Napleton. The excitement on that visit was being introduced to Mina the cairn, a fascinating creature, who while already obviously on the friendliest of terms with Marco was still determined to be given her fair share of attention.

The first chorus rehearsal of the Worcester, Hereford and Gloucester contingents took place on 8 July, and Elgar conducted *The Apostles*, *The Kingdom* and *For the Fallen*.

It was, I think, on our next visit to Napleton that Elgar, probably in response to some question of mine on orchestration, put on the Weingartner records of the *Symphonie Fantastique* and explained Berlioz' orchestral colouring. He had received these records a few weeks earlier, and they were great favourites with him. He particularly loved the 'March to the Scaffold', and to my father's amusement insisted, for my benefit, on playing this over two or three times, carefully explaining to me with a full score the reason for the use of instruments at each point, especially at the falling of the guillotine blade and the rolling away of the head.

My father was determined to replace the not-to-be *King Arthur Suite* in the Friday night concert with some other orchestral work by Elgar but he had not responded to hints made during our Sunday visits that he should suggest one. Having got nowhere by the end of July, when we went on holiday to Lake Windermere, my father wrote to Elgar suggesting *Sospiri*. Whether he was serious or only putting it up to provoke an alternative work I do not know.

Kempsey   Augt. 4th 1926

My dear Firapeel:

I have not the remotest notion of what *Sospiri* is, was, or will be. I do not imagine it could possibly be a thing for your Concert, but if you will let me see it I will decide.

I hope you are all having a lovely time in what I know to be a lovely place.

Yrs ever
Reynart.

My father then replied suggesting *Dream Children*.

Kempsey   Friday [13 August 1926]

My dear Firapeel:

I do not think the little piece worth a place in such a concert as yours in the Coll. Hall. As to 'Dream Children', I have no recollection of them— or it. But I do not want them or it done. They, or it would be too experimental. Better leave me out of the programme. I am so glad to know that you are so happily placed for your rest.

Yrs ever
Reynart.

We returned to Worcester on 15 August, and on the 17th Elgar, Marco and Mina called upon us and my father persuaded him to agree to *Dream Children* being included in the Friday evening concert, but Elgar insisted that my father should conduct it.

I was at this time a keen photographer, and it was on this morning that I took the now well-known photograph of Stanley Baldwin, then prime minister, Elgar and my father outside the cathedral, and photographs of Elgar, Marco and Mina on the steps to our house.

The full-chorus rehearsal in the cathedral was on 25 August, at which Elgar was conducting *The Kingdom*. He lunched with us and it was then arranged that though he would sleep at Napleton, he and Carice would use our house as his festival base and, as in 1923 when he stayed with us, form part of our festival house-party, which included Muriel Foster and Charlton Palmer, the organist of Canterbury Cathedral.

We all went to London on 30 August for the soloist and orchestral rehearsals. Elgar had Carice with him and was in wonderful form. The rehearsals went without a hitch and everybody seemed in unusually good humour.

A theatre party was arranged for the Wednesday evening to see *The Ghost Train*. Billy Reed, Elgar, Carice, the three of us, Charlton Palmer, the Brewers and the Hulls all came. It was a wonderful evening with everybody in boisterous mood.

The Worcester rehearsals all went well, and the festival itself, having started with a most impressive opening service, which had included Elgar's orchestral transcription of Battishill's *O Lord, look down from Heaven* and Handel's Overture in D minor, moved steadily on with fine performances one after the other. With the chorus and orchestra at their best, and Agnes Nicholls, Olga Haley, John Coates, Herbert Heyner, Horace Stevens and Norman Allin as soloists, *The Apostles* was bound to be, as it was, a moving experience, and *The Kingdom*, performed the next morning, continued that experience to an overwhelmingly emotional point. Such feelings are highly personal, and dependent on one's own participation, but for me these two performances reached a height that has never been surpassed. Elgar had also conducted the *Enigma Variations* and *For the Fallen* with Ethel Suddaby as soloist.

Dream Children, Op 43, conducted by my father, introduced me to a charming work which had its first performance in the Queen's Hall on 4 September 1902. Why Elgar had had reservations on its being included in the Friday evening concert, for which it proved ideal, I have never understood.

Elgar and Billy Reed were, as always, the life and soul of every gathering they were at, and as far as our own house-party was concerned they were more boyish than ever, and every day managed to have some 'jape' or other. I can only recall one of these, and that only because I photographed an early stage of it.

As in 1923, my mother had asked Billy Reed to do some shopping for her, and Elgar, who had just come in from Napleton, insisted on going along to help him. One of my mother's requirements had been onions for soup and as a vegetable for supper. At the shop Elgar spotted, thrown on one side, an enormous coarse onion which he begged from the owner, and carried it on an empty tray separately from the 2lb of onions which Billy had bought. On the steps of our house Elgar replaced Billy's onions with the single one, and sent him in to my mother with a story that, owing to the enormous demand for onions due to a bout of colds, this was all that he could get, but he had been told that when cut up this would meet all her requirements. Elgar followed Billy in with his hands behind his back, and when my mother expostulated and told Billy not to be so gullible, he produced the bag of onions, roaring with laughter.

Billy Reed had his car with him this year, and he left us on the Saturday to spend the weekend at Napleton. As Elgar would have Billy and Carice with him, he decided to give a special 'festival supper' on Sunday, 12 September, and on this occasion my mother came with us. The Brewers were also there and, I think, the Hulls. It was a delightful end to the Festival.

During the festival week Herbert Heyner, one of the artists, had introduced me to some friends of his, a Mr and Mrs David Hay. Mr Hay, on learning that I had just taken my degree at Cambridge, suggested that when I was next in London I should call upon him in Westminster where he had an office. He was a civil engineer, but at that time I knew no more. I had actually been offered an appointment as junior maths master at Ardingly College, but as I privately doubted if I would make a good schoolmaster, I had asked for a few days to think about it. Sydney Nicholson, later Sir Sydney, the organist of Westminster Abbey, had already asked me to go and stay with him for a few days. I did so, and while in London I met David Hay's partners and was offered a pupilage to start at the beginning of 1927. This, though I little knew it, was to be the start of 7 years most exciting bridge and tunnel work with Mott, Hay & Anderson.

At our next visit to Elgar I was naturally full of this, and he was not only most encouraging, but made useful suggestions regarding where I should try and get accommodation in London, and offered introductions to the various concert hall officials, which resulted in a number of free tickets to concerts and, later, Sunday Zoo passes. Elgar was a Fellow of the Zoological Society.

Towards the end of September my father arranged for a cheque for Elgar's conducting fees at the festival to be sent to him. Elgar had, as on earlier occasions, offered to forgo them, but the festival had been a financial success and my father felt that they should be paid.

Napleton Grange, Kempsey, Worcester.
Sepʳ 29th 1926

My dear Firapeel:
Many thanks for the unexpected: the formal receipt accompanies this. Three tails wagged (profusely) at the sight of the cheque and the owner's prophesied *Bones*.

After the festival I can never make up my mind as to whether I enjoyed it or no. We must talk this point over—next Sunday?
Yours ever
Reynart.

The following Sunday we did talk about this point, my father having raised it. But from the animated discussion about the merits of the different works—especially the new ones—and their performances, it quickly became obvious that, as indeed had appeared at the time, Elgar had really enjoyed the festival enormously, and as always nothing had escaped his eagle eye.

He never sat in a fixed seat—he always gave his steward's tickets away—and loved roaming in and out of the cathedral via the south cloister or west doors since almost invariably he stayed on the artists' side of the screened-off west end of the cathedral.

Earlier in the summer I had been able to help two young freelance professional photographers, Edgar and Winifred Ward, who had come to Worcester to take a series of pictures illustrating the city and its churches, with particular interest in the cathedral. I spent some days with them and they had become personal friends. At that time I had told them about the forthcoming Worcester Festival, and of Elgar's connection with it, and his love of dogs. Later they sent me copies of some of their photographs, and also told me that they had decided to come down again in September to take a further series of photographs, but this time with special reference to the festival and those taking part. Would I help? They particularly wanted a photograph of Elgar. I showed Elgar the photographs they had sent to me and he readily agreed to meet them. Some of their festival photographs, including the now well-known one of Elgar with Marco, first appeared in the 8 September issue of *The Queen*. Some weeks after the festival Elgar decided that he would like them to take more photographs of himself and the dogs, and asked me for their address.

St. J[ames]'s S.W.   Thursday [25 November 1926]

My dear Wulstan

Many thanks for the address of the charming photograph*ists*,—which terminal I think is beyond *ers*, as Mr. & Mrs. Ward are beyond ordy snapshotters—always excepting yourself.

Fog here
Yrs v sincy
Edward Elgar.

I stayed at home for most of the last 3 months of 1926. The Dean and Chapter had agreed that I should reorganise the choir music, which at that time consisted of large folio bound volumes, many of them in single parts. These months at home were wonderful because time was largely my own, and in addition to visits to Napleton almost every Sunday Elgar had now taken to calling on us nearly every time he came into Worcester, which was often daily.

What fun these visits were! He would come in, perhaps with his latest purchase, a second-hand book or engraving, an old Worcester plate or maybe cocktail glasses from Woolworth's—at that time they had a wonderful collection of cheap Czechoslovakian glass. His excitement at showing us what he had bought! Often he would spend some time talking to my mother about horseracing, which they both loved, although neither of them ever seemed to be very successful in spotting the winners.

Elgar, his dogs, his smart saloon car, which this year had replaced his open car, and Dick Mountford his chauffeur, were familiar and greatly appreciated sights in Worcester and Worcestershire those days, and indeed until 1933, when he became seriously ill. He often asked my father and myself to accompany him on his car jaunts, and I, having time on my hands, was glad to do so. Sometimes we exercised the dogs on Kempsey Common, on Bringsty Common and the Old Hills, or on Corse Common and often there were visits to Evesham or Pershore. Pershore, I remember, was a particular favourite of his because he had found a shop there which sold marvellous pork pies. I remember eating many of them on Sunday evenings. Elgar loved horses, and always carried lumps of sugar in his pockets for them when we roamed the commons.

On 30 November the WFCS was giving a rather special Christmas concert which included Bach's *Christmas Oratorio*, Corelli's *Christmas Concerto* and Handel's *Concerto Grosso* in B minor. To our delight Elgar decided to attend the rehearsal and have supper with us before the concert. Much of his time during the concert was spent in the organ loft with Edgar Day or below the orchestral platform. He hated sitting still, and undoubtedly was missing the dogs.

1927

There are no letters for this year, which is not surprising since Elgar and my father were now meeting several times each week.

In January I had taken up my pupilage with Mott, Hay & Anderson and was living in London. I generally went home for about one weekend in three, and by catching the first train to London on the Monday mornings I was able to go out to Napleton for our Sunday evenings. These were a special joy for me and I looked forward to them greatly.

In London I was greatly enjoying being able to attend, generally free, thanks to Elgar, concerts in the Wigmore Hall, Queen's Hall, etc, and I was having a wonderful world of symphonic and chamber music offered up to me.

On 4 April, at Elgar's instigation, I was invited to attend a reception-recital at Gillett & Johnston's foundry in Croydon. The Canadian Government had commissioned them to cast a peal of bells to be erected in the new Victory Tower recently built as a War Memorial at Ottawa. Elgar had been requested to write a carillon to be played at the opening ceremony. I was delighted to find Billy Reed among the distinguished guests, and we sat together for the bell recital, which included as the main work Elgar's composition, based on *Land of Hope and Glory*. The bells had been mounted on a temporary steel scaffolding.

I was home for Easter, and on Tuesday, 19 April, Elgar collected us all and we had a most exciting day at the Croome Races. He and my mother had a wonderful time going into the paddock, examining the horses, discussing form, odds, etc, and placing bets on every race. I can see Elgar now, immaculately dressed, with grey top hat and racing glasses.

June 2nd was Elgar's seventieth birthday. My father had written an article on it for the *Evening Standard*, and in the evening the BBC broadcast a special concert in his honour which he conducted. At the end of it he made a short speech and ended it with the words, 'Good-night, everybody. Good-night, Marco.'

Elgar loved this incident, to which over several years he was apt to refer, and he always claimed that according to Madge Grafton, who was listening at Napleton, Marco became terribly excited and rushed round the room barking, looking for him.

June had brought me an unusual voluntary task out of working hours which intrigued Elgar very much. During the early hours of 29 June, there was to be a total eclipse of the sun, which would be best seen in the north-west of England, and David Hay had asked me to try and work out the best spot from which to photograph it. I had spent many hours studying maps and making contour cross-sections, and as far as I can now remember we had agreed that a certain point in the Craven area of the Pennines high up on the Fells near Whernside seemed the most promising photographic viewpoint for Hay's requirements, and one remote from crowds.

Both Elgar and my father were keenly interested in the spot chosen, Elgar because the area was well known to him from his visits to Dr Buck at Settle in the 1880s, and my father because Whernside overlooked his favourite rail route to Scotland over the Settle–Carlisle section of the Midland Railway. At one time they talked of going up to see the eclipse, but I knew that in the end neither would make the long journey north.

I was to have accompanied the Hays by car on the expedition, but at the last moment they decided to take their daughter and make a long holiday of it. I was allowed, however, to take time off and go on a special LMS rail excursion to see it at Southport. It was a thrilling and indeed an awesome sight, but I was in the midst of jostling crowds, and my own photographs were very poor. Elgar was very interested in the scenic photographs that the Hays had taken, including the actual eclipse.

Our Napleton evenings continued to follow their normal pattern, but I had been taking an interest in Elgar's microscope, and he now often showed me slides of insects, butterflies, leaves and other natural objects which he had prepared over the years, and occasionally sections of fossils and rocks. More time was also being devoted to crossword puzzles, my father having now become an addict. On one occasion I recall that Elgar gave me a red cloth-bound dictionary specially designed for crossword-solvers, but I never became a regular follower of the art, though it was fun on these evenings.

Supper was almost always cold, and was therefore a movable feast, which meant that in good weather we generally started by taking the dogs on a long walk over Kempsey Common. There were a number of horses grazing on the common and, now being used to Elgar and the dogs, they always came up to receive their sugar. For me, used to town life, it was fascinating to see Elgar with the horses, and their obvious affection for each other. To watch them hurrying to him, often neighing with pleasure, and his handling of them was a remarkable sight.

I was often able to persuade Elgar and my father to talk about the past, and learnt a great deal, most of which has already been written under the respective years concerned. It was a Hereford Festival year and relevant matters were obviously alluded to, but I can now only recall two instances.

On one Sunday Elgar told my father that HMV had now completed their recording van, that the difficulties of recording the LSO no longer existed since their contract with Columbia had now lapsed, and that the Dean, with a little persuasion from Elgar had agreed to records of the festival performances in Hereford Cathedral being made.

The other instance referred to Elgar's writing of the *Civic Fanfare*. At the Three Choirs opening service on the Sunday afternoon there were three processions: the Lord Lieutenants of the three counties; the Mayors and Corporations and the civic heads of the boroughs; and the clergy. Up to that time the National Anthem had been played at the entry of each of the first two processions. In 1927, however, some expert of ceremonial etiquette had drawn the festival authorities' attention to the fact that the National Anthem should only be played in such circumstances for the entry of the King's official representative, and when the Lord Lieutenant of the county was present it was not appropriate to play it for the Mayor as well as for him. This raised the difficulty of appropriate music to be played on the entry of the mayors. Hull had approached Elgar in his capacity as Master of the King's Musick for a ruling, but had hinted strongly that the ideal solution would be for Elgar to write a special composition for the mayors. Elgar confirmed that the point raised was correct, and responded to Hull's challenge by immediately writing the *Civic Fanfare*. This decision was taken after all the programmes had been printed.

The *Civic Fanfare* was first played on 4 September, and received in effect a 'double-first' performance. Elgar was very punctilious about timings, and when the time shown on his schedule came up he immediately started the fanfare, and on its completion prepared to leave the rostrum. Unfortunately the mayoral procession was delayed and only arrived as the fanfare ended. Elgar, accordingly, had to repeat it. HMV included part of the opening service in their recordings, and with it the fanfare, and the work therefore had its first live and recorded performance simultaneously. Surely a unique première!

At the festival we took a house for the week as usual, and as Carice and Elgar were staying with Mrs Underwood close by we saw a lot of them.

I had not been able to attend any of the London rehearsals and thus greatly looked forward to the Hereford ones. 'PC' had prepared a fine programme which included new works by Brewer, Brent-Smith, Charles Wood and Walford Davies.

Elgar conducted his new *Civic Fanfare*, *Gerontius*, *The Music Makers*, *Cockaigne*, the Second Symphony and the Violin Concerto with Albert Sammons as soloist. Vaughan Williams conducted his *Pastoral Symphony*, and his *The Shepherds of the Delectable Mountains* was conducted by Hull. Bach's Mass in B minor, Beethoven's *Choral* Symphony and the César Franck

Symphony in D minor, which I did not know, were for me the highlights of the festival, but every day had its own rewards.

Elgar was somewhat depressed on 2 October, my last visit to Napleton Grange. His existing lease terminated in October, but he had been negotiating to continue it or buy the house, and until a few days earlier had hoped to remain there. Now his search for an alternative house had become urgent. He had discussed the position with my parents some weeks earlier, and my mother suggested that he should get in touch with the owner of Battenhall Manor, a house off the London Road, who was going away for some months. The house was not ideal, but met most of Elgar's needs, and later in October he took it for 6 months, with a possible extension. Towards the end of October, with Carice's help, he moved into Battenhall Manor.

Battenhall Manor was an interesting house, mainly built in the eighteenth century, and was then in open country. Before the coming of the railway to Worcester in 1850 it had extensive grounds and a large home farm. The railway had separated most of the land from the house, and this had later been sold off. The London Road was now carried over the railway by a bridge, which had necessitated a long steep approach on the city side. This had cut off the old front drive to the house from London Road and left it with a narrow strip of garden only on the road side, now some 20ft or so below the London Road. Dense shrubs growing on the main road bank had produced externally a rather gloomy house, with only the south-east face providing open views, and these were restricted by the railway which ran fairly close to the house, although on a slightly lower level. Trees had been grown in the grounds to obscure some of the road bridge.

The house itself had a beautiful old dark oak staircase, and although the main reception rooms had good proportions, the furniture which went with the house was generally large and in dark wood, though there were some very fine pieces. The result, except in sunshine, was to add to the gloomy first impression, and at times to create an almost sinister atmosphere. Battenhall Manor was reputed to be haunted, but Elgar never saw anything, though he did complain of creaking sounds at night on the old staircase. In the evening, however, with a fire and the lights on, the rooms took on an entirely different aspect and were comfortable and restful.

From our point of view the house had one great advantage. It was much nearer and a frequent bus service went along the London Road. As the road rose steadily from cathedral level bicycling would have been hard work. Any exercise needed after our evenings could easily be obtained by walking back home. My mother, too, could now accompany us, though this was usually for a lunch-party.

Carice and her husband stayed with Elgar for Christmas, and on Christmas Eve they all came to tea with us. Elgar was thrilled at this time, I remember, with a new electrical gramophone which HMV had recently sent him, and we were all invited to go to lunch after Christmas and hear it. It was, however, well into the New Year before I did so, as Carice and Elgar developed chills—it was a white Christmas that year—and the visit was postponed.

1928

The year began with wonderful news. The New Year's Honours List published on the Monday announced a KCVO for Elgar. My father had spent the Sunday evening with Elgar, but he had been given no hint, possibly because there had been others present. My father had therefore the added pleasure of going to see him again on the Monday to offer him all our congratulations.

I returned home for a weekend towards the end of January, and spent the Sunday evening at Battenhall Manor. I remember congratulating Elgar on his KCVO, and how he made light of it, but was really very pleased by the continued recognition of himself and his music. Most of the evening was devoted to playing records on his new gramophone, of which he was very proud, saying, 'Notice how much rounder and natural the instruments now sound.' I think it was on this occasion that Elgar played over some test records made at the Hereford Festival, and told us that it had been 'touch and go' if any records were to be issued. HMV's experts had found a number of technical faults, and felt that no commercial records should be made. Elgar, who had been much involved in the venture, had intervened, and it was finally agreed that a few of the best sides should be released.

When I was home in January I imagined that I would be staying in London for some months working on the widening of the City

& South London Tube, but on 3 February Jock Anderson told me that within the next fortnight they were sending me to Newcastle to work on the Newcastle–Gateshead Bridge then under construction. I accordingly went down to Worcester to tell my parents over the weekend of 4 February. Elgar, who was keenly interested in what I was doing, was as delighted as I was of this forthcoming new experience for me, and said that he would set about finding people to introduce me to.

As I was starting in Newcastle on 15 February, I returned to Worcester the weekend before to prepare for my move. On Sunday we spent the evening with Elgar, and that was my last visit to Battenhall Manor, which was demolished some years later. (A school now stands on the site.)

When my father wrote to me in the early part of March he told me of the sudden death (1 March) and the funeral of Sir Herbert Brewer. He also wrote that Elgar had found a furnished house in Stratford-upon-Avon which he liked and which he had decided to rent from Easter. This was Tiddington House, the home of Lady Muntz.

In March my father had conducted two Elgar concerts, *Gerontius* in the cathedral on the 13th, and a WO&LCS concert with the *Wand of Youth Suite* No 1 and *The Snow* on the 17th. Carice had been staying with Elgar and they attended both concerts and greatly enjoyed them. My parents dined at Battenhall Manor after the concert, and reported that Elgar, surrounded by four dogs, for Carice had her Bridget with her, was in exceptionally good humour. To have settled on a house for when he left Battenhall must have been a great relief to him, and he was still filled with enthusiasm for his new gramophone, playing a number of recent records, amongst others 'proof copies' of all the records that had been made at the Hereford Festival.

Elgar first slept in Tiddington House on 21 April, and on the 28th, he and Carice fetched my father to Stratford for the weekend. My father wrote to tell me that Tiddington House was a delightful place with a large garden and a private boathouse which adjoined the river Avon.

Elgar was obviously very taken with Stratford and its many visitors. My father said that Bernard Shaw and his wife were coming to stay in the town the next week and that Elgar was hoping to see a lot of them. Elgar was also clearly thrilled with the house and was already planning improvements in the garden and considering the possibility of having a boat on the Avon. Apparently the only disturbing thing for him were the portraits in the house. He hated family pictures, and was considering how, if he could not replace them, he could cover them up in some way.

The dogs, four including Carice's Bridget, were having a heavenly time rushing around. Marco was enjoying a 'digging-up' fit, but Elgar did not seem to mind his dirty feet at all. A lovely sight were the swans sailing magnificently up and down the river in front of the lawn.

My father's visits were now usually on Saturdays, there being no Sunday trains, and unless he had an important choir practice he generally went for lunch, tea and an early supper, which enabled him to catch the last train home. Elgar also came over to Worcester frequently. He was obviously very happy in Stratford and in good health, but just now he was worried about his brother Frank who was very ill.

My father went over on 2 June, Elgar's birthday, and found Elgar and Dick Mountford attempting to remove a large half-sunken log from the river. Elgar was depressed as Frank was not expected to live for more than a few days. (He died on 8 June.) May arrived in her car in the afternoon and he cheered up a little. He said that he had seen a small grand piano in Leamington and was considering hiring it.

Tiddington House, near Stratford-upon-Avon.
June 7th 1928

My dear Firapeel:
I hope you saw dear Billy's honour [W. H. Reed] in The List on Monday: he is *M.V.O.* Do write & congratulate him and I *wish* you could write a good paragraph & send it to the Worcr. *papers*.
In haste
Yrs ever
Reynart.

My father had seen it, and was sure that Elgar had had a hand in it.

While I had been in London I had for some months worked on stress calculations and structural steel work for the proposed bridge, which Mott, Hay & Anderson were then designing, across the Firth of Forth near South Queensferry. Trial borings in the

Firth for the piers were now to be put down, and on 4 June I left the Newcastle bridge to take charge of this work, my first big responsibility. After we had been drilling on various sites for some weeks our drilling gear jammed about 17ft into the rock beneath the bed of the Firth. I was temporarily held up, and as I wanted to discuss certain matters with Jock Anderson in London it was agreed that I should take a long weekend and combine a visit home with my discussions.

I was accordingly in Worcester on 14 July, and went over to Stratford with my father. On our arrival we found Elgar fishing from a boat which he had bought a few days earlier. He told me that Dick and he had already rowed up and down the river to Stratford Bridge several times, and he intended soon to make a real fishing expedition. The new grand piano had arrived and Elgar played over to us a sketch with a charming eighteenth-century atmosphere. When I asked him what it was he said, 'Oh, only an idea I am thinking about.' Some months later I realised that this must have been the beginning of the incidental music for Bertram Matthews' play *Beau Brummel*.

Elgar then asked me to play to them some records which he had recently received and were lying by the gramophone. They proved to be the National Gramophonic Society's recording of his *Introduction and Allegro for Strings*, conducted by Barbirolli. I well remember how pleased Elgar was with the performance and his discussion with my father regarding the warmth and expressiveness of the string playing. I recall asking Elgar if the story that I had read somewhere about it being Welsh in origin was true, and he told me that this was only partially true. He had written the work in Hereford in 1905, but the theme which had really started it had been heard by him some 3 years earlier while he was staying at Llangranog in Cardiganshire. While walking along the cliff he had heard the sound of singing coming across the water, too distant to recognise the tune, but the fall of a third recurred, and from this half-heard melody had come his 'theme'.

For most of the time, however, we sat out in the garden. I was naturally full of my Firth of Forth borings work, and Elgar was fascinated. He asked me for a few of our rock samples when we had finished with them, as he wished to cross-section them for his microscope. His sections, when ready, made a wonderful microscope study.

I next saw Elgar at the Gloucester Festival. I arrived on 2 September, in time for the opening service. It was Herbert Sumsion's first festival, and a great success. He had taken over Brewer's programme. 'John', as he was known to his friends, and his charming American wife Alice, fitted in at once, and until his retirement she was to be the life and soul of Gloucester Festival social activities and the trusty friend of all.

Elgar was conducting *Gerontius* and *The Kingdom* in the Cathedral, and on the Wednesday evening in the Shire Hall the Cello Concerto, with Beatrice Harrison as soloist. In the same concert my father was conducting his orchestral arrangement of *The Shepherdess* and *Thou art come*, sung by Roy Henderson, and Vaughan Williams was conducting *The Lark Ascending*, with Billy Reed as the solo violin. This was my introduction to one of Vaughan Williams' most delightful works.

It was an adventurous programme which included Granville Bantock's new work *The Burden of Babylon*, Honegger's *King David*, Ethel Smyth's Mass in D and Zoltan Kodály's *Psalmus Hungaricus*, with Steuart Wilson as soloist. The last two works were conducted by their composers. The Mass was interesting, and it was fascinating to watch Dame Ethel Smyth's very masculine forceful beat, but it was the Kodály work which moved me profoundly. It was to start a love of his music that has only intensified as the years have gone by.

There was one great disappointment for me and for many others. HMV wanted to make records at this festival as they had now completely overcome their difficulties in Hereford the year before. Elgar and the three conductors were now all strongly behind the proposal, but the Dean and Chapter refused permission, and despite a letter from Elgar to the Dean, Dr Gee, they held to their refusal, with the result that what might well have been annual HMV records of the Three Choirs Festivals never got off the ground.

Early in October I returned temporarily to Newcastle in connection with the final preparations for the official opening of the 'New Tyne Bridge', as it was now called, by King George V accompanied by Queen Mary, on 10 October. I was granted a few days leave before returning to Scotland.

On 13 October my father and I went over to Stratford for what proved to be a fascinating day. After lunch we took the dogs for a long walk and, tea over, we then settled down comfortably before a large fire. Elgar was very interested in the ceremonial arrangements for the opening of the bridge. Conversation then turned to the incidental music for *Beau Brummel*, which he was then completing. He had the sketches there, and with a little persuasion he sat down at the piano and played sections over to us. Soon, however, he jumped up and asked my father to play, and a little later, to my great joy, Elgar joined him at the piano and together they gave a magnificent representation of *Beau Brummel*.

My father went over to Birmingham on 5 November to hear Elgar conduct the opening night of *Beau Brummel* at the Theatre Royal. He wrote telling me that the theatre orchestra was small and rather unimpressive, but it was remarkable what Elgar had got out of them.

Over several visits to Elgar my father had been discussing a first draft programme for the 1929 Worcester Festival, and Elgar, who now seemed to have regained his interest in composing, had volunteered to write a new work for the festival, and towards the end of November he was giving serious thought to setting two poems of Shelley, *The Demon* and *Adonais*. My father accordingly sounded the Dean (Dr Moore Ede) upon the matter and sought his views.

Deanery, Worcester.
Dec 3 1928

Dear Sir Ivor,

It will be a great thing if Sir Edward Elgar will produce a great work for the Festival. It will be good for the Festival, good for England and good for the world to be enriched by another of Sir Edward's masterpieces. I would do anything in my power to assist Sir Edward.

I have looked through the two poems you mentioned—'The Demon' and 'Adonais'—As poems they are beautiful—'Adonais' is the best, but it is frankly pagan. I have been trying to see if it can be twisted into a Christian poem. It is not possible. The Festivals aim at the encouragement of Church music, or great works of music, Christian in character, and suitable for a Cathedral as a Christian Temple. I do not see how we can regard Shelley's poems, even if somewhat edited, as suitable for the Cathedral. Can Sir Edward not find some poem suitable? He found the right thing in Gerontius. Is there no other poem of that class which he can take as basis of his work?

Yours sincerely,
W. Moore Ede.

My father sent the Dean's letter on to Elgar.

Tiddington House, near Stratford-upon-Avon.
6th Decr. 1928

My dear Firapeel:
    Here is the Dean's letter: I don't see (really) what else he *could* say but
Shelley is 'off'.
    I fear I cannot turn on another subject so easily as it seems to the D.
Weather dull & dogs bored.
Yrs ever
Reynart.

On 14 December my father had conducted the BBC Northern
Ireland Orchestra in Belfast in a broadcast concert.

8, College Yard, Worcester.
Christmas Eve 1928

My dear Reynart,
    Just a line to wish you and all in your cluse a very happy Christmas. I
wanted to come over and see you last week but alas! you had fled Stratford
and it came to nothing. Perhaps in these holidays it may be possible. You
might let me have a line. Are you likely to be at home and free on Friday
next if I could get away? On Wednesday afternoon we do your 'I sing the
birth'. They love it.
    Belfast went off very well. They have a nice orchestra there and played
the Second 'Wand of Youth' Suite in good style.
    I hope you may have been able to think out an idea. But in any case I
want to see the dogs. My love to them and to you all.
Yours ever
I.A.

The cathedral choir sang Elgar's new carol *I sing the Birth*, the
words by Ben Jonson, at Evensong on 26 December. My father told
me that Elgar had only finished this carol at the end of October and
it had received its first performance by the Royal Choral Society in
their Royal Albert Hall concert conducted by Malcolm Sargent on
10 December. This was therefore only its second performance.

1929

8, College Yard, Worcester.
Jan. 9th, 1929

My dear Reynart,

It is only the ninth day of this New Year and I am so anxious that it should be made memorable by a great work from you that I am going to write to you what I cannot bring myself to put into words by way of the mouth. I ask you for the moment to discount the fact that such a work would bring cosmic distinction (a good phrase) to my own Festival; such distinction it would indeed give. But my motives are thoroughly dispassionate. I know you to be a sleeping volcano. I want you, for the sake of all of us who love you and your music, to cause yourself to erupt. None of us can help you to get a start. I know that once started the Reynartian lava would sweep everything before it and lo! at once the works of the Puny Men would be seen in their proper scale.

You and I both love Worcester. And Worcester is unchanging in its love of, and pride in you. It is of no use belittling it by word or thought. The thing is there. I see it in the eyes of the humble Festival Choral singer: I see it in the eyes of greater people. These people have faith in you: you stand for Worcester to the great world.

Are you not going to stir yourself? You alone can choose subject, but if it cannot be choral then let it be orchestral.

When I listen to the marvellous music you have written, when I remember all that you have taught us, I could weep to see you keeping silence as you do. One day succeeds another and you will not break it. And yet I *know* that the old magic is there. You cannot keep back the little flashes that show me that it is *there*.

And what are you getting out of it all? Certainly not *otium*. Your mind, the greatest mind I have ever known, was made to cope with the very greatest problems and to solve them.

Let us have great days again; I will come and compare notes with you week by week. Think how much it would give me to look forward to.
Yours ever,
I.A.
Why not the Third Part? It *is quite* possible.

On my father's next visit to Stratford he took up the matter again, but Elgar had lost all interest in a new choral work. He was successful, however, in interesting Elgar in orchestrating Purcell's motet *Jehovah, quam multi sunt hostes mei*, which he proposed to include in the festival programme.

Tiddington House, near Stratford-upon-Avon.
24 Jan 1929

My dear Firapeel:
I am off to Manchester—back soon.
Purcell. I have made a skeleton but—the wretched Bach Choir edn.
says Purcell left only a *figured* bass: Novello [in the Vincent Novello folio
edition] prints the bass & no figures: there are discrepancies, which edn.
shall you use for the Choir? Shall you make a new one? Can the *original* be
seen anyhow? Resolve me these: I feel at sea with the inadequate
Cummings affair. Poor old Novello 'saw' things better than these rotten
pedants.
Yrs ever
Reynart.

William Hayman Cummings (1831–1915) was a founder of the
Purcell Society, edited many Purcell works and wrote a book on
Purcell, later found to be somewhat unreliable on factual
information.

8, College Yard, Worcester.
Jan. 26th, 1929.

My dear Reynart,   Purcell
I am so delighted to hear about the skeleton. I know those skeletons and
what they develop into! I believe the score which Purcell left is in
Christchurch, Oxford. I thought of getting out a new edition—unless you
would do so!—and, certainly, there is room for it. Cummings should have
confined himself to his own masterpieces. I hope you have seen the full
score of his Te Deum. Life is incomplete unless one has seen that.
Wonderful as the work is in itself, the full score is far more wonderful—
full of nutrition; thoroughly bloody.
Now I will take the opportunity of a visit to Oxford which I am obliged
to make for a dryasdust paper which is in the proof stage and will go and
spy out the land at Christchurch. In course of a very short time I will
report to you.
In the meanwhile I should take dear old Vincent to be right in the main.
Yours ever,
I.A.
In classic phrase: Vincent hath Bowels.   That seal was
                                                       rather masterly.

The envelope of Elgar's letter had been superbly sealed by him
in red wax with a lozenge-shaped seal containing a single 'E'. The
simplicity gave it unusual dignity.

In the end Elgar worked from an edition which my father had prepared from the original in the British Museum and another at Christ Church, Oxford. This was later published by Bayley & Ferguson. Elgar's full score, which he gave to my father, is now in my possession.

On 12 February Elgar came over for the WFCS concert to hear Alexander Brent-Smith's *Choral Dances* for Chorus and Orchestra and a Suite for Strings arranged by Julius Harrison from harpsichord works by Domenico Scarlatti.

I was in Worcester on 20 March on my way to Durham, and was fortunate to be able to go to the WO&LCS concert that night. Elgar had come over to hear his own *Aspiration* and *False Love*, both poems written by Alice (from the *Bavarian Highlands*).

I was able to come down again for a weekend in April, and my father and I went over to Tiddington on the 27th. Elgar was recovering from severe bronchitis but had been out for some days and seemed to be almost his usual self. Marco was in attendance, but was missing Mina and Meg who were away with the Graftons. Elgar asked if my father had heard from Bayley & Ferguson about publishing his new edition of the Purcell, but no firm acceptance had so far arrived.

College Yard.
April 30, 1929

My dear Reynart,
I was delighted to see that you had made such a quick recovery. You really have a wonderful physique.

Bayley and Ferguson are going to take the Purcell. They are anxious to get on with it at once. I was wondering whether you would like to score it when it is in type, or whether you would prefer to go ahead with it now. It shall be just as you like. In any case I should appreciate it enormously if you would make any alterations you like in the accompaniment. You suggested, for example, that it should begin with the bare key-note. Then, again, I must certainly incorporate the independent bass which Vincent Novello got from another MS.

Another point I should like you to consider is the ending of the sections—when they should have Tierce de Picardie, when not.

Do look at the accompaniment through those wonderful eyes of yours.

Yours ever
I.A.

I hope *Marco* is more reconciled now.

Tiddington House, Stratford-upon-Avon.
6 May 1929

My dear Firapeel: *Purcell*
   I have not been well—hence the delay. The more I look at IT the more I want a simple Bass note to open (Novello)—also on *your* p.6, *Largo*, I think the same thing wd be right: I cannot do without the Novello idea in the 3rd & 4th bars of this section—but where does the bass come from? On your page 8 *I* propose a *comma* & rf or ff—the words do not matter. Some of the slurs are misleading [on the uncorrected proofs which my father had sent to him] and should come out. I return the *four* 'editions' & await a rough proof from the pub.^{rs} & *your* revision.

In great haste
Yrs ever
Reynart.

My father put the following note on this letter:

Now p.7 of the Bayley and Ferguson edition. The passage is there marked *Maestoso*. The bars alluded to are bars 3 and 4 of this page. The Bass was taken from a MS at one time in the possession of Hawes. The comma he proposes would come after the 5th quaver of p.9. He also asked for one at the end of bar 2, p.7.

I had a few days holiday in Worcester in the middle of May before moving to Liverpool, where I was 'loaned' to the Mersey Tunnel contract until my new Lancashire Railway Bridges contract was ready. I went over to Stratford with my father on 18 May. Elgar as usual was interested in my new work, and he gave me an introduction to the Liverpool Philharmonic authorities. More orchestral music was once again assured to me. Elgar and my father talked mainly about the Purcell, but he mentioned that he would not be renewing his lease of Tiddington House, and though it would not terminate until the end of the year, he must now start looking for a new house. He seemed uncertain where it should be, probably Warwickshire, Worcestershire or Herefordshire, but he also talked about a house on the coast, perhaps in Sussex. He would look at advertisements, and would my mother keep a look-out for houses, and also for a house in Worcester for the festival week.

   In June my father received advance copies of the Purcell from Bayley & Ferguson and he sent a copy to Elgar together with a few festival programmes and a poem which he had recently come across and thought Elgar might set.

413

S-on-A.
Monday 24th June 1929

My dear Firapeel:
   First thank you for the complete copy of the Purcell. I am so glad you added rehearsal numbers.
   Now as to dates.—I *think* I can come to your *Worcester people* next Monday. I am not sure of this and the weather is the chief factor in helping me to a decision. I will be definite before the week is out. On the 11th I am with you [for the combined chorus rehearsal for the festival held in the cathedral] & shall get over in good time.
   No: the words will not do—they are too 'indefinite'— It's difficult to find the exactly right thing.
   I hope to send the f.sc. in a day or two.
                          Yours ever
                            Reynart.
I am glad to have the programmes also.

[Tiddington House]
27th June 1929

My dear Firapeel:
   Here is the score. It is an awkward thing to do, as it is intrinsically contrapuntal in the chorus bits—save of course the unaccpd.
   I have only put a 'guide' in red ink for the chorus—if the thing is copied decently the voc: parts can easily be taken from the print. There are one or two quite trifling things I have marked in blue pencil [two misprints and some omitted rests in the vocal edition]—It does not lend itself to orchl. climaxes—I have done what I could: if you object to the full (org. & brass) ending, just knock it out.
   Cast an eye to the organ part *generally* & decide if there's too little, too much, or too bad—what's there.
                          Yrs ever
                            Reynart.
I telephoned this morning to say I knew nothing of the newspaper paragraph.

   A paragraph had appeared in a London paper to the effect that Sir Edward Elgar had written a new choral work for the forthcoming Three Choirs Festival in Worcester in September.

8, College Yard, Worcester.
June 28, 1929.

My dear Reynart,
   I have just been feasting my eyes upon your full score. I am only just in from Malvern so have only been able to turn over the leaves and recognize

414

Sir Ivor Atkins, Dr Percy Hull, Dr Herbert Sumsion and Sir Edward Elgar. A photograph taken outside the West Porch of the Cathedral. Three Choirs Festival at Hereford, 2 September, 1933; photograph by Vivian of Hereford

the well-known master manner. But oh! there are some hopeful moments. When I have got rid of a bl—ted pupil whom I momentarily expect I shall settle down to the enjoyment of it. This is just to acknowledge receipt and I take the opportunity to enclose a mysterious half sheet of music paper which I found mixed up with the f.s. Farewell. I hear the Bl—one.

Yours ever,

I.A.

On 6 July I went to Tiddington House with my father. When we arrived it was hot and sunny and we found Elgar in the boat fishing. He had apparently had no luck and gave it up and rowed us to the bridge and back in a most professional manner. After lunch we lazed in the garden and Elgar told us about a most interesting visit he had received from Lionel Tertis about a fortnight earlier.

Tertis had made a viola arrangement of the Cello Concerto, and Elgar had agreed to hear a play-through before making a firm decision about such an arrangement. Tertis had arrived with George Reeves, and they had given a performance of the whole concerto with Reeves accompanying on the piano. Elgar told my father that it had been a most impressive demonstration of the capabilities of Tertis' specially designed large viola, and that he had gladly agreed to the arrangement being published with his sanction. Nine months later, Elgar conducted the first public performance of the arrangement in London with Tertis as soloist.

The day was not to end, however, without fresh excitement, especially for me. Some reference must have come up about Hull, and Elgar said to my father,

'You know how P.C. has often tried to persuade me to write another *Pomp and Circumstance March*. Well, a theme occurred to me suddenly the other day while I was out with the dogs, and I jotted it down on the back of a map I had with me. I have ideas about developing it, and I think it will be as another March.'

Naturally I was thrilled and asked if I might see the map, and on our return indoors Elgar showed it to me. Such was the start of the *Pomp and Circumstance March* No 5 in C major, which Elgar

(*opposite*) Sir Edward Elgar outside the West Porch of Hereford Cathedral in September 1933. This was the last Three Choirs Festival that Elgar attended. Within a few weeks he had to have an operation from which he never recovered, dying on 23 February 1934. Photograph by Vivian of Hereford

dedicated to P. C. Hull, and which received its first performance in the Queen's Hall on 20 September 1930.

This was to be my last visit to Elgar at Tiddington House.

At the beginning of August my parents went on a tour of Scotland with Thomas Whitney Surette and his wife, and I was able to join them for a long weekend.

8, College Yard, Worcester.
August 20, 1929

My dear Reynart,

Just a line to express my unqualified admiration of your Shaw speech. It was splendid: unfailing in the really clever touches which I looked for.

I am just back from a short holiday. May I remind you of the next Combined Rehearsal. August 29 (Thursday).

I hope I may see you before then, so as to compare notes. I want a verbatim account of Saturday's proceedings [the première of Shaw's new play *The Apple Cart*]. I shall put you on early at the Cathedral (on the 29th)—that is, if you wish it.

Lunch will be at 1 p.m. You are expected to be present in force. Can you not bring G.B.S.?

I *was* vexed to miss Saturday.

Yours ever
I.A.

Elgar had made a speech opening the Shaw Exhibition at the Malvern Festival.

Tiddington House, Stratford-upon-Avon.
21 Aug 1929

My dear Firapeel:

Thank you for the rehearsal scheme: do send me $\frac{1}{2}$ dozen more. I am sorry you were not in Malvern. I am really there for the week but come back here for posts & return tomorrow. Barry Jackson has taken Lawnside & he has a large house party there.

I will put the matter before *G.B.S.* but I fear the pf. accompt. will be too meagre to attract him: I wish we cd. have that *and* the organ.

The Apple Cart is an astounding piece of work—marvellous. You shd really see it at Malvern.

Haste
Yrs ever
Reynart.

Sir Barry Jackson was largely responsible for organising the Malvern Festival. Elgar was staying with him.

The Three Choirs full-chorus rehearsal on 29 August in the cathedral began at 2.30pm, and my father, as he had promised, put *The Kingdom* on near the beginning. Elgar brought Sir Barry Jackson and the Bernard Shaws to lunch with my parents. The latter created a slight difficulty as they only liked salads with raw cabbage and no meat. They all left with Elgar after he had rehearsed *The Kingdom*.

The Worcester Festival was from 8 to 13 September. The next time I met Elgar, on the Sunday evening, he was installed in Marl Bank, Rainbow Hill, Worcester, which he had rented for the week. We were much impressed with Marl Bank and the view over Worcester to the Malvern Hills.

The opening service included three items of special interest for me, the slow movement of César Franck's Symphony in D minor, the hymn by Charles F. Grindrod, 'Eternal God, Who quickening light', set to the tune 'Lasst uns erfreuen', which had been specially orchestrated by Billy Reed, and Bach's *Fantasia and Fugue in C minor*, orchestrated by Elgar. I had been thrilled by the glorious sound rolling down the nave, and I remember Elgar telling my father, who had conducted it, how he had enjoyed the service and how interested he had been to hear the Bach *Toccata, Adagio and Fugue* in C minor, played by Edgar Day on the main Harrison organ almost immediately afterwards. He and my father had quite a long talk about the differing 'colour' of the two systems of sound—organ pipework and orchestral instruments. They compared the more precise tone of the organ pipe with the warmer and more sensitive quality of stringed instruments.

On the Tuesday morning *Elijah* was preceded by Elgar's arrangement of the National Anthem, the Purcell and a Byrd five-part motet *Laetentur Caeli*. I had been told a great deal about my father's new edition and Elgar's orchestration of Purcell's *Jehovah, quam multi sunt hostes mei*, and I had heard it in rehearsal on the Monday morning, but the actual performance, with Steuart Wilson and Horace Stevens as the soloists, exceeded all my expectations. Purcell, like Byrd, had always been a favourite composer of mine, but with Elgar's orchestration this particular motet stands out entirely on its own.

Over the succeeding days Elgar conducted *Gerontius*, *The*

Kingdom, Introduction and Allegro for Strings and the Second
Symphony. New works conducted by their composers included
Brent-Smith's *Choral Concerto*, Edgar Bainton's *Epithalamion*,
and Sumsion's Idyll, *At Valley Green*, the last a light but charming
work. Walford Davies had also composed for the festival *Christ in
the Universe* for soprano, tenor, chorus, piano and orchestra, with
himself at the piano.

Myra Hess had been the soloist in Beethoven's Concerto in G
major. Her playing was an absolute revelation to me, enhanced
perhaps by the fact that I had been privileged to be allowed to sit by
her during the rehearsal.

The great event of this festival was the first performance of
Bach's *St John's Passion* in a new edition prepared by my father,
with verse translation by Dr T. A. Lacey, who at that time was a
canon of Worcester. I did not know this masterpiece among Bach's
great works, and I was stunned by its greatness.

As usual we entertained largely during the festival, and GBS and
his wife came to lunch on 10 September. GBS was in splendid
form, keeping all around him in fits of laughter. As he was going I
rather diffidently asked him to sign my copy of *St Joan*, a play for
which I have always had a special affection. He graciously replied,
'Bring all my plays that you have and I will sign them for you.'

I rushed off, but could find only three, *St Joan, You never can
Tell* and *Caesar and Cleopatra*. I well remember his remark as he
was signing them: 'What! only three, and those the least
representative of my work.' With a twinkle in his eye he added,
'What an opportunity you have lost. You could have sold them at a
great profit!' Needless to say, I did not do so.

Elgar and Carice lunched with us on the Friday, and he told us
that he had decided to buy Marl Bank and that some time in
November or early December he would take up residence there.

In October I took up my duties on the railway bridges contract
for the 'Liverpool East Lancashire Road', and moved to Newton-
le-Willows midway between Liverpool and Manchester. From
now on until 1933 I was to enjoy the privilege of spending many
Sundays in the organ lofts of Liverpool and Manchester Cathedrals, with Walter Henry Goss-Custard and Archibald Wayett
Wilson, both of whom showed me great kindness and hospitality. I
was also able to attend the concerts of both the Liverpool
Philharmonic and the Hallé—a marvellous musical experience.

For the next few months I was unable to get to Worcester, but I now owned a Standard 9 Saloon, and towards the end of the year I started going to Worcester for about one weekend in three. By driving back through the night I was able to spend Sunday evenings at Marl Bank with Elgar.

Elgar moved into Marl Bank on 5 December. On Sunday 15 December, my father resumed his Sunday evenings with Elgar, and on Saturday 21 December I came down to Worcester for a long Christmas visit. On the Sundays of the 22nd and 29th I drove my father to Marl Bank, and we spent generally similar happy evenings to those which had begun in 1923 at Napleton Grange.

Elgar was once more back in his beloved Worcester, and this time in what was to be his home for the rest of his life. His love of animals prompted him to send a Christmas card with wording as reproduced here.

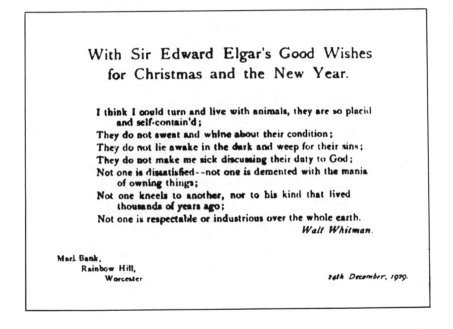

With Sir Edward Elgar's Good Wishes for Christmas and the New Year.

I think I could turn and live with animals, they are so placid and self-contain'd;
They do not sweat and whine about their condition;
They do not lie awake in the dark and weep for their sins;
They do not make me sick discussing their duty to God;
Not one is dissatisfied--not one is demented with the mania of owning things;
Not one kneels to another, nor to his kind that lived thousands of years ago;
Not one is respectable or industrious over the whole earth.

Walt Whitman.

Marl Bank,
   Rainbow Hill,
      Worcester.   *24th December, 1929.*

PART 8
1930–1935

1930

With Elgar now firmly established in Marl Bank he and my father were once more meeting most days, since Elgar usually called on my parents when he shopped or took the dogs on one or other of the commons. If my father could spare the time he often went on these walks. As a result there are no letters during 1930, but on the other hand I spent more time than before with Elgar.

No doubt, partly because of having my first car and loving motoring, I often came down to Worcester on consecutive weekends to make up for the time which I had to spend in Lancashire on my bridge work. We could only obtain possession of the railway at weekends, and then but a single track at a time, when we would gradually move our constructed bridge sections into place. Elgar found these operations most interesting, and as we always took photographs of them for record purposes, I was expected to bring these down every time I came to Worcester, and a part of our evenings at Marl Bank was always given up to discussing progress.

At the beginning of 1930 I spent three evenings with Elgar, 12 and 25 January, and 9 February. The evening of 12 January was almost entirely spent listening to records.

At the end of 1929 Elgar had received from HMV a new gramophone—their very latest model (No 551)—and it had been installed in the dining-room. This was the first fully electric gramophone with built-in loudspeaker that he had been sent. He was naturally very proud of it and was still experimenting with its possibilities.

When supper was over Elgar placed a record on the turntable, set the volume control as high as it would go and left me to start up the gramophone after he and my father had settled down in his study across the main entrance hall. Both doors were left open, but before I could even get into the study there was a roar from my father, 'Turn the volume down—it's awful!' During the next quarter of an hour or so either Elgar or I was rushing between the two rooms altering the volume control, adjusting the doors of the machine, opening, shutting, leaving ajar the doors of the two rooms, etc. I can see my father now, sitting there, looking benevolently on the two excited children.

Much of the 25 January visit was devoted to a detailed

description of the moving in of half a bridge under the fast main line of the LMS during the previous weekend.

The evening of 9 February was another gramophone one, and a good example of Elgar's interest in mechanical 'gadgets', and of helping his friends. For the Christmas I had brought down with me my portable HMV gramophone, to which I had attached an 'auto-stop' which I had designed myself. No portable at that time had such a device. Elgar had seen it when he called on us and was most interested. On 25 January he had asked me if I could bring it down again on my next visit. I brought it with me on 9 February. After supper I demonstrated it, and Elgar spent quite a long time playing with it and satisfying himself that it was simple, robust and did work. We then played records over on my portable and his wonderful new machine. How feeble, and in some ways raucous, mine sounded compared with the glorious tone of his. As we left Elgar told me that he would write to HMV and try to persuade them to take up my gadget. He did indeed write—to Trevor Osmond Williams, a leading member of their International Artists Department.

Marl Bank, Rainbow Hill, Worcester.
12 Feb 1930

My dear Trevor:
　This is not your business but perhaps you will put it before the authority who deals with such 'gadgets' if you think it worth while.
　Wulstan Atkins (son of Sir Ivor A.) has devised a little adjunct for the *small* portable gramophone to stop the motor when the record is played through: I believe no 'portable' has such a thing. If the idea is of any use his address is 8 College Yard, Worcester. He shewed the thing to me which is quite simple & works.
Best regards
Yours ever
Edward Elgar.

Later, by request, I sent the gadget to HMV. Weeks went by and then they returned it to me saying that they had tested it thoroughly but had decided that the additional cost that would be involved could not be justified. Interestingly, however, an 'auto-stop', but of a totally different design, was included in the new model of the HMV portable issued some months later. Decca also incorporated yet another type of 'auto-stop' in their portable about this time. Thought transference, maybe!

I did not see Elgar again until 16 March, when an amusing incident occurred. Elgar enjoyed a good dinner with fine wines, but normally lived simply on traditional English fare washed down occasionally with beer, but more usually with Bulmer's cider or Weston's perry, of which he was very fond. On this visit, however, my father and I were surprised on entering the dining-room to find in front of our places a squat unlabelled black bottle, and to see a very mischievous smile on Elgar's face. The reason for his merriment was quickly apparent when we opened the bottles and began drinking an exceedingly fine old Audit ale.

It was a wonderful drink, but extremely potent. Elgar reminded us of an argument that my father and I had had some weeks before about the relative merits of Oxford and Cambridge Audit ales, and told us how he had persuaded a Burton-on-Trent friend to let him have a few bottles of their private Directors' Audit. The dining-room table at Marl Bank was oval, and Elgar always sat with the dogs on chairs on each side of him, Mina to his left and Marco to his right. This evening we were understandably in very talk-ative mood, and during an animated discussion between Elgar and my father I glanced at Marco, who to my surprise was busy lapping up Elgar's ale. Before I could say anything there was a loud crash and Marco was sprawled on his back, feet in the air, on the carpet. We could not wake him up and there we had to leave him to sleep it off.

On my next visit a fortnight later the evening was much less eventful, but I remember that conversation included a discussion on Kodály's part-songs, two of which, *The Straw Guy* and *See the Gipsy*, had been sung at the WO&LCS concert the previous afternoon. Elgar had not attended the concert but he had been at the rehearsal when he had met the Polish violinist, Sonia Moldawsky, who was the soloist in Vaughan Williams' *Lark Ascending*.

Another excitement at this visit had been the news that the BBC's Midland Region had decided to broadcast my father's performance of *The Apostles* with the WFCS from Worcester Cathedral on 10 April.

On my return to Newton-le-Willows I decided to buy at once, on hire-purchase, a powerful Pye portable radio set with built-in loudspeaker to enable me to listen to this broadcast, as I did not feel that I could risk using my now old crystal set. As it happened, I had to go to London and was able to get to Worcester for the actual performance. Elgar and Carice came in afterwards and they were both obviously delighted. The local orchestra had, as usual, been increased, and the soloists were Joan Elwes, Millicent Russell, Percy Manchester, Keith Falkner, Richard Watson and Roy Henderson. Most of the soloists joined us afterwards, and I remember Elgar talking to them about early performances.

I was in Worcester again for the weekend of 12 April, and with Easter Sunday and another visit to London, I spent three consecutive Sundays at Marl Bank. The evenings were very cold, and a glowing fire was conducive to lazy conversation leading to reminiscences between my father and Elgar, and with Sunday succeeding Sunday I was able to direct their talks to the writing of various Elgar compositions and their first performances.

It was, in fact, largely over 1930 and 1931 that I learnt so much about his earlier works. Many of these reminiscences have already been given under the actual years involved. It was during one of these three visits that, having listened to Elgar and my father reminiscing about the *Enigma Variations*, I asked Elgar what the 'Enigma' was. I can see him now, with his eyes twinkling, when he said to me, 'Well, you had better ask Troyte that. He could tell you what it was.' Troyte Griffith, the subject of one of the Variations, was no musician, so I said, 'But how could Troyte tell me?' Elgar laughed, and he told me a story, but I still don't know if he was pulling my leg, or whether there was any truth in it. This is the story he told me:

One day, when I knew Troyte was coming, I marked with sticky paper certain keys on the piano, and on each piece of paper I put a number showing the sequence in which they were to be played. When Troyte came in I asked him to play these in the sequence in which they were marked, and he did so. I then removed the sticky paper and told him, 'Troyte, you now know the "Enigma"!' I knew I was safe because I knew he wouldn't remember which notes he had played.

I was at home again on 18 May, and on our visit to Marl Bank we found Carice there, and our evening was devoted to records and roulette, a game which she much enjoyed. It was on this occasion that on our arrival we found Elgar's sister Pollie and her son Gerald about to return to Perryfields, Bromsgrove. They turned back and we were all together for perhaps an hour.

I had heard a great deal about Pollie. When Elgar left his

parents' home at the music shop in 1879 he stayed with her and her husband William Grafton until 1883. On Grafton's appointment as manager of the Salt Works at Stoke, near Bromsgrove, they had to leave Worcester. Elgar then lived with another sister, Lucy Pipe, in Worcester, until his marriage in 1889. He was very attached to both the sisters, but there was a very special relationship between him and Pollie. It was to her that he would go when he wanted a change and complete rest. May, Madge and Claire were her daughters. The nieces had always spent a lot of their time with the Elgars, and after Alice's death one or other of them lived with and looked after him. He had great faith in Pollie and she was in some ways almost like a mother to him. It was absolutely fascinating to see them together. They had a wonderful understanding and brought the very best out of each other. There were lovely little touches of humour and twinkling of eyes. Pollie was definitely a powerful character and a benign influence. This was the only opportunity I had of seeing them together in a homely atmosphere, and I wish that I had been able to know her better. Elgar was very close to his relations, and often went over to Bromsgrove on Sundays for family lunches.

This weekend had been crowded with interest for me. On the Saturday the Precentor, Rev H. S. Payne, who lived just beyond us at No 9, College Yard, had come to tell us that in clearing out an old cellar he had found an opening which he invited us to explore with him. The old monastic Charnel Chapel had stood in the area between our houses, and it seemed almost certain that this opening must lead into the crypt below that demolished chapel. Great preparations for our exploration were made—old clothes, electric torches, candles to test the atmosphere, etc.

After further clearing of debris and finding that a candle projected well into the space burnt brightly, I, being the youngest, clambered down into the chamber, and after a little more clearing I was quickly followed by the Precentor and my father. Torches revealed a vaulted crypt and many bones. It was an eerie sight, and part of the chamber was blocked, but such architectural detail as could be seen was clearly thirteenth century, and there was no doubt that it was the Charnel Chapel crypt. Over the years the chapel had been neglected, and by the seventeenth century had fallen into decay, apart from the crypt, and with the exception of a low section of one wall which had been incorporated into No 9, nothing now remained above ground.

We could not explore more than a small area, but Valentine Green in his *History of Worcester* published in 1796 describes the crypt as being 58ft long, 22ft broad and 14ft high, containing a vast quantity of bones piled up on each side of a central passage. When we saw it the bones appeared to have covered the whole of the floor area.

On the Sunday we told Elgar all about this and, as we anticipated, he was thrilled. He and Carice visited my parents the next day—I had returned to Lancashire—and the Precentor showed them the discovery.

I was in Worcester again for two weekends at the end of May. On the first Sunday Elgar played to us some records he had just received, among which was an advance copy of *Carissima* and *Salut d'Amour*, due to be publicly released in June. Afterwards we played roulette with Carice and I remember it was a most exciting game. On the second Sunday—Carice having gone home—Elgar delighted us by playing over some sketches which I later learnt were part of the *Severn Suite for Brass*.

Bridge work kept me in Lancashire for the rest of June, but on 6 July I went to Marl Bank. The great event of the previous week had been the Worcester Races on Pitchcroft, where Elgar had been my mother's guest since she was at that time chairman of the Worcester City Corporation Race Committee.

Pressure of work during the remainder of July and August meant that I could not get to London for the Hereford Festival rehearsals, and I had to drive straight to Hereford, where I found, as usual, a large house party.

My father told me that Elgar was recovering from a bad attack of lumbago and was experiencing considerable difficulty in getting on and off the platform and rostrum, even with assistance. He was adamant, however, that he would conduct as usual. This I was to see for myself during the week, and it was most noticeable, though he must have been in pain and had to sit to conduct, that his disability in no way affected his performances.

The opening service was preceded by Elgar's *Civic Fanfare*, which led straight into his arrangement of the National Anthem, since it had been arranged that the Lord Lieutenant's procession would enter the cathedral as the mayors were taking their seats. The service had been my father's *Magnificat* in A and *Nunc*

Dimittis in D and the anthem Parry's *Blest Pair of Sirens*. Elgar had intended to conduct his *Introduction and Allegro for Strings*, in which Billy Reed was leading the quartet within the orchestra, but he was in considerable pain on the Sunday and Hull conducted it with the rest of the service.

Having missed all the rehearsals so far I was determined to be present for all the Monday ones. I spent most of the morning in the organ loft. The chorus and orchestral platform at Hereford, as at Worcester, is in the two westernmost bays of the nave, and the Nicholson temporary organ in Hereford is erected on the decani side with the console high up, giving a commanding view of all that takes place on the platform. It is always fascinating to stand in the organ loft and watch the conductors controlling their forces each in his own way.

Elgar may not have been a great conductor in a strictly technical sense, but no one could obtain finer performances of his own works. His 'command' came not from the movements of his arms or great gestures, but from his own vital personality and an absolute understanding of his forces. He used his left hand very sparingly, but very expressively, and his baton movements were small. But every movement, and especially his expression and his magnetic eyes held each member of the chorus and orchestra and made his performances unique.

From my perfect viewpoint I watched all this as he rehearsed *The Apostles*. He made virtually no stops in the Prologue or 'The Calling of the Apostles', but he was not happy with Scene 2, 'By the Wayside'. Having discussed some point he then called out,

'Right! two bars before 62 please, "Blessed are the meek for they shall inherit the earth."'

Before he could lift up his baton a voice from the orchestra was heard to say very clearly and expressively, 'Yes, six feet by two!'

Elgar's half-raised hand dropped, and slowly a smile broadened over his face with no attempt to hide it, and raising his hand again he said, 'Yes, Gentlemen', and smartly brought his baton into action. This time all went well and the rehearsal continued without a stop for the rest of the section. Over the years I was privileged to overhear many examples of the LSO's dry humour, but, alas, this is the only one that I can now recall.

On the Wednesday morning Elgar conducted his Symphony in A flat, and perhaps it was because it was in the small cathedral, or perhaps it was my own mood, but I can remember feeling that I was more 'wrapped up' in it than ever before. His conducting of *Gerontius* on Thursday evening, with Astra Desmond, Steuart Wilson and Horace Stevens will also long remain with me.

On the Friday I sat in the organ loft for the *Messiah*, and wandering round at the back of the platform was Elgar. He loved the *Messiah* and never missed being present for at least part of it.

On Sunday 28 September my father and I went to Marl Bank and Elgar greeted us warmly, though he was walking stiffly and seemed in pain. He was, however, in splendid form over supper and when we had moved into the Study he took my father to his desk and handed him a somewhat faded green folder. It contained a number of manuscript sheets loosely stitched together with no cover, but on the front page was an ink sketch of a knight in armour.

'Oh, you have found it!', my father said with obvious pleasure. 'Yes,' Elgar replied, 'it was in a bundle of old music which I was turning over recently and had not seen since we went to Severn House.'

It was the manuscript full score of the *Froissart* Overture.

'I will put it in the Cathedral Music Library,' my father said.

'No, I have already given the original score of *Lux Christi*,' Elgar replied. I want you to keep this personally as a memento of our forty years' friendship. I had originally intended to post it to arrive on the actual anniversary, September 10th, but as that was in the middle of the Hereford festival it did not seem suitable, and I wanted to have the enjoyment of handing it to you in person.'

My father was deeply moved; one of the rare occasions on which he allowed his emotion to show. We then moved to the fireside and I well remember watching my father as he turned the pages over, smiling every now and then when he was clearly savouring orchestral passages which had attracted him at the first performance in 1890. Elgar, pipe in mouth, was watching him closely, with the firelight playing on his contented and happy face.

Some weeks later Elgar gave the Worcester Cathedral Library his fair copy manuscript score of *Froissart* from which the printed copies were engraved. This copy does not have the drawing, but like the original score was prepared by Alice, the name of the instruments, etc., being written in by her. Elgar acknowledged Alice's help by getting her to write her initials C.A.E. on the final page under his own signature. The Dean and Chapter presented this fair copy and the manuscript of *The Light of Life* on permanent loan to the Elgar birthplace Museum in 1985.

On our next visit, 5 October, we were all much more subdued, as Elgar was suffering from a bad attack of what he now described as sciatica. This was certainly the beginning of something much more serious, though I did not know it at the time.

There was plenty to talk about at Marl Bank on 12 October. My mother had broadcast an appeal for the Worcester Royal General Infirmary that day, of which she was then chairman, and Elgar and all of us were delighted at how well she had 'come over'.

The greater part of the evening centred, however, around the recent performances of the *Faery Fantasy* by Winifred Barrows, based on Elgar's *Wand of Youth* music given by the staff and pupils of Lawnside School, Malvern, and conducted by my father. Elgar was obviously enthralled about the whole business, and talked about the original little play and how each of his brothers and sisters had contributed their part to it. It was quite clear, however, which of them, even at the age of 10 or 12, had really been the spirit behind it all. He talked about one of his earliest sketches, in 1867, becoming the 'Fairies and Giants' section, but I also remember him giving 1869 as the date of the original play.

He contrasted the delightful settings of Winifred Barrows' *Faery Fantasy*, as described by my father, with the real little wood and small stream near the cottage in Broadheath which had inspired the original conception. He closed his eyes and was clearly 'day-dreaming' about his parents and childhood, and his face grew gentle with a reminiscent happy smile

On 19 October Elgar seemed better and he was much more cheerful. I got heavily teased at my failure to solve an engineering clue in the crossword puzzle. Needless to say it was not long before Elgar himself found the word, 'caisson', and I kicked myself for once found it was so obvious, especially to a bridge engineer. I was puzzled, however, as to how Elgar could possibly know so technical and unusual a word. He explained to me that he had come across the word some months earlier, had looked it up in a dictionary, as he always did on such occasions, and with his uncanny memory it was there for all time.

I did not see Elgar again until 9 November. On 2 November I had taken delivery of a Morris Oxford 6-cylinder car, and so we took Elgar and the dogs for a short run.

Elgar had a number of sketch books on his table, which indeed were there on several of my earlier visits. This time, however, he also had on the piano some sheets of manuscript music, and after supper he played them over to us and explained that for some weeks he had been going over his old sketch books with the idea of producing another suite. I think it was the 'Merry Doll', but anyway this and other sketches became the *Nursery Suite*. Elgar's thoughts about the *Wand of Youth* and his early sketches may well have turned his mind to the *Nursery Suite*, since some of the sketches used in its preparation, such as 'The Waggon Passes', date from the same period as some of those used in the two *Wand of Youth Suites*.

I was next at Marl Bank on 24 November, my birthday, when we all went there for a celebration supper.

On 27 December, there was another special recital of Christmas music in the College Hall, including music by Bach, Corelli and Handel, and carols by Byrd, Holst and Vaughan Williams and two by Elgar: *A Christmas Greeting* and *I sing the Birth*, written in 1928. Elgar had promised to come, but did not feel well enough to go out, and sent good wishes to all instead. He was better the next day and we went up to Marl Bank. Carice was there, and the evening was spent in listening to Verdi's *Requiem* on records. HMV had sent them to him a few days earlier.

1931

There are again no letters this year, but I was able to spend many Sundays at Marl Bank.

The year began well with a delightful evening with Elgar on 4 January. He had just finished the *Nursery Suite*, and he and my father, to my joy, spent a happy time playing to each other the different movements. At my request, though I do not think that it was needed, they played together several times 'The Waggon Passes', with a number of extempore additions. It was indeed a merry occasion.

My next visit was on 25 January. Carice was there, and the supper party was larger than usual since May was also there, and her brother Gerald. I cannot remember any music that evening. Part of the time was spent on Torquemada's crossword puzzle in the *Observer*—unusually, Elgar had hardly looked at it until that evening. General talk and some games, popular then but now forgotten, filled in the evening.

February and March were much more satisfactory and I was able to spend several Sunday evenings at Marl Bank. Elgar was not completely his old self, but there were now only occasional twinges of lumbago. On most of these evenings I was able to get Elgar or my father, or both, to play over the various movements of the *Nursery Suite* to me, and over the period I heard the whole work, though not in its entirety at one session.

It was on one of these evenings with sketch-books still all around, that I asked Elgar if he had kept all the sketches that he had made throughout his life.

'Certainly', he said, 'sketch-books are vital for a composer or author. They record ideas which may well have no use at the time when they are jotted down but which will one day generate other ideas from which new works will be created. Some of them may, as in the case of the *Nursery Suite*, be worked straight into the work, others while not used directly may well influence it. Mind you, I often use them in a totally different way to that which was in my mind when I jotted them down.'

He added that he had not, of course, kept all the 'draft sketches' from which his published works had been written, and, looking at my father with a twinkle in his eye, he added, 'You had better ask your father to show you a few. I have given him, or he has begged, quite a number. But sketch-books are quite another matter. One should never part with those.'

On 3 March the WFCS performed the *Dream of Gerontius* in the cathedral, with Enid Cruickshank, Steuart Wilson and Harold Williams as soloists. I had been in London but managed to get to Worcester in time for the performance. On going into the cathedral I was delighted to find Elgar talking to Edgar Day in the north choir aisle. He said that he would not sit down but would wander around. Afterwards he came into the house and seemed pleased with the performance, though his back was clearly still giving him trouble.

I was at Marl Bank again on three Sundays in April. Elgar was in poor shape. He had strained a tendon and was hobbling around with a stick. On one of these occasions he said that the orchestral parts of the *Nursery Suite* were now all printed and that as soon as he was fit enough he would go up to the HMV studios and record it. The work was dedicated, with royal permission, to the Duchess of York and the Princesses Elizabeth and Margaret Rose, and Elgar was hoping that their Royal Highnesses would attend the recording session.

I next went to supper with Elgar on 17 May. He had now recovered and was looking forward to conducting the following Saturday in Hyde Park, as part of the *Daily Express* 'Empire Celebration'. While he was in London he was going to record the *Nursery Suite* at Kingsway Hall, and was eagerly anticipating this session.

When we saw Elgar on 31 May he told us about his conducting in London and how well the recording for the *Nursery Suite* had gone. The last movement and possibly one of the others would have to be re-recorded, but that could be done on 4 June, when he expected that the Duke and Duchess of York would be present and the whole suite would be played to them. He was in great form; clearly these recording sessions were cheering him up enormously.

June was a great month for all Elgar's friends, for the Birthday Honours List announced that a baronetcy had been conferred upon him, and on 17 June London University made him an honorary Doctor of Music.

Our visit to Marl Bank on 21 June not unnaturally became something of a celebration. Elgar was in magnificent form, with eyes sparkling, and still full of his recording session on 4 June, when the *Nursery Suite* had been played to Their Royal Highnesses the Duke and Duchess of York, who had been most complimentary. There had been a number of distinguished guests, including Bernard. Shaw and Sir Landon Ronald. Elgar was particularly pleased that Their Royal Highnesses had asked him to present to them Billy Reed, who had been leading the LSO.

It was 19 July before I saw him again, and it was a very quiet evening. He was not at all his usual self. My father told me afterwards that he had become ill shortly after my previous visit and had been really very poorly indeed, but was now recovering.

The next time I saw Elgar was in London at the beginning of September, at the rehearsals for the Gloucester Festival. When I arrived at the Royal College of Music Elgar was in the middle of the *Nursery Suite* but soon moved on to the Violin Concerto, with Albert Sammons as soloist. He sat throughout, but his conducting had its normal vigour. It was wonderful to hear the *Nursery Suite* with an orchestra. I had to hurry away, but not before I had joined my father and Elgar for a short talk. I remember his telling us that HMV were planning for 1932, when he would be seventy-five, a recording of the Violin Concerto with Fritz Kreisler. For a long time he had hoped that a recording with Kreisler would be possible and was excited at the prospect, but it was not to be.

We had taken a house as usual for the Gloucester Festival, and rather more than normal fell to my lot that weekend, since Miss Agnes Done was dying, and my mother spent much of the weekend and all the Monday with her in Worcester. Elgar shared our grief since her father, Dr William Done, organist of Worcester Cathedral from 1844 to 1895, had encouraged him as a boy in every way that he could, and allowed him to borrow from him and from the cathedral music library any music which was not available from the music shop.

Miss Done was herself a very fine pianist, and in addition to playing for the Worcester Festival Choral Society's rehearsals had been soloist in festival concerts on a number of occasions.

The opening service included Elgar's orchestral transcription of Handel's Overture in D minor, which he conducted, and as I write this I can recall those rich harmonies rolling down Gloucester's great Norman nave. He conducted *Gerontius* on the Tuesday evening, preceded by Holst conducting his new *Choral Fantasia*. In the Wednesday evening concert in the Shire Hall Elgar conducted the *Nursery Suite*. The audience loved it, and Elgar was obviously very moved by its reception. The next morning he conducted the Violin Concerto with Albert Sammons, and again one noticed how Gloucester Cathedral enhances orchestral music.

The previous evening Vaughan Williams had conducted his *Job—a Masque for Dancing* in the Shirehall. How thrilling it was, but I wished it could have been heard in the cathedral. On the Thursday evening he conducted his *The Lark Ascending* in the cathedral with Billy Reed as the solo violin, where the work immediately gained in sonority.

This year I had heard *Gerontius* from the spacious organ loft on top of the Choir screen. The sound is naturally quite different from that which an audience normally hears, but how exciting, and because of the wonderful acoustics even the words of the soloists could still be clearly heard. The opportunity to watch Elgar's every movement, hands and eyes, took me back to 1917, when I had first sung under his baton.

My bridge-building in Lancashire kept me fully occupied until the end of the year, but I did get down to Marl Bank on 25 October. I remember this visit very clearly for earlier in the month my father had received a number of papers concerning nineteenth-century Worcester Festivals which Miss Done had left to him in her will. Among them was a plan of the orchestra platform for the 1878 festival, the first Worcester Festival in which Elgar played as a second violin. He and my father were both very excited about it, and Elgar had marked on it the exact position in which he had sat, and added a signed note.

On 22 October my father received an additional incomplete and undated drawing which had only just been found, and he was taking this and the 1878 one to Marl Bank on our visit. They were both thrilled with the new discovery, and almost our entire visit was given up to discussions as to the probable date for this second, earlier plan.

I was also able to visit Marl Bank on 15 November. Elgar was in an exuberant mood. He had been staying with Billy Reed in Croydon and had conducted the Croydon Philharmonic Society in a performance of *Gerontius*, which had given him intense pleasure. The orchestra, led by Billy Reed, was made up of LSO and Croydon players, and the chorus, trained by Alan Kirby, comprised members from the Croydon Philharmonic Society and other associated choirs. The programme was an entirely Elgar one, and began with his arrangement of the National Anthem, followed by the Meditation from *The Light of Life*, *For the Fallen*, with Kate Winter as the soprano soloist, and the *Dream of Gerontius* with Enid Cruickshank, Heddle Nash and Horace Stevens as the soloists.

Alan Kirby, a London stockbroker, had founded the Croydon Philharmonic Society in 1914. He was a gifted amateur musician and a very fine chorus trainer and conductor. He was also a great lover of Elgar's works and had specialised in his choral music. Elgar was delighted when Kirby invited him to conduct at Croydon. I remember him saying that when he attended the rehearsal he was amazed at the perfection of this chorus and at their complete understanding of his work. His music, Elgar said, would always be safe in Kirby's keeping.

Elgar's almost boyish delight was not, however, entirely due to his Croydon performance, though this clearly had meant a great deal to him, for two other events had also just taken place both of which pleased him greatly. On 6 November he had been invited to attend a dinner in London given by the Worshipful Company of Musicians. This company traces its descent from a city guild of about 1500 and a charter of James I. It had never been wealthy, but owing to the generosity of a former Master was able to create the Collard Fellowship in 1931 to make grants to a British musician of proved ability, and scholarships and prizes at the Royal Academy of Music, the Royal College of Music, and elsewhere. The dinner was in connection with these awards, and at it Elgar had been made the first honorary freeman.

Six days later he had opened HMV's new recording studios in Abbey Road, St John's Wood, in the presence of a number of friends, including Bernard Shaw, Sir Barry Jackson, Sir Landon Ronald and Sir Walford Davies. After a short speech he had conducted the LSO, led by Billy Reed, in *Land of Hope and Glory*, and the proceedings had been filmed by Pathé for their news-reel service. Elgar was eagerly looking forward on his next visit to London to seeing a private showing of the film. He was thrilled with the new studio and felt that the records of *Falstaff* made the same day might well be the finest he had ever done.

I did not see Elgar again until 13 December. A few days earlier he had received the test records of *Falstaff* and he was delighted with them. We played them over after supper on his new gramophone. This looked to me exactly like his earlier one, and it was in fact a replacement of the same model which he had before. There were sketches lying about, and I hoped that he would play them, but clearly it was a record night.

I was in Worcester for Christmas, and on 27 December we went to Marl Bank. It was another gramophone evening. Elgar, I remember, played over all the *Falstaff* test records again and was apparently not too happy about some passages, but we were all thrilled at their general excellence.

1932

Throughout 1932 and much of 1933 I was able to spend most of my weekends in Worcester. During this time our visits to Marl Bank were to take a slightly different pattern. Before supper, when the weather was suitable, we still spent time walking the dogs or sitting in the garden, and supper, generally cold, was the same as before with May, Madge or Mary Clifford with us, who usually disappeared after the meal. It was in the study after supper that the change came. Up to now conversation had tended to be general and at some stage often reminiscent, but now it was much more about the present—the coming festival, racing at Worcester or Cheltenham, a local point-to-point meeting or some other outside activity. Elgar's 'country gentleman' attitude seemed to be changing to something more vital and positive.

In years when the festival was to be in Worcester conversation at this time and for weeks before and afterwards had always tended to occupy much of the evening, and this year there was much to talk about. Elgar had agreed to conduct *Gerontius*, the Symphony in A flat, *The Music Makers* and *For the Fallen*; Vaughan Williams was writing a new work, *Magnificat*; my father was giving the first performance in England of a Polish work, *Stabat Mater*, by Karol Szymanowski (Elgar was delighted about this).

Most important of all, Elgar was writing an orchestral version of the *Severn Suite* as a result of my father's persuasion. This would have its first performance at the Wednesday evening concert. Elgar was working on it during the first 3 months of 1932, and finished the orchestration early in April. For weeks, in addition to sketchbooks, there had been manuscript loose sheets all over the place, and on several Sundays Elgar and my father had played over one or other of the movements.

Some months earlier my father had told me that Elgar was contemplating writing an opera, and had approached Bernard Shaw for help with a libretto. Shaw was not very helpful, however, and Elgar accordingly turned to a number of Ben Jonson's plays as a possible basis, and had decided on *The Devil is an Ass*, and began to select sections and scenes for a libretto. He had then consulted Sir Barry Jackson who agreed to provide a complete libretto, and this he did over the next few months.

Elgar had, however, made a start with the material which he

himself had already selected, and had decided on the title—*The Spanish Lady*. He had actually played some of it to us, and showed us some of his sketches for stage sets and entrances. I began to realise that a new side of Elgar was emerging for me, and he and my father were now beginning to enter a world which I could only dimly and partially understand. Now I was, quite unconsciously to them for most of the time, an almost unseen listener, albeit an enthralled and fascinated one.

Elgar's table again took on the appearance that my father had known at the beginning of the century, and manuscripts were everywhere in piles, on the piano, even pinned to picture frames and bookcases, if Billy Reed was expected or had just been. I remember that I asked Elgar on one occasion what all the pinned-up loose sheets meant, and he explained that they were different ways of presenting an idea, and that Billy's playing helped him to make a decision. There was a beautiful polished wood music-stand (which he later gave to my father), but it was still easier for Billy to play the passages arranged in this way, while he moved from one to the other.

It gradually became obvious to me that Elgar had a number of projects on the go apart from one which seemed to be pre-dominantly in his mind, the one in which Billy Reed was now clearly involved. There was the *Severn Suite*, now almost completely orchestrated, and *The Spanish Lady*, which at that stage appeared to be progressing well for he played over sketches from time to time, and very jolly they were. He was also working on some old sketches for piano pieces. One of these he played to us in its finalised form, *Sonatina*. I remember this one clearly because it was dedicated to May Grafton. There were two or three others in rough form, but these were put on one side until later in the year.

Apart from the *Sonatina* Elgar was working on a larger piano work for which there were a number of manuscript sheets, mostly piano, but some for piano with orchestral outline. None of them looked new, and many of them were written all over with amendments to such an extent as to make them almost unplayable. Elgar frequently discussed details with my father and often asked his advice. On several Sundays odd sections were played over, but soon these sketches faded out of the picture, no doubt partly because Elgar could not make up his mind whether the work should become a piano solo or a piano concerto, but mainly, I

441

believe, because he did not appear to have any real interest in it, and seemed glad to put it on one side, and it was shortly afterwards to disappear altogether. The main basis for the new piano composition, if anything had come of it, would have been the old *Concert Allegro*, written in 1901 for Fanny Davies after continuous pressure from her. Nearly 40 years later, in 1969, John Ogdon resurrected this old work and gave a number of performances of it.

Another work at this time was *Apostles III*. For months Elgar's reference books and manuscripts lay around, and on a number of occasions, to my delight, he and my father played over sketches and had discussions on them. How many of these sketches were new I do not know, but I suspect that most of them dated back to 1903. My father told me that he would have preferred Elgar to start concentrating on one work, and I know which that would have been—*Apostles III*—but clearly the fact that his mind was now on serious composition was the important thing, and any attempt to direct his inspiration might at this stage be disastrous. As the months passed, however, although nothing was said when I was there, Elgar seemed to me to be moving towards the new orchestral work, though the *Apostles III* sketches still remained in prominent view. *The Spanish Lady* material was still about, but did not seem to have been touched since my last visit.

Of course composition did not take up every Sunday. Towards the end of March Elgar told us all about Ninette de Valois' ballet based on his music in the *Nursery Suite*, which had been produced at Sadlers Wells. He had attended a performance conducted by Constant Lambert and was really thrilled about it.

His interest in recording for HMV was as great as ever, and a number of sessions were taking place or contemplated. It was probably on the same occasion that he told us that HMV wanted to make records of the new orchestral version of the *Severn Suite*, and that he was recording them on 14 April. I remember that when he told us this my father was quite perturbed, until Elgar explained that though the records would be made there would be no public release until after the first performance at the Worcester Festival in September. I can still see my father's great relief, when he realised that his hard-earned festival 'scoop' would not be spoilt. Elgar had watched his face fall, and his eyes twinkled mischievously at the now happy change in his expression.

On 8 May I had a great surprise. The evening was warm, and on our arrival Elgar without saying anything took us down the garden. Erected there were two sections of the Worcester Old Bridge parapets. Somehow I suspect that my father had already seen them, but my cry of surprised delight gave Elgar great satisfaction. The Old Bridge was being widened at this time, and some of the original parapet was surplus to requirements. Elgar had a special love for the bridge, over which he had frequently walked to school. I shared his joy at its rescue, and although to be honest it was a little incongruous in the garden, it remained a continuous pleasure, and often have I stood or leaned against it alongside Elgar and my father, looking across at the cathedral and the distant Malvern Hills, sometimes with the sun setting behind them.

About this time HMV gave Elgar another gramophone, one with wireless and an automatic record changer. It was a new toy for all of us, and on several evenings it was put through its paces. But more important things were happening.

Later in May Elgar told us that HMV had asked him to record the Violin Concerto in July with a brilliant 16 year old violinist, Yehudi Menuhin, who had fallen in love with the work and was planning to play it at a concert in London during November. Elgar, who obviously had heard a lot about Yehudi, was delighted, and keenly looking forward to the recording.

On 18 June I was present in the College Hall in Worcester when Elgar made the main speech at a meeting of the 'Friends of the Cathedral'. His speech was largely about his long connection with Worcester Cathedral, and he acknowledged that he had learnt his first ideas of music from the cathedral, and had always found it a place of rest, contemplation and refreshment in the highest sense of the word.

He said that he began borrowing books from the Music Library when he was about 8, and he described how barbarously printed they were in eight different clefs, and how before he was 12 he had mastered them all. He recounted stories of former deans and paid a glowing tribute to the lay clerks. It seemed odd to him that their musicianship was not widely recognised.

'A man in a cathedral,' he said, 'had to be a musician who could read off a composition and in two or three rehearsals be note-perfect. When they had a Melba or a Caruso who had to learn a short part in an opera, it had to be hammered out note by note for 3 or 6 months beforehand.'

He referred to James Smith, a Worcester tenor lay clerk, then aged ninety, and told of an incident that had occurred at an earlier Worcester Festival.

I was a child when I first knew Mr Smith. At one of the Worcester festivals they had certain great London artists. One was Albani, there was a tenor of the same class, and so on. They were doing a quintette in the cathedral. Smith was standing by, and the bass (an international artist too) entirely lost his place. Smith, who knew nothing about it at all, but simply had a copy of the music, sang the whole thing through, putting on as near a bass voice as he could. The London critics—one of the most distinguished was there that afternoon—never noticed what had happened. That was so usual—it would be rather surprising if they had!

Madame Albani first sang in Worcester in the 1878 festival. It seems likely therefore that this was a slip of the tongue. Elgar perhaps meant to refer to Mademoiselle Tietjens, who in her day was just as well known and popular.

On the next evening Elgar, who was clearly delighted with the reception given to his speech, enlarged upon his reminiscences, and some of these are included in Appendix 1.

Proofs of the Book of Words for the festival were beginning to come in, and my father reminded Elgar that he would soon be needing the notes for the *Severn Suite* and the Piano Quintet, which were to be included.

Marl Bank, Worcester.
Tuesday [28 June 1932]

Me dear F.
   I *am* so sorry. This will do for the Suite: the Quintet I cannot manage. I have no copy & no old programme & have really quite forgotten all about it. Let it go!
Your
R.

With this letter Elgar sent the note regarding the orchestral version of the *Severn Suite* which he wished to appear in the festival programme. It was very simple: a dedication to G. Bernard Shaw, the five movements, the fact that it was a first performance in this form, and the following note:

The Suite was written for brass band in 1930. The movements at first bore some fanciful titles connected with the river after which the Suite is named. The orchestral version is now to be heard for the first time, there is no addition to or alteration from the original form.

On Sunday 17 July, there was much to talk about at Marl Bank. The first full-chorus rehearsal had taken place in the College Hall on 7 July. Elgar had not been well, but having conducted the *Music Makers* early in the afternoon, he stayed on after tea to hear the Szymanowski, and he and my father were delighted at how well the work had gone, and Elgar said again what an achievement it was that my father had secured the first performance in England for the festival, and he commented on the fine choral writing.

Most of the evening was, however, taken up by Elgar recounting his first meeting with Yehudi Menuhin—'wonderful boy'—his short rehearsal and the actual recording sessions on 14 and 15 July. He was clearly tremendously impressed by Yehudi's musicianship, his technique and his remarkable understanding of the concerto. Two days had been reserved for rehearsals in Menuhin's room at Grosvenor House, and it had been arranged for Ivor Newton to accompany him. Elgar said he took an immediate liking to the boy. They played the work right through, and Elgar and Yehudi both felt no more rehearsal was needed. Elgar told us that he excused himself from lunch in order to go to the races! He reminded me of a boy who had been playing truant.

Our visit to Marl Bank on 14 August was a very interesting one. Elgar played over some test records of the Menuhin concerto sessions and was tremendously enthusiastic about them, as was my father. I naturally asked when they would be available to the public, but Elgar told me this would not be until the end of the year, after Yehudi's performance of the concerto, which he was conducting in the Albert Hall on 20 November.

He then played some of his recent sketches which, for the first time as far as I was concerned, were referred to as the Third Symphony. I asked my father about the symphony on our way home, and he told me that the subject was still confidential but that Elgar had actually been considering another symphony 'off and on' for some years, and some of the sketches dated back to those earlier times. I assumed that my father must by now have heard played through what had been written up to then, and asked questions about it. To my surprise he said, no, he had heard and seen a lot of sketches but that Elgar would never play them through or let him see them in consecutive order. Apart from the fact that he thought they would all be part of the first movement, but even this he was not sure about, he really knew little except that Elgar had hinted that it would be on a different scale to his first two symphonies.

My father explained that though Elgar was more secretive than usual, there was nothing new about the way he composed, namely, sections at a time. He had often done this before. If he was working on a section that pleased him, he would often, unlike most composers, orchestrate that section all on its own, perhaps before he had even thought seriously about what would precede or follow it. When he came to planning the movements many of the first sketches would be abandoned, or maybe rewritten and used in other movements, or other works, in quite a different way to those originally contemplated. At this stage, my father told me, Elgar's mind regarding the ultimate form of the symphony was obviously completely flexible. I found all this very puzzling, as I did the fact that whenever Elgar played from a sketch he always played much more than appeared on the paper. The only thing that was clear was that Elgar's creative genius was again taking control and driving him on.

I did not see him again until the Worcester Festival, at which he was in wonderful form. He had a large house-party at Marl Bank which included Carice, Bernard Shaw and his wife, Charlton Palmer and his brother, and he also kept 'open house', especially between the afternoon and evening performances. At other times he was to be seen around the Cathedral, in the Public Hall, being entertained at lunches; in fact, everywhere. He was always at his best at festivals, especially Worcester ones, surrounded by friends, musicians—professional and amateur—and by fellow citizens of all interests, not least racing. To see his boyish enthusiasm made it almost impossible to realise that he had passed his seventy-fifth birthday.

On Saturday 3 September, although none of his works was being rehearsed, Elgar spent much time at the rehearsal, and he was back in the cathedral in the evening with most of his house-party to attend the private organ recital which my father was giving with Billy Reed for a few specially invited guests. It was a wonderful occasion. After everybody was seated the lights were turned off and the cathedral was mysteriously lit only from the external floodlighting. The organ never seemed more noble and its soft passages more haunting than it did that evening in a virtually empty building. As a well-kept secret, Billy played the slow movement of the Violin Concerto to organ accompaniment. Everybody, including Elgar, was deeply moved. He had believed that one movement of his Sonata in G was to be played, and was therefore taken completely by surprise.

He was again in the cathedral for the opening service, behind the platform, and he and Carice came to tea with us afterwards. I remember Edgar Day's shy reception of Elgar's warm con-gratulations on his *Magnificat* and *Nunc Dimittis*.

On the Monday Elgar conducted at the morning, afternoon and evening rehearsals, and he was present on Tuesday morning for *Elijah*, which always gave him great pleasure. His energy was astonishing. He conducted *Gerontius*, with Astra Desmond, Frank Titterton and Harold Williams as soloists, on Tuesday evening, 6 September, the Symphony in A flat on the Wednesday morning, the first performance of the orchestral version of the *Severn Suite* the same evening, and *The Music Makers*, with Muriel Brunskill as soloist, on the Thursday morning, and in the evening *For the Fallen* with Isobel Baillie as soloist. All of these performances were memorable ones, with Elgar showing no signs of fatigue.

On the Friday morning he came in for the *Messiah*, and sat in his steward's seat with Carice and Bernard Shaw and his wife. It was one of the very few occasions on which I saw him sitting throughout a performance.

I have referred earlier to Elgar spending most of his time during festivals on the performers' side of the platform, and among my father's papers I found a note of his about Elgar at Three Choirs Festivals. It gives a vivid timeless picture of the Three Choirs, Elgar and of his love for *Elijah*.

To Elgar the festivals of the Three Choirs were supreme events, landmarks in his life. 'Who will ever love these Festivals as you and I have', he wrote to me during the war, when the future of music seemed so dark and hopeless. At these Music Meetings he was in his own country—near his own Malvern Hills—and he was amongst people who loved him. And how we used to watch for him behind the scenes in a performance. We all knew he was somewhere about, for he would be uneasy anywhere except amongst players and singers. I have seen him sitting in the nave during rehearsals, but I do not recall any occasions when he sat there for a performance. His place was amongst the people who were making the music. And he loved to watch them. He could rarely keep still for long but would move from one side of the orchestra to the other, or pay a visit to the organ loft. In a performance of the 'Elijah' there were always certain features that he would be looking out for. He had a great admiration for Mendelssohn's orchestration and often drew my attention to touches of mastery. I remember how he would always keep his eyes upon the trombones in the Overture, or in the recitative 'O that Thou wouldst rend the heavens', where he particularly admired their use. At other times he would move off to get a good view of the chorus. But wherever he had wandered he was always sure to be found standing near the double-basses for the chorus 'Then did Elijah the prophet break forth like a fire', watching the players in the great arpeggio figures which are so alive with fire and energy. His face was a picture as he listened. And of course every double bass player knew that he was there and his presence was such an inspiration that they would almost make the place rock with the sound. Indeed it seemed by the sound of it as if the very boards of the platform were being ripped up.

For many people the Three Choirs Festivals of the thirties were thought of as Elgar Festivals, and indeed they were, but they also provided performances of many of the great classics and opportunities for performances of new works by young composers, and Worcester 1932 was no exception. The programme included the first performance of Vaughan Williams' *Magnificat*, written for the festival, and his *Benedicite*, both of which he conducted. William Walton conducted his Concerto for Viola and Orchestra and *Portsmouth Point*. Edward Norman Hay's *Paean* was a first performance in England, as was also the eagerly anticipated Szymanowski work, *Stabat Mater*, conducted by my father. Holst conducted his *Hymn of Jesus*, by then recognised as the remarkable work that it is, and the ballet music from *The Perfect Fool*.

The Friday evening concert in the College Hall included a performance of *Three Songs*, written by Molly Hull, which gave great pleasure to her many friends. They were sung by Cynthia Perrins, accompanied by the composer. I can still recall the applause and P.C.'s delighted smile.

The performances of *Gerontius*, *Elijah*, the *Messiah* and Bach's Mass in B minor this year will always be remembered for the outstanding soloists and choral singing and for the glorious playing of the London Symphony Orchestra, but for me it is also to be remembered for Brahms' Concerto in D minor in the cathedral with Myra Hess as the soloist, and for her playing with the Griller String Quartet in the College Hall of Elgar's Quintet in A minor.

I have already referred to Elgar's open hospitality at Marl Bank during the festival week. My father and I, often accompanied by Billy Reed, usually looked in for a quick cup of tea or a drink before we took the walk on one of the commons which was my father's normal relaxation at that time. There were always interesting people to meet on these occasions. The festival weather in 1932 was warm and sunny, and Elgar delighted to sit in the garden, dogs at his feet, with his guests sitting or standing around him. On one of these evenings when the surrounding party included my father, myself, Billy Reed, Charlton Palmer, his brother, H. C. Colles and one or two others, someone asked if there would be a Third Symphony.

Elgar said with an enigmatic smile something like, 'Oh, I am working on that, but of course nobody is interested in my music these days!' At which, needless to say, everybody expostulated, although the remark was clearly not intended to be taken seriously, and conversation turned to the doings of Marco or some such important matter. Elgar was furious when the *Daily Mail* came out with a demand for the production of the new symphony, with the implication that it had already been written.

We had a short holiday immediately after the festival, and I did not go to Marl Bank until 25 September. Elgar played over to us the two piano sketches he had earlier in the year put on one side and which he had now completed. These were *Adieu* and *Serenade* for piano. I remember he told us he was dedicating the serenade to John Austin as a token of appreciation of their long friendship and for his help in 'editing' over 40 years. It was to be a surprise for him, however, and we must keep it secret. My father was delighted, for he also shared Elgar's affection for a mutual friend and the leader of the orchestras of both the WFCS and WO&LCS.

Most of the evening was taken up in a long discussion about an organ arrangement of the *Severn Suite*, from which it became clear that for some months my father had been trying to persuade Elgar to rearrange the material as an organ sonata. Elgar had given my father in 1925 a manuscript fugue dated Napleton, June 1923, to be played by him at the re-opening recital of the reconstructed cathedral organ. It was now evident that this fugue came from the sketches used by Elgar in writing the *Severn Suite*, and my father was hoping that he would convert the other movements of the suite into a sonata. My father had already, at Elgar's suggestion, edited for publication the 1923 fugue. Elgar said that my father should himself arrange the organ sonata and he would have the full scores of the band and orchestral versions sent to him. They had several sessions together over the next few weeks, and in April 1933, my father's organ version was published by Keith Prowse, with Elgar's full approval, as the Organ Sonata No 2 in B flat, Op 87A. In this the fugue, originally in C minor, was now transposed to B flat minor. My father wrote the cadenza and coda, but otherwise all the material came from Elgar's sketches and scores.

On my next visit to Marl Bank, on 16 October, Carice, Madge and Troyte were there and conversation was general. There was no music, but sketches were still pinned up everywhere and my father told me that Billy had been down for the previous night but had left that morning. As we were leaving Elgar told my father that he was very much looking forward to going to Belfast later in the week to conduct *Gerontius*. The orchestral version of the *Severn Suite* would also be broadcast in another programme.

Godfrey Brown, the BBC Belfast Music Director, was by now an old friend of my father's. Brown had recently been in Worcester, where he had met Elgar, and had told my father how much they would welcome Elgar in Belfast. My father had accordingly suggested the visit to Elgar and extolled the hospitality in Belfast.

The Grand Central Hotel, Royal Avenue, Belfast.
Thursday [Postmarked 20 October 1932]

My dear Firapeel:
You see I am safe here & your good friend Godfrey Brown is taking wondrous care of me: he *is* a good cicerone. I don't wonder you like Belfast.

Back next week
Yrs ever
Reynart.

On 29 October Elgar had a pile of manuscript with 'B.J.' (Ben Jonson) stamped on the sheets, and he told us that he was again working on the opera as Barry Jackson had now sent him more of the libretto. There were also separate piles in connection with the symphony and *Apostles III*, but the reference books were no longer in evidence. Elgar played over the latest B.J. sheets but seemed rather listless, and we then played gramophone records including the Menuhin concerto. Elgar had received some additional test records early in September which he told us were going to replace some of those he had played to us in August. The more we heard the records the more impressive they were, and Elgar quickly recovered his vitality.

At my next visit, on 13 November, Elgar was in his most exuberant mood. He told us in strict confidence that Bernard Shaw had suggested to Sir John Reith that the BBC should commission from him the Third Symphony, and that Landon Ronald on their behalf was discussing terms with him for the commission. Elgar was clearly thrilled about the proposal.

Conversation then moved to Yehudi Menuhin's forthcoming performance of the Violin Concerto in the Albert Hall on 20 November, which Elgar was conducting.

I did not see Elgar again until 11 December, when he was in splendid form. He told us that all had now been settled regarding the commissioning of the Third Symphony and that the BBC would announce it on 14 December. My father asked how the Violin Concerto had gone at the Albert Hall on 20 November, and Elgar said that it had been a great success with the audience. He spoke enthusiastically about the 'Wonder Boy', and told us that Menuhin Senior now wanted to repeat the performance in Paris and had invited him to conduct, which he had agreed to do after some initial doubts. There was talk of his flying to Paris from Croydon, and he was very excited at what would be his first flight.

This evening we did have some music, since Elgar had written more of *The Spanish Lady*, which he played to us, and also a sketch entitled 'Mina' (named after his cairn), which Keith Prowse was to publish in 1934. It was very slight but had a nostalgic charm about it.

I did not get down to Worcester again until Christmas. On Christmas Day it was very foggy, but I took my father up to Marl Bank to convey our Christmas greetings and to thank Elgar for his Christmas–New Year card; though we did not know it, the last he was to send. Elgar's Christmas cards were always original and characteristic. This year's one was obviously his own literary invention.

1932 - 1933

With all good wishes for

CHRISTMAS and the NEW YEAR

from

Edward Elgar.

In a gorgeous, illimitable, golden corridor, several of the Higher-Beings were in waiting.
  Around, and in mysterious depths, great and marvellous works were making.   . . .

But the New World, it seemed, was not going well.
  ' I do not see why a New World,' said Gabriel.
Uriel surveyed, with hesitating discontent, a trumpet.
  ' Have you to play that thing ? ' asked Raphael.
  ' Some day,' Uriel answered, without enthusiasm. . . .

A vast Purple Shadow filled the space and Lucifer sat.   Ithuriel slightly shifted his spear.
  ' How,' asked One, ' do you, Intellect, picture what is coming ? '
Lucifer answered,—' I shall like it ; there will be much to amuse besides the religions.'
  ' Nonsense,' said Gabriel, ' they are dull.'
  ' Also,' continued the Purple One with considerable relish, ' I shall enjoy Shakespeare ; he will say I am a gentleman.   Milton—'
  ' We are sick of Milton,' hastily interrupted the Others,—' of Milton and a whole lot of insufferable bores. Why, oh why, must it be ? ' . . .

Michael fingered a sword and saw his effigy as the everlasting maître d'armes ; Raphael groaned, ' Think of me in pictures of that wretched boy with his eternal fish ! '

Uriel, Ithuriel and the rest yawned, ' Unhappy Earth, why, oh why ? '   .   .   .

.   .   .   .   .

From somewhere near came a curiously pleasant sound; pleasant and not unmirthful.

If the MAKER-OF-ALL could be pleased beyond ordinary with any single piece of work, it would seem that the last created thing was of an excellence surpassing those grisly gewgaws which HE had seen and found good.   .   .   .

Michael drew the draped curtain ; then backed away, radiant.

' HE is pleased,—HE laughs,—HE has made, (Michael whispered) —a Puppy ! '

The august features of the Higher-Beings relaxed. ' The Earth is well,' they chanted, ' a Puppy ! '

.   .   .   .   .

The Purple Shade heaved outward and sank below.

Lucifer knew that through the ages Man could be serenely happy with his DOG.

When we arrived we found Carice and her husband there, and they were preparing for a large family supper—seven Graftons were expected. Elgar teasingly said that after his card we had clearly come to see the dogs and not him, but he was obviously pleased at our coming over in the fog. I did not think, however, that he looked at all well.

1933

The BBC commission was a tremendous encouragement to Elgar, and from now on I was to see his manuscript sheets steadily increasing, and generally, as Billy Reed was coming down more and more frequently, there were sketches pinned up all around the room awaiting his next visit. These were usually in connection with the Third Symphony, but sometimes for the opera. Elgar appeared to be composing both these works simultaneously.

On my first visit that year Elgar was worried because he could not replace the Italian handmade music paper which he loved and which was running out. On my second visit, on 15 January, however, he was very happy since Landon Ronald had found a man who was prepared to make up and supply handmade paper to Elgar's requirements, and on my visit at the end of the month the first sheets had arrived which he proudly showed to my father. It certainly was beautiful paper, and Elgar was very happy with it, but from the way he handled it and the old Italian paper, first one, then the other, I felt that he still had a longing for his original choice, with its memories of when he had first found it in Italy, some 25 years earlier.

I remember my visit to Worcester of 14–16 January very well because my father told me when I arrived that Elgar had just received the first rough proof of the Organ Sonata No 2 Op 87A, and was bringing it down after Evensong for him to play before they passed the proof. It would be the first time it had been played complete, and both were eagerly looking forward to hearing it, as indeed we all were, including my mother and Edgar Day. We were all in the organ loft, but as soon as it was finished Elgar wanted to hear it again from the nave, and so it received a second performance, with my mother and I sitting and Elgar roving around the cathedral. He was in marvellous form on our return to the house, and obviously delighted with the work.

The symphony and the opera were shaping well during the first months of the year, and Elgar seemed pleased, and occasionally he played some of the sketches to my father, but I noticed that those he played were more often for the opera than the symphony. I gained the impression that if it had not been for the BBC commission priority might well have been given to the opera, though clearly both had now captured his creative imagination.

Elgar was not wholly occupied with his composing. Recording for HMV and the forthcoming visit to Paris took up part of the conversation, as did references to racing. He was a keen and frequent attender at race meetings at this time, especially if Carice was staying with him. His energy was amazing for his age, but it came in bursts, and he no longer took long walks with the dogs but now preferred to motor to one or other of the commons and after a short walk would often then sit in the car, leaving the dogs to rush around.

At this time I was in Worcester for most weekends and every now and then I could arrange to be there for a weekday. Elgar normally looked in on my parents on the way to or from exercising the dogs, and if I was at home I generally went out with him. He loved company on these occasions, and he was a wonderful companion himself, with anecdotes about every place we visited. There did not seem to be a village in Worcestershire or Herefordshire which he did not know, and most of them, especially those near Worcester, were regular haunts for him.

He was putting on weight and becoming tired more quickly than previously, but mentally he was as active and his kindly wit as pungent as ever. During the first half of 1933 he showed a restless activity, and judging from his conversation life seemed for him to be coloured in vivid hues, no longer in the soft pastel shades of nostalgia. There was a vividness in whatever he did. When one was with him one could feel the 'hum' as it were of a great dynamo. I mentioned this to my father and he said that I was letting my imagination run away with me, but he did agree that Elgar was now mentally in the state in which he remembered him in the days of his greatest creativity.

Our evenings at Marl Bank had a new quality. I was an interested spectator for much of the time. Elgar and my father, though they said very little, seemed in some strange way to be closer than ever. The silences were longer than usual, but their thoughts must have been in communion, for often some sketch shown to my father would be looked at and put down silently, but each seemed to be satisfied, and sometimes Elgar would pick up a pen and make an alteration. For me, those evenings when Elgar talked about what he had been doing or we played records were the easy-going, pleasant ones, but the other evenings had a deeper, exciting and disturbing quality, because only partially understood, that I shall never forget. To have been in the presence of an *active* creative genius leaves an indelible mark on one.

On 16 March the WFCS concert in the cathedral included Elgar's *Sursum Corda* for Organ and Orchestra, the first and second movements of Brahms' Symphony in E minor and his *Requiem*, and Elgar, who loved Brahms and the organ, came to the performance that evening and looked in afterwards for a short while. He told me that it was a long time since he had heard *Sursum Corda* and hoped that I had noticed what a difference the great cathedral organ made to the work. I had to confess that I did not know the work, but that I had motored down from Lancashire especially to be at the concert and was returning later that night.

He seemed pleased, and indeed commented on it when I saw him again at Marl Bank the following Sunday.

Elgar had about a month earlier recorded *Froissart* with the LPO, and he now had the test records which we played over several times. They were astonishingly realistic and among the finest recordings that Elgar had made. I had recently built an electric gramophone unit and presented it to my father, so I was not greatly surprised when he asked Elgar to get him a similar test set, especially as I knew their first meeting had been at the première of this work in 1890. (The records were not issued publicly until 1934.)

Elgar laughed and said, 'Oh! I have anticipated you, and I have already ordered a second set for you as a celebration present of 43 years' friendship.' My father's face glowed with pleasure, and a few days later Elgar delivered the records in person.

On 9 and 16 April most of the evening was devoted to gramophone records, mainly Mozart, Bach and Brahms, but I particularly remember Chabrier's *Marche Joyeuse*, since I had to search for it in a stack of records, mostly without covers. When I found the record, an American Victor, it showed many signs of wear but was a delightful piece. Elgar told us that HMV had sent it to him with a batch of records some weeks earlier and that it was a constant joy to him.

On our way home I expressed surprise that there had been no talk about the opera or the symphony, and my father told me that Elgar had left the opera on one side for some days now and was concentrating hard on the symphony, but no doubt wanted to forget all about it for the weekend.

On our visit on 30 April the symphony sketches were again in evidence, and to my joy Elgar played some of them to us, but they were fragments only and played in no particular order. These were discussed and Elgar seemed to me to have several different ideas about them. I could of course make little out of all this, but noticed that he played over several times certain passages with minor variations. I also saw that one or two of the sheets had been fully scored. To hear a composition in the making was a strange and fascinating experience.

The rest of the evening was taken up with Elgar telling us about his plans for the next fortnight. He was keenly looking forward to going to Croydon on 5 May for a long weekend with Billy and

'James' (Mrs Reed), and to conducting the Croydon Philharmonic Society and the LSO on the Saturday night in a performance of *The Apostles*. Alan Kirby had engaged Isobel Baillie, Astra Desmond, Eric Green, Frank Phillips, Harold Williams and Arthur Cranmer, and the chorus would know the work through and through—it was bound to be a wonderful performance. He and Billy would play over some of the Third Symphony, and on the Monday Dick Mountford, his chauffeur, who had driven him down, would motor him to Newmarket for a week's racing. To watch the change in Elgar's mood from the serious composer to the easy-going race-goer was quite astonishing. When we left him he was still in his most boyish mood, and one would have thought that racing was the most important thing in his life.

On our next visit, on 21 May, Carice was there and Elgar played us test records he had just received of *Cockaigne*, *Pomp and Circumstance March* No 4, *Elegy*, and the prelude to *The Kingdom* played by the BBC Symphony Orchestra. He told us that he had greatly enjoyed conducting them, and what a fine orchestra they had become under Adrian Boult.

I noticed on his desk a small onyx clock, and Elgar said that Alan Kirby had presented it to him on behalf of the Croydon Philharmonic Society at a small ceremony after he had conducted *The Apostles*. This was, in fact, the last time that he conducted this work.

Carice referred to Elgar's forthcoming Paris concert, and he told us again that he was going to fly there from Croydon, and how Fred Gaisberg (HMV) and Dick Mountford would be going with him.

When I went to Marl Bank on 4 June it was something of a celebration evening. We congratulated him both on his GCVO, which had been gazetted in the King's Birthday Honours List on 1 June, and on his seventy-sixth birthday the following day, and he told us all about his wonderful French trip. He was most enthusiastic about his flight and had clearly loved every moment of it, and the hotel had been most comfortable. On 29 May, Mr Menuhin had taken him to lunch at their home overlooking the Seine at Ville d'Avray, St Cloud, and he had met the family, including Yehudi's sisters Hephzibah and Yaltah. He had greatly liked the three children, and when he discovered that they now had no grandfathers on either side, he offered to become a foster grandfather to them. He loved young people, and was obviously delighted with his new relationship. Some years later I was to hear from Yehudi Menuhin that he and Hephzibah had immediately taken to Elgar, and they were very happy to become his 'foster grandchildren'.

Elgar had told us that he had been most impressed with Georges Enesco's rehearsal of his concerto. The Orchestre Symphonique de Paris knew the work well and Yehudi had been in great form. After lunching, Elgar and Gaisberg motored some forty miles through the Fontainebleau forest to Grez-sur-Loing to call on Delius. He told us how delighted Delius had been with their visit, with the records Elgar had brought, and with news from England, especially of the great interest now being taken in his music. The visit ended with the opening of a bottle of champagne in his honour, and the exchange of toasts of mutual good wishes.

The next afternoon he had been invited to attend a State function in the Artillery School, where the President presented him with a decoration. He amused us very much by his description of being kissed on both cheeks as part of the ceremony, and how the President's waxed moustache had tickled him so much that he could hardly avoid making a grimace, which he told us he was sure would have created an international incident.

The concert that evening in the Salle Pleyel was given to a distinguished audience, including the President, ministers and other representatives of the French government. Elgar told us that Yehudi had repeated the wonderful interpretation of the concerto that he had given in the Albert Hall and the performance had been very good, though the French orchestra lacked the finer touches of the London Philharmonic. He had been given a good reception by the audience, but he said that it had lacked warmth, and despite all the congratulations that he received afterwards he felt that the French concert public did not understand his music.

At the beginning of July Elgar became unwell and was under doctor's orders, and at the end of the month the weather was very hot, which seemed to worry him since he complained that he was finding it difficult to work and that he was falling behind schedule.

On our visit on 30 July, Elgar seemed anxious that my father should see how far he had proceeded with the symphony. Billy Reed had been down for a couple of nights the previous week and they had worked over a number of passages. Elgar sat down at the piano and began to play, my father and I standing behind him.

From what he said it seemed that the structural form was now complete in his mind, and indeed much of the material, but he still did not start at the beginning and there were clearly many sections missing. What was evident to me, though, was that he had not lost his power of making a piano sound orchestral, and that he was playing far more than was written down. It was a thrilling evening because although I did not really understand it, I gained a definite impression that Elgar now knew where he was going.

As I was taking over new work in Somerset in September, I was very busy tidying up in Lancashire, and as a result did not get down to Worcester until 1 September, in time to go to Hereford for the festival.

My father went to Marl Bank on 27 August, where he found Fred Gaisberg, who was staying the weekend. Gaisberg told him that Elgar had played over the Third Symphony to him that afternoon, and how complete it now was. My father on leaving, and being alone with Elgar, told him how pleased he was to hear how rapidly the symphony had progressed during August (my father had been away). Elgar, however, said that in fact he had not been well, the continual heat had upset him, and he had also been in London to conduct the Second Symphony at the Proms. He said he didn't think that he had added anything material to what he had played when my father was last with him at the end of July.

We had our usual house-party at Hereford for the festival, and Elgar had taken 'The Priory', a house with a large sunny garden. This year for the first time he did not make his usual 'bacon-sniffing' tours, and in fact he only came to our house twice.

Elgar had always been a stylish dresser, and he was as immaculate as ever this festival. When he was not in formal clothes he wore a very smart light linen suit with a coloured bow tie. He now walked continuously with a stick and tired very quickly. He was still surrounded by his friends, but this year they called upon him. The weather was warm and sunny and he kept open house, usually sitting in the garden. Carice, May and Madge Grafton and Mary Clifford provided generous hospitality, especially between the afternoon and evening performances. For once Elgar seemed to want to talk about music, and I recall listening to him telling a group of musicians how much he owed to Bach, Handel, Haydn and Beethoven, and how he loved Berlioz, Mendelssohn, Rossini and the romantic symphonies of Schumann and Brahms. His knowledge of chamber music was profound, and he had a long discussion about the early and late Beethoven quartets, which I am ashamed to confess I then hardly knew.

None of this reduced energy showed, however, in his conducting. At the opening service, wearing his full court dress, he conducted his March in B flat (so named in the programme—the Triumphal March from *Caractacus*, transposed from C) and the *Civic Fanfare*. (The Civic Fanfare is in B flat.) On the Tuesday evening he obtained a very fine performance of *Gerontius*, and at the Wednesday evening concert he conducted the viola arrangement of his Concerto in E minor, with Lionel Tertis as soloist.

The Elgar climax of the festival, however, came on the morning of the Thursday with the performance of *The Kingdom*, the last time, though we did not know it then, that Elgar was to conduct. I remember that morning very clearly. My father was that year playing the organ for the morning performances, and he and I had walked across from the house that we had taken to the west end of the cathedral, and as we were standing there Elgar came up. The three of us stood in the sun talking and chatting, with Elgar greeting all his old friends in the orchestra and chorus as they moved into the cathedral. I recall he drew our attention to the Sinclair head which is carved over one of the doors and reminded my father of bicycle rides the three of them had taken together. Then my father and Elgar passed into the darkness of the cathedral and I wandered round to the north door and to my seat for the performance of *The Kingdom*.

I can see it again today: Elgar conducting, with Elsie Suddaby, Astra Desmond, Frank Titterton and Harold Williams around him, and Billy leading the orchestra, and the chorus and orchestra following his every movement and quietly and surely meeting his every wish. Elgar's movements were slight and less demonstrative than they would have been years before, and at times it was as if he was himself being carried away by his own music. But the performance was perfect and strangely intimate and reflective. Perhaps memories were passing through his mind of his writing this work in Hereford 27 years before, or more likely later events have added poignancy to my own memories. Elsie Suddaby's singing of 'The Sun goeth down', and the last chorus, 'Thou O Lord art our Father and we are Thine', with Elgar very quietly putting down his stick after the last chord had faded away, will always remain in my memory.

On our visit to Marl Bank on 17 September we found Elgar in good form. Billy Reed had spent the previous weekend with him and Elgar had made additions and alterations which he played over and discussed with my father. The symphony appeared to be progressing.

There was some talk about the Hereford Festival and then Elgar asked me to play to us the test records which he had just received of the *Serenade for Strings* and *Elegy*, recorded in the Kingsway Hall at the end of August. They were very good, and Elgar seemed pleased. I remember he made me repeat the second movement of the *Serenade*, and he discussed some point with my father. I very much regret now that I did not question my father about the discussion, for these records were to be the last ones that Elgar made.

On 19 September I went to live in Bath, and for some months I was only able to spend occasional weekends in Worcester. Knowing my keen interest in Elgar's affairs, especially the symphony, my father kept me closely in touch. On 24 September Elgar complained to him about an attack of lumbago which was very painful, but otherwise he seemed normal, and on the following Sunday they spent a quiet, uneventful evening. On 8 October, however, my father rang up to tell me that Elgar had become really ill and the previous day had been taken to South Bank Nursing Home for an operation, and was expected to be there for some time. On the few weekends that I was able to get to Worcester I would take my father up to South Bank. Elgar had a pleasant room, somewhat remote from the main part of the building, and he was able therefore to have a gramophone, which during the first few weeks was a constant pleasure for him. Gaisberg, as soon as he heard of Elgar's operation, had immediately sent to South Bank the latest model gramophone and a supply of records.

Carice came to live at Marl Bank and spent as much time as possible with her father, as did his nieces and Mary Clifford, to whom he was able to dictate letters. Over the weeks he saw many old friends, including Landon Ronald and Ernest Newman. Billy, naturally, came down whenever he could.

As the weeks passed the pain grew stronger and he was increasingly heavily sedated, but when awake he often liked his visitors to put on records for him, and I well remember an occasion while I was sitting with my father by his bedside and he asked me to put on the record which was on the turntable. It was the slow movement of his own Quintet, played by Harriet Cohen and the Stratton Quartet, who had only very recently recorded it. On another occasion he asked for the slow movement of one of the last of the Beethoven Sonatas, the one in E, Op 109. He seemed now to like to listen to chamber music. It calmed and eased him, but seldom did one play a second side; usually before the end of a record he had fallen asleep. At other times we would find him sleeping. We would creep in and my father would sit close to him and usually after a little time Elgar would open his eyes and smile, often saying nothing.

Towards the end of November his friends thought that the end was drawing near, and although nothing was ever said to suggest this, I am sure that Elgar himself knew how ill he was. It was about this time, my father told me, when Billy and Carice had been with him, that Elgar referred to the incomplete symphony and begged that no one would ever 'tinker with it'. After his death Sir John Reith, when the 'fragments' were handed over to the BBC by Carice and Reed, gave a firm promise to this effect.

Early in December, to everybody's surprise, Elgar seemed to take a new interest in life. My father told me that he had asked Gaisberg to bring his own photographer down to take some pictures of him at South Bank, for him to give to a few special friends.

At Christmas we all three went to South Bank to give him the season's greetings and good wishes, and he was well enough to remind my father of some earlier Christmas event of years before.

1934

On 1 January, Elgar was moved from the South Bank Nursing Home to Marl Bank, and after an initial set-back appeared to be maintaining his improvement, though his close friends knew that the end could only be a matter of weeks or months at best.

I saw him very briefly with my father on 7 January, when he was drowsy, but talked for a moment or so and seemed happier back in his own home. This was the last time that I was to see him awake.

Carice told us before we left that Gaisberg was doing everything he could to interest Elgar, and that, with approval, he was contriving a very special event, if Dr Moore Ede (his doctor) would agree, namely, that her father should from his bed via a telephone line to London take charge of a gramophone recording session of some of his music, probably from *Caractacus*.

My father telephoned me a few days later to tell me that Dr Moore Ede had agreed, and that Elgar had shown him a letter from Gaisberg outlining the proposal. He was obviously absolutely thrilled with the whole idea. He told my father that Dick was already making up a special stand to hold the full score over his bed so that he could control proceedings.

Some days later my father telephoned again to tell me that the forthcoming recording session had now been fixed for 22 January, and it was still having a wonderful effect on Elgar. The only fear now was that he might be in great pain on the day and unable to take part. Fortunately this was not so, and my father who was present wrote me an account of this historic event.

He had been invited to be at Marl Bank at 3pm. Carice told him on arrival that Gaisberg and his electrical engineer had been there since midday, and that the land-line was all connected up in the room next to Elgar's bedroom. A microphone and loudspeaker would later be placed near his bed. She said her father had been very excited all the morning, but had then fallen asleep. The recording session was expected to start about 3.30pm. Troyte Griffith arrived, and at 3.30 they went up to Elgar's room. Carice, Dr Moore Ede and the nurse were already there. Elgar was sitting propped up with pillows, and Dick was arranging the special stand he had made across the bed and placing a full score of *Caractacus* upon it. Madge Grafton, Mary Clifford, Dick's wife and the maid came in. The microphone and speaker had been installed, and Elgar opened the score and was very keen to begin. Gaisberg, however, explained that although the post office lines had been in use since 2pm, they had become noisy at about 3, and until the disturbance had been traced they could not use them. Everybody, especially Elgar, was becoming restless with the delay, when suddenly, shortly after 4 o'clock the loudspeaker came to life and Lawrance Collingwood and Billy Reed sent greetings to Elgar, and the LSO cheered. Elgar responded with a short speech thanking them and expressing pleasure at being able to take part in this great experiment. He then called upon them to start and they played the Triumphal March from *Caractacus*. Collingwood then asked for comments, and Elgar drew his attention to a number of points— 'the tempo was not quite right,' 'strings should bring out the melody more,' etc. The March was then repeated to his satisfaction, and he then called for 'The Woodland Interlude', which was played and at his request repeated slower. The recording ended at about 5.15, with repeated mutual good wishes from all involved. Elgar fell back exhausted but looking happier than he had for a long time. My father added that Elgar's vigour had amazed everybody, especially Dr Moore Ede, and that the movements of his hands during the proceedings made it quite clear how much he would have liked to have done the conducting himself.

The recording session had given Elgar a new interest in life, and a day or so later he told my father that he wished there could be another one, but from this time on he steadily declined and his pain increased until he soon had to be under drugs almost continuously.

I drove my father to Marl Bank on 4 February. We saw Carice, but Elgar was sleeping deeply and we crept away. My father called at Marl Bank every day, and he told me that after this visit Elgar gradually faded away, and a little before 8am on Friday 23 February he died peacefully.

My father had some days previously discussed with the Dean the holding of a memorial service in the cathedral as soon as possible after Elgar's death, and on news of the sad event he immediately went to London to discuss the matter with Billy Reed and to find the first day on which the LSO would be available. Billy returned with my father and stayed with my parents until after the funeral.

On Monday 26 February, at 10am, with the morning mists still on the Malvern Hills that he had loved so much, Elgar was laid to rest next to Alice, who had been buried there nearly 14 years earlier, in the churchyard of St Wulstan's Roman Catholic Church, Little Malvern. By his own request and Carice's, the service was a very simple one without music and with only family and intimate friends present—indeed, the time of the service had not been announced.

My father was present and told me how moved he was by the very simplicity of the service. Throughout there had been bright sunshine, but as the holy water was sprinkled over the oak coffin in the grave there was a sudden fall of snow, which lay upon the coffin as a soft white blanket. Before they left the churchyard the sun was again shining. The service was taken by Dom G. Cyprian Alston, OSB, and those attending were Carice and her husband, Elgar's nephews and nieces—Gerald, Roland, May and Madge Grafton—Mary Clifford, Alderman Hubert Leicester and his son Philip, Troyte Griffith, my father, Sir Landon Ronald, Billy Reed, Dr Moore Ede, Nurse Harrison, Dick Mountford and his wife, and Mrs Keble and her sister who lived close by and provided coffee after the service. The only flowers were a single bunch of early daffodils, and there were no mourning or formal clothes.

The funeral over, my father, the Dean and Billy Reed made the final arrangements for the national memorial service to be held in Worcester Cathedral on 2 March. The London Symphony Orchestra were giving their services as a mark of affection for their old friend and one-time conductor.

I had not been in Worcester since 4 February, due to pressure of work, but naturally I made special arrangements to be present at this great service. Special trains from London and elsewhere had been laid on, and the cathedral was absolutely packed with those who wished to show their respect and love for this great man who had stirred their imagination more than any other English composer, and whose music had reflected so many aspects of the English character and countryside. They came from all walks of life—musicians, literary men, actors, clubmen, country folk, Worcester citizens, sportsmen, and the racing fraternity from near and far to whom he had become so well-known over the years as a regular race-goer. Elgar's interests had been so wide that it would be difficult to name any section of our community which was not represented individually or officially. Eminent musicians representing the music colleges, the universities, music associations and societies were to be seen thronging each other to go into the cathedral, and official representatives were everywhere mingling with the crowd of those attending. The King was represented by Admiral Sir Henry Buller and by the Lord Lieutenant, Viscount Cobham; and the Prime Minister, Stanley Baldwin, and other Members of Parliament sent official representatives. The mayors and corporations of the three cathedral cities and from other towns and boroughs attended in state, and representatives of the clergy of the dioceses formed another long procession.

Outwardly there was all the pomp and ceremony appropriate to the passing of a Master of the King's Musick, but the feeling within the cathedral was very different. Here one sensed something much simpler and deeper—a very real affection for and wish to honour one who in his lifetime had helped them to see visions of something greater and more lasting.

The chorus included units from Hereford and Gloucester. The LSO was led by Billy Reed, and P. C. Hull and John Sumsion were there as friends and as conductors of the Hereford and Gloucester Festivals.

The service had been chosen by my father to include music not only from representative compositions but also works for which Elgar had a special affection. There was no organ voluntary or music for the processions, which entered silently. The service opened with the LSO playing the Introduction to Part 2 of *The Apostles*, and then the words 'I am the Resurrection . . .' were said by the Archdeacon, followed by the first lesson and two prayers. The LSO then played the *Enigma* Theme and three Variations, I (C.A.E.), IX (Nimrod) and XIII (***). The Dean read the second lesson and two more prayers. The Prelude to *Gerontius* then followed, and Harold Williams sang '*Proficiscere, anima Christiana de hoc Mundo*' (Go forth upon thy journey, Christian soul), and the chorus sang 'Go in the Name of Angels and Archangels' to the end of Part 1. This was followed by Astra Desmond singing 'My work is done' and 'Softly and gently dearly-ransomed soul', and the chorus joined in with 'Lord, thou hast been our refuge' and 'Praise to the Holiest'. The Bishop read the third lesson and two more prayers, and Elsie Suddaby then sang from *The Kingdom* 'The sun goeth down', with the chorus singing 'Our Father', 'Ye have received the Spirit of Adoption', and 'Thou, O Lord art our Father, our Redeemer, and we are Thine', which ends *The Kingdom*.

The processions and congregation then silently moved out of the cathedral, deeply moved by this most impressive service.

After this service, in response to a growing feeling that there should be a permanent memorial to Elgar in the Cathedral, the Dean and my father on 12 March circulated an appeal for funds to erect a memorial in the form of a stained-glass window. Originally a window in the cloisters was contemplated, but when it was clear that adequate funds would be available, it was decided that the window should be in the north aisle of the nave, near the spot where Elgar so often stood watching orchestra and chorus during Worcester Festivals. It was also felt that the design of the window should be chosen by competition from the greatest stained-glass window artists of the day. Archibald K. Nicholson's design was finally selected, and it was arranged that the window should be dedicated at the 1935 Worcester Festival.

The Gloucester Festival of 1934 included three Elgar works. *The Kingdom*, performed 'In Memoriam Edward Elgar', was conducted by John Sumsion, with Elsie Suddaby, Olga Haley, Percy Manchester and Harold Williams as soloists. The Second Symphony was conducted by Percy Hull, and *Gerontius* by my father with Astra Desmond, Heddle Nash and Harold Williams as soloists.

All, as might be expected, were beautiful performances, but the one which stands out in my memory is *Gerontius*. Only one other performance, that in Worcester a year later, moved me as much as this, and perhaps even that did not have the devastating emotional effect on me of this one. Soloists, chorus and orchestra were determined to make this, the first Three Choirs performance since Elgar's death, something entirely special. It was as if it was each performer's personal contribution and act of devotion to Elgar's memory. Unashamed tears rolled down many cheeks that evening.

Gaisberg had wished to make a gramophone recording of what he realised would be an absolutely unique performance of *Gerontius*, and one which he felt would be a worthy memorial to Elgar. The conductors, the festival authorities and all concerned in the performance were in agreement, but sadly once more the Dean and Chapter could not see their way to changing their earlier decision that recordings should not be made in Gloucester Cathedral, and the opportunity was lost for ever.

1935

The Elgar Memorial Window in Worcester Cathedral was finished in the late summer of 1935, ready for dedication at the Three Choirs Festival. This was the first Worcester meeting after Elgar's death, and his music figured in each day's programme.

Again, each performance seemed to have a special significance, as though Elgar himself were present. Two of the performances stand out very clearly in my memory as if they had been heard only yesterday. One was *The Apostles*, with Isobel Baillie, Astra Desmond, Heddle Nash, William Parsons, Roy Henderson and Harold Williams, with the evening sun setting through the great west window behind the chorus. The other was *Gerontius*. The performance began half an hour early, to allow for the inclusion of a special dedication service of the memorial window. After the playing of Elgar's arrangement of the National Anthem, a procession headed by the Bishop (A. W. T. Perowne) and the newly appointed Dean (Arthur W. Davies), Viscount Cobham, the Lord Lieutenant of Worcestershire, Sir Ivor Atkins, Sir Hugh Allen, Sir Walford Davies, Dr Vaughan Williams, Dr Percy Hull, Herbert Sumsion, Dr C. Lee Williams, W. H. Reed, A. K. Nicholson and Roy Harrison, the festival secretary, moved to the north aisle of the nave. After prayers the Dean requested the Lord Lieutenant to unveil the window. Beethoven's *Equale for Trombones* was played, and the Bishop dedicated the window in memory of Edward Elgar. The 'Nimrod' Variation was then played. The rich colours in the window and in the ceremonial robes as the group returned to their places added a touch of pageantry to the occasion.

The soft opening notes of the Prelude to *Gerontius* sounded through the cathedral, and as one listened with half-closed eyes, it was easy to imagine that it was Elgar himself who was conducting.

The soloists were Frank Titterton, Harold Williams and Astra Desmond. Again there were tears in many eyes, and the memory of this great performance will remain with me until I die.

EPILOGUE

After Elgar's death his music continued to dominate the Three Choirs Festivals up to their cessation in 1939, when the outbreak of World War II caused the abandonment of the Hereford Festival. The Three Choirs were revived by Hull at Hereford in 1946.

My father conducted his last Three Choirs Festival at Worcester in 1948. He retired as Organist and Master of the Choristers at Worcester in 1950, but remained Librarian of the Worcester Cathedral Library until his death in 1953.

As for myself, I have maintained my close connection with the Three Choirs Festivals. I began in 1908 by being taken regularly to festival rehearsals up to World War I, and since the revival of the Three Choirs Festival at Worcester in 1920 I have been present at every festival. I continued my engineering career until my retirement in 1969. At Sir Adrian Boult's request (he was then chairman) I agreed to become a Trustee of the Elgar Birthplace Trust and I was elected in 1972, when Sir Adrian became president and Sir Gerald Nabarro was elected chairman. On the advice of the Charity Commissioners Sir Gerald instigated the formation of The Elgar Foundation—a Charitable Trust—to raise money to finance the Elgar Birthplace Trust and the Elgar Birthplace. After the death of Sir Gerald I was elected chairman of both the above Elgar Charitable Trusts in 1973, a position I still hold. My father had a prominent part in the original formation of the Elgar Birthplace Trust, and my mother was at one time also a Trustee. I am proud to be able to continue helping to preserve the Birthplace and its unique treasures for future Elgar music lovers.

APPENDIX 1
Reminiscences of early Worcester Festivals and Elgar's childhood and youth

Under suitable intimate circumstances, such as by the fireside in his home or perhaps walking around the cathedral at Worcester, Elgar would often talk about his childhood and early days, and about his family's connection with the Three Choirs Festivals at Worcester. I heard these anecdotes and reminiscences over a period of nearly 20 years, and those relating to the years before he met my father are grouped here in chronological order.

His earliest story relates to the Worcester Festival of 1848, and was told to him by his father. Elgar told it to me during the Worcester Festival of 1926 while we were walking round the cloisters.

The incident occurred during a secular concert of the festival in the College Hall. Two celebrated and popular singers, Mademoiselle Alboni, a contralto, and Signor Lablache, a tenor, had just sung a *duo buffo*, '*Oh! Guardate che figura*', from Gnecco's *La Prova*, at that time a well-known and greatly appreciated work, and to great applause, bowing together, hand in hand, they retreated to the small stone passage which led from the platform down to the cloisters. When they got there they bowed again, and they went on bowing—and still they went on bowing. It was some time before it was realised that both of them, being rather stout, had become inextricably stuck in the narrow archway. Stewards eventually had to free them.

Some years later at Marl Bank I heard him tell this story again, and this time he added that his father had quickly appreciated the two great artists' predicament, but in those days it was not for a back-desk second violin player to deal with such celebrities.*

The earliest reminiscence which Elgar told me about himself referred to a visit with his father to the cathedral chapter house. He said that when he was 8 he was already giving his father some help

* There is no mention of an Elgar in the printed list of the festival Band for 1848, but neither is an Elgar shown in the lists for 1851 and 1854, in all of which festivals Elgar told me that his father had played. His father's and uncle's names first appear in the festival Band of 1857. The probable explanation is that his father had played in the earlier festivals in the secular concerts only either as an extra player or as a substitute. The Elgars never played in the Three Choirs Festivals in either Gloucester or Hereford.

in the shop, and one day he went with him to the chapter house where the Precentor and the organist wished to discuss the supply of some services and anthem parts required by the choir. Elgar ventured to remind his father that the publisher's traveller had told him there would be a delay in obtaining one of the anthems. Dr Done, the organist, who took an interest in the boy, and had already given him permission to study the cathedral music folios, smiled, but the Precentor was not amused and ordered him to leave the chapter house immediately, saying that such matters were not for children.

He also recalled that in 1866 he was allowed for the first time to attend the Monday rehearsal for the festival and, knowing that they would be rehearsing Beethoven's Mass in C, he had run from the shop to the cathedral with a large score—'nearly as big as the small boy'—the only copy he could find. He was 9 by this time, and he told me years later with some pride that he could already read all the individual choir parts of the cathedral music, which was still written in the C as well as the F and G clefs.

Elgar told me that when he was 9 or 10 he used to play the piano for the daughter of a canon's widow who lived in a house on the far side of College Green, and how fond he was of going through the cathedral, which was a natural short cut for him. This practice was absolutely forbidden. His description of how he used to dodge the vergers kept my father and myself in fits of laughter, the more so since I had myself as a chorister often done the same thing.

Referring to the same period he spoke about a piece of music which he had written during a holiday in Broadheath when he was 10. This was the 'Humoreske', which became 'Fairies and Giants' in the Elgar family play *The Wand of Youth*, given in 1869 as a present for their parents (see also page 433).

The festival in 1869 was at Worcester, and Elgar's father was helping Mr Goodwin, the festival librarian, to check and correct the hired orchestral parts and had taken Edward with him to help. Elgar told us that he could not resist adding some extra notes for the brass to play in Handel's *Messiah*, which he felt would provide added colour. His additions went unnoticed at the time, but, alas, he never heard them since they were detected at the rehearsal. In spite of this misdemeanour he was allowed for the first time to attend all the cathedral performances, and he recalled his wonder and delight at the orchestral effects in *Elijah*, *Judas Maccabaeus*, and especially in *The Messiah*. His father and uncle were playing in the orchestra, but it was the London professional players who so excited him by their expertise and fine playing. He spoke also of hearing Sims Reeves, Santley and Tietjens for the first time. 'Ah!,' he said, 'now they *were* singers, and what an impression they made upon me.'

It was after this festival that Elgar decided to take up the violin.

Another reminiscence of 1869 or 1870 related to a visit with his father and uncle to Pershore for a concert in which they were both playing. After the concert they were driving home in their pony and trap. They usually stopped for beer at a hostelry in the town, but this evening they had been delayed and it was shut. His father had been grumbling that there was no hope of a drink now, when to their surprise they noticed that all the lights were on at an isolated country inn. They called in, to find that a relative of the owner was giving a stag party prior to his marriage the next day. On learning that they had come from playing at a concert, they were invited in to join the solitary violinist there, and a merry night of it they made, not leaving until the early hours of the morning. Elgar told us that he personally remembered little after the first hour, having been persuaded to drink draught cider. He next remembered being carried upstairs by his father, and his mother's annoyance at their late return home.

The following reminiscences also refer to the late 1860s and early 1870s, though I cannot give precise dates.

One evening in Marl Bank Elgar told us about his 'self-teaching period', and described how after going to bed he would wait until his parents were asleep and then creep downstairs and collect the score he had been studying in the shop, perhaps a Mozart or Rossini Mass or a Beethoven sonata, take it up to bed with him and pore over it for half the night by the light of a candle and with his bedclothes drawn up into a sort of tent to prevent his mother seeing the light under the door. He went on to tell us how whenever he could get a few hours free he would take bread and cheese and a score and walk out to the quiet Claines churchyard, north of the city where his mother's parents were buried, and he said that in these surroundings he could concentrate for as long as he wanted without the constant interruption in a busy shop. At other times he would retire to 'hide-outs' on the banks of the river Severn, and, especially while he was at school at Littleton House, on the banks of the Teme near the point where it joins the Severn. This was a favourite retreat of his. Elgar had a very special love for the river Teme, every reach of which he seemed to know, and this river was very much in his mind during his last illness.

On one occasion he told us another story about his youthful retreats, this time relating to the banks of the Severn. He always carried a sheet or two of blank music paper, and one day a passer-by spotted him scribbling and went over to ask what he was doing. 'I am trying to write down what the wind in the reeds is singing,' Elgar said, and the questioner went away, shaking his head and muttering to himself.

This reminds me of a similar story that Elgar told me, though I think that it applies to a later date. Someone asked him where his music came from and he replied, 'Music is in the air, music is all around us. You have only to reach out and take as much as you need.'

His story about his headmaster's lesson on *The Apostles*, told on page 90, belongs to this 'self-teaching period', as does also that of the bell-ringing at St Helen's, a small church close to the music shop. The bell-ringer there was old and suffered from rheumatism, and when Elgar was about 14 or 15 he often acted as a deputy and rang the bells for him. It was the custom in those days for the day of the month to be struck on the bell immediately after the 8pm evening curfew had been rung. On one occasion when it was the 31st of the month his great friend Hubert Leicester had a bet with Elgar that he would not toll the bell 33 times instead of 31. Elgar, who was always up to any lark, immediately took the bet, and that night the bell rang 33 times. Alas! however, some dear old lady, who had been counting, objected very strongly and wrote to the rector, with the result that Elgar got the sack.

I recall another evening when Elgar spoke warmly about the 1872 Worcester Festival. He was then 15 and had left school. He was apprenticed to Mr William Allen, an understanding local solicitor and an old friend of his father, who had given him leave to attend the festival. He told us that his score-reading and violin playing enabled him now to notice the special features in the orchestration of the various composers and in their treatment for voices. My father was immensely interested in this conversation and on our return home wrote down part of what Elgar had said:

473

I remember how struck I was by the way in which Handel treated the second violins when strengthening a lead for altos, bringing that part into prominence by throwing it into the upper octave. I noticed also the wonderfully resonant effect Handel obtained by the spacing of his chords in a chorus like 'Their sound is gone out.'

My father told me that this must have been the time when Elgar's instinctive genius for orchestral colour first began to show itself.

On this same occasion Elgar referred also to the year that he had spent working in the solicitor's office. He told us how indebted he was to Allen for training him to deal with matters immediately and precisely, and he spoke of the hours he had devoted to preparing the sealing wax and seals for legal documents. His own love of seals and the immaculate impressions he obtained on his own envelopes throughout his life obviously stemmed from this training. He stated also how it was this short experience which clarified his mind and convinced him that only as a musician and composer would he be able to satisfy his creative ability.

At another time, when we were in the cathedral, he talked about the 1875 Mock Festival, and how the Dean and Chapter, largely at the instigation of the Earl of Dudley, had refused to allow an orchestra to be employed or charges to be made for tickets for performances in the cathedral, and would only agree to what Elgar called the Services and Anthems Festival. Worcester citizens as a whole had been outraged by this curtailment of the traditional Three Choirs Festival, and Elgar vividly described the streets and shops decked with black funeral flags as a protest, and the cabbies with black crepe on their whips. Despite the large choir being drawn from the three cathedral cities and from St George's, Windsor and Christ Church and New College, Oxford, Elgar said it was a gloomy week without an orchestra and that the only redeeming feature had been S. S. Wesley's wonderful organ playing at the end of the evening services of Bach's *Wedge* and *Giant* Fugues. Elgar delighted to tell us that it had rained incessantly during the Mock Festival, though it had been fine up till then, and brilliant sunshine returned the day it was over.

He and my father often talked about Wesley's playing, and I can recall one occasion in the late 1920s when Elgar made my father play the *Giant* Fugue, pointing out to him as he did so the special features and the registrations that Wesley had used. In my father's presidential address to the Royal College of Organists in July 1935, he devoted a paragraph to it which I quote:

Elgar heard him [S. S. Wesley] at Worcester in 1875, and often spoke to me of the thrilling effect Wesley's playing had upon him. The occasion was the outgoing voluntary at a Three Choirs Festival evensong. Wesley began with a long extemporisation, designed to lead up to Bach's Choral Prelude *'Wir glauben all an einen Gott'* [*Giant* Fugue], breaking off the extemporisation in an arresting way before entering upon the Prelude. The effect upon Elgar was so great that in after years when he returned to live in Worcester and would constantly slip into the old cathedral which had so many memories for him and which he greatly loved, he almost invariably asked me to play him something, and we always had to end with the *Giant*. But I do not know that I was ever able to recapture the impression left upon him by Wesley.

One evening at Marl Bank some reference was made to Mendelssohn's *Elijah*, a favourite work of Elgar's, and I remember well the look on his face as he told us how thrilled he had been when he had first played in *Elijah* as a back-desk first violin in the Worcester Philharmonic Society's performance in the summer of 1876, conducted by W. Done. This must have been one of Elgar's earliest public appearances as a violinist in an important concert, though he had accompanied singers and played the violin in Worcester Glee Club evenings at the Crown Hotel some 3 years earlier and had also played in other small groups. He told me, with a most boyish grin, that his early appearances as an accompanist at Glee Club evenings had not been without criticism. Singers had complained to his father that Edward confused them with his 'enrichments'. Elgar's habit of playing more than appeared on the paper, already commented on, clearly started at a very early age.

Elgar sometimes talked about the wind quintet comprising Hubert and William Leicester (flute and clarinet), Frank Exton (flute), his brother Frank (oboe) and himself. He had to learn the bassoon specially to enable him to play with them, and it was his duty to make arrangements or write music for their Sunday meetings. He spoke also about his work at Powick Asylum between 1877 and 1884. His salary had been £32 a year plus 5s for each polka or quadrille which he composed for them. The money had been very useful, but his experience in writing music for the asylum band and for the wind quintet had been absolutely invaluable for him as a young composer.

On another Sunday our thoughts turned to the British Medical

Association and how it had been founded in Worcester in 1832. This reminded Elgar of the BMA's jubilee in Worcester in 1882 and the soirée, including a concert, in the Shire Hall. He told us that the Worcester Amateur Instrumental Society's orchestra, of which he was then leader, was providing the music and that he had been invited to write a piece for the occasion. A year before he had written an *Air de Ballet* which had proved popular in Worcester, and he had accordingly now written a second one of the same name for performance at the soirée. The orchestra was short of strings at that time, he said, and when John Beare, an old professional friend of his father, told them that the doctor at Giggleswick, near Settle, in Yorkshire, who would be attending the BMA meeting, was a very keen amateur musician who not only played the cello but also conducted the local music society, he was immediately sent an invitation to play the cello at the soirée. Elgar told us how delighted they were at his acceptance, but that he had no idea then of what the consequences of their meeting were to be. He said that when he met Dr Charles Buck they found that it was not only music that they had in common but also a love of nature and the countryside. An immediate friendship was formed and within 3 weeks Elgar made his first visit to Giggleswick. He went on to tell us that from then on up to his marriage in 1889 he went frequently to Yorkshire where he accompanied Buck on his professional visits in the extensive moorland country, and in playing with him in trios and quartets. In the mid-1880s Buck greatly encouraged him in his writing, and some of his compositions were actually written in Giggleswick, including *Salut d'Amour*.

Buck loved dogs, and Elgar told us that on one of his visits north in 1885 Buck gave him a collie called Scap. He recounted his experience in the train while bringing Scap to Worcester and their many adventures together. Scap was his constant companion up to his marriage, when he had to leave him with his sister Lucy and her husband, with whom he had been living. Buck attended Elgar's wedding and whenever the Elgars were near enough they would visit him.

I well remember this evening, because while Elgar was talking about Scap, Marco, who had been asleep in front of the fire woke up and nuzzled his head into Elgar's lap, pawing him and demanding attention just as if he sensed that Elgar was talking about another dog and was jealous.

In 1932 and 1933 Elgar very often spoke of the early years of his professional life, and almost always he brought in a reference to what he owed in those days to Dr Buck's constant encouragement to continue with his composing. His mind clearly turned frequently to the happy days that he had spent in the company of his old friend in Settle. It was on one of my father's visits at this time that Elgar told him about his first engagement in 1883 and how by mutual consent the engagement had been broken off the next year. I was not present, and my father did not tell me about it until some years after Elgar's death. He said that he was in a difficult position. Elgar had not stipulated that the matter was confidential, but for nearly fifty years he had never disclosed his first engagement, and my father was certain that Carice did not know about it. On the other hand he felt that this experience had profoundly affected much of Elgar's music and should, therefore, at some time be revealed. After much thought my father considered that in order to avoid any possible distress it should be kept secret until fifty years after Elgar's death, and hence his disclosure to me on the understanding that I would ensure that this information became known in 1984. The original intention was to do this by means of a letter to be sent to the Trustees of the Elgar Birthplace, but as this book will not be published until after the 50th anniversary of Elgar's death on 23 February, it would now seem that inclusion here will be a more effective method of releasing the information.

The Elgars were acquainted with the Weaver family who owned what was considered to be the leading bootmakers' business in the county, not far away at 84, High Street, Worcester. The families were not intimate because of the difference in their religion, the Weavers being Unitarians, but they were keen musicians and Edward and Frank, the son, became good friends. Frank was a violinist and played in various string combinations including the Worcester Amateur Instrumental Society, of which Edward was the leader. He also played the double bass. Frank Weaver's sister, Helen Jessie, and her friend, Edith Groveham, were at the time students at the Leipzig Conservatory of Music. Helen was studying the violin with a view to becoming a professional performer. Elgar would have liked to have been a student there himself some years earlier, but this was financially impossible. In 1882, however, he had saved up enough money to make a visit to

Leipzig to go to concerts and opera there. He consulted Frank Weaver on where he should stay with the result that it was arranged for him to stay at the same pension as the two girls.

Elgar arrived in Leipzig on New Year's Day, 1883, and stayed for a fortnight. He was apparently very popular with both girls, but he fell deeply in love with Helen, who returned his love. They agreed to meet again in Worcester on her return at the end of the Leipzig term, and they became engaged. Their families, however, stipulated that no engagement should be announced until Helen had finished the remaining two years at Leipzig and the difference in their religions could be resolved. Many letters were exchanged during Helen's stays in Leipzig.

Events, however, were not to run smoothly. In the autumn of 1883 Mrs Weaver became seriously ill and Helen decided in November to abandon Leipzig and return home to nurse her dying stepmother. She and Elgar continued to enjoy their companionship, meeting often and going to concerts together. After their stepmother's death Frank took over the business, and Helen, to Elgar's delight, decided to remain in Worcester and their companionship continued, but neither family showed any desire for a change in religion. By April Helen had decided to give up any idea of pursuing her career as a performer, and to take up teaching instead, which would mean leaving Worcester. Some weeks later, probably in June or July, 1884, they agreed to break off their engagement, mainly, my father gathered, because of their different religions, and as was the custom in those days, to return each other's letters. Miss Weaver went away to teach and to stay with her friend Edith in Bradford. At some stage she contracted smallpox which left her with distressing asthma.

In the autumn of 1885 Helen Weaver decided to go to New Zealand, and later died there.

I understand that Elgar never had any direct contact with Helen after the breaking off of their engagement, but he clearly was kept informed by both Frank Weaver and by Edith Groveham whose friendships he maintained.

With the knowledge that Elgar was engaged to Helen Weaver it is not difficult to find confirmation of this incident in Elgar's early life. References are to be found in Elgar's letters to Dr Buck of 21 December 1882, 13 May and 23 August 1883, but the most interesting ones are:

478

1 July 1883: 'The vacation at Leipzig begins shortly, my "Braut" arrives here on Thursday next; remaining 'till the first week in Septr: of course I shall remain in Worcester 'till her departure.'

11 Nov 1883: 'Well Helen has come back! Mrs Weaver is so ill, dying in fact, so the child thought it best to return and nurse her so we are together a little now and then and consequently happy.'

14 Jan 1884: 'P.S. Miss Weaver is remaining in Worcester and the little Music &c that we get together is the only enjoyment I get and more than I deserve no doubt.'

21 April 1884: 'My prospects are about as hopeless as ever. . . . Miss Weaver is very well. I do not think that she will remain in Worcester much longer now.'

20 July 1884: '. . . my prospects are worse than ever & to crown my miseries my engagement is broken off & I am lonely.'

Sunday, 8 March 1885: '. . . Of course all these things are of no account, but they serve to divert me somewhat & hide a broken heart.'

Wednesday, 7 October 1885: 'Miss W. is going to New Zealand this month—her lungs are affected I hear & there has been a miserable time for me since I came home.'

Musicologists will, I am sure, find 'influences' of the effects of this earlier engagement in many passages of Elgar's music. I will only refer to two where my father felt this incident explained hitherto unsatisfying dedications. The first is the 13th of the *Enigma Variations*. Knowing Lady Mary Lygon, as she then was, and even allowing for Elgar's admiration for her and what she did for music in one of the earliest of the Competitive Festivals—the Madresfield Festival—he could not understand how the lady could have inspired this Variation, with all its depth and tenderness. The dedication becomes even more surprising when it is remembered that Elgar had already dedicated to her the revised *Three Characteristic Pieces for small Orchestra*, Op 10, published in 1899. Is the solution now to be found in the quotation 'Calm Sea and Prosperous Voyage'? Surely this is really a reference to Helen Weaver's sailing to New Zealand in 1885. If so, the intimate nature of the rest of the Variation becomes understandable. Alice must have wondered about the Mendelssohn quotation in this Variation, and Lady Mary Lygon's forthcoming sea voyage to Australia in April 1899 with her brother, Earl Beauchamp, who had been appointed Governor of New South Wales, would seem to have been a tactful explanation if Helen was the real dedicatee. The omission in the published copies of the letters 'L.M.L.' on the manuscript sketch seems to bear this out.

The other dedication is that of the Violin Concerto, (translated) 'Herein is enshrined the soul of . . . . .' The five 'points' are significant. There have been many suggestions as to who was concealed in these. Alice always maintained that the five points represented Julia Worthington, nicknamed PIPPA, in whose home at Careggi in Italy some of the sketches of the Violin Concerto and of the Second Symphony were written. Others have thought that they referred to Alice Stuart-Wortley, who was closely connected with the Violin Concerto. My father was never satisfied with either of these suggestions. With our knowledge of Elgar's engagement to Helen, a violin student, is it not more likely that the five points stand for HELEN, and that the soul enshrined was hers?

APPENDIX 2
Worcester Festivals and the Elgar family

	William Henry (father) Violin	Henry (uncle) Viola	Edward William Violin	Frank (brother) Oboe
1848	†			
1851	†			
1854	†			
1857	*	*		
1860	*	*		
1863	*	*		
1866	*	*		
1869	*	*		
1872	2nd V	*		
1875	The 'Mock Festival'—no orchestra			
1878	2nd V	*	2nd V	
1881	2nd V	*	1st V	
1884	2nd V	*	1st V	
1887	2nd V	*	1st V	3rd Oboe
1890	2nd V	*	1st V	
1893			1st V	
1896	No Elgars were in the orchestra of the festival			

† Elgar said that his father played in these three festivals, but his name does not appear in the printed programmes. He probably played in some of the secular concerts as an additional violin or as a deputy. The names of Elgar's father and uncle appear for the first time in the printed programme in 1857.

Elgar's first festival engagement was as a second violin, at £4, in 1878. In the same year Pollie (Elgar's sister) sang in the chorus as a soprano. Frank (Elgar's brother) made his only festival appearance in 1887, when a third oboe was needed. Elgar's last festival as a member of the orchestra was in 1893.

APPENDIX 3

Some Worcester Festivals of special interest to Elgar and Atkins

Elgar and my father were fascinated by some of the eighteenth- and nineteenth-century Three Choirs Festivals at Worcester, and especially in the arrangements made for the bands, soloists and chorus. Up to and including 1836 all the Cathedral Festival performances at Worcester, with one exception, had been given in the choir, the nave not being used. Virtually no structural work had been involved since the small musical forces then available, including the band, had been easily accommodated, and also the audience. Additional space for the increasing numbers of listeners in the 1820s had been provided by building a gallery. The exception was the 1788 Worcester Festival which had been attended by King George III, Queen Charlotte, the Princess Royal and the Princesses Augusta and Elizabeth who were staying as the guests of Bishop Hurd at the Bishop's Palace. For this Festival a special gallery was erected at the west end of the nave for the royal party, and other arrangements made for the assembly. Valentine Green, the Worcester historian, who was present, describes the scene as follows:

At half past eleven, their Majesties and the Princesses, with their retinue, proceeded from the palace to the cathedral, and were received at the great north entrance by the bishop in his episcopal robes, and the dean and prebendaries in their surplices and hoods, and conducted by them to a magnificent gallery, prepared for their reception, under the great west window. The gallery was spread with a rich Worcester carpet, lined and faced with crimson silk, and shaded with a lofty canopy of the same, terminating in a crown. In a division of the gallery on the right were seated the bishops of Worcester, Gloucester, and Hereford, and the stewards of the meeting; on the left, the dean and prebendaries. In front of the royal gallery, a lower one was prepared for the nobility and persons of distinction; and from the corners of this were extended seats for the mayor, corporation, and their families. The area was benched for the people in general. As soon as their Majesties and the Princesses had taken their places, the music band (consisting of the first vocal and instrumental performers in the kingdom) immediately began the coronation anthem.

482

A second platform was also erected at the east end of the nave over the steps leading into the choir for the band of sixty-nine players, the soloists and the chorus of fifty singers.

His Majesty graciously offered the Festival authorities the services of his private band and twelve royal players joined the normal Festival band. The works performed at that time were almost exclusively by Handel, and the private band was thoroughly familiar with Handel's music, but nevertheless Elgar and my father were convinced that the addition of these players must have presented difficulties to Thomas Pitt, the Cathedral organist, who was conducting.

It was fortunate that the authorities had decided to move the Festival into the nave as it is recorded that the performances were attended by more people than ever before, and for *The Messiah* the audience exceeded 2,000.

For the 1791 Festival the choir was used again, and until the 1839 Festival, when the ever increasing audiences and music forces of the nineteenth century resulted in a permanent move into the nave, no special accommodation appears to have been required for the performers.

The attendance of the Duchess of York and the Princess Victoria in 1830, however, caused substantial temporary structural alterations. A special gallery was erected in the South Choir aisle with its own access through a window in the Dean's Chapel, now St John's Chapel, to accommodate them and their retinue.

It was, however, the extensive wooden platforms for the performers erected in the nave in 1839 and later years which were of the greatest interest to Elgar and my father. From 1839 until 1863 these were all at the east end of the nave, a few feet in front of the closed choir screen. The platforms of 1839, 1842 and 1845 were probably generally similar to the one specially erected for 1788, though the 1842 one was certainly extended to allow for the augmented chorus. Charles Clarke, the Cathedral organist, was an old man then in ill health and was unable to conduct that Festival, and the Festival committee had at short notice to engage an outsider, Joseph Surman of Exeter Hall, London, the well-known conducter of the Sacred Harmonic Society, to take his place. His choir had sung many of the works in the Festival programme, and it was decided that he should bring his singers with him. The band, which included the usual Festival instrumental performers, augmented this year from the orchestras of the Ancient and Philharmonic Concerts in London, consisted of 84 players, and the chorus, drawn from the Worcester, Liverpool and Birmingham Choral Societies, with singers from the Sacred Harmonic Society and Exeter Hall, made up 218 singers which with the 11 soloists provided 313 performers, a larger number than at any previous Three Choirs Festival.

William Done, who had been articled to Charles Clarke in 1828 and later became deputy organist, succeeded him in 1844, but too late for him to make any alteration in the orchestral platform for the 1845 Festival, his first as conductor. He was, however, very dissatisfied with the sound balance achieved, and he designed a very original lay-out for his musical forces for the 1848 Worcester Festival. The arrangements on this very unusual orchestral platform were understandably of special interest to Elgar and my father, and provided the main subject of discussion on several Sunday evenings. Dr Done, then an old man, appears to have told Elgar something about it in the late 1880s, and Elgar's father knew something about it also, but it was not until my father came across a copy of the *Illustrated London News* of 9 September 1848, with an engraving and description that enlarged on the *Worcester Journal*'s and *Gloucester Journal*'s accounts that the full originality of the lay-out became apparent. The illustration on page 485 shows clearly the position of the musical forces.

The unusually high-tiered platform was erected some feet in front of the closed screen with the organ upon it which then separated the choir from the nave, and extended westwards across the tower space and approximately one and a half bays into the nave. The solo voices, male and female, were placed in the front of the lowest tier, with the conductor several feet behind them and the chorus to each side of him and extending eastwards, filling up the first nine rows of benches—the ladies to the right and the gentlemen to the left. Behind the chorus on higher tiers was the band. Nearest the chorus were placed the double basses and the cellos with Howell, the principal double bass, and Lindley, the principal cello, in the centre. On the tier above were the 1st violins and the 2nd violins. Above them were the woodwind and on the top tier the drums, with Chipps in the centre with his great drum, and on the right the brass instruments and the ophicleide. Several feet behind the platform was the great organ, played by Mr Amott,

The 1848 Festival: note the high platform and unusual positioning of soloists, singers and band

the Gloucester organist, who could only see the conductor through mirrors. How Done could control the soloists who were all behind his back and below him was one of the points first discussed, but how this original lay-out could be thought to improve the general sound balance was another. Elgar naturally was particularly intrigued as to what orchestral effects could have been thought to have been achieved by the curious string arrangements and the extreme difference in the height of the various sections.

Done clearly realised that his platform arrangements had not provided any material improvements in sound distribution, and he must also have appreciated its disadvantages since for the 1851 Festival he reverted to a more conventional positioning and to a lower platform with the rostrum placed in front of it.

The band again contained the usual players, but this year was augmented from the orchestras of Her Majesty's Theatre, the Royal Italian Opera and the Ancient and Philharmonic Concerts, and the chorus came from the London, Liverpool, Birmingham and Gloucester Choral Societies, some 300 performers.

For the 1854 Worcester Festival, however, all the members of the band were individually engaged, a practice that continued up to the abeyance of the Three Choirs Festivals in 1914. The overall number of performers was now always about 300, and the orchestral platform remained virtually unchanged in front of the closed choir screen at the east end of the nave up to 1866.

For the 1866, 1869 and 1872 Festivals the orchestral platforms were erected at the west end of the nave under the great west window. This change had been brought about by the removal of the closed choir screen in 1865 as part of the Cathedral restoration. The placing of the orchestra at the west end of the nave necessitated the provision of a separate organ there, and the 1866 platform provided accommodation for the erection of an organ specially designed by Nicholsons, the Worcester organ builders.

In 1875 the Dean and Chapter refused permission for the Three Choirs Festival in Worcester Cathedral, and instead replaced it with a week of sung services and organ recitals. 1875 became known as the 'Mock Festival'.

In 1878 the Three Choirs Festival was again held in Worcester, but the Dean and Chapter would only agree to a low platform over the raised steps to the now open choir screen. This was Elgar's first Festival as an orchestral player, and the plan of this low platform with the exact position in which Elgar sat is shown opposite.

It would appear from the sketch plan reproduced on p 488 that the erection of a platform at the east end of the nave was originally contemplated for the 1881 Festival, and the architect had clearly been trying to comply with the Dean and Chapter's requirements that the platform should be as low as possible.

The Festival conductor had always been unhappy about this low platform, and the performances at the 1878 Festival fully confirmed his fears. A number of discussions took place between

The 1878 Festival: plan showing the low platform over raised steps to the new open choir screen
The 1878 Festival: Elgar's annotated copy of the programme

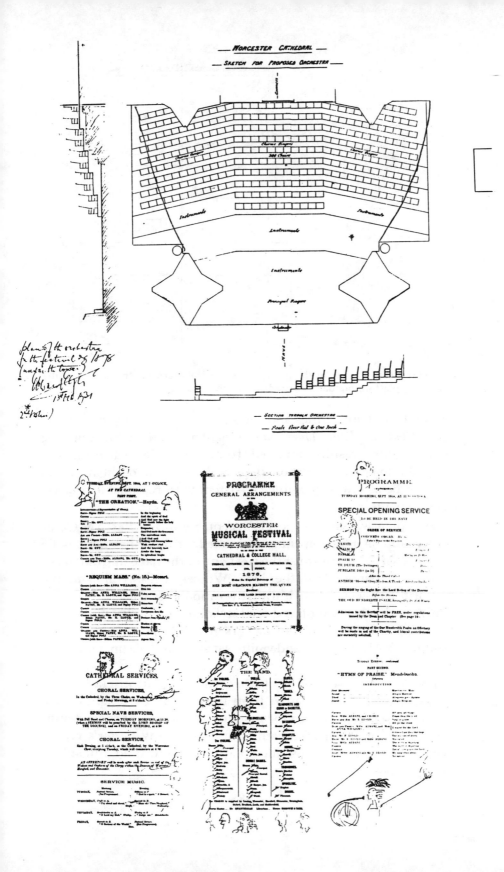

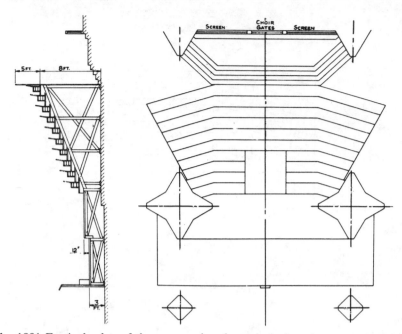

The 1881 Festival: plan of the proposed orchestral platform at east end of the nave. The platform actually erected was at the west end

the Cathedral authorities and the Festival Committee before the 1881 Festival. The Dean and Chapter, while admitting the unsatisfactory results obtained from the 1878 platform, still wanted it to be over the choir steps at the east end of the nave and for it to be as low as possible consistent with reasonable musical requirements.

This plan was not, however, acceptable to the Festival Committee, and later agreement was reached for the construction of a large orchestral platform at the west end of the nave in front of the great west window for the 1881 Worcester Festival, and the platform has been erected in that position ever since.

Elgar, who this year played as a 1st violin, drew a sketch showing the exact seating of all the players in 1881. He himself sat at position 13. His father, a 2nd violin, sat at 11, and his uncle, a viola, at 7.

The general lay-out of this large orchestral platform in front of the great west window, apart from being widened to allow for a larger orchestra, remained for practical purposes unchanged until many years after Elgar's death, and, indeed, my father's retirement. A modern steel scaffolded platform is now used, but still in the same position.

488

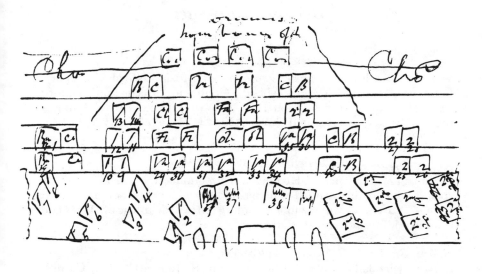

The 1881 Festival: Elgar's own sketch showing the positions of all the orchestral players on the platform erected at the west end of the nave under the great west window

The 1881 Festival: the list of players in the band. The numbers (keyed-in by Elgar himself) refer to the players' positions in the sketch above.

Biographical Notes

Allen, Sir Hugh (Percy) (1869–1946)
Organist, conductor, scholar. Professor of Music Oxford University.
Director Royal College of Music. Conductor Leeds and Oxford
Festivals, Oxford and London Bach Choirs. Director Royal Philhar-
monic Society. Knighted in 1920, CVO 1926, KCVO 1928,
GCVO 1935.

Atkins, Frederick Pyke (1830–1897)
Organist and choirmaster. He moved from Gloucestershire as a boy and
spent all his life in Llandaff and Cardiff. For many years organist of St
John's Church, Cardiff, he took a leading part in the music of Wales and
the Eisteddfod movement. Father of

Atkins, Sir Ivor (Algernon) (1869–1953)
Born in Llandaff, he assisted his father in St John's Church, Cardiff.
Organist Stonehaven, Scotland. Assistant to George Robertson Sinclair
at Truro Cathedral, 1886, and moved with him to Hereford Cathedral in
1889. Organist Ludlow Collegiate Church, 1893. Organist and Master of
the Choristers Worcester Cathedral, 1897–1950. Conductor Three
Choirs Festivals Worcester 1899–1948. Cathedral Librarian 1933–1953.
Knighted in 1921 in recognition of his part in the revival of the Three
Choirs Festivals at Worcester in 1920 after their abeyance during World
War I.

Atkins, Katharine May Dorothea (née Butler)
Married Ivor Atkins; one son, Edward Wulstan Ivor, born 1904. Sang in
Elgar's Worcestershire Philharmonic Society and in the Worcester
Orchestral and Ladies Choral Society. Keenly interested in music. She
took a leading part in local affairs, becoming in 1935 the first woman High
Sheriff in England and Mayor of Worcester in 1936/37. Chairman
Worcester Royal General Infirmary. Died in 1954.

Bantock, Sir Granville (1868–1946)
Composer. Music Director at the Tower, New Brighton, Cheshire.
Principal, School of Music in the Midland Institute, Birmingham.
Succeeded Elgar as Peyton Professor of Music at Birmingham Un-
iversity. He wrote a number of large works of which the best known was
Omar Khayyam. A close friend of Elgar and Atkins. Knighted in 1930.

Blair, Hugh (1864–1932)
Organist and composer. Assistant organist Worcester Cathedral
1886–1895. Organist 1895–1897. Organist Holy Trinity, Marylebone,
London, from 1897.

Blake, Mrs Carice Irene (née Elgar) (1890–1970)
Elgar's only child. Married Samuel Blake (d 1939) in 1922. After Elgar's death Carice devoted much of her time to looking after his musical interests and for some years lived at Broadheath so that she could be at the Elgar Birthplace Museum during the initial stages. The arrangement of Elgar's possessions there and the planning of the rooms were almost entirely due to her. She was a Trustee until her death.

Brewer, Sir Herbert (Alfred) (1865–1928)
Pupil of Charles Harford Lloyd at Gloucester Cathedral. Brewer was appointed Organist and Music Master at Tonbridge School in 1892, and on Charles Lee Williams' retirement he was elected organist of Gloucester Cathedral, 1897–1928. Conductor Three Choirs Festivals, Gloucester 1898–1925. Knighted in 1926.

Buck, Charles William (1852–1932)
Had an extensive medical practice in and around Giggleswick, near Settle, Yorkshire. He was a keen amateur musician, played the viola and 'cello, organised local chamber-music concerts and conducted the local orchestra. Elgar met him in Worcester in 1882. They found they had many interests in common and an immediate friendship was formed which resulted in Elgar making frequent visits to Settle and in Buck attending Elgar's marriage in London in 1889. During the mid-1880s Buck greatly encouraged Elgar in his composing. They remained lifelong friends.

Buths, Julius (1851–1920)
Pianist and conductor at Düsseldorf from 1890. Was present at the first performance of *Gerontius* in Birmingham in 1900. He produced a German edition and conducted the work at Düsseldorf in 1901 and again at the Lower Rhine Festival held there in 1902.

Chadwick, George Whitefield (1854–1931)
Professor at New England Conservatory of Music. Conductor Worcester (Mass) Music Festivals.

Clarke, Douglas (1893–1962)
Composer and conductor. Dean of Music McGill University, Montreal 1930–1955.

Claughton, Thomas Legh (1848–1915)
Apart from his ecclesiastical duties as Canon of Worcester Cathedral and Rector of St Andrew's, he was an accomplished amateur violinist who for a number of years had played in Worcester orchestras, and in 1890 played among the 1st violins in the Worcester Festival.

Colvin, Sir Sidney (1845–1927)
Director Fitzwilliam Museum, Cambridge, 1876–1884. Keeper of the

Department of Prints and Drawings, British Museum, 1884–1912. Knighted 1911.

Coward, Sir Henry (1849–1944)
Was recognised as one of the finest choral conductors and chorus masters of his day. He founded the Sheffield Music Union. In 1895 he was appointed Chorus Master of the newly formed Sheffield Music Festival, which was conducted by August Manns. He later toured Germany, France and Canada with the Choruses of the Sheffield Music Union and the Leeds Choral Union. He was knighted in 1926.

Cowen, Sir Frederic (Hymen) (1852–1935)
Composer and conductor. Conducted Hallé Orchestra 1896–99, Liverpool Philharmonic Society 1896–1913, Cardiff Festival 1902–1910, and the Handel Festivals. Knighted 1911.

Damrosch, Frank Heino (1859–1937)
Composer and conductor. Founded and conducted the Musical Arts Society of New York. Conductor Oratorio Society. Director of the Institute of Musical Art in New York.

Damrosch, Walter Johannes (1862–1950)
Composer and international conductor. Conductor Metropolitan Opera House, New York, Oratorio Society and New York Philharmonic Society. Re-organised and conducted the New York Symphony Orchestra.

Davies, Sir (Henry) Walford (1869–1941)
Organist, composer and well-known broadcaster. Organist Temple Church, London. Professor of Music at the University College of Wales, Aberystwyth 1919–1926. On the death of Elgar was made Master of the King's Musick.

Ede, William Moore (1850–1935)
Dean Worcester Cathedral 1908–1934. Chairman British Council of the World Alliance of Churches. Keenly interested in the welfare of Worcester he started a 'garden village' and a housing association which resulted in many houses being built for low rentals. He collected money for the restoration of Edgar Tower and the maintenance of the Cathedral, was a great supporter of the Three Choirs Festivals and took a leading part in their revival at Worcester in 1920.

Elgar, Caroline Alice (née Roberts) (1848–1920)
Daughter of Major-General Sir Henry Gee Roberts, a retired Indian Army officer. Married Edward Elgar in 1889; one daughter, Carice Irene (1890–1970). She was an author and a poet, and wrote a number of poems which were set by Elgar. She devoted her married life to furthering Elgar's musical career.

Elgar, Sir Edward (William), Baronet (of Broadheath), OM GCVO (1857–1934)
Composer. Knighthood 1904, OM 1911, KCVO 1928, GCVO 1933. Master of the King's Musick 1924–1934.

Elgar, William Henry (1822–1906)
Elgar's father. Born in Dover, he came to Worcester in 1841 and with his younger brother Henry built up a successful piano-tuning practice and music shop. William was a fine violinist and with his brother, who played the viola, they became leading lights in the orchestras around Worcester and Hereford. Organist of St George's Roman Catholic Church in Worcester 1846–1885.

Embleton, Henry Charles (1854–1930)
A rich man deriving much of his money from a fleet of colliers which he operated from Newcastle-upon-Tyne. He was a very enthusiastic amateur musician and a lavish patron of the Leeds Choral Union, not only in Leeds, but by subsidising them for concerts in York, London, Canterbury and in Germany and France. He was a strong supporter of Elgar's music, and most of his choral works, some of them first performances, were given by the Society, including an Elgar Festival in 1909. After 1905 the Elgars were usually Embleton's guests in Leeds, and Elgar had acknowledged his indebtedness to his friend by dedicating to him *The Reveille*, Op 54.

Gaisberg, Frederick (1873–1951)
In 1889, while still a schoolboy, Gaisberg earned pocket money by playing the piano for the Columbia Phonograph Company who recorded music on wax cylinders. Gaisberg had found his career, and later came to England to record discs for His Master's Voice. He became Recording Artists Manager and as such was responsible for many of HMV's greatest records, including the unique Elgar recordings. He became a close friend of Elgar.

Griffith, Arthur Troyte (1864–1942)
A Malvern architect and watercolour painter; a close friend of Elgar and No 7 in the *Enigma Variations*.

Hadow, Sir (William) Henry (1859–1937)
Fellow of Worcester College, Oxford. Scholar, musician and composer. Vice-Chancellor of Sheffield University 1919–1930. Knighted in 1918 and given CBE in 1920.

Halford, George (1859–1933)
Was introduced to Birmingham by Swinnerton Heap as a pianist and subsequently became conductor of various choirs within the area. In 1896 he started the Halford Concert Society and succeeded William Cole

Stockley as the chief orchestral conductor in Birmingham. Elgar had a high opinion of him and of his work in performing the compositions of contemporary European composers in Birmingham.

Heap, Charles Swinnerton (1847–1900)
Composer, pianist and conductor. Appointed conductor Birmingham Philharmonic Union 1870. Founded music societies in Malvern, Leamington, Walsall, Wolverhampton and Stoke-on-Trent. Conducted Wolverhampton Festivals of 1883 and 1886. Founded the North Staffordshire Musical Festival 1888. Chorus Master Birmingham Festival Choral Society 1895–June 1900. A fine musician who understood Elgar's music. His sudden death before the start of the rehearsals for *Gerontius* was a bitter disappointment to Elgar.

Hull, Sir Percy (Clarke) (1878–1968)
Chorister Hereford Cathedral 1889. Pupil of G. R. Sinclair and Assistant Organist from 1896. Interned in Germany during World War I. Organist Hereford Cathedral 1918–1949. Conductor Three Choirs Festivals, Hereford 1921–1949. Knighted 1947.

Jackson, Sir Barry (Vincent) (1879–1961)
Author and playwright. Founder of the Birmingham Repertory Theatre. Produced the Elgar–Shaw and Malvern Summer Festivals 1929–1937. Director Stratford-upon-Avon Festivals and Shakespeare Memorial Theatre. Knighted 1925.

Jaeger, August Johannes (1860–1909)
Born Düsseldorf. Joined the staff of Novellos in 1890 and acted as special negotiator for the firm, with Elgar becoming a close friend. 'Nimrod' in the *Enigma Variations*.

Kreisler, Fritz (1875–1962)
This eminent Viennese violinist gave the first performance of Elgar's Violin Concerto in London in 1910. Elgar dedicated the Concerto to him.

Leader, Benjamin Williams (1831–1923)
Was born in Worcester, and at the end of the nineteenth century and beginning of the twentieth was held in great esteem as an English landscape painter. After a decline in popularity his work is now again highly thought of and eagerly sought after.

Lee Williams, Charles (1851–1935)
Organist Llandaff Cathedral 1876–1882, Gloucester Cathedral 1882–1897. Conductor Three Choirs Festivals, Gloucester 1882–1895. Retired but maintained his interest in the Festivals and (with Godwin Chance) wrote the *Annals of the Three Choirs Festivals 1864–1930*.

Lloyd, Charles Harford (1849–1919)
Organist Gloucester Cathedral 1876–1882. Conductor Three Choirs
Festivals, Gloucester 1877–1882. Later organist Christ Church Cathedral, Oxford, Eton Chapel and the Chapel Royal.

Mann, Arthur Henry (1850–1929)
An outstanding choir trainer; was elected Organist and Director of the
Choir at King's College, Cambridge in 1876.

Menuhin, Yehudi, KBE (Hon) (born 1916)
This eminent American-born violinist will always be associated with the
Elgar Violin Concerto, which as a boy of 16 he recorded with the London
Symphony Orchestra conducted by the composer.

Norbury, Florence (1858–1927) and *Norbury, Winifred* (1861–1938)
The sisters lived at Sherridge, an eighteenth-century house near
Malvern, and although only the initials 'W. N.' appear above the 8th
Variation in the *Enigma Variations*, it is known that Elgar had Sherridge
and both the ladies in mind when he wrote this Variation.

Ord, Bernhard ('Boris') (1897–1961)
Organist, conductor, teacher. Organ Scholar Corpus Christi College,
Cambridge. Elected Fellow King's College, 1923. 1927 went to Cologne.
On Dr Mann's death in 1929 succeeded him as Organist of King's
College, Cambridge, when he instituted the famous Christmas Eve
Festival of Nine Lessons and Carols. 1937 conductor of the Cambridge
University Musical Society. CBE 1958.

Palmer, Charlton Clement (1871–1944)
Assistant Organist Lichfield Cathedral 1890–1897, Organist Ludlow
Parish Church 1897–1908. Organist Canterbury Cathedral 1908–1937.

Parker, Horatio William (1863–1919)
Professor of Music at Yale University 1894–1919. Composer. His *Hora
Novissima* received its first performance in England at the 1899
Worcester Festival and was the first American work to be heard at a
Three Choirs Festival. *A Wanderer's Psalm* was written for the 1900
Hereford Festival and conducted by him. He conducted the third part of
his *The Legend of St Christopher* at the 1902 Worcester Festival.

Peyton, Richard (1825–1910)
A wealthy supporter of the arts in the Midlands and a generous
benefactor to music. He founded a scholarship at the Royal College of
Music. He was heavily involved with the Birmingham Triennial Festival,
and in 1904 he endowed a Chair of Music at Birmingham University
conditional on Elgar becoming the first holder of the Professorship.

495

Ramsden, Archibald (1835–1916)
Came from Yorkshire and was a well-known and prosperous piano dealer with showrooms in Leeds and in Bond Street, London. He was an old friend of Elgar's father, with whom he dealt professionally, and was very popular with the Elgar family.

Reed, William Henry (1876–1942)
Violinist, composer. Associated with the Three Choirs Festivals from 1902. Leader of the London Symphony Orchestra from 1912. He was a well-known quartet leader and was generally considered to be the most distinguished orchestral leader in England in his day. He became an intimate friend of Elgar and Atkins. He was the author of *Elgar* in the Master Musicians Series and of *Elgar as I knew him*.

Richter, Dr Hans (1843–1916)
Hungarian-born conductor. Was an assistant to Richard Wagner, and he conducted *The Ring of the Niebelung* at Bayreuth in 1876, coming to London the next year. Conducted the Hallé Orchestra 1900–1911. A great admirer of Elgar's work. He conducted the first performance of the *Enigma Variations*, *Gerontius* and other works. Elgar dedicated his Symphony No 1 to Richter.

Rodewald, Alfred E. (1861–1903)
Built up his considerable fortune as a cotton broker but devoted much of his time to developing music in Liverpool. His standing as a conductor was greatly appreciated by Hans Richter and Elgar, who became an intimate friend. He formed the Liverpool Orchestral Society as an amateur organisation, but later re-organised it to include the engagement, mainly at his expense, of professional players. Adequate rehearsal was the keynote of the outstanding high standards of performance that he always achieved. He had a delightful sense of humour and was one of the founder members with Bantock and Elgar of the 'S. T. P.' Society. In 1901 Elgar dedicated his *Pomp and Circumstance March* No 1 to Rodewald and the Liverpool Orchestral Society.

Ronald, Sir Landon (1873–1938)
Started his professional life as a concert pianist, became a conductor and had a special appreciation for Elgar's orchestral music. He did much to bring the two Symphonies before the London concert-goers, and before World War I was considered by many to be a greater interpreter of the Symphonies than Elgar himself. He was Principal of the Guildhall School of Music 1910–1937, and Chairman of the HMV Quality Committee for many years. He was knighted in 1922.

Rootham, Cyril Bradley (1875–1938)
Lecturer and composer. Elected organist and Musical Director to St John's College, Cambridge, in 1901 and a Fellow in 1914.

Sanford, Samuel Simons ('Gaffer') (1849–1910)
Professor of Applied Music at Yale University. Financially independent.
He used his wealth as well as his great musical abilities to advance music
and young musicians. He studied with Rubinstein and accompanied him
in his tours of America. He was an exceptionally gifted pianist of concert
calibre, but too retiring to give more than an occasional public recital. A
Trustee and one of the original organisers of the Institute of Musical Art
of New York, and President of the New York Symphony Orchestra. At
Rubinstein's suggestion he was invited to be the solo pianist at the 1890
Three Choirs Festival at Worcester but declined. In 1899, however, he
attended, with Horatio Parker, the Worcester Festival and later became a
great friend of Elgar and Atkins. Elgar dedicated his *Introduction and
Allegro for Strings* to him in 1905. Elgar usually referred to him as
'Gaffer'.

Schuster, Francis Howard Leo (1852–1927)
A wealthy supporter of the arts who, with his elder sister Adela, became
close friends of the Elgars who frequently stayed with them in their
Westminster and Bray houses. Schuster surrounded himself with the
leading musicians and artists of the day, but had a special admiration for
Elgar and his music which he furthered in every way he could.

Sgambati, Giovanni (1841–1914)
A pupil of Liszt and a friend of Wagner. Concert pianist, composer and
conductor. He founded the series of orchestral concerts given in the Sala
Dante, then Rome's only concert hall, and was co-founder of the Licee
Musicale at the Accademia di S. Cecilia, Rome.

Sinclair, George Robertson (1863–1917)
Organist Truro Cathedral 1881–1889, Hereford Cathedral 1889–1917.
Conductor Three Choirs Festivals, Hereford 1891–1912 (festivals in
abeyance 1914–1919). Conductor Birmingham Choral Society
1899–1917. His name will always be associated with his bulldog *Dan*.

Speyer, Sir Edgar (1862–1932)
The head of the banking firm. He was a cousin of Edward Speyer and
married a well-known professional violinist, Madame von Stosch (known
to her friends as Todi), who on occasions played through with Elgar his
violin music, including the Violin Concerto, before publication. Sir
Edgar was Chairman of the Queen's Hall Orchestra and very influential
in the London musical world.

Speyer, Edward (1838–1935)
A rich banker and patron of the arts with close connections with the
German music world. He was one of Elgar's most influential friends. The
Elgars often stayed with him and his wife Antonia at their house,
Ridgehurst, in Shenley, Hertfordshire. Lalla Vandervelde, the wife of
the Belgian Minister of Justice, was their daughter.

Stanford, Sir Charles (Villiers) (1852–1924)
Irish composer. Professor of Music Cambridge University 1887–1924.
Professor of Composition Royal College of Music. Conductor London
Bach Choir 1885–1902. Leeds Festival (1901–1910).

Strauss, Richard (1864–1949)
Composer and conductor. Elgar's great European contemporary. They
first met in London in 1897. Strauss's famous speech at Düsseldorf after
the performance of *Gerontius* at the 1902 Lower Rhine Festival was the
beginning of Elgar's European reputation.

Stuart of Wortley, Lady (Alice Stuart-Wortley) (1862–1936)
Her husband, Charles Stuart-Wortley, MP for Sheffield, was created a
Baron in 1916. The Elgars first met the Stuart-Wortleys at a Sheffield
Festival and the families became close friends. Alice Stuart-Wortley was
a keen musician and encouraged Elgar in the composition of the Violin
Concerto and in parts of Symphony No 2.

Sumsion, Herbert Whitton ('John') (born 1899)
Organist, composer, conductor. Pupil of Herbert Brewer at Gloucester
Cathedral. Director of Music at Bishop's Stortford College 1923–1926.
Professor of Harmony Curtis Institute of Music, Philadelphia. Organist
Gloucester Cathedral 1928–1967. Conductor Three Choirs Festivals,
Gloucester, 1928–1965. CBE 1961.

Surette, Thomas Whitney (1862–1941)
A graduate of Harvard University he started lecturing on music in 1895
and was one of the first Americans to appreciate the importance of music
in education, especially for children and young people. He quickly
established a reputation throughout Eastern America and in England as a
Music Educationist. In 1914 he founded a 'Summer School of Music' in
Concord, Massachussetts, which became internationally famous.

Terry, Charles Sanford (1864–1936)
Professor of History Aberdeen University 1903–1930. A good musician
and a great Bach scholar, he wrote a number of books on Bach and his
biography of Bach received high praise in Germany, where he was
recognised as an authority. Leipzig University gave him an honorary
doctorate. He became a great friend of Elgar and Atkins, both of whom
stayed with him on several occasions.

Tolhurst, George (1827–1877)
He came of a musical family and was born and lived in Shoreditch. He
later spent some years in Australia, where he was Acting Organist at
Melbourne Cathedral. *Ruth*, published privately by him in London,
received its first performance in Melbourne in 1867. After his return to
England it was performed in London. He died in Barnstaple.

Trench, Frederick Herbert (1865–1923)
Poet and playwright. He was known for his 'ear for the music of words', which no doubt first brought him to Elgar's attention.

Whewall, James (1850–1909)
He was a miner who had been a chorister in the Parish Church of Kingsley near Cheadle, a mining district. He moved to the Tungstall area as a youth and became choirmaster at the Wesleyan Chapel, where he founded a juvenile choir which quickly began to win prizes in the local musical competitions. Shortly afterwards he met with a serious pit accident, became an insurance agent and begant organising his adult Choral Society, which went from strength to strength under his conductorship.

Williams, Trevor Osmond (1885–1930)
A leading member of HMV's International Artists Department with a flair not only for artistic matters but also for administration and finance. He was also a director of the Covent Garden Opera Syndicate.

Wilson, James Maurice (1836–1931)
Headmaster Clifton College. Rector of Rochdale, where he assisted in the formation of the Co-operative Movement. Canon Worcester Cathedral 1905–1926. Cathedral Librarian 1907–1924. Did much for Worcester and its citizens. Largely responsible for the provision of public parks and other amenities. Authority on the Cathedral Library and the Cathedral architecture, and a great supporter of its music.

INDEX

Numbers in *italic* type refer to photographs
Numbers in **bold** type refer to major entries

Aberdeen, 162, 192, 195, 245, 376
Aberdeen University, 145, 154, 162
Acworth, H.A., 374
Alassio, 107, 111
Albani, Dame Emma, 26, 44, 46, 104, 170, 444
Alboni, Mlle, 470
Alexandra, HM Queen, 113
Alexandra Palace Male Voice Choir, 198
Allen, Sir High P., 247, 322, 349, 383, 468, 490
Allen, Perceval, 173
Allen, William, 473
Allin, Norman, 350, 394
Alston, Dom G. Cyprian, 465
America, 102, 127, 129, 133, 139, 145, 149–50, 158, 207, 214–15, 297, 372
Amphlett, Rev Paul, 302
Amsterdam, 298
Amsterdam Orchestra, 98
Anderson, Mary (Madame de Navarro), 238
Arbos, Enrique Fernandez, 210
'Ark, The', 186, 189
Arnold, Richard P. (in *Variations*), 35
Athenaeum, The, 114, 328, 334, 337–8, 378–9, 383
Athens, 140
Atkins, Edward Wulstan Ivor (the author): birth and early days, 125, 183, 205, 212–13, 231, 245–6, 247, *257*, 266–7, 281; sings in *For the Fallen*, 281–4; *290–1*, 297, 301–2, *309*, 322–5, 337; at Festival rehearsals and performances, (Worcester) 313–18, *344*, 419–20, 446–8, 467–8, (Gloucester) 348–50, 407, 436–7, 467, (Hereford) *343*, 377, 400–1, 430–2, 459–61; at Cambridge, 370–3, 375–6, 384, 392; visits to Napleton Grange, 365–6, 369–70, 380, 388–9, 392–3, 397–8, 400; visits to Battenhall Manor, 402–4; to Tiddington House, 406–8, 412, 417–18; to Marl Bank, 421, 425–8, 430, 433–6, 438–43, 445–6, 449–51, 453–8, 462, 464; civil engineering, 398, 403–7, 413, 420, 425–6, 438; general, 322–5, 327, 337, 339, 341, 350–2, 379, 396–400, 429–30, 443–4, 454, 461–2, 456–6, 469
Atkins, Florence (sister of I.), 21
Atkins, Frederick Pyke (father of I.), 21, 490
Atkins, Sir Ivor Algernon: LIFE birth, 21; organist at Stonehaven, 22; assistant to Sinclair at Truro, Hereford, 22, 25; first meeting with Elgar, 25; attends Birmingham Festival and sees Dvořák and Richter, 27; at Gloucester Festival, 28; Elgar discusses works with, 29; becomes organist at Ludlow, 29; appointed organist at Worcester, 30; takes over WFCS, 31; conducts first concert, 32; meets 'Variation' friends, 35; letters from Elgar re Birchwood, 36; plays *Organ Sonata in G*, 37; a possible 'Variation', 38; receives proofs of *Variations*, present at first performance, 39–40; plans for first Worcester Festival, 41–4; marries Dora Butler, 42; artists for *Light of Life*, 43–4; rehearsals, 45; hears first performance of *Sea Pictures*, 46;

Variations for organ, 47; visits to Elgar during writing of *Gerontius*, 51; Coleridge-Taylor works at WFCS concert, 51; writes about first performance of *Gerontius* at Birmingham, 52; later memories of performance, 53–4; discussion about new Elgar work for Festival, 54; at first performance of *Cockaigne*, 57; note on *Gerontius* in Düsseldorf, 60–1; music at Craeg Lea, 61; plans for Festival, 61–2; sketch of *Pomp and Circumstance* March No 3 dedicated to, 62; refers to *Reynard the Fox*, 62, 64; Elgar gives nickname 'Firapeel', 66; rehearsals for Festival, 66, 69, 72; doctrinal problems over *Gerontius*, 70–72; receives proofs of *Grania and Diarmid*, 72; work on words of *Gerontius*, 72–3; letters about Festival, 76–85; first letter from 'Reynart', 78; trouble with Book of Words, 80; successful Festival, 86–7; becomes member of STP, 88–9; hears music of *Apostles* as written, 91–7, 99; scoring *Magnificat in A and Nunc Dimittis in D*, 99–100; letter to Mrs Elgar re *Apostles*, 101; checking proofs of *Apostles*, 103; at first performance, 104; conducts *King Olaf* at WFCS concert, 113; last visit to Craeg Lea, 116; first visit to Plas Gwyn, 116; *Magnificat and Nunc Dimittis in G* at Gloucester Festival, 121; plans for Worcester Festival, 128–9; receives *Hymn of Faith* libretto, 129; first performance of *Pomp and Circumstance March* No 3 (dedicated to A.), 131; considering new Worcester Orchestral Society, 132; present at Elgar's first lecture at Birmingham University, 132–3; working on *Hymn of Faith*, 133–5; offered appointments in New York, 135–6, 139; *Hymn of Faith* completed, 135; conducts Worcester Festival, 140; formation of Worcestershire Orchestral Society, 141–3; hears work on *The Kingdom*, 145–6, 148–9; conducts London concert, 146–7; *Too Late* and *Thou art come* for Hereford Festival, 148; conducts first WOS concert, 150; correcting proofs of *The Kingdom*, at first performance in Birmingham, 153–5; at Hereford Festival, 153–4; planning 1908 Festival, 158–61; shooting with Elgar, 160; cycling in Scotland, 162; Elgar encourages him to write, 158, 160–1, 164, 173–6, 347–8, 368; programme and soloists for Festival, 169–70, 173–6; hears work on Symphony, 177; declines hon D.Mus from Canterbury, 182; Worcester Festival rehearsals and concerts, 182–4; *Hymn of Faith* performed, 183–4; at first performance of Elgar's Symphony, 186; performs Symphony at WFCS concert, 188–9; edits Schubert's *Lazarus*, 195; receives proofs of Violin Concerto, 203; holiday in Austria, 205; at first performance of Violin Concerto and at Schuster's supper, 209–12; discussing new edition of *St Matthew Passion*, 212; new WOLCS' first concert, 212; hears work on Second Symphony, 214; working on *Passion*, 213–16; discusses ideas for Festival with Elgar, 215–19;

final work on *Passion*, 217–19, 227–8; Rothenburg-on-Tauber inspires idea for Chorales, 227–8; 1911 Festival finest so far, 229–33; visits Severn House, 238; hears first performance of *Music Makers*, 241; conducts it at WFCS concert, 241; sketches of work, 242–4; receives score of *Falstaff* and hears work at Leeds, 247–8; plans for Festival, 249–53, 262–4; outbreak of war, Festival abandoned, 264–5; memorial services and war charities, 265–8; work on Cathedral Music Library, 272–4; receives proofs of *For the Fallen*, 276; performance for Cathedral, 276–84; *Light of Life* and *Froissart* proposed for Music Library, 284–5; dedicates *Organists of Worcester Cathedral* to Elgar, 288; Armistice Service, 290; receives proofs of Violin Sonata, 290; hears about Elgar's chamber music, 290–1; performances, 292–3; plans to revive Festival, 295–8, 302–5; programme, 315; rehearsals and performances, 312–14, 316–18; Festival a great success, 318–21; D.Mus Oxon, 321–3; Knighthood, 323, 326–7; WFCS perform *Caractacus*, 329; Elgar proposes for Athenaeum, 337–8; rebuilding of Cathedral organ, 340–2, 366, 371; rehearsals and concerts at Gloucester, 341, 345–50; first visits to Napleton Grange, 360, 365–6; Worcester Festival, 368–70; mother dies, 373; election to Athenaeum, 378–9, 383; HMV recording in Cathedral considered, 387–90; evenings at Napleton, 388–90, 400; at Battenhall Manor, 402–3; hears Hereford test records, 403; visits to Tiddington House, 404–6; hears *Beau Brummel* music, 406, 408; urges Elgar to write the Third Part of *Apostles*, 410; editing Purcell work for Elgar to orchestrate, 411–14; Worcester Festival, 419–20; Sunday evenings at Marl Bank, 425–8; WFCS performance of *Apostles* broadcast, 427–8; exploring the Charnel Chapel, 429–30; at Hereford Festival, 430–32; is given *Froissart* MS, 432; conducts *Faery Fantasy*, 433; plans for Worcester Festival, 440; hears sketches of *Spanish Lady*, *Sonatina*, *Apostles III* and Third Symphony, 441–2, 445–6; Festival performances, 447–9; edits Organ Sonata No 2, 449–50; performance, 454; receives *Froissart* records, 456; hears further work on Symphony and opera, 453–5; Symphony only, 456, 458–9, 461; hears records of *Serenade for Strings* and *Elegy*, 461; Elgar's final illness, visits to Nursing Home, 461–2; at Marl Bank, 461; present at recording session, 462–4; death of Elgar, 464; at funeral, 464–5; arranges Memorial Service, 465–6; conducts *Gerontius* at Gloucester Festival, 467; Elgar Memorial Window and special performances at Worcester Festival, 467–8; conducts last Worcester Festival, 469; retires as organist, 469; death, 469, 490; PLATES *Frontispiece, 33, 34, 67, 172, 224, 257, 309, 310, 343, 363, 381, 415*; WORKS Original **Works**, Arrangements and Editions: *Abide with me*, 368, 370; *Chorale Prelude* on tune 'Worcester' (Tomkins), 347; *Hymn of Faith*, 129–30, 133–6, 140, 156, 163, 176, 183–4, 307, 312–13, 317, 379; *Jehovah quam multi sunt hostes mei* (Purcell: ed Atkins, orch Elgar), 410–14, 419; *Lazarus* (Schubert; edited), 170, 173, 195; *Magnificat in A* and *Nunc Dimittis in D*, 99–100, 430; *Magnificat and Nunc Dimittis in G*, 121; *Organists of Worcester Cathedral*, 288–9, 379; Organ Sonata No 2 in B flat (Elgar: arrgt of *Severn Suite*), 384, 449–50, 454; *St John's Passion* (Bach: edited), 420; *St Matthew Passion* (Bach: edited with Elgar), 205, 207, 212–19, 224, 226–7, 231, 269, 308, 313–14, 317; *Shepherdess, The*, 407; 'She walks, the Lady of my delight', 347; *There be none of Beauty's Daughters*, 377; *Thou art come*, 148, 407; 'Three Kings from Persian Lands' (Cornelius: carol

arrangement), 286; 'Too Late', 148; *Year at the Spring, The*, 377; 'Virgin's Lullaby, The', 242, 287, 354; 'Worcester' (hymn tune), 40

Atkins, Katharine May Dorothea (Lady Atkins, *née* Butler. 'Dora'), 32, **42**, 83, 140, 152, 186, 192, 218, 240, **267**, 284, 327, 331, 377–8, 397, **430**, 433, 454, 469, 490

Atkins, Reginald Mozart (brother of I.), 21

Austin, John W., 31, 56, 103, 154, 208, 449

Austin, W., 73

Australia, 479

Austria, 205, 245

Bach, Johann Sebastian, 61–2, **76**, 162, 179–80, 183, 205, 212, 218, **231**, 284, 286, 294, 306, **317**, 330, 334, 336, **338**, 340, 347, 375, **377**, 379, **386**, 389, 398, 401, **419–20**, 434, 448, 456, 459, 474–5

Baillie, Isobel, 447, 457, 468

Bainton, Edgar, 377, 420

Bairstow, Sir Edward, 366

Baker, Dalton, 163

Baker, William Meath (in *Variations*), 35, 37

Baldwin, Stanley, 363, 465

Bantock, Sir Granville, 20, 51, 58, 59, 86, 87–9, 100, 102, 106, 122–4, 184, 195, 216, 229, 231, 247, 349, 407, 490

Barbirolli, Sir John, 406

Barrie, Sir James, 342

Barrows, Winifred, 433

Battenhall Manor, Worcester, **402**, 403–4

Battishill, Jonathan, 366–7, 370, 394

Bax, Sir Arnold, 216, 334, 370

Bayle's Dictionary, 269–70

Bayley & Ferguson, 366–8, 376, 412–13

Bayreuth, 77, 79, 81, 87, 90

BBC (British Broadcasting Corporation), 384, 399, 409, 427, 450–1, 454, 462

Beare, John, 476

Beauchamp, Earl, 226, 250, 479

Beel, Antonie, 60

Beethoven, Ludwig van, 35, 126, 145, 174, 184, **199**, **202**, 268, 294, **317**, 401, **420**, 459–60, 462, **468**, 471–2

Belfast, 384, 386, 409, 450

Belgium, 265, 267, 332

Bellasis, Father Richard, 71–2

Bell, Nellie, *see* Welch, Nellie

Bennett, A.W., 375

Benton, Alfred, 121

Beresford, Admiral Lord Charles, 140, 292

Berkeley, Robert, 275, 318

Berlioz, Hector, 313, 316, 393, 459

Bettws-y-coed, 59, 99

Binyon, Laurence, 268, 359, 365, 390

Birchwood Lodge, 35–7, 45, *68*, 79, 94, 100, 136

Birkenhead, *see* New Brighton

Birmingham, 29, 61, 87, 113–14, 125, 266, 271, 278, 327

Birmingham Festival, 19, 27, **51–3**, 56, 76, 90, 99, **103–4**, 146, 154, 156, 195, 241

Birmingham Festival Choral Society, 133, 149

Birmingham Oratory, 71, 73

Birmingham University, 124, 127, 132, 143, 145, 156, 161, 163, 164, 180

Bizet, Georges, 144

Black, Andrew, 44, 104, 106, 121

Blackwood, Algernon, ('Starlight'), 270, 294–5

Blake, Samuel (Carice's husband), 331, 337, 453, 465

Blair, Hugh, 28, 29, 30, 37, 77, 81, 82, 139, 490

Blanche, Jacques Emile, 210

Bliss, Sir Arthur, 349

Boito, Arrigo, 247

Boosey & Co, 126

Boughton, Rutland, 195

Boult, Sir Adrian, 210, 457, 469
Bramah, Ernest, 355
Brahms, Johannes, 55, 61, **126**, 143, 210, 215, 294, 314, 336, **377**, **448**, 455–6, 459
Bray ('The Hut), 202, 245, 246
Brema, Marie, 44, 46, 83–4, 162, 267
Brent-Smith, Alexander, 197, 307, 313, *343*, *344*, 370, 377, 401, 412, 420
Brewer, Sir Herbert, 31, 37, **57**, *67*, 78, 229, 246, 319, 336, 338, 341–2, *344*, 346, **348–9**, 352, 377, 394–5, 401, **404**, 407, 491
Brian, Havergal, 217
Bridge, Sir Frederick, 136, 292–3, 374
Brillat–Savarin, 200
Brinkwells, Fittleworth (E's Sussex cottage), 286, 288–9, 291, 294–5, 308, 331
Bristol, 88
Bristol Festival, 19
British Medical Association, 476
Broadheath, Worcester (E's Birthplace), 20, 433, 471
Brodsky Quartet, 105
Bromsgrove, 139, 428
Broughton, Alfred, 19
Brown, Godfrey, 384, 450
Browning, Robert, 160, 174
Brunskill, Muriel, 447
Brussels, 214, 298
Buck, Dr Charles, 399, 476–7, 478–9, 491
Buck, Percy Carter, 322
Buller, Admiral Sir Henry, 465
Burley, Rosa, 35, 114
Buths, Julius, 52, 60–1, 73–4, 114, 126, 491
Butler, Katharine May Dorothea, *see* Atkins, Katharine May Dorothea
Butt, Dame Clara, 46, 210
Butterworth, George, 247
Byrd, William, 419, 434

Cambridge, 160, 268
Cambridge University, 294, 339, 349, 359, 370–3, 375–6, 392, 427
Cammaerts, Émile, 267–8
Cammaerts, Tita Brand, 267
Canada, 207, 215, 398
Canterbury, 182, 251, 254, 262, 342, 345, 394
Capri, 158–9
Cardiff, 21, 123, 373
Cardiff Festival, 19, 163–4
Careggi, 190–1, 480
Caruso, Enrico, 443
Cavalcanti, Guido, 191
Caxton, William, 64
Chabrier, Emmanuel, 456
Chadwick, George W., 46, 491
Chaminade, Cecile, 55
Chance, H. Godwin, 333
Charles, II, King, 232, 345
Charnel Chapel, 429–30
Chelsea Barracks, 266
Cheltenham, 151, 440
Cheshire, 79, 81
Chester, 100
Chester Festival, 19, 20
Chicago, 158–9
Chilworth (Carice's home), 331, 347
Church Stretton, 232
Cincinnati Music Festival, 145, 150, 158
Claines, 182, 472
Clark, Charles W., 173, 182–3
Clarke, Charles, 483, 484
Clarke, Douglas, 375, 491
Claughton, Alban, 69, 73

Claughton, Canon Thomas Legh, 43, 70–2, 129, 392, 491
Clayton, Henry R., 285, 366
Clef Club, 125
Clifford, Mary, 384, 440, 459, 461, 463, 465
Coates, John, 83–4, 88, 96, 102, 104, 163, 173, 256, 307–8, 317, 350, 394
Cobham, John, 83–4, 88, 96, 102, 104, 163, 173, 255, 307–8, 317, 350, 394
Cobham, Viscount: John Cavendish Lyttelton, 465, 468
Cohen, Harriet, 462
Coleridge-Taylor, Samuel, 45, 51, 106, 199, 241
Colles, Henry Cope, 449
Collingwood, Lawrance, 463
Cologne, 74, 114, 124, 126
Colvin, Sir Sidney, 290, 491–2
Colwall, Herefordshire, 69, 232
Columbia Graphophone Co, 389, 400
Concord, Massachusetts, 370
Connaught, HRH Prince Arthur of, 308
Constantinople, 140
Corelli, Arcangelo, 286, 398, 434
Cornelius, Peter, 286
Covent Garden, 75, 176
Covent Garden Elgar Festival, 111, 113
Coward, Sir Henry, 342, 492
Cowen, Sir Frederic (Hymen), 106, 492
Craeg Lea, (E's Malvern home), **42**, 51, 61, 62, 65, 88, 93, **94–5**, 100, 101, 102, 103, 104, 114, 115, **116**, *118*, 123, 136, 146
Craigher, Jacob Nicolas von, 41
Cramer, Francois, 375
Cranmer, Arthur, 457
Cromwell, Oliver, 182
Crossley, Ada, 46, 162
Croydon, 398, 451, 456
Croydon Philharmonic Society, 438–9, 457
Cruickshank, Enid, 435, 438
Crystal Palace concerts, 21, 54, 170
Culp, Julia, 173
Cults (Aberdeen), 162, 192–3
Cummings, Williams Hayman, 411

Damrosch, Frank Heino, 115, 134, 136, 150, 492
Damrosch, Walter Johannes, 115, 150, 492
Dan (Sinclair's bulldog), *34*, 38
Davidson, Malcolm, 370
Davies, Dr Arthur Whitcliffe, 468
Davies, Fanny, 442
Davies, Sir Henry Walford, 20, 54–5, 61–2, 76, 173, 184, 199, 231, 313, 385, 401, 420, 439, 468, 492
Day, Edgar, *258*, 282, *343*, 398, 419, 435, 447, 454
Delius, Frederick, 458
Derenburg, Mrs. Carl (*née* Eibenschütz), 210
Desmond, Astra, 307–8, 311, 432, 447, 457, 460, 466–8
Done, Agnes, 437–8
Done, William, 28, 437, 471, 475, 484–6
'Dorabella', *see* Powell, Dora
Dore, Philip, 375
Dover, 264
Dublin, 57, 377
'Duchess, The', *see* Underwood, Miss Alice
Dudley, Earl of, 474
Durham, 340, 412
Durham, University of, 111, 115
Düsseldorf, 60–1, 74–5, 98, 114, 126
Dutton, S.T., 285
Dvořák, Antonin, 27, 78, 144–5, 329

Ede, Dr. William Moore (Dean of Worcester), 346, 408–9, 492
Ede, Dr. W.E. Moore (E's doctor), 463–5
Edinburgh, 237–8

Edward, HRH Prince of Wales (later HM King Edward VIII), 30
Edward VII, HM King, 75–6, 111, 113, 202
Edwards, F.G., 136
Ehrke, Dr F., 164
Eisteddfod, 21
Elgar, Anne (E's mother), 20, 85
Elgar Birthplace, 38, 139, 469, 477
Elgar, Caroline Alice (Lady Elgar, *née* Roberts), **20**, 27, 28, 37, 47, 58, *68*, 74, 81, 98, 112, 113, 136, *138*, 150, 151, 153, 154, 157, 163, 169, *171*, 180, 186, 189, 195, 218, *222*, *223*, 238, 249, *260*, **266**, 269, 271, 275, 281, 289, 301–2, 304, **306**, 354, 374, 464, 492
Elgar, Sir Edward William, 1st Baronet (of Broadheath), OM, GCVO: LIFE birth, 20; early signs of genius, 20; 'Humoreske', 21; plays violin and other instruments, 21; engagement to Helen Weaver, 477–80; first published compositions, 21; marries Caroline Roberts, 20; goes to live in London, 20; first meeting with Atkins, 25–6; *Froissart* at Worcester Festival, 25–6; plays in Herefordshire Philharmonic concert as leader, 26; moves from London to 'Forli', Malvern, 27; first performance of *The Spanish Serenade* in Hereford, 28; *The Black Knight* in Worcester, 29; first performances in Worcester of *Sursum Corda*, Organ Sonata in G, 29; *From the Bavarian Highlands, The Light of Life*, 30; *King Olaf* at Hanley, 30; letter to Atkins on appointment at Worcester, 30; *Imperial March* for Hereford Festival, 31; Worcestershire Philharmonic Society launched, 35; rents Birchwood Lodge, 35; works on *Caractacus*, 36; *Lux Christi*, 37; *Enigma Variations* sketches, 38; *Variations* completed and first performance, 39–40; final form of ending, 40; proposed *Gordon* Symphony for Worcester festival, 41; *Light of Life* substituted, 41; moves to Craeg Lea, 42; artists for *Light of Life*, 43–4; first performance of *Variations* in final form, 46; *Sea Pictures*, first performance at Norwich, 46; *King Olaf* at Sheffield, 46; working on *Dream of Gerontius*, 51; Hereford Festival, 51; first performance of *Gerontius* at Birmingham, 52–3; later memories of the disappointing performance, 53–4; hopes for *Gerontius* at Worcester Festival, 54; hon D.Mus from Cambridge, 55; *Serenade* for Strings at WFCS concert, 55; Selection from *Gerontius* and *Sea Pictures* at WPS concert, 56; first performance of *Cockaigne* in London, 57; at Gloucester Festival, 57; tobacco from Sanford, 57–8; *Pomp and Circumstance* Marches 1 and 2 at Liverpool, 58; support from Rodewald, 58–9; *Gerontius* in Düsseldorf in German version, 60–61; first performance of *Grania and Diarmid*, 61; plans for *Gerontius* at Worcester Festival, 61–2; doctrinal problems, 70–2; rehearsals, 72, 82–5; performance at Festival, 85–7; conducts WPS concert, *Pomp and Circumstance* Nos 1 and 2, 72; work on *Dream Children* and *Coronation Ode*, 73; *Gerontius* at Lower Rhine Festival, 73–5; Richard Strauss' famous toast, 75; starts work on *Apostles*, 76; letters to Atkins about Festival, 76–9; first one signed 'Reynart', 78; in Bayreuth, 79; conducts *Cockaigne* and *Gerontius* at Festival, 86; first performance of *Coronation Ode* at Sheffield, 88; work on *The Apostles*, 91–8; unique *Apostles* libretto, 91; *Coronation Ode* by WFCS, 93; *Gerontius* at Hanley, 96; first performance of *Gerontius* in London, 98; Hereford Festival, 102; first performance of *Apostles* in Birmingham, 104; in Italy, 106–7, 111; Covent Garden Festival, 111; Lower Rhine Festival, 114; comparison of chorus tone, 114–15; doctorate from Durham, 115; Knighthood, 115–16; moves to Plas Gwyn, Hereford, 116; conducts

Apostles first time in a cathedral (Gloucester), 121; considering accepting Birmingham Professorship, 124; Oxford D.Mus, 128; first performance of *Pomp and Circumstance* March No 3 (dedicated to Atkins), 131; first professorial lecture at Birmingham University, 132–3; in America, doctorate from Yale University, 134; Freeman of Worcester, 139; conducts at Festival, 140; working on *The Kingdom ('Apostles II')*, 142–3, 145; second visit to America, 150; scoring of *The Kingdom* and first performed in Birmingham, 151–5; hon LL.D from Aberdeen, 154; in Italy, 158; third visit to America, 158; LL.D from Pennsylvania University, 158; working on *Wand of Youth* Suite, 160–2; first performance of *Pomp and Circumstance* March No 4, 162; Gloucester festival, conducts *The Apostles* and *Kingdom* in consecutive performances, 162; in Italy for six months (Rome), 165; writes about Worcester Festival plans, 169–70, 173–6; resigns Birmingham Professorship, 180; conducts at Festival, *The Kingdom* and first performance of *Wand of Youth* Suite No 2, 183; Symphony finished, 184; first performance in Manchester, 186; invents H2S apparatus, 185; despondency and ill-health, 188–90; stays with Julia Worthington in Florence, 189–91; death of Jaeger, 190; takes a flat in London, 198; completes Violin Concerto, 202; First Symphony on pianola roll, 204; working on Second Symphony, 202, 208–9; first performance of Violin Concerto with Kreisler and at Schuster's supper, 209–12; sends walking-stick to Wulstan Atkins, 212–13; completes Second Symphony, 214; visit to America and Canada, 215–16; work on *St Matthew Passion* with Atkins, 217; first performance of Second Symphony in London, not so well received, 217; award of OM, 219; family and financial problems, 220–5; advice on editing, 227; scores brass parts for Chorales, 228; 'japes' at Worcester Festival, 229–30, 232; conducts Second Symphony and Concerto, 231; 'The Flight from Worcester', 232; leaves Plas Gwyn for London, 232; moves into Severn House, 237; *Crown of India* at Coliseum, 238; working on *The Music Makers*, 239–40; first performance in Birmingham, 241; in Italy, unwell and restless, 245; *Falstaff* finished, 245–6; first performance at Leeds, 247; unable to write new work for Worcester Festival, 250–1; committed to writing *Apostles III* for Embleton, 263; abandons this for war effort, 265; patriotic works, 267–8; writing *The Starlight Express*, 270; performances in London, 271; arrangements for performing *For the Fallen* in Worcester Cathedral, 276–84; MSS for Cathedral Music Library, 284–5; wartime London a strain, takes 'Brinkwells' cottage, 286; writes chamber music here, Violin Sonata, 288–90; String Quartet, 290–4; Quintet for piano and strings, 288, 290–4; Cello Concerto, 291, 295; death of Alice, 306; suggestions for 1921 Worcester Festival, 307–8, 311; conducts at rehearsals and concerts, 313–14; pleasure at Atkins' D.Mus and Knighthood, 322, 324, 326; interest in microscopes, 329; Carice's engagement, 331; conducts Cello Concerto and *The Apostles* at Hereford, 332; leaves Severn House for London flat, 333; conducts *The Apostles* and *The Kingdom* at Gloucester, first consecutive performance since war, *344*, 350; gives EWA another walking-stick, 350; letter to Atkins about the writing of *King Olaf*, 354; leases Napleton Grange, 360; scores Battishill and Wesley anthems, 366; voyage to S. America, 372; Master of King's Musick, 376; works performed at Hereford Festival, 377; Philharmonic concert and Gold Medal, 385; ill-health, 385–6; recording works with HMV,

389; buys Mina, 389; japes at Worcester Festival, 395; carillon at bell-foundry, 399; 70th birthday broadcast, 'Good-night, Marco', 399; *Civic Fanfare* written for Hereford, 400–1; moves to Battenhall Manor, 402; KCVO conferred, 403; takes Tiddington House, 404; writes music for *Beau Brummel*, 406, 408; recording of *Introduction and Allegro for Strings*, how it came to be written, 406; conducts *Gerontius*, *The Kingdom* and Cello Concerto at Gloucester, 407; proposed new works for Worcester refused by Dean, 408–9; orchestrates Purcell's *Jehovah, quam multi sunt hostes mei* for Festival, 411–14; Tertis' viola arrangement of Cello Concerto, 417; *Pomp and Circumstance* March No 5 for P.C. Hull, 417; meetings with Bernard Shaw, 418–19; decides to buy Marl Bank, 420–21; interest in EWA's gramophone 'auto-stop', 426; story of *Enigma* 'solution', 428; conducts at Hereford, 430–2; attacks of 'lumbago', 430, 432; writes *Nursery Suite*, 434–5; recorded, 436; baronetcy conferred, 436; *Nursery Suite* at Gloucester, 436–7; *Gerontius* in Croydon, 438; *Falstaff* recorded, 439; working on opera (*Spanish Lady*), orchestral version of *Severn Suite*, *Sonatina* and *Apostles III*, 440–1; love of Worcester Cathedral, 443; Menuhin records Violin Concerto, 445; work on Third Symphony, 445–6; commissioned by BBC, 451; love of *Elijah*, 447–8; last Christmas card, 452; intense work on Symphony and opera, 453–5; GCVO conferred, 457; Violin Concerto in Paris, 458; visit to Delius, 458; conducts at Hereford Festival, his last, 460; Symphony progressing, 461; illness and operation in South Bank Nursing home, 461–2; returns to Marl Bank, 462; Gaisberg arranges recording session, 463–4; death, 464; funeral, 464–5; Memorial Service in Worcester Cathedral, 465–6, 493; PLATES Frontispiece, 34, 68, 117, 118, 119, 120, 137, 138, 171, 172, 221, 223, 224, 259, 309, 310, 343, 344, 361, 362, 363, 364, 381, 382, 415, 416; WORKS (inc. projected and unfinished works referred to in text), *Adieu* (pf), 449; *Adonais* (poem by Shelley, projected), 408–9; *Air de Ballet*, 476; *Apostles, The* (Op 49), 51, 61, **76**, 88, **90–1**, 99, 101, **102–4**, 113–14, 121, 124, **126**, 131, 134, 140, 145, **150**, 153, 154, 158, 161–3, 169, 173–5, 193, 195, 272–3, 331–2, 336, 345–8, **350**, 385, 388–9, 393–4, 427, 431, 457, 466, **468**, 473; *Apostles II, see The Kingdom; Apostles II, see The Kingdom; Apostles III (The Last Judgement*, projected), 250–1, 263, 265, 346, 371, 388–9, 442, 451; *Aspiration (From the Bavarian Highlands)*, 412; *Beau Brummel* (incidental music), 406, 408; *Black Knight, The* (Op 25), 28, 29; *Caractacus* (Op 35), 36–7, 52, 121–4, 329, 460, 463–4; *Carillon* (Op 75), 267–8, 386; carillon chimes for Ottawa War Memorial, 399; *Carissima*, 430; Chorales, two, arranged for brass from Bach's *St Matthew Passion*, 227–8, 231, 317–18; *Christmas Greeting, A* (Op 52), 169, 287, 354, 434; *Civic Fanfare*, 400–1, 430, 460; *Cockaigne* Overture, (Op 40), 57, 131, 195, 218, 389, 401, 457; *Concert Allegro* (pf), 442; *Coronation March* (Op 65), 217, 220, 226, 231, 246, 262; *Coronation Ode* (Op 44), 61, 66, 73, 75, 88, 93; *Crown of India, The* (Op 66), 237–8; 'Death on the Hills' (Op 72), 253, 335; *Deep in my Soul*, 169; *Demon, The* (poem by Shelley, projected), 408–9; *Dream Children* (Op 43), 61, 73, 160, 393–4; *Dream of Gerontius, The* (Op 38), 51, **52–3**, 54, 59, **60–1**, 61–2, 65–6, **69–75**, 82–6, 88, 96, 98, 104, 140, 150, 154, 173, 175, 182–3, 195, 206, 215, 241, 246, 253, 256, 262–3, 266–7, 307–8, 313, **317**, 319, 331, 370, 377, 401, 404, 407, 419, 432, 435, 437–8, 440, 447–8, 460, 466, **467**, 468; *Elegy* (Op 58), 461; Empire March, 372–3,

377; *Evening Scene*, 139, 156; *False Love (From the Bavarian Highlands)*, 412; *Falstaff* (Op 68), 239, 245–9, 261, 341, **439**; *Fantasia in C minor* (Bach, arranged for orchestra, Op 86), 336, 338, 389, see also Fugue in C minor; *Feasting I watch* (Op 45, No 5; *Greek Anthology* partsongs), 156, 342; *Fly, Singing Bird, fly* (Op 26, No 2), 55, 212, 374; *For the Fallen (The Spirit of England*, Op 80, No 3), 268, 272, 276–84, 313–14, 336, 345, 347–8, 365–6, 370, 385, 393, 438, 440, 447; *Fountain, The* (Op 71, No 2), 253; *Fourth of August (The Spirit of England*, Op 80, No 1), 285–6; *Fringes of the Fleet, The*, 285–6; *Froissart* Overture (Op 19), 25–6, *33*, 284–5, 432, 456; *From the Bavarian Highlands* (Op 27), 30, 246, 412; Fugue in C minor (Bach, arranged for orchestra), 330–2, 334, 336, 341, 389, see also *Fantasia for C minor;* Fugue in C minor (the 'Napleton' Fugue; became movement of Organ Sonata No 2 in B flat), 384, 449; *Give unto the Lord*, Psalm 29 (Op 74), 256, 261, 262, 305; *Go, song of mine* (Op 57), 191–2, 195, 219; *Gordon* Symphony (projected), 41–3; *Grania and Diarmid* (Op 42), 61, 72, 131; *Great is the Lord*, Psalm 48 (Op 67), 205, 253, 262; *Greek Anthology, Five Partsongs from the* (Op 45), 212, 342; *Grete Malverne on a Rock*, 32; *Herald, The*, 376–7; 'Humoreske', 21, 471; *Imperial March* (Op 32), 31; *In Memoriam — In Memory of a Seer* (unpublished), 177; *In the South*, 'Alassio' Overture (Op 50), 111–13, 121, 124, 126, 131, 150, 156, 180; *Introduction and Allegro for Strings* (Op 47), 127, 128, 130–31, 140, 150, 154, 263, 311, 313, 377, 406, 420, 431; *I sing the Birth*, 409, 434; *Jehovah, quam multi sunt hostes mei* (motet by Purcell, orchestrated), 410–14, 419; *Jerusalem* (Parry, orchestrated), 370; *King Arthur* (incidental music), 359, 365, 390, 393; *Kingdom, The (Apostles II*, Op 51), **38**, 90–1, 123, 124, 142, 145–6, **148–9, 150–6,** 158, 160–4, 169, 173, 182–3, 336, 341, 345–6, 348, 350, 366, 370, 377, 393–4, 407, 419–20, 457, **460**, 466, **467**; *King Olaf, Scenes from the Saga of* (Op 30), 30, 35, 45, 46, 96, 112–13, 121, 165, 238, 353–4, 373–4; *Land of Hope nd Glory* (from *Pomp and Circumstance* March No 1), 372, 399, 439; *Let us Lift up our Hearts* (motet by Wesley, orchestrated), 366–8, 370; *Light of Light, The (Lux Christi*, Op 29), 30, 37, 41, 43–5, 284–5, 432, 438; *Love's Tempest* (Op 73, No 1), 253; March in B flat, 460; 'Mina', 451; *Music Makers, The* (Op 69), 209, 239–44, 302, 307–8, 313, 317, 401, 440, 445, 447; *My Love dwelt in a Northern Land*, 27, 32, 55, 156, 335; *National Anthem*, 75, 209, 370, 401, 419, 430, 438, 468; *Nursery Suite*, 434–7, 442; *O Lord, look down from Heaven* (motet by Battishill, orchestrated), 366–7, 370, 394; Organ Sonata in G (Op 28), 29, 37, 447; Organ Sonata No 2 in B flat (arrangement of *Severn Suite* by I.A.; Op 87A), 384, 449, 454; *O soft was the Song* (Op 59, No 1), 197; Overture in D minor (Handel, transcribed for orchestra), 366–8, 370, 394, 437; *O Wild West Wind* (Op 53, No 3), 169; *Owls* (Op 53, No 4), 169; *Polonia* (Op 76), 268, 386; *Pomp and Circumstance* Marches (Op 39): No 1 in D, 58–9, 61, 111, 389; No 2 in A minor, 58–9, 61, 389; No 3 in C minor, 38, 62, 124, 126, 130–31, 134, 190, 389; No 4 in G, 160, 162, 389, 457; No 5 in C, *381*, 417–18; Psalm 29, see *Give unto the Lord;* Psalm 48, see *Great is the Lord;* Quartet in E minor (strings; Op 83), 290–4, 306; Quintet in A minor (pf and strings; Op 84), 288, 290–4, 444, 449, 462; 'Reveille, The' (Op 54), 342; *Rosemary* (pf), 21; *Salut d'Amour (Liebesgrüss*, Op 12), 21, 430, 476; *Salve Regina)*, 21; *Sanguine Fan, The* (Op 81), 279, 281, 284; *Sea Pictures* (Op 37), 46, 131, 180, 386;

Serenade (Op 73, No 2), 253; *Serenade* (pf), 449; *Serenade* in E minor for Strings (Op 20), 28, 55, 461; *Serenade Mauresque* (Op 10, No 2), 21, 53; *Severn Suite* for Brass (Op 87), 430; *Severn Suite* (arranged for orchestra), 384, 440–2, 444–5, 449; *Sevillana* (Op 7), 21; *Shower, The* (Op 71, No 1), 253; *Snow, The* (Op 26, No 1), 212, 374, 404; Sonata in E minor for Violin and Piano (Op 82), 288–94; *Sontina* (pf), 441; *Sospiri* (Op 70), 257, 393; *Spanish Lady, The* (Op 89; unfinished), 441–2, 451, 454; *Spanish Serenade* ('Stars of the Summer Night', Op 23), 28–9, 384; *Spirit of England, The* (Op 80), 285–6; *Starlight Express, The* (incidental music, Op 78), 270–1; *Sursum Corda* (Op 11), 29, 82–3, 85, 314, 455; Symphony No 1 in A flat (Op 55), 165, 177–8, 180–1, **184–9**, **193–5**, 199, 204, 206, 209, 212, **214**, 298, 385, 431–2, 440, 447; Symphony No 2 in E flat (Op 63), 202, 208, 213–14, **217**, 232, 246, 269, 307, 401, 420, 459, **467**; Symphony No 3 (Op 88, unfinished), *382*, 445–6, 449–51, 453–4, **456–9**, 461–2; *Te Deum* and *Benedictus* in F (Op 34), 31, 51–2, 195; *There is sweet music* (Op 53, No 1), 169; *Three Pieces* (orchestra, Op 10), 53, 480; *Torch, The* (Op 60, No 1), 197; *To Women* (*Spirit of England*, Op 80, No 2), 268, 272; *Twilight* (Op 59, No 6), 199; *Variations on an Original Theme* ('Enigma', Op 36), **35**, **38–40**, 42, 46, 47, 54, 128, 131, **147**, **158**, 175, 180, 199, 207, 388, **428**, 466, 468, **480**; Violin Concerto in B minor (Op 61), 165, 191, 195, 199–200, **202–4**, 205–6 **208–9**, 213–14, 218, **231**, 298, 335, *382*, 390, 401, 436–7, 445, 447, 451, 458, 481; Violoncello Concerto in E minor (Op 85), 291, 295–6, 328, 331–2, 370. 377, 407, 417, 460; *Wanderer, The*, 369; *Wand of Youth, The* (Suite No 1, Op 1A), 160–2, 165, 170, 180, 433–4, 472; *Wand of Youth, The* (Suite No 2, Op 1B), 176, 178–9, 182–3, 201, 384, 409, 433–4, 472; *Weary Wind of the West*, 156; *Zut! Zut! Zut!*, 369.

Elgar, Frank (E's brother), 28, 374, 405, 475, 481
Elgar, Helen Agnes ('Dot', E's sister), 225
Elgar, Henry (E's uncle), 25, 26, 274, 281, 314, 470, 481
Elgar, William Henry (E's father) 20, 25, 26, 140, 470, 481, 493
Elgar Blake, Carice Irene (E's daughter), 81, 112, 116, 129, 133, 139, 150, 152, 154, 163, 165, 169, 180, 189, 195, 197, 214, *221, 222, 223*, 304, 306, 311, 313–14, 316, 318, 328, **331**, 333, **337**, 385, 388, 394–5, 401–5, 420, 428, 430, 434, 446–7, 450, 453, 457, 459, 461–5, 477, 491
Elijah (Mendelssohn), 45, 53, 253, 255, 307, 317, 320, 385, 419, **447–8**, 475
Elizabeth, HRH Princess (now HM The Queen), 436
Elman, Mischa, 184
Elwes, Joan, 428
Elwes, Gervase, 162, 173, 307–8, *310*, 316–17
Embleton, Henry, 121, 251, 263, 280, 308, 493
Enesco, Georges, 458
Esser, Heinrich, 179, 183
Ettal Monastery, 246
Ettling, Henry ('Uncle Klingsor'), 35, 72–3, 96, 125–6
Evesham, 398
Exton, Frank, 475

Falkner, Sir Keith, 428
Farnaby, Giles, 286
Ffrangcon-Davies, David, 96, 102, 104–5, 163
'Firapeel' (E's name for Atkins, first letter to), 66
Fittleworth, 295 *see also* Brinkwells
Fitton, E.B. (mother of Isabel), 374
Fitton, Isabel ('Ysobel' in *Variations*), 35, 141, 374
Fitz Clarence, H.E., 253

Florence, 162, 189–91
Foregate Street, Worcester, 205
Forli (E's Malvern home), 27, 35, 37, 42, *68*, 353
Forrest, Dr Robert William (Dean of Worcester), 70
Foster, Muriel, 46, 74, 81, 84, 88, 96, 104, 140, 198–199, 210, 215, 218, 394
Franck, César, 313, 401, 419
Franke, Professor F.W., 61, 74
Fry, Charles, 189
Fuller-Maitland, J.A., 372

Gairloch, 264
Gaisberg, Fred, 457–9, 461–3, 467. 493
Gardiner, Henry Balfour, 216
Garmisch, 29, 205, 245, 275
Gee, Dr (Dean of Gloucester), 407
George III, King, 482–3
George V, HM King, 218, 238, 308, 323, 407, 465
German, Sir Edward, 144, 349
Germany, 28, 75, 114, 205, 212, 227, 245
Gillet & Johnston, 398
Gladstone, Herbert John, Viscount Hawarden, 349
Glasgow, 376
Gloucester, 113, 131–2, 161, 374; Cathedral, 86, 116, 140, 205, 229, *259*, 350, 467; Festival, 28, 36–7, 57, 121, 205–6, 246, 253, *259*, 336, 345–50, 385, **407**, 436–7, **467**
Gloucester Festival Chorus, 78, 131, 466
Gloucestershire, 21
Gluck, Christoph, 35
Gnecco, Francesco, 470
Godard, Benjamin, 55
Goodwin (Festival librarian), 471
Goetz, Muriel, *see* Foster, Muriel
Goldsmith, Oliver, 336
Goossens, Eugene, 334, 349
Gordon, General Charles George, (projected Symphony), 41–3, 53
Gordon, Mrs Granville, 375–6
Gore, Charles (Bishop of Worcester, 1902–4), 71–3
Görlitz, Jugo, 98
Gorton, Canon C.V., 93, 123, 133, 139, 169, 276
Goss-Custard, Walter Henry, 420
Gounod, Charles, 35, 55
Grafton, Claire (E's niece), 429
Grafton, Gerald (E's nephew), 428, 434, 465
Grafton, Madge (E's niece), 360, 370, 384, 399, 429, 440, 450, 459, 461, 463, 465
Grafton, May (E's niece), 116, 133, 135, 139, 150, 152, 154, 165, 169, 238, 384, 405, 429, 434, 440–1, 459, 461, 465
Grafton, Roland (E's nephew), 465
Grafton, Susanna ('Pollie', E's sister), 20, 250, 266, 268, 274, 285, 336, 353, 374, 428–9, 481
Grafton, William (E's brother-n-law), 429
Gray, Alan, 373
Green, Eric, 457
Green, Valentine, 430, 482
Green, William, 46, 83
Greene, H. Plunket, 26, 28, 46, 83–4, 163, 198
Grez-sur-Loing, 458
Grieg, Edvard, 165
Griffith, Arthur Troyte, 35, 57, 58, 113, 213, 238, 306, 428, 450, 463, 465, 493
Griller String Quartet, 449
Grindrod, Dr Charles, 97, 152, 206, 273, 419
Groveham, Edith, 477–78
Grover, Herbert, 122

Hadow, Sir Henry, 360, 493
Haley, Olga, 394, 467
Halford, George, 125, 493–4
Hallé Orchestra, 96, 133, 420
Hamilton, Henry, 238

Handel, George Frederic, 28, 284, 286, 366–8, 370, 394, 398, 434, 437, 459, 471, **474;** see also *Messiah*
Hanley, 19–20, 30, 95–6, 133, 156
'Harleyford Musical Festival', 195–6
Harris, Dr Charles, 207
Harrison, Arthur (of Harrison & Harrison), 340, 384
Harrison, Beatrice, 332, 370, 407
Harrison, Julius, 271, 307, 313, 316, 412
Harrison, Percy, 238
Harrison, Roy, 468
Harty, Sir Hamilton, 218, 247
Harwood, Basil, 247, 385
Hay, David (of Mott, Hay and Anderson), 395–6, 399
Hay, Edward Norman, 448
Haydn, Franz Joseph, 459
Heap, Charles Swinnerton, 53, 96, 494
Heidleberg, 60
Henderson, Roy, 407, 428, 468
Henry, O., see O. Henry
Henwick, 205
Hereford, 26, 38, 76, 113, 131–2, 133, 135–6, 163, 169, 209, 232, 237, 406, 459–60; Cathedral, 22, 25, 78, 133, 169, 195, 278, 400; Festival, 27, 30–31, 38, 51, 99, 148, 153–4, 193, 195, 241, 331–3, **377,** 400–1, 430–2, **459–61,** 469
Hereford Festival Chorus, 131, 177, 466
Herefordshire, 69, 78, 185, 347, 413, 455
Herefordshire Philharmonic Society, 26–7, 28, 113
Hess, Myra, 420, 449
Heyner, Herbert, 307, 317, 350, 394
Higley, William, 165, 173
HMV (His Master's Voice), 286, 294, 365, 387, 389–90, 400–1, 403, 407, 425–6, 434, **439,** 441–2, 454, 456–7
Holbrooke, Joseph, 20, 217
Holland, 332
Holst, Gustav, 332, 349, 385, 388, 434, 437, 448
Honegger, Arthur, 407
Horseracing, 397, 399, 430, 440, 454, 457
Housman, Rev. Henry, 40–1
Howells, Bernard, 375
Howells, Herbert, 206, 349, 352, 385
'Howle, Orlando', 56–7, 58
Hughes, Talbot, 127
Hull, Molly (Lady Hull, *née* Hake), 394–5, 448
Hull, Sir Percy Clarke ('P.C.'), *34*, 78, 197, 323, 331, **333,***344,* 394–5, 401, *415,* 417–18, 431, 448, 466–9, 494
Humperdinck, Engelbert, 35
Hurd, Richard (Bishop of Worcester, 1781–1808), 482
Hyde, Thomas Garmston, 35, 73
Hyde, Walter, 170–1, 174

India, 238
Ingleborough, 372
Innsbruck, 205, 246
Ireland, 377, 432
Irving, Sir Henry, 125
Italy, 106–7, 111, 157–8, 165, 189–91, 201, 245, 263, 452

Jackson, Sir Barry, 381, 418–19, 439–40, 450, 494
Jaeger, August Johannes ('Nimrod' of *Variations*), 35, 39–40, 52, 56–7, 58, 60, 74, 87, 91, 114, 121, 139, 153, **190, 198–199,** 494
Jaxon, Henry, 373
Jeremy, Raymond, 293, 306
Joachim, Joseph, 210
John, King, 273
Johnstone, Arthur, 74
Jonson, Ben, 409, 440, 450

Kalisch, Alfred, 58, 74, 88, 102, 106, 145, 156
Kelly, F.S., 210

Kempsey, see Napleton Grange
Kilburn, Nicholas, 197, 319, 323, 374
King, Shuttleworth, *344, 351*
King's School, Worcester, 276, 282
Kipling Rudyard, 285
Kirby, Alan, 438, 457
Knight, Father T., 53
Kodály, Zoltan, 407, 427
Koenen, Tilly, 175, 177, 180, 182–3
Kramskoi, Ivan Nicoliavitch, 93, 102
Krefeld Music Festival, 212
Kreisler, Fritz, 206–7, 209, 212, 214, 218, 231, 335, 390, 437, 494

Lablache, Signor, 470
Lacey, Canon, 420
Lake District, 269, 274
Lakin, Alice, 183
Lamb, Charles, 251
Lambert, Constant, 442
Lancashire, 413, 425, 430, 455
Lawnside School, Malvern, 276–7, 433
Lawson, Hon Harry L., 159
Leader, Benjamin Williams, 261, 494
Leck Hall, Westmorland, 237, 252, 275, 301, 327, 337, 372, 383
Leeds, 88, 133, 268, 277, 280–1, 286, 301, 374
Leeds Choral Union, 121, 345
Leeds Festival, 19–20, 36–7, 161, 163–4, 246–7, 249
Lee Williams, Charles, 55, 80–1, 129, 139, 206, 304, 314, 333, 468, 494
Leicester, Hubert, 141, 261, 268, 306, 319, 331, 374, 465, 473, 475
Leigh Sinton, 36
Leipzig, 478–79
Lempriere, Dr John, 103
Lett, Phyllis, 175, 182–3, 317, 350
Ley, Henry G., 332
Lightowler, Frederick, 122
Lincoln, 202
Liszt, Franz, 35, 77–8
Littleton House, Worcester (E's school), 90, 275, 472
Liverpool, 58–9, 87, 88, 150, 413, 420
Liverpool, Orchestral Society, 58–9
Liverpool Philharmonic Orchestra, 59, 413, 420
Llandaff, 21
Llandrindod Wells, 157, 188–9, 245
Llangranog, 406
Llantwit Major, 274, 312
Lloyd, Charles Harford, 206, 317, 495
Lloyd, Edward, 26, 28, 43–4, 46
Lloyd George, David, 323
Lodge, Sir Oliver, 132–3
Loeb, S., 156
London, 19, 20, 88, 113, 124, 131, 136, 156, **187, 198–199,** 201–2, 245, 252, 271, 286, 291, 296, 334, 354, 398, 463
London Philharmonic Orchestra, 385, 456, 458
London Symphony Orchestra, **8**6, 126, 130–31, 146–7, 185, 198, 207, 232–3, 237–8, 271, 296, 304–5, 318, 340, 389–90, 400, 431, 436, 438–9, 448, 457, 463–6
London University, 436
Longfellow, Henry Wadsworth, 160
Lower Rhine Festival, 52, 60–1, 73–5, 114
Ludlow, 318
Ludlow Collegiate Church, 29, 135, 152
Lugg, River (at Mordiford), 209
Lunn, Louise Kirkby, 173, 256, 261, 307, 311, 317
Lygon, Lady Mary, 479–80

MacDonald, J. Ramsay, 383
McEwen, Sir John, 385
Mackenzie, Sir Alexander, 184–5, 188

507

McNaught, William G., 169
Madresfield Musical Competition, 105, 480
Mainz, 35, 124, 126
Malvern, 35, 58, 81, 99, 115, 156, 207–8, 232, 265, 267
Malvern Choral Society, 329, 373
Malvern Concert Club, 105
Malvern Festival, 418–19
Malvern Hills, 20, 51, 232, 345, 419, 443, 447, 464
Malvern Link, 20, 27
Manchester, 133, 154, 185–6, 271–2, 420
Manchester, Percy, 428, 467
Mann, Arthur Henry ('Daddy Mann'), 373, 375, 495
Manns, Sir August, 21, 54
Marco, (E's spaniel), *362, 363,* 365, 379–80, 385, 388, 392, 394, 397, **399,** 405, 412, **427,** 449, 477
Marden, Richard (Elgar), 369
Margaret Rose, HRH Princess, 436
Marl Bank, 26, 98, 114, 285, *382,* **419–21,** 425, 427–8, 432–6, 438–43, 445–6, 449–51, 455–9, 461–4, 470, 471
Marlowe, Christopher, 190
Mary, HM Queen, 308, 407
Masefield, John, 265
Mason, Charles, 35
Massenet, Jules, 35
Matthews, Bertram P., 406
Meg (E's Aberdeen terrier), *362, 364,* 365, 380, 388, 392, 412
Melba, Dame Nellie, 170, 443
Mendelssohn, Felix, 37, 448, 459, 475, 479; see also *Elijah*
Menuhin, Hephzibah, 457–8
Menuhin, Moshe, 451, 457
Menuhin, Yaltah, 457
Menuhin, Yehudi, *382,* 443, 445, 451, 458, 495
Messchaert, Johannes, 74
Messiah (Handel), 45, 46, 53, 265, 308, 316–18, 320, 432, 447–8, 471–2, 483
Metzmacher, Willy, 60
Meyerbeer, Giacomo, 144
Meynell, Alice, 347
Milan, 162
Mills, Watkin, 28
Mina (E's cairn), *362, 363, 364,* 365, 389, 392, 394, 412, 427, 451
'Mock' Festival, 293, 474
Moldawsky, Sonia, 427
Montaigne, Michel de, 338
Moore, George, 72
Morecambe Competitive Festival, 93, 133, 139, 159, 342
Mordiford, 209
Morris, Thomas, 182
Mossel, Max, *34,* 125
Mott, Charles, 256, 261, 266–7, 271
Mott, Hay and Anderson, 398, 405
Mountford, Dick, 383–4, 398, 405–6, 457, 463, 465
Mozart, Wolfgang Amadeus, 145, 215, 386, 456, 472
Munich, 205, 245
Muntz, Lady, 404
Murdoch, William, 293
Musical League, 216
Music Festivals, 19–20

Nabarro, Sir Gerald, 469
Naples, 157–8, 245
Napleton Grange, Kempsey, 359–60, *362,* 365–6, 370–1, 376–80, 383–4, 385, 392, 399, **402,** 421
Nash, Heddle, 438, 468
National Gramophonic Society, 333, 406
Navarro, Antonio de, 238
Neville, Father William, 71, 73, 241
Nevinson, Basil G. (in *Variations*), 35, 41

Newcastle-upon-Tyne, 269, 308, 311, 404, 406–7
Newman, Ernest, 86, 88, 102, 156, 185, 292, 461
Newman, Cardinal John Henry, 52, 71, 73, 241
Newmarket, 457
New Radnor, 150
New Symphony Orchestra, 305
Newton, Ivor, 445
Newton-le-Willows, 427
New York, 134, 150, 158
New York Institute of Musical Art, 115, 134
New York Oratorio Society, 115
New York Philharmonic Orchestra, 115
New Zealand, 479–80
Nicholls, Agnes, 88, 163, 173, 277, 281, 317, 350, 394
Nicholson, Archibald K., 467–8
Nicholson, Sir Sidney, 395
Nikisch, Arthur, 27, 247
'Nimrod', *see* Jaeger, A.J.
Norbury, Florence, 495
Norbury, Winifred ('W.N.' in *Variations*), 495
North Staffordshire District Choral Society, 96
North Staffordshire Festival, 19, 30, 96
Norwich Festival, 19, 46, 140–1
Novello & Company (publishers), 35, 40, 52, 59, 91, 101, 103, 113, 128, 146, 156, 165, 186, 187, 216, 220, 225, 233, 247, 285, 290, 331, 336, 366–8
Novello, Vincent, 411–13

Oban, 136
Oberammergau, 205
Ogdon, John, 442
O. Henry (pseudonym of William Sidney Porter), 280
Opening Service (Festival), 31, 45, 82, 99, 121, 183, 304, 314, 400–1, 430–1
Orchestrelle Company, 204
Ord, Bernhard, 375, 495
Ostend, 180
Ottawa, 399
Oxford University, 127–8, 322–3, 339, 411–12, 427, 474

Paderewski, Ignaz Jan, 268
Palestrina, Giovanni Pierluigi, 286
Palliser, Esther, 44
Palmer, Charlton, 152, 154, 394, 446, 449, 495
Paris, 151–2, 189, 451, 454, 457
Parker, George, 350
Parker, Gilbert, 197
Parker, Horatio, 45, 46, 87, 495
Parratt, Sir Walter, 374
Parry, Sir Hubert, 20, 28, 46, 55, 72, 106, 164, 184, 199, 231, 317, 347, 349, 370, 431
Parsons, William, 468
Patmore, Coventry, 139
Patersons (publishers), 376
Payne, Rev H.S., 429
Pearce, Ernest Harold (Bishop of Worcester, 1919–30), 320, 322, 337, 383
Pearsall, Robert Lucas, 286
Penmaenmawr, 246
Pennsylvania University, 158
Penny, Dora ('Dorabella' in *Variations*), *see* Powell, Dora
People's Orchestral Society, Liverpool, 59
Pepys, Samuel, 69
Perowne, Arthur William Thompson (Bishop of Worcester, 1931–41), 468
Perrins, Cynthia, 448
Perrins, Dyson, 302
Pershore, 398, 473
Peyton, Richard, 125, 132, 495
Philharmonic Society, 209, 385
Phillips, Claude, 326
Phillips, Frank, 457

Pietro d'Alba (Carice's rabbit), 133, 135, 169, 197, 222
Pipe, Lucy (E's sister), 20, 385, 429, 476
Pitt, Percy, 55, 156
Pittsburgh, 158
Plas Gwyn (E's Hereford home), 113, 116, 123, 124, 126, 127, 128–9, 135, *138*, 145, 148, 150, 152, 160, 161, 177, 180, 186, 189, 201–2, 204, 206, **212**, *221*, *223*, **226–7**, **232**, 331
Pompeii, 158
Pope, Alexander, 159
Powell, Dora (Mrs Richard Powell, *née* Penny), 35, 206
Powick, 302, 475
Prout, Ebenezer, 125
Prowse, Keith, 450–1
Purcell, Henry, 55, 336, 410–14, 419

Queenstown (now Cobh, Co Cork), 216

Radford, Robert, 307
Ramsden, Archibald, 79, 90, 496
Ramsgate, 151–2
Randall, John, 370
Reed, William Henry, 28, 86, 203–4, 205–6, 231, 288–90, 292–3, 306, *310*, 313, 316, 318, 332, 336, *344*, 348, *364*, 369–70, 376–7, *381*, 389, 394–5, **405**, 407, 419, 431, 436–9, 441, 446–7, 449–50, 453, 456, 458, 460–6, 468, 496
Reed, Mrs W.H. ('James'), 206, 457
Reeve, Francis, 90
Reeves, George, 417
Reeves, Sims, 472
Reith, Sir John, 451, 462
'Reynart' (Elgar), first letter from, 78
Richter, Hans, 27, 35, 39–40, 42, 44, 54, 59, 102–3, 113, 133, 142, 176, 185–7, 198–199, 238, 496
Rimsky-Korsakov, Nikolay, 313
Roberts, Caroline Alice, *see* Elgar, Caroline Alice
Roberts, Field-Marshall Lord, 266
Robinet, Mme Paul, 268
Robinson, Dr Armitage (Dean of Westminster), 111
Rodewald, Alfred E., 58, 74, 79, 81, 87–9, 99, 102, 106, 496
Rome, 157–8, 164–5, 169, 245
Ronald, Sir Landon, 289 292, 340, 436, 439, 451, 453, 461, 465, 496
Rootham, Cyril, 268, 373, 497
Rossetti, Dante Gabriel, 191
Rossini, Gioacchino, 459, 472
Rothenburg-on-Tauber, 227
Rothenstein, William, 301
Rotterdam, 124, 126
Royal Academy of Music, 86, 200–1, 439
Royal Amateur Orchestral Society, 111
Royal Choral Society, 131, 409
Royal College of Music, 322, 436, 439
Royal College of Organists, 475
Rumford, Kennerley, 104, 210
Russell, Millicent, 428

St George's Church, Worcester, 21, 52
Saint-Saëns, Camille, 55, 246
St Wulstan's Church, Little Malvern, 306, 464
Salmond, Felix, 293, 296, 306
Salzburg, 205
Sammons, Albert, 293, 306, 401, 436–7
Sanford, Henry (S.S.S.'s son), 198
Sanford, Professor Samuel Simons, 46, 57, 87, 115, 116, 124, 127, 128, 134, 139, 150, 151–2, 158, *171*, **197–8**, *221*, 497
Santley, Sir Charles, 472
Sargent, Sir Malcolm, 409
Saughall, Cheshire, 59, 79, 81

Scap, (E's collie), 476
Scarlatti, Domenico, 412
Schmitt, Florent, 252
Schott & Co (publishers), 82
Schubert, Franz, 41, 72, 77, 170, 173, 195, 386
Schumann, Clara, 210
Schumann, Robert, 144, 210, 459
Schuster, Sir Felix V., 210
Schuster, Leo Francis (Frank), 102, 111–12, 124, 126, 131, *138*, 139, 140, 147, 148, 156, 162, 186, 195, 201, 206, **209–12**, 217, 289, 306, 497
Scotland, 162, 184, 193, 263–4, 340, 399, 418
Scriabin, Alexander Nicholaevich, 349–50
Sennis (tenor), 170, 173
Settle, Yorks, 399, 476–7
Severn House (E's London home), 217, 232, 237, 239, 245, 246, 288, 291–2, *309*, 328, 331, 333
Severn, River, 274, 345, 473
Sgambati, Giovanni, 165, 169–70, 497
Shaw, George Bernard, 292, 301–2, *381*, 404, 418–20, 436, 439–40, 444, 446–7, 451
Sheffield Festival, 19, 45, 46, 61, 88, 114
Shelley, Percy Bysshe, 408–9
Shorthouse, J. Henry, 345
Shrewsbury, 301, 306
Shrub Hill, Worcester, 142, 158, 205, 206, 354, 359
Sibelius, Jean, 241
Sinclair, George Robertson, 22, 25, 27, 29, 31, 32, *33*, *34*, 38, *67*, 76, 78, 113, 131, 132, 148, 151–2, 156, 160, 162, 169, 177, 186, 189, 195, 205, 214, *221*, 227, 241, 276, **278–9**, 314, 317, 331, 460, 497
Smith, James, 444
Smyth, Dame Ethel, 407
Sobrino, Luise, 81, 122
Somerton, J.W., 80, 86
Southall, Samuel, 78, 128, 351
South Bank Nursing Home, 386, 461–2
Spanish monks, 294–5
Spetchley, 275, 318–19
Speyer, Sir Edgar, 156, 217, 497
Speyer, Edward, 156, 180, 217, 245, 497
Spohr, Louis, 43
Squire, Emily, 162
Stallard, John, 302
Stamboul, 141
Stanford, Sir Charles Villiers, 20, 55, 160–2, 169, 184, 287, 306, 349, 374, 498
Steinbach, Dr. Fritz, 114, 124, 126
Sterndale, Bennett, Sir William, 209
Steuart-Powell, Hew David (in *Variations*), 35
Stevens, Horace, 394, 419, 432, 438
Stockley, William Cole, 21, 53
Stoke Prior, 250, 266, 273, 286, 295, 306, 318, 325, 333, 336, 340, 354, 429
Stoll, Oswald, 238
Storridge, 36
Stosch, Leonora von, 497
'STP' ('Skip the Pavement' Society), 58, 87–9, 91, 102, 105–6
Stratford-upon-Avon, 404–7, 410
Stratton Quartet, 462
Strauss, Richard, 58, 74–5, 77, 81–2, 93–4, 125, 140, 498
Stroud, 226
Stuart-Wortley, Alice ('Windflower', later Lady Stuart of Wortley), 217, 220, 269, 480, 498
Stuart-Wortley, Charles (later Lord Stuart of Wortley), 217, 269
Suddaby, Elsie, 394, 460, 466–7
Sullivan, Sir Arthur, 55, 125, 314
Sumsion, Alice, 407
Sumsion, Herbert Whitton ('John'), 407, *415*, 420, 466–8, 498

509

Surette, Thomas Whitney, 46, 163, 164, 297, 370, 418, 498
Surman, Joseph, 483
Swift, Jonathan, 353
Swinnerton Heap, Charles, see Heap, Charles Swinnerton
Switzerland, 263, 304
Szymanowski, Karol, 440, 445, 448

Tchaikovsky, Peter Ilyich, 35, 55, 144
Teme, River, 473
Tennyson, Alfred Lord, 174
Terry, Charles Sanford, 154, 162, 192–3, 195, 201, 206, 217, 220, 225, **231–2**, 245, 246, *258, 259,* 265, 287, 306, 376, 383, 498
Tertis, Lionel, 417, 460
Tewkesbury, 184
Thomas, Lily, 35, 148, 150, 158, 227
Thompson, Herbert, 73, 369
Three Choirs Festivals, 19, 27, 29, 31, 46, 57, 86, 121, **269,** 314, 329, 350, 351, 407, **447–8,** 469; see also Gloucester, Hereford and Worcester Festivals
Tiddington House, Stratford-upon-Avon, 404–6, 412-13, 417–18
Tietjens, Mlle, 444, 472
Tilbury, 176
Titterton, Frank, 447, 460, 468
Tolhurst, George, 65, 498
Tomkins, Thomas, 345, 347
Torquay, 201
Townshend, Richard Baxter (in *Variations*), 35
Tree, Charles, 122
Trefusis, Lady Mary (*née* Lygon), see Lygon, Lady Mary
Trench, Frederick Herbert, 160–1, 499
Truro Cathedral, 22, 25, 278
Tubb, Carrie, 277–9, 284
Turin, 233
Turkey, 140

Ullswater, 269, 274
'Uncle Klingsor', see Ettling, Henry,
Underwood, Alice ('The Duchess'), 35, 148, 150, 158, 227
Underwood, Mrs. E.M., 279, 401
Upton-upon-Severn, 182, 274, 276

Vaga (River Wye), 191
Valois, Dame Ninette de, 442
Vaughan Williams, Ralph, 20, 206, 216, 231, 322, 332, 388, 401, 407, 427, 434, 437, 440, 448, 468
Venice, 162, 191
Verdi, Giuseppe, 215, 434
Verona, 191
Vert, Nathaniel, 39, 44
Vigornia (Worcester), 173, 188, 191, 237, 351
Volbach, Fritz, 126

Wagner, Richard, 27, 35, 77, 144, 232
Wales, 245, 274, 301, 432
Wales, Edward, Prince of (later HM King Edward VIII), 30
Walpole, Hugh Seymour, 210
Walthew, Richard, 55
Walton, Izaak, 189
Walton, Sir William, 448
Ward, Edgar and Winifred, 396–7
Warrender, Lady Maud, 200
Watson, Richard, 428
Weaver, Frank, 477–8
Weaver, Helen Jessie, 477–80
Weingartner, Felix, 393
Welch, Henry, 237, 252, 275
Welch, Nellie, 237, 275

Wembley Exhibition, 372, 375, 377
Wesley, Samuel Sebastian, 366–8, 370, 474–5
West, John E. (Novellos), 294
Westminster Abbey, 111, 395
Westminster Cathedral, 98
Westmorland, 237
Whernside, 399
Whewall, James, 96, 499
Widows, and Orphans of the Clergy (Charity), 321
Wiesbaden, 74
William III, King, 182
Williams, Charles Lee, see Lee Williams, Charles
Williams, Harold, 435, 447, 457, 460, 466–8
Williams, Trevor Osmond (of HMV), 426, 499
Wilson, Archibald Wayett, 420
Wilson, Canon James Maurice, 230, 273, 277, 280, 499
Wilson, R.H., 149, 156
Wilson, Sir Steuart, 407, 419, 432, 435
Winter, Kate, 438
Winterbottom, Charles, 42
Wolfrum, Philip, 60
Wolverhampton, 205
Wood, Charles, 385, 401
Wood, Mrs Henry (novelist), 345
Wood, Sir Henry J., 74, 162, 165, 385
Worcester, 20–1, 55, 113, 127, 134, **139,** 153, 189, **202, 213,** 220, 226, **232,** 272, 274, 286, 287, 305, 336, 345, 359, 371, 380, 396–8, 402, **410,** 443, 478–79
Worcester Amateur Instrumental Society, 476–7
Worcester Cathedral, 29, 30, 82, 106, 130, 180–1, 184, 202, 207, 226, 247, 265–6, 290, 324, 340–1, **345,** 347, **384,** 427, 437, **443, 465–8,** 475; Music Library, 266, 272–3, 284–5, *309,* 332, 432, 443, 469
Worcester Festival, 25, 29, 30, 41–3, 54–5, 61–2, 65, 75, 127, 130, 140, 158, 160, 165, 183–4, 202, 216–19, **229–31,** 241, 249–53, **262–5,** 267, 269, 284, 292–3, 295–8, 302–5, 307–8, **311–21,** 359, 366, **368–70,** 375, 386–8, 390–1, **393–6,** 408, 413–14, 418–20, **438,** 440, 444, 446–9, **467–8,** 469, 470, 473, 481, 482–9
Worcester Festival Choral Society, 28, 30, 31, 32, 51, 55, 59, 62, 66, 73–5, 93–4, 106, 112–13, 121, 157, 165, *172,* 184, **188,** 195, 202, 238, 241–2, 276, 278, 329, 334–5, 338, 340, 374, 380, 385, **398,** 412, 427, 435, 437, 449, 455
Worcester (Massachusetts) Festival, 297
Worcester Royal General Infirmary, 267, 275, 433
Worcestershire, 20, 21, 27, 185, 245, 275, 286, 296, 323, 359, 398, 413, 455
Worcestershire Musical Competitive Festival, 272
Worcestershire Orchestral and Ladies Choral Society, 212, 267–8, 295–6, 323, 388, 404, 412, 427, 449
Worcestershire Orchestral Society, 141–3, 150, 164, 171, 190, 201, 202, 213
Worcestershire Philharmonic Society, 35, 51, 55, 56, 60, 72, 131, 164, 212
Worshipful Company of Musicians, 439
Worthington, Julia, ('Pippa'), 134, 139, 140, 150, 154, 156, 158, 160, 162, 169, 189, 191, 192, 195, 206, 217, **245,** 480
Wüllner, Ludwig, 60, 74, 98
Wye, River, 38, 113

Yale University, 46, 115, 127, 134, 139
Yeats, William Butler, 72
York, HRH Duchess of (later HM Queen Elizabeth), 436
York, HRH Duke of (later HM King George VI), 436
York Minster, 121, 133
Ysaÿe, Eugene, 214

Zimmermann, Louis, 126